全国英语专业博雅系列教材/总主编　丁建新

英美研究

主　编　廖益清　李　贻
　　　　曹金蓉　燕甜甜

·广州·

版权所有　翻印必究

图书在版编目（CIP）数据

英美研究/廖益清，李贻，曹金蓉，燕甜甜主编．—广州：中山大学出版社，2014.12

（全国英语专业博雅系列教材/丁建新主编）

ISBN 978 - 7 - 306 - 05030 - 4

Ⅰ．①英…　Ⅱ．①廖…　②李…　③曹…　④燕…　Ⅲ．①英语—阅读教学—高等学校—教材　Ⅳ．①H319.5

中国版本图书馆 CIP 数据核字（2014）第 151061 号

出 版 人：	徐　劲
策划编辑：	熊锡源
责任编辑：	熊锡源
封面设计：	曾　斌
责任校对：	刘学谦
责任技编：	黄少伟
出版发行：	中山大学出版社
电　　话：	编辑部 020 - 84111996，84113349，84111997，84110779
	发行部 020 - 84111998，84111981，84111160
地　　址：	广州市新港西路 135 号
邮　　编：	510275　　　传　真：020 - 84036565
网　　址：	http://www.zsup.com.cn　　E-mail:zdcbs@ mail. sysu. edu. cn
印 刷 者：	广州中大印刷有限公司
规　　格：	787mm × 1092mm　1/16　21 印张　496 千字
版次印次：	2014 年 12 月第 1 版　2014 年 12 月第 1 次印刷
印　　数：	1 ~ 4000 册　　定　价：39.00 元

如发现本书因印装质量影响阅读，请与出版社发行部联系调换

英语专业博雅系列教材编委会

总主编　丁建新（中山大学）

编　委　会

李洪儒（黑龙江大学）
司显柱（北京交通大学）
赵彦春（天津外国语大学）
田海龙（天津外国语大学）
夏慧言（天津科技大学）
李会民（河南科技学院）
刘承宇（西南大学）
施　旭（浙江大学）
辛　斌（南京师范大学）
杨信彰（厦门大学）
徐畅贤（湖南城市学院）
李玉英（江西师范大学）
李发根（江西师范大学）
肖坤学（广州大学）
宫　齐（暨南大学）
张广奎（广东财经大学）
温宾利（广东外语外贸大学）
杜金榜（广东外语外贸大学）
阮　炜（深圳大学）
张晓红（深圳大学）

博雅之辩（代序）

大学精神陷入前所未有的危机，许多人在寻找出路。

我们的坚持是，提倡博雅教育（Liberal Education）。因为大凡提倡什么，关键在于审视问题的症结何在，对症下药。而当下之困局，根源在于功利，在于忘掉了教育之根本。

博雅教育之理念，可以追溯至古罗马人提倡的"七艺"：文法、修辞、辩证法、音乐、算术、几何、天文学。其目的在于培养人格完美的自由思考者。在中国教育史上，博雅的思想，古已有之。中国儒家教育的传统，强调以培养学生人格为核心。儒家"六艺"，礼、乐、射、御、书、数，体现的正是我们所讲的博雅理念。"学识广博，生活高雅"，在这一点上，中国与西方，现代与传统，并无二致。

在古罗马，博雅教育在于培育自由的人格与社会精英。在启蒙时代，博雅教育意指解放思想，破除成见。"什么都知道一点，有些事情知道得多一点"，这是19世纪英国的思想家约翰·斯图亚特·密尔（John Stuart Mill）对博雅的诠释。同一时期，另外一位思想家，曾任都柏林大学校长的约翰·亨利·纽曼（John Henry Newman）在《大学理念》一书中，也曾这样表述博雅的培养目标："如果必须给大学课程一个实际目标，那么，我说它就是训练社会的良好成员。它的艺术是社会生活的艺术，它的目的是对世界的适应……大学训练旨在提高社会的精神格调，培养公众的智慧，纯洁一个民族的趣味"。

博雅教育包括科学与人文，目标在于培养人的自由和理性的精神，而不是迎合市场与风俗。教育的目标在于让学生学会尊重人类生活固有的内在价值：生命的价值、尊严的价值、求知的价值、爱的价值、相互尊重的价值、自我超越的价值、创新的价值。提倡博雅教育，就是要担当这些价值守护者的角色。博雅教育对于我们来说，是一种素质教育、人文教育。人文教育关心人类的终极目标，不是以"有用"为标准。它不是"万金油"，也无关乎"风花雪月"。

在美国，专注于博雅教育的大学称为"文理学院"，拒绝职业性的教育。在中国香港，以博雅教育为宗旨的就有岭南大学，提倡"全人教育"；在台湾大学，博雅教育是大学教育的基础，课程涉及文学与艺术、历史思维、世界文明、道德与哲学、公民意识与社会分析、量化分析与数学素养、物质科学、生命科学等八大领域。在欧洲，博雅教育历史中的七大范畴被分为"三道"（初级）与"四道"（高级）。前者包括语法、修辞与辩证法，后者包括算术、几何、天文与音乐。在中国大陆的中山大学，许多有识之士也提倡博雅之理念，让最好的教授开设通识课程，涉及现代学科之环境、生物、地理等各门。同时设立"博雅学院"，学拉丁，读古典，开风气之先。

外语作为一门人文性很强的学科，尤其有必要落实博雅之理念。对于我们来说，最好的"应用型"教育在于博雅。早在20世纪20～40年代，在水木清华的外文系，吴宓先生提倡"语""文"并重，"中""西"兼修，教学上提倡自主学习与互动研究。在《西洋文学系学程总则》中，吴宓明确了"博雅之士"的培养目标：

> 本系课程编写的目的为使学生：（甲）成为博雅之士；（乙）了解西洋文明之精神；（丙）熟读西方文学之名著，谙悉西方思想之潮流，因而在国内教授英、德、法各国语言文字及文学，足以胜任愉快；（丁）创造今日之中国文学；（戊）汇通东西方之精神而互为介绍传布。

博雅之于我们，不仅仅是理念，更重要的是课程体系，是教材，是教法，是实践，是反应试教育，是将通识与专业熔于一炉。基于这样的理念，我们编写了这套丛书。希望通过这样的教育，让我们的学生知道人之为人是有他内在的生活意义，告诉我们的学生去求知，去阅读，去思考，去创造，去理解世界，去适应社会，去爱，去相互尊重，去审美，去找回精神的家园。

无需辩驳，也不怕非议。这是我们的坚守。

中山大学外国语学院　教授、博士生导师
中山大学语言研究所　所长
丁建新
2013年春天

前　言

　　进入21世纪以来，国际商务与文化交流迅速发展，我国对具有国际视野的复合型人才出现多层次、多样化需求。在强调英语专业技能的基础上，跨文化交际能力的重要性也日益凸显。培养学生对文化差异的敏感性、宽容性和处理文化差异的灵活性，才能适应日益广泛的国际交流的需要。根据《高等学校英语专业英语教学大纲》（2000年版）"对英美等英语国家的地理历史和发展现状有一定的了解，熟悉英语国家的地理、历史、发展现状、文化传统、风俗习惯""注重培养获取知识的能力、独立思考的能力和创新的能力，提高思想道德素质、文化素质和心理素质"的精神，我们编写了这本《英美研究》，用于英语专业英语国家文化或英美概况课程的教学。

　　本教材在选材上本着"权威性、思辨性、启发性、丰富性、时新性"的原则，选择学生关心和感兴趣的内容，充分再现原汁原味的地道英语。概况部分强调内容的权威性和语言的准确性，文本多选自英美政府官网，如英国的directgov和美国国务院的IIP等；深度阅读部分则强调一定的研究深度和学术思辨性，是有态度有色彩的论述，文本选自高端英语媒体或有影响力的学者之手，如英国的 *The Economist* 和美国卡托研究所的David Boaz。在本书的编排上，我们致力于满足学生了解英美文化的需求，也注重培养学生独立思考的能力，是一本以"通识教育"+"思辨能力"理念培养学生核心竞争力的教材。我们视本教材为一个多元的工具，承载着观念的多元，要求读者关注文本的背景和立场，进行批评性阅读。

　　本书主要讨论英、美两国文化，兼顾加拿大、澳大利亚和新西兰，以地理、历史、政府、经济、教育、传媒和文学为主线，每章包括概况和深度阅读两部分。全书共分15章，外加附录1章。简介如下：

　　第一章：英国地理。概况部分主要选自About.com和Buzzle.com网站。这两大网站均为英文搜索平台，其中About.com是美国网络公司IAC旗下子公司，网站内容涵盖从家庭到旅游等各方面；Buzzle.com是一个获取新闻、文章和信息的动态网络搜索平台。关于人文地理的数据信息主要选自英国官网The Office for National Statistics（ONS）。在深入阅读部分的第一篇，美国旅行作家、自由写作者Ferne Arfin分享她眼中的一个英国小镇Rye，从旅行家的角度描绘

英美研究

一个独具英伦风情的英国小镇地道风光；第二篇摘自 BBC Weather 网站，波兰籍英国气象学家 Tomasz Schafernaker 从科学的角度对英国人口口相传的气象谚语进行分析。

第二章：英国历史。概况部分选自英国广播公司 BBC 官网的历史栏目，以英国历史文化发展为线索，展现英国历史进程中的国家概况，语言材料真实地道，涉及内容全面翔实。深度阅读部分旨在提供对英国历史的个性理解。第一篇选自英国著名学者 P. J. Marshall 编纂的 *Cambridge Illustrated History—British Empire*，概述大英帝国的发展史，并从新的视角诠释大英帝国对整个世界的影响；第二篇，英国埃克塞特大学历史系教授 Jeremy Black 对"二战"之后英国各方面的变化进行论述。

第三章：英国政府。概况部分主要摘自英国政府官网及英国议会官网，包括英国宪法、三权分立、英国政党、大选等方面，内容真实权威，文字简明扼要。深度阅读部分从不同的角度解读英国政治体系。第一篇为大家介绍一些有趣的习惯法，体现英国宪法的不成文性及其奉行的遵循先例原则；第二篇对比英美大选，包括时间、程序、经费等方面的不同之处。

第四章：英国经济。概况部分首先介绍英国经济整体状况，然后分阶段阐述 1945 年至今英国经济的发展历程。主要选自 Wikipedia 英国经济板块。深度阅读部分的第一篇选自 BBC News，经济学家 Douglas Fraser 探讨苏格兰经济的发展现状和未来；第二篇选自阿巴斯诺特银行集团（Arbuthnot Banking Group）经济顾问和非执行董事 Ruth Lea 在 *Daily Mail* 上的一篇文章，主要讨论英联邦能否在英国经济未来的发展中发挥更大的作用。

第五章：英国教育。概况部分选自英国政府官网 Directgov 以及英美学术期刊、主流媒体上刊载的关于英国教育的内容。主要关注英格兰的义务教育、高等教育情况，对其中的流弊也有相当中肯的批判。深度阅读部分先扬后抑：第一篇出自《卫报》（*The Guardian*），肯定世人瞩目的英国公学精英教育的成功之道；第二篇论调急转直下，抨击英国私立教育逐渐拉大与公立教育之间的鸿沟，展现英国教育界和民众对缩小教育不公现象的思考和辩论。

第六章：英国传媒。概况部分选自 BBC 等主流英语媒体，对英国的传媒受众、媒体中心、著名报纸杂志、平面媒体、电视广播以及互联网均有涉猎。深度阅读部分：第一篇出自爱尔兰广播电台，梳理具有 168 年历史的英国老报《世界新闻报》轰然倒塌的来龙去脉；第二篇是新闻集团少东家 James Murdoch 对旗下报纸电话窃听丑闻的致歉和反省，言辞坦诚而不卑微。

第七章：英美节假日。概况部分主要介绍英国银行节日和其他节日。由于英美节日存在部分重合，美国节日在该章练习的答案中呈现，不另章介绍。主要内容选自美国政府网站 USA. gov 和 全球第一个国际网络社区 InterNations。

前　言

深入阅读部分讨论英美文化中的两个重要节日，第一篇选自BBC官网，英国历史学家David Cannadine从美国化、国家身份等角度论述Bonfire Night的兴衰；第二篇是美国学者Jacqueline Keeler揭示感恩节华衣之下美国印第安人的悲凉，视角独特，引人深思。

第八章：英国文学。概况部分选自耶鲁大学文学教授Henry A. Beers为美国学生编写的 *Brief History of English and American Literature*，将英国文学按照时间顺序分为中古文学、英国文艺复兴、18世纪文学、英国浪漫主义、维多利亚文学和20世纪文学六个阶段，思想性和艺术性兼顾，让学生在了解西方文学的同时，感受英语语言的魅力。深度阅读部分讲述两位英国文学巨匠：第一篇简述莎士比亚对现代英语的影响和贡献；第二篇，英国导演Simon Callow从一位导演兼演员的角度阐释狄更斯的作品对舞台剧的影响。

第九章：美国地理。概况部分介绍美国地理基本状况，内容主要选自About.com, usa-facts.com, The Encyclopaedia of the Nations和usa.usembassy.de等网站。深入阅读部分的第一篇，著名获奖地理学家Matt Rosenberg介绍美国自1776年以来国土发展和边界扩充史；第二篇是旅行作家Christy Karras关于美国旅行的小贴士，从侧面反映美国风土人情。

第十章：美国历史。概况部分主要选自美国国务院国际情资计划局向全球公开发行的 *U.S.A. History in Brief*，内容全面扼要，语言文字深入浅出，兼具可读性与权威性。深度阅读部分，第一篇是世界著名的卡托研究所执行副所长、学者David Boaz对华盛顿拒不称帝的评论与反思；第二篇摘自 *Journal of Historical Review*，学者Samuel Taylor探讨如何从多元文化视角看待美国的历史和未来。

第十一章：美国政府。概况部分主要摘自美国白宫官网，系统介绍美国宪法、三权分立、两党制、总统大选、联邦制等。深度阅读部分从不同角度剖析美国政治体系。第一篇来源于美国政府官网，简述在美国这个联邦制国家里，地方、州、联邦三个层次政府之间的关系和各自的职能；第二篇来源于美国国家档案记录管理局官网，介绍美国总统选举特有的计票方法——选举人团制度。

第十二章：美国经济。概况部分包括对美国经济的整体介绍和阶段性梳理。主要内容选自Wikipedia。深入阅读部分的第一篇选自MarketWatch.com，资深记者Jeffry Bartash报道美国经济在2014年初的复苏迹象并不明显；第二篇选自美国科学杂志 *Scientific American*，美国经济学家Jeffrey David Sachs讨论如何摆脱美国2006年开始的经济危机。

第十三章：美国教育。概况部分主要精选自美国国务院国际情资计划局向世界介绍美国教育的 *U.S.A. Education in Brief*，以"教育开民智"为主线，从规模化、地方化、多样化三方面阐明美国的 K12 义务教育体制,并从不同切入点略述美国高等教育的现状与挑战。深度阅读部分:第一篇引自 *The Economist*,分析导致美国高等教育学费高涨、性价比日渐降低的几大问题;第二篇出自美国教育部 12 位"教师大使 TAF"之一的 Dan Brown,从文中我们可以窥探美国各地大中小学一线教师们对本国教育的看法和诉求。

第十四章:美国传媒。概况部分综述美国主要的广播电台、电视台、电影产业、著名报刊以及互联网。深度阅读部分:第一篇选自美国国务院国际信息局数字资料库,总结自 1769 年起至 21 世纪,美国新闻传播手段发展的 13 个里程碑;第二篇是美国亚利桑那州州立大学 Dan Gillmor 教授的研究成果:如何做一个善于摄取信息和利用媒体的现代人。

第十五章:美国文学。概况部分选自剑桥大学出版社出版的 *The Cambridge History of American Literature*,对美国多种文学流派以及各个时期的文学作品进行广泛的论述。深度阅读部分主要介绍两位美国文学巨匠,第一篇讲述海明威的生平事迹及其作品所获得的批评和赞誉;第二篇介绍马克·吐温是如何利用幽默之琴弹奏文学之歌的。

附录为英美研究的延伸部分,涉及加拿大、澳大利亚和新西兰三个国家。主要介绍三国地理、主要城市、历史与政治,内容均来自三国的政府官网、官方旅游网站等,内容权威,真实可读。

本书编排了丰富的习题,概况部分的 Exercises 围绕本章内容设计了选择题、是非题和简答题,深度阅读的每一篇文章之后也针对性地提出了启发性讨论题,以激发读者讨论的欲望,引发读者的认知冲突,从而培养读者独立思考的能力。本书末尾附有练习的参考答案,为读者提供便捷的自主学习平台。同时应注意:讨论题的多元性决定了答案并非唯一。

书中不当之处,敬请方家指正。

主　编

2014 年 9 月

Contents

Part A: The United Kingdom of Great Britain and Northern Ireland 1
   Chapter 1   Geography 2
   Chapter 2   History 17
   Chapter 3   Government and Politics 39
   Chapter 4   Economy 55
   Chapter 5   Education 72
   Chapter 6   Media 93
   Chapter 7   Holidays 108
   Chapter 8   Literature 123

Part B: The United States of America 143
   Chapter 9   Geography 144
   Chapter 10   History 165
   Chapter 11   Government and Politics 191
   Chapter 12   Economy 207
   Chapter 13   Education 223
   Chapter 14   Media 242
   Chapter 15   Literature 255

Appendix: Canada, Australia and New Zealand 277

Key to Exercises 297

Part A:
The United Kingdom of Great Britain and Northern Ireland

Chapter 1

Geography

Section One: A Brief Introduction

1. The Geography of Britain

A group of about 5,000 islands off the north-west coast of mainland Europe form what we call the British Isles. The largest island, which is also the largest isle in Europe, is Great Britain. Ireland is the second largest after Britain. The geography of Britain is discussed below.

1.1 Physical Geography

The British Isles is the geographical term for a group of about 5,000 islands off the north-west coast of mainland Europe between the latitudes 50°N and 61°N. The largest island is Britain or Great Britain, which is also the largest island in Europe. It consists of England, Wales and Scotland.

The next largest island is Ireland, which is made up of Northern Ireland and the Irish Republic. Britain and Northern Ireland, together with a number of small islands, form the United Kingdom of Britain and Northern Ireland, more commonly known as the United Kingdom (which is almost 20% smaller than Italy). In every usage, however, Great Britain or Britain is used to mean the United Kingdom. **The Isle of Man**①, between Ireland and Britain, and **the Channel Islands**②, off north-west coast of France, though recognizing the Crown, have their own parliaments and

---

① The Isle of Man: 马恩岛（或是 Mann），英格兰与爱尔兰间的海上岛屿，是英国的皇家属地。此岛的自治政府有着长远的历史，他们在公元 10 世纪就已经有自己的国会，首府为道格拉斯（Douglas）。

② the Channel Islands: 海峡群岛是位于英吉利海峡中的群岛。这些岛屿分为两个行政区：根西（Bailiwick of Guernsey）和泽西（Bailiwick of Jersey）。英国对这些地方有宗主权，但是这些地方并不被视为英国本土，而算是英国的属地。

are self-governing.

Great Britain is just under 1,000 km long and just under 500 km across in its widest part. The most mountainous region is Scotland (with Britain's highest peak, Ben Nevis-1 343 m), which also has a wide lowland area between the Grampians and the Southern Uplands, where most of the large towns, including Edinburgh and Glasgow, and three-quarters of the population are located. Much of Wales is also mountainous and in England, **the Pennine Range**① (the "backbone of England") extends to 224 km (although the highest peak is only 895 m high). The rest of England tends to be rather undulating, and not even the large agricultural plains of East Anglia are perfectly flat. In Ireland all the highland areas are around the edge, but there are no peaks over 1,100 m.

Rivers in Great Britain are quite short—the longest rivers are **the Severn**② and **the Thames**③—but their easy navigability has made them an important part of the inland transport network for the transportation of bulk products such as coal, iron ore and steel.

1.2 Human Geography

Population

With 57 million people, the United Kingdom ranks about fifteen in the world in terms of population, with England (46 million) by far the most populous part (followed by Scotland 5 million, Wales 2.8 million and Northern Ireland 1.5 million). The population is increasing very slowly and in 1976—1978 and 1982 actually fell. The estimated age distribution in 1985 was 21% <16; 64% 16-64; 15% >64. Although there are more than 6% more male than female births, the higher mortality of men at all ages means that there are more females than males (29 million against 27.6 million).

The **average population density**④ in Britain is about 239 per sq. km, compared with, for example, 190 per sq. km in Italy. England, with 361 inhabitants per sq. km, is one of the most densely populated countries in the world (the rest of Britain is much lower: Wales 135 per sq. km, Scotland 65 and Northern Ireland

---

① the Pennine Range: 奔宁山脉，旧译"佩奈恩山脉"。英国英格兰北部的主要山脉和分水岭，从北部的南泰恩河谷地到南部的特伦特河谷地，南北延伸241公里，东西平均宽度为48公里。

② the Severn: 塞文河。全长354公里，源出威尔士普林利蒙（Plynlimon）东北坡，注入大西洋布里斯托海峡。流域面积11,266平方公里（4,350平方英里）。

③ the Thames: 泰晤士河（或 River Thames），位于英格兰东南，源自科茨沃尔德山（Cotswold Hills），大致向东流，流经的第一个小镇是克里克莱德，流经伦敦，在诺尔注入北海。全长约338公里，为英格兰最长之河流（英国第二长河，次于354公里的塞文河），也是全世界水面交通最繁忙的都市河流和伦敦地标之一。

④ average population density: 平均人口密度。

Map of the United Kingdom
From: http://geography.about.com/od/findmaps/ig/Country-Maps/UK-Map.htm

111).

The UK population estimates for 2013 show that the population of the UK grew to 64.1 million in mid-2013—a gain of 400,600 (0.63%) over the previous year mid-2012. This growth is slightly below the average since 2003. This means that the UK's population has increased by around 5 million since 2001, and by more than 10 million since 1964.

Natural change (that is, the number of births less the number of deaths) contributed slightly more than net international migration to the population increase in the year. There were 212,100 more births than deaths (53% of the increase) and 183,400 more immigrants arriving than emigrants leaving (46% of the increase).

The estimated populations of the four regions of the UK in mid-2013 are 53.9 million (growth of 0.70%) in England, 5.3 million (growth of 0.27%) in Scotland, 3.1 million (growth of 0.27%) in Wales and 1.8 million (growth of 0.33%) in Northern Ireland.

Conurbations and New Towns

The highest densities are to be found in conurbations, which are groups of once separated towns that have grown to form a single community. Although Britain is short of housing, planners like to keep a belt of undeveloped land around cities known as green belt to reduce pollution and provide open spaces for leisure. This has meant that the only alternative to the redevelopment of slum areas in conurbations (such as the Docklands development in London) has been the creation of New Towns as Harlow in Essex. The industrial area in these towns is separated from housing and there are greener, open spaces. New Towns have partially failed, however, especially since many are near enough to conurbations, people to use them as dormitory towns (towns where a large percentage of the population commutes daily to work in a conurbation) and recent government policy has been to expand existing towns like Telford and Milton Keynes (formed from the amalgamation of a group of villages), which is cheaper than creating an entirely new town.

Weather and Climate

Britain has a generally mild, temperate climate. The weather, however, tends to be very changeable as a result of constant influence of different air masses. There are few extremes in temperature, which rarely goes above 32℃ or below −10℃. Annual rainfall is fairly evenly distributed, but ranges from more than 1,600 mm in the mountainous areas of the west and north to less than 800 mm over central and eastern parts. This is because depressions from the Atlantic bring frontal rainfall first to the west and because western Britain is higher and so gets more relief rain.

2. Geographic Regions of the United Kingdom

The United Kingdom is an island nation in Western Europe on the island of

The Office for National Statistics (ONS) is the UK's largest independent producer of official statistics and is the recognised national statistical institute for the UK. It is responsible for collecting and publishing statistics related to the economy, population and society at national, regional and local levels. It also conducts the census in England and Wales every ten years. ONS plays a leading role in national and international good practice in the production of official statistics. It is the executive office of the UK Statistics Authority and although they are separate, they are still closely related.

http://geography.about.com/od/unitedkingdommaps/tp/united-kingdom-regions.htm

About.com (an IAC Company) is one of the largest sites on the Internet that helps nearly 90 million people each month discover, learn about, and be inspired by topics ranging from parenting and healthcare to cooking to travel. About.com is for anyone who has a question, a problem, a passion or just wants to learn something new.

Exercises

I. Choose the one that best completes each of the following statements.

1. Which of the following names is NOT related to the United Kingdom?
   A. Northern Ireland.   B. Scotland.
   C. Wales.   D. Toronto.
2. In which region of the UK is the city of Edinburgh located?
   A. In Wales.   B. In Scotland.
   C. In Northern Ireland.   D. In Ireland.
3. The River Thames is in _____.
   A. Wales   B. Scotland   C. England   D. Northern Ireland
4. Big Ben was named after _____.
   A. Christopher Wren   B. Benjamin Hall
   C. Ben John   D. G. Stephenson
5. The Capital of Wales is _____.
   A. Swansea   B. Cardiff   C. Rhonda   D. Belfast
6. _____ is England's biggest naval base.
   A. Portsmouth   B. Southampton   C. Plymouth   D. Dover
7. British food is _____.
   A. unlimited   B. abundant   C. limited   D. changeable
8. The British people usually have a small quantity of _____ as a first course.
   A. soup   B. sweet   C. vegetable   D. dessert
9. What the Englishmen usually talk about in their daily life is _____.
   A. price   B. tax   C. weather   D. sports

10. The highest mountain in Britain is _____.
    A. Scafell   B. Ben Nevis   C. the Cotswolds   D. the Forth
11. The longest river in Britain is _____.
    A. the Clyde   B. the Mersey   C. the Severn   D. the Thames
12. The largest lake in Britain is _____.
    A. the Lough Neage   B. Windermere Water
    C. Coniston Water   D. the Lake District
13. The immigrants coming to Britain are mainly from _____.
    A. Europe   B. the United States
    C. Africa   D. the West Indies
14. Britain is separated from the rest of Europe by the English Channel in the ____ and the North Sea in the east.
    A. east   B. south   C. west   D. north
15. In Britain only _____ of the population are farmers but they manage 70% of the land area.
    A. 2%   B. 3%   C. 4%   D. 5%

II. Read the following statements carefully and decide whether they are TRUE or FALSE.

1. Great Britain is the largest island of both the British Isles and Europe.
2. In Ireland all the highland areas are around the edge, and the peaks are over 1,100 m.
3. England is the most populous part of the UK.
4. In the UK, there are more females than males.
5. England is one of the most densely populated countries in the world.
6. Edinburgh is both the capital and largest city of Scotland.
7. Wales is one of the wettest regions in Europe.
8. Geographically speaking, the north and west of Britain are highlands, while the east and south-east are mostly lowlands.
9. Welsh is located in the west of Great Britain.
10. Britain has, for centuries, been slowly tilting with the North-West slowly rising and the South-East slowly sinking.

III. Give brief answers to the following questions.

1. What is the British Isles?
2. How did New Towns develop?

Section Two: In-depth Reading

Britain may sometimes be confused with England. Actually, they are totally different. Britain refers to the United Kingdom of Great Britain and Northern Ireland;

just like an old English pub should look—even though you can order tapas there. Its vaulted cellars and underground passages were probably used by smugglers to hide their booty. In the 18th century Rye was a notorious smuggler's haven.

While you're in Rye, stop in at one of the two branches of the Rye Castle Museum (the Ypres Tower and the East Street Museum), to find out more about this town's fascinating past.

References

http://gouk.about.com/od/Day_Trips_From_London/ss/Rye-The-Prettiest-town-In-The-South-Of-England.htm

About the Author

Ferne Arfin, your Guide to UK Travel, is an American abroad. A freelance writer, guidebook author and native New Yorker, she has lived in the UK for many years. A writer all her life, Ferne started out as a newspaper journalist in Boston. She wrote corporate literature, advertising copy and public relations before seeing the light and turning her attention to full time journalism and travel writing. Now, with her constant traveling companion Wallace—a very discerning and well traveled West Highland Terrier—she spends as much time as she can discovering new places around the UK.

Discussions

1. Why does the author recommend travelers to visit small towns, like Rye, rather than cosmopolis?
2. Can you recommend some towns worth visiting in other parts of the world?

Reading Two

The British people always talk about weather because weather in the British Isles is very changeable. So people believe "*Our national obsession comes from our seasons seeming to be so unpredictable*". Will it rain on your picnic/camping trip/festival? Old weather sayings may sound like fanciful folklore, but some can help amateur forecasters. Here are six that are backed up by science.

Weather Lore: What's the Science?
Tomasz Schafernaker

Is there any truth to weather sayings, or are they merely a whimsical interpretation of reality?

Some of the earliest examples of weather lore date back to the *Bible*. With farmers and mariners so dependent on the weather, we have undoubtedly been looking for signs from the heavens since the dawn of man.

Forecasting the weather accurately can be a challenge, even with today's supercomputers.

But an experienced weather observer can get a fairly good idea of an impending storm well in advance, just by looking at the sky. The signs can be clearer than you think.

Over the millennia we have learnt to recognise these patterns, and a rhyme handed down from generation to generation is a good way to share and remember knowledge—especially in the days before literacy was widespread.

While many old sayings are unreliable and of little practical use, here is the meteorological logic behind six traditional weather rhymes.

1. "Red sky at night, shepherd's delight; red sky in the morning, shepherd's warning"

Deep red sunsets are often associated with dry, settled weather and high pressure. A deep red sunset may indicate a prolonged spell of good weather. But the key sign is in the red sky around the sun—and not the colour of the cloud itself.

Red sky in the morning can be interpreted in a slightly different way. As the sun rises at a low angle in the east, it may light up the impending clouds associated with a weather front coming in from the west.

It may also indicate that rain is on its way and due to arrive later in the day, hence the "shepherd's warning".

2. "Three days rain will empty any sky"

This saying is very much open to anyone's interpretation, but the simplest logic behind it is that, in our climate, heavy rain doesn't really last for very long.

Cloudy and gloomy weather may persist for many days at a time, but torrential rain usually clears in a day or two, and almost certainly in three.

3. "When the wind is out of the east, it is neither good for man nor beast"

This is a classic weather rhyme and an easy one to interpret for meteorologists in the UK and in any other part of Europe.

It simply implies that our harsh winter weather usually comes in from eastern Europe and Russia. A strengthening icy wind blowing from the east would indicate to a farmer hundreds of years ago that snow and frigid conditions were on the way.

Cold "easterlies" often bring spells of heavy snow to eastern Britain, but the wind chill from a cutting Siberian wind is felt right across the country. In the summer months, on the other hand, an easterly wind may carry pollutants and poor quality air from the near continent, giving us hazy skies. However, the latter link is more open to debate.

news coverage. The service maintains 44 foreign news bureaux and has correspondents in almost every country. James Harding, a former editor of *The Times* newspaper, was named on 16 April 2013 as Director of News and Current Affairs.

About the Author

Tomasz Schafernaker (born 8 January 1979) is an Anglo-Polish meteorologist for the Met Office, best known for his appearances for BBC Weather.

Discussions

1. What does the sentence "*Our national obsession comes from our seasons seeming to be so unpredictable*" mean?
2. Why do the British like to talk about the weather?
3. Do you think weather rhymes are still trustworthy as they used to be?

Chapter 2

History

Section One: A Brief Introduction

1. The Founding of the Nation

1.1 Prehistory & Antiquity

England was settled by humans for at least 500,000 years. The first modern humans (homo sapiens) arrived during the Ice Age (about 35,000 to 10,000 years ago), when the sea levels were lower and Britain was connected to the European mainland. It is these people who built the ancient megalithic monuments of Stonehenge and Avebury.

Between 1,500 and 500 BC, Celtic tribes migrated from Central Europe and France to Britain and mixed with the indigenous inhabitants, creating a new culture slightly distinct from the Continental Celtic one. This was the Bronze Age.

The Romans tried a first time to invade Britannia (the Latin name of the island) in 55 BC under Julius Caesar, but weren't successful until 43 AD, during the reign of Emperor Claudius I. Britain subsequently became a Roman province and it remained so until the beginning of the 5th century.

The Romans controlled most of present-day England and Wales, and founded a large number of cities that still exist today. London, York, St Albans, Bath, Exeter, Lincoln, Leicester, Worcester, Gloucester, Chichester, Winchester, Colchester, Manchester, Chester, Lancaster, were all Roman towns, as in fact were all the cities with names now ending in -chester, -cester or -caster, which derive from Latin "castrum" (fortification).

1.2 The Anglo-Saxons

The Romans progressively abandoned Britannia in the 5th century as their

was in fact murdered, so that William's second son, Henry, could become king. Henry I's succession was also agitated, with his daughter Matilda and her cousin Stephen (grandson of William I) starting a civil war for the throne. Although Stephen won, Matilda's son succeeded him as Henry II (1133—1189). It is under Henry II that the University of Oxford was established.

The following struggle of Henry II's two children was made famous by the legend of Robin Hood. **Richard I "Lionheart"**① was hardly ever in England, too busy defending his French possessions or fighting the infidels in the Holy Land. After Richard was killed in France, his brother **John "Lackland"**② usurped the throne and startled another civil war. Dissatisfied with John's leadership, the lords forced him to sign the *Magna Carta* on June 15, 1215. The *Magna Carta* contained 63 clauses, the most important being the following: the king could not exact payment from the vassals without their consent; no freeman should be arrested, imprisoned, or deprived of their property unless they are convicted by a jury; merchants would be allowed to move about freely; there should be the same weights and measures throughout the country; traditional rights and privileges should be given to the towns.

Portrait in Westminster Abbey, thought to be of Edward I
From: http://en.wikipedia.org/wiki/Longshanks

---

① Richard I "Lionheart": 狮心王理查德一世。亨利二世之子，约翰兄长。因其在战争中总是一马当先，犹如狮子般勇猛，因此得到"狮心王"的称号。在10年国王生涯中，几乎全部时间都花在戎马弓刀之上，他参与过包含十字军东征之内的许多战争，而他的军事表现也使他成为中世纪最杰出的军事指挥官之一。后在法兰西征战时驾崩。

② John "Lackland": 无地王约翰。13世纪初的英格兰国王。好战却又屡战屡败，在连年战争中，他失去了英格兰在欧洲大陆大部分的领地。为维持战事，约翰王加紧了对市民和贵族征税，与此同时，牛、羊、小麦的价格也都出现了成倍上涨。

John's grandson, Edward I "Longshanks" (1239—1307) spent most of his 35-year reign fighting wars, first against his barons led by **Simon de Montfort**①, then on the 9th Crusade, back home annexing Wales, and last but not least against the Scots, led by William Wallace and Robert the Bruce, whose proud resistance was immortalised in the Hollywood movie *Braveheart*②.

Edward I's son, Edward II, was all his father wasn't. He didn't like war, preferring to party with his friends. He also happened to be gay, which led to his imprisonment and tragic murder by his wife and her lover.

1.6 Hundred Years' War & War of the Roses

Edward III (1312—1377) succeeded his father at the age of 15 and reigned for 50 years (the second longest reign in English history after Henry III, queens excluded). His reign was marked by the beginning of the **Hundred Years' War**③ (1337—1416) and epidemics of "Black Death", which killed one third of England (and Europe's) population.

The Hundred Years' War was a series of wars fought between England and France. Each side drew many allies into the fighting. The war had its roots in a disagreement dating back to the time of William the Conqueror, who became King of England in 1066 while retaining possession of the Duchy of Normandy in France. As the rulers of Normandy and other lands on the continent, the English kings owed feudal homage to the King of France. In 1337, Edward III of England refused to pay homage to Philip VI of France, leading the French King to claim confiscation of Edward's lands in **Aquitaine**④.

At first, the war went in England's favor. As time went on, however, guns and gunpowder appeared in war, which greatly reduced the effectiveness of the English bows and arrows. Most of the English possessions in France was lost to Joan of Arc. By the time the war ended, the English has lost all the territories they had gained during the war except the French port of Calais.

In 1455, the Wars of the Roses broke out. This civil war opposed the House of Lancaster (the Red Rose, supporters of Henry VI) to the House of York (the White Rose, supporters of Edward IV). The Yorks argued that the crown should have

---

① Simon de Montfort：西蒙·德·蒙特福特，英格兰男爵，英国国会之父。

② *Brave Heart*：电影《勇敢的心》，讲述在"长腿爱德华"暴政之下，英雄之后华莱士带领苏格兰人民为自由抗争的故事。

③ Hundred Years' War：百年战争。世界最长的战争，长达116年，参战方包括英国和法国，以及后来加入的勃艮第。百年战争中，发展出不少新战术和武器。战争胜利使法国完成民族统一，为日后在欧洲大陆扩张打下了基础；英格兰几乎丧失所有的法国领地，但也使英格兰的民族主义兴起。

④ Aquitaine：阿基坦，法国西南部的一个地区。1137年阿基坦女公爵与法国国王路易斯七世结婚后，阿基坦公国加入法国，但在她再嫁给英国国王亨利二世后，其归属权便存在争议。

passed to Edward III's second son, Lionel of Antwerp, rather than to the Lancasters descending from John of Gaunt. One of the key players was Richard Neville, **Earl of Warwick**①, nicknamed "the Kingmaker", for deposing Henry VI for Edward IV, then again Edward for Henry 9 years later.

Edward IV's son, Edward V, only reigned for one year, before being locked in the Tower of London by his evil uncle, Richard III (1452—1485). The reason is that Lancastrian Henry Tudor (1457—1509), the half-brother of Henry VI, defeated Richard III at the Battle of Bosworth Field in 1485, and became Henry VII, founder of the House of Tudors. Henry Tudor's son is maybe England's most famous and historically important ruler, the magnificent Henry VIII (1491—1547).

King Henry VIII by Hans Holbein the Younger, Walker Art Gallery
From: http://en.wikipedia.org/wiki/Henry_VIII

2. Transition to the Modern Age

2.1 Religious Reformation

Henry VIII is remembered in history as one of the most powerful kings of England. Except for getting married six times, desperate for a male heir, Henry changed the face of England, passing the ***Acts of Union with Wales***(1535—1543)②,

---

① Earl of Warwick:沃里克伯爵。英格兰大贵族,玫瑰战争中著名的立王者。1461 年帮助约克家族的爱德华四世登基,后来又使被废黜的兰开斯特家族的亨利六世恢复王位。

② Acts of Union with Wales:《威尔士法案》,也称《联合法案公章》。英格兰王国以《1535 年联合法案公章》合并威尔士公国,以《1707 年联合法案》合并苏格兰王国,成为大不列颠联合王国,再以《1800 年联合法案》合并爱尔兰王国,成为大不列颠与爱尔兰联合王国。1922 年,爱尔兰自由邦脱离联合王国,但北爱尔兰留下。1927 年,爱尔兰共和国成立,英国国名于是改为大不列颠及北爱尔兰联合王国。

thus becoming the first English King of Wales, then changing his title of Lord of Ireland into that of (also first) King of Ireland (1541).

In 1533, Henry divorced his first wife, Catherine of Aragon (Queen Mary's mother) to remarry Anne Boleyn (Queen Elizabeth I's mother), the Pope excommunicated Henry, and in return, Henry issued the *Act of Supremacy*, and proclaimed himself head of the Church of England. To assure the control over the clergy, Henry dissolved all the monasteries in the country (1536—1540) and nationalised them, becoming immensely rich in the process. The Religious Reformation was in essence a political movement in a religious guise.

Henry VIII was the last English king to claim the title of King of France, as he lost his last possession there, the port of Calais. It was also under Henry VIII that England started exploring the globe and trading outside Europe, although this would only develop to colonial proportions under his daughters, Mary I and especially Elizabeth I (after whom Virginia was named).

The 10-year old Edward VI inherited the throne at his father's death in 1547, but died 6 years later and was succeeded by his elder half-sister Mary. Mary I (1516—1558), a staunch Catholic, intended to restore Roman Catholicism to England, executing over 300 religious dissenters in her 5-year reign, which owned her the nickname of Bloody Mary. Mary died childless of ovarian cancer in 1558, and her half-sister Elizabeth ascended the throne.

The great Virgin Queen Elizabeth I (1533—1603) saw the first golden age of England. It was an age of great navigators like Sir Francis Drake and Sir Walter Raleigh, an age of enlightenment with the philosopher Francis Bacon (1561—1626), and playwrights such as Christopher Marlowe (1564—1593) and William Shakespeare (1564—1616).

Her reign was also marked by conflicts with France and Scotland (bound by a common queen, **Mary Stuart**①), then Spain and Ireland. Elizabeth never married, and when Mary Stuart tried and failed to take over the throne of England, Elizabeth kept her imprisoned for 19 years before finally signing her act of execution. Elizabeth died in 1603, and ironically, Mary Stuart's son, James VI of Scotland, succeeded Elizabeth as **King James I of England**②—thus creating the United Kingdom.

---

① Mary Stuart：玛丽·斯图亚特出生后 6 天成为苏格兰女王，17 岁成为法国王后。因为她是伊丽莎白一世的表侄女，有继承英格兰王位的资格，因而被伊丽莎白一世所忌惮，被其判下狱 19 年，并于 1587 年因企图刺杀女王罪被处以极刑。

② 苏格兰的詹姆斯六世为玛丽·斯图亚特之子，1603 年，伊丽莎白一世指定詹姆斯为其继承人后驾崩，詹姆斯即位为英格兰国王，自封为大不列颠王国，称詹姆斯一世。

The "Darnley Portrait" of Elizabeth I
From: http://en.wikipedia.org/wiki/Elizabeth_ I

2.2 Civil War & Restoration

James I (1566—1625) was a **Protestant**①, like Elizabeth, and aimed at improving relations with the Catholics. But 2 years after he was crowned, a group of Catholic extremists attempted to place a bomb at the parliament's state opening, when the king and his entourage would be present, so as to get rid of all the Protestant aristocracy in one fell swoop. This incident was called Gunpowder Plot.

The divide between Catholics and Protestant worsened after this incident. James's successor Charles I (1600—1649) was eager to unify Britain and Ireland, and wanted to do so as an absolute ruler of divine right, like his French counter-part Louis XIV. Despite being an (Anglican) Protestant, his marriage with a French Roman Catholic combined with policies at odd with Calvinist ideals and his totalitarian handling of the Parliament eventually culminated in the **English Civil War** (1642—1651)②. The country was torn between Royalist and Parliamentarian troops, and most of the medieval castles still standing were destroyed during that period.

Charles I was beheaded, and the puritan leader of the Parliamentarians, **Oliver**

---

① Protestant: 新教是由16世纪宗教改革运动中脱离罗马天主教的一系列新教派的统称，主流教派有路德宗、加尔文宗和圣公会。

② English Civil War: 英国内战是1642年至1651年在英国议会派与保皇派之间发生的一系列武装冲突及政治斗争；英国辉格党称之为清教徒革命（Puritan Revolution）。此事件对英国和整个欧洲都产生了巨大的影响。

Cromwell (1599—1658)①, ruled the country as a dictator from 1649 to his death. He was briefly succeeded by his son Richard, whose political inability prompted the Parliament to restore the monarchy in 1660, calling in Charles I's son, Charles II (1630—1685).

Charles II was better at handling Parliament than his father, although as ruthless with other matters. It is during his reign that the Whig and Tory parties were created, and that the Dutch colony of New Amsterdam became English and was renamed New York.

Charles II was the patron of the arts and sciences. He helped found the **Royal Society**② and sponsored architect Sir Christopher Wren, who rebuilt the City of London after the **Great Fire of 1666**③, and constructed some of England's greatest edifices. Charles acquired Bombay and Tangiers through his Portuguese wife, thus laying the foundation for the British Empire.

Although Charles produced countless illegitimate children, 14 of whom he acknowledged, his wife couldn't bear an heir, and when he died in 1685 the throne passed to his Catholic and unpopular brother James II.

2.3 The Glorious Revolution

James II's religious inclinations and despotism led to his quick removal from power in the Glorious Revolution of 1688. His Protestant daughter Mary, married to his equally Protestant nephew, William of Orange. The couple was "invited" by the Protestant aristocracy to conduct an invasion from the Netherlands. They defeated James' troops at the Battle of the Boyne, and deposed James II with limited bloodshed. James escaped to France in 1688, where he remained the rest of his life under the protection of Louis XIV. The new ruling couple became known as the "Grand Alliance". In the following year, the parliament passed the *Bill of Rights*, which limited the power of the monarch and guaranteed the authority of Parliament. In 1707, the ***Act of Union***④ joined the Scottish and the English Parliaments thus creating the single Kingdom of Great Britain and centralising political power in

---

① Oliver Cromwell：奥利弗·克伦威尔为新模范军（New Model Army）指挥官之一，在英国内战中击败了保皇党。1649年在查理一世被处决后，克伦威尔开始使用护国主的头衔统治着英格兰、苏格兰和爱尔兰。

② Royal Society：英国皇家学会成立于1660年，是世界上历史最长而又从未中断过的科学学会。它在英国起着全国科学院的作用。英国皇家学会目前最知名的院士包括物理学家霍金、胚胎移植及肝细胞研究权威安妮·麦克莱伦、互联网发明人蒂姆·伯纳斯·李。

③ Great Fire (of London)：伦敦大火发生于1666年9月2日-5日，是英国伦敦历史上最严重的一次火灾，烧掉了许多建筑物，包括圣保罗大教堂，但这次火灾终止了自1665年以来伦敦的鼠疫问题。

④ 见本章2.1节注释 Acts of Union with Wales。

London.

2.4　Industrial Revolution

The Industrial Revolution was the transition to new manufacturing processes in the period from about 1760 to sometime between 1820 and 1840. This transition included going from hand production methods to machines, new chemical manufacturing and iron production processes, improved efficiency of water power, the increasing use of steam power and the development of machine tools. It also included the change from wood and other bio-fuels to coal.

Textiles were the dominant industry of the Industrial Revolution in terms of employment, value of output and capital invested. Textiles were also the first to use modern inventions, like the Spinning Jenny, the water frame, the spinning mule, the power loom and the steam engine. These inventions completed the mechanization of the textile industry and prepared the way for a new system of production: large scale industry.

Model of Spinning Jenny in the Museum of Early Industrialization, Wuppertal, Germany
From: http://en.wikipedia.org/wiki/Spinning_jenny

The Industrial Revolution marks a major turning point in history; almost every aspect of daily life was influenced in some way. In particular, average income and population began to exhibit unprecedented sustained growth. But what brought it about and why did it happen first in Britain? Political, economic and intellectual conditions would all contribute. But at the heart of the revolution was the use of energy.

Coal was the fuel which kick-started the Industrial Revolution, and Britain was very fortunate to have plenty that could be easily mined. Britain had an advantage over other European countries because its mines were near the sea, so ships could carry coal cheaply to the most important market—London.

Newcomen and other inventors benefited from the intellectual climate. There was a prolific exchange of scientific and technological ideas. And Britain, unlike many

European countries, did not suffer censorship by Church or state. Alongside the new discoveries was a growing movement of people, trying to find practical applications for these new discoveries. Men of action and men of ideas, industrialists and scientists-often from very different backgrounds – met to share their ideas and observations, in what was to be called the Industrial Enlightenment. They unleashed a wave of free thinking and creativity.

Britain also had the right political background for free-market capitalism. The system of parliamentary government that followed the Glorious Revolution of 1688—1689 provided the background for stable investment and for a basis of taxation favourable to economic expansion. France, by contrast, was home to some of the finest scientific minds, but had an absolute monarchy which wielded great control over economic and political life.

Naval power and imperial possessions enabled Britain to dominate trans-oceanic trade and to profit accordingly. Entrepreneurship was at the heart of economic success in the colonies. There was a considerable human cost to this free trade however, which enabled landowners to buy huge numbers of slaves, transported from Africa. They were treated as a natural resource to be used and exploited in the quest for maximum profit.

3. The Rise and Fall of the British Empire

3.1 The British Empire & Victorian England

In 1837, William IV died of liver disease and the throne passed to the next in line, his 18-year old niece Victoria (1819—1901), although she did not inherit the Kingdom of Hanover, where the Salic Law forbid women to rule.

Victoria didn't expect to become queen, was still unmarried and inexperienced in politics, and had to rely on her Prime Minister, Lord Melbourne (1779—1848), after whom the Australian city is named. She finally got married to her first cousin, Prince Albert of Saxe-Coburg-Gotha (1819—1861), and both were respectively niece and nephew of the first King of the Belgians, Leopold I (of Saxe-Coburg-Gotha).

Prince Albert organised the **Great Exhibition** [①](the first World Fair) in 1851, and the profits were used to found the great South Kensington Museum (later renamed the Victoria and Albert Museum) in London.

Britain asserted its hegemony on virtually every part of the globe, although this resulted in numerous wars, as for example the Opium Wars (1839—1842 and

---

① Great Exhibition：伦敦万国博览会，即第一届世博会，它已经历了百余年的历史，最初以美术品和传统工艺品的展示主为，后来逐渐变为荟萃科学技术与产业技术的展览会。

1856—1860) with Qing China, or the **Boer Wars** ①(1880—1881 and 1899—1902) with the Dutch-speaking settlers of South Africa.

In 1854, the United Kingdom was brought into the **Crimean War** ②(1853—1856) on the side of the Ottoman Empire and against Russia. One of the best known figure of that war was **Florence Nightingale**③ (1820—1910), who fought for the improvement of the women's condition and pioneered modern nursing.

In 1861, Albert died prematurely at the age of 42. Victoria was devastated and retired in a semi-permanent state of mourning. She nevertheless started a romantic relationship with her Scottish servant John Brown (1826—1883), and there were even talks of a secret marriage.

The latter years of her reign were dominated by two influential Prime Ministers, Benjamin Disraeli (1808—1881) and his rival William Ewart Gladstone (1809—1898). The former was the favourite of the Queen, and crowned her "Empress of India" in 1876, in return of which Victoria creating him Earl of Beaconsfield. Gladstone was a liberal, and often at odd with both Victoria and Disraeli, but the strong support he enjoyed from within his party kept him in power for a total of 14 years between 1868 and 1894. He legalised trade unions, advocated both universal education and universal suffrage.

Queen Victoria was to have the longest reign of any British monarch (64 years), but also the most glorious, as she ruled over 40% of the globe and a quarter of the world's population.

3.2 The Two World Wars

Victoria's numerous children married in about all European Royal families, which owned her the affectionate title of "grandmother of Europe". Her son, Edward VII (1841—1910) was the uncle of German Emperor Wilhelm II, Tsar Nicholas II of Russia, King Alphonso XIII of Spain, and Carl Eduard, Duke of Saxe-Coburg-Gotha, while George I of the Hellenes and King Frederick VIII of Denmark were his brothers-in-law; and King Albert I of Belgium, Manuel II of Portugal, King Ferdinand of Bulgaria, Queen Wilhelmina of the Netherlands, and Prince Ernst August, Duke of Brunswick-Lüneburg, were his cousins.

The alliances between these related monarchs escalated in the WWI (1914—

---

① Boer Wars：布尔战争是英国与南非布尔人为争夺南非殖民地而展开的战争。荷兰殖民者17世纪到达南非，他们与葡萄牙、法国殖民者的后裔被称为布尔人。

② Crimean War：克里米亚战争是因争夺巴尔干半岛的控制权而在欧洲大陆爆发的一场战争，奥斯曼帝国、英国、法国、撒丁王国等先后向沙皇俄国宣战，以沙皇俄国的失败而告终。

③ Florence Nightingale：弗洛伦斯·南丁格尔出生在意大利的一个优裕家庭，因在克里米亚进行护理而闻名。"5.12"国际护士节设立在南丁格尔的生日这一天，就是为了纪念这位近代护理事业的创始人和现代护理教育的奠基人。

1918) when Archduke Franz Ferdinand of Austria was assassinated in Sarajevo, and Austria declared war on Serbia, which in turn was allied to France, Russia and the UK. The First World War left over 9 million dead (including nearly 1 million Britons) throughout Europe, and financially ruined most of the countries involved. The monarchies in Germany, Austria, Russia and the Ottoman Empire all fell, and the map of central and eastern Europe was redesigned.

The consequences in Britain were disillusionment with the government and monarchy, and the creation of the Labour Party. The General Strike of 1926 and the worsening economy led to radical political changes, and women were granted the same universal suffrage as men (from age 21 instead of previously 30) in 1928.

In 1936, Edward VIII (1894—1972) succeeded to his father George V, but abdicated the same year to marry Wallis Simpson, a twice divorced American woman. His brother then unexpectedly became George VI (1895—1952) after the scandal.

Nazi Germany was becoming more menacing as Hitler grew more powerful and aggressive. Finally Britain and France were forced to declare war on Germany after the invasion of Poland in September 1939, and so started the WWII.

WWII involved the vast majority of the world's nations—including all of the great powers—eventually forming two opposing military alliances: the Allies and the Axis, the former included Germany, Austria-Hungary, later joined by the **Ottoman Empire**① and Bulgaria, and the later were mainly comprised of France, the Russian Empire, the British Empire, Italy and the United States.

The charismatic Winston Churchill (1874—1965) became the war-time British Prime Minister in 1940 and he encouraged the British to fight off the attempted German invasion. Britain won the war, but at great costs. Britain was drained of its manpower. As a result, Britain lost the sea supremacy forever to the United States. In addition, the country has exhausted its reserves of gold, dollars and overseas investment, and was deeply in debt to the United States.

3.3 The Postwar

In 1945, the UK was bankrupt and its industry destroyed by the Blitz war, and the British Empire was dismantled little by little, first granting the independence to India and Pakistan in 1947, then to the other Asian, African and Caribbean colonies in the 1950's and 60's (in the 70's and 80's for the smaller islands of the eastern Caribbean).

Most of these ex-colonies formed the British Commonwealth, now known as the

---

① Ottoman Empire：奥斯曼帝国。奥斯曼土耳其人以小亚细亚为核心建立的跨欧、亚、非三洲的军事封建帝国，又称奥斯曼土耳其帝国。

Commonwealth of Nations. 53 states are now members of the Commonwealth, accounting for 1.8 billion people (about 30% of the global population) and about 25% of the world's land area.

In 1952, Elizabeth II ascended the throne at the age of 26. Although she somewhat rehabilitated the image of the monarchy, her children did not, and their sentimental lives have made the headlines of the tabloid newspapers at least since the marriage of Charles, Prince of Wales, with Lady Diana Spencer in 1981.

Pop and Rock music replaced colonial remembrances in the 1960's with bands like the Beatles, Pink Floyd, the Rolling Stones or Black Sabbath. The Hippie subculture also developed at that time.

The 70's brought the oil crisis and the collapse of the British industry. Conservative PM Margaret Thatcher was elected in 1979 and stayed until 1990. She privatised the railways and shut down inefficient factories, but also increased the gap between the rich and the poor by cutting on the social security. Her methods were so harsh that she was nicknamed the "Iron Lady".

Margaret Thatcher
From: http://en.wikipedia.org/wiki/Margaret_Thatcher

Thatcher was succeeded in her party by the unpopular John Major, but in 1997, the "New Labour" (more to the right than the "Old Labour") came back to power with Tony Blair. Blair's liberal policies and unwavering support of neo-conservative US President George W. Bush (especially regarding the invasion of Iraq in 2003) disappointed many **Leftists**[①], who really saw in Blair but a **Rightist**[②] in disguise.

---

① Leftist：工党和自民党为英国的左派党，在近现代政治中，左派是指社会中维护社会中下层利益、支持改变旧的不合理社会秩序、创造更为平等的财富和基本权利分配的群体。

② Rightist：保守党为英国最大的右派政党，其强调民族主义、传统和宗教，且反对社会主义、共产主义和国际主义。

But Blair has also positively surprised many by his intelligence and remarkable skills as an orator and negotiator.

Nowadays, the English economy relies heavily on services. The main industries are travel (discount airlines and travel agencies), education (apart from Oxford and Cambridge universities and textbooks, hundreds of language schools for learners of English), music (EMI, HMV, Virgin...), prestige cars (Rolls Royce, Bentley, Jaguar, Lotus, Aston Martin, MG...), fashion (Burberry, Dunhill, Paul Smith, Vivienne Westwood, French Connection...), and surprisingly to some, food (well especially tea, biscuits, chocolates and jam or companies like Unilever and Cadburry-Schweppes).

References

http://www.bbc.co.uk/history/0/

BBC History is a British website devoted to history articles on both British and world history and is aimed at all levels of knowledge and interest. This website includes such sections as Ancient History, British History, World Wars, Historic Figures, Family History, History for Kids and On This Day.

http://www.eupedia.com/

Eupedia.com was founded in December 2004 by Maciamo. The concept of this website is similar to that of a combined Wikipedia, Wikitravel and Wikicommons dedicated exclusively to Europe, so as to facilitate navigation and keep visitors focalized on European travel, history, linguistics and genetics. Reference articles were written only by authors with specialized and first-hand knowledge of the countries, including unique insights about European history, linguistics and genetics.

Exercises

I. Choose the one that best completes each of the following statements.

1. Which of the following tribes first came to Britain?
    A. Anglos.   B. Saxons.   C. Jutes.   D. Celts.
2. The three great Germanic tribes: the Anglos, the _____ and the Jutes, which invaded Britain, form the basis of the modern British people.
    A. Saxons   B. Scots   C. Welsh   D. Essex
3. William, Duke of Normandy, is now known as _____.
    A. William the Confessor   B. William Lion-Heart
    C. the father of the British navy   D. William the Conqueror
4. Because of the _____ in 1066, a lot of French words entered into the English vocabulary.
    A. Norman Conquest   B. Crusades

C. Invasion of the Vikings D. Wars of the Roses
5. The Wars of Roses are fought between _____.
   A. France and Britain B. England and Scotland
   C. England and Wales D. two branches of the English royal family
6. During the reign of _____, England was separated from the Roman Empire religiously.
   A. Henry VII B. Henry VIII C. Elizabeth I D. James II
7. The Great Charter (Magna Charter) was signed by _____ in 1215.
   A. King Henry II B. King John C. King William D. King Richard
8. During the 14th century, an epidemic named _____ spread over Europe and caused millions of deaths.
   A. Black Death B. Malaria
   C. Rift Valley Fever D. Scarlet Fever
9. Mary I is remembered less by her official title than the nickname "Bloody Mary" because _____.
   A. she was a devout Catholic and had a lot of Protestants burnt to death
   B. she launched a series of wars
   C. she showed no mercy to Catholics
   D. she killed all her brothers and sisters in order to get the throne
10. _____ was the founder of the Plantagenet Dynasty and ruled England for 35 years.
    A. Henry I B. King Stephen C. Henry II D. Count of Anjou
11. _____ became the first prince to hold the title of Prince of Wales, which continues to be borne by the eldest son of the reigning monarch.
    A. Richard I B. Henry III C. Edward II D. Edward III
12. Mary died childless and her half-sister _____ came to the throne in 1558.
    A. Ann B. Victoria C. Elizabeth D. Catherine
13. The Great Civil War, as it became known, was fought between _____.
    A. Royalists and Parliamentarians
    B. the House of Lancaster and the House of York
    C. king and church
    D. England and Scotland
14. The longest reign in British history was the monarch of _____, which lasted from 1837 to 1901.
    A. Queen Elizabeth I B. Queen Victoria
    C. Queen Mary I D. Henry VIII
15. An empire "on which the sun never sets" is a nickname of the Britain during the reign of _____.
    A. Queen Elizabeth I B. Queen Victoria

C. Queen Mary I   D. Henry VIII

II. Read the following statements carefully and decide whether they are TRUE or FALSE.

1. Julius Caesar, the great roman general, invaded Britain for the first time in 55 BC. For nearly 400 years, Britain was under Roman occupation.
2. The Norman conquest of England is perhaps the best-known event in English history. Under William, the feudal system in England was completely established.
3. In the mid-5th century a new wave of invaders, Saxons, Angles and Celts came to Britain, they were three Teutonic tribes.
4. The Hundred Years' War was fought between England and France, and the war went in England's favor.
5. The War of Roses was a series of civil wars between two great noble families: the House of York and the House of Tudor.
6. In an effort to make a compromise between different religious factions, Queen Elizabeth I actually defended the fruit of the Religious Reformation.
7. When Oliver Cromwell died in 1658 and was succeeded by his son Richard, the regime began to collapse. The parliament was elected in 1660 and resolved the crisis by asking the late King's son as King Charles II to return from his long exile in France.
8. William and Mary jointly accepted the *Bill of Rights* which excluded any Roman catholic from the succession and confirmed the principle of parliamentary supremacy. Thus the age of constitutional monarchy began.
9. During World War II, Winston Churchill, the prime minister of the UK, led the British people to fight against the Fascist.
10. Britain's first woman prime minister was Margaret Thatcher.

III. Give brief answers to the following questions.

1. What were the two camps in World War II?
2. Why did Industrial Revolution happen first in Britain?

Section Two: In-depth Reading

At the peak of its power, the phrase "the empire on which the sun never sets" was often used to describe the British Empire, because Britain enjoyed a period of almost unchallenged dominance and expanded its imperial holdings across the globe. However, WWI placed enormous financial and population strain on Britain, and since then it was no longer a peerless industrial and military power. The two articles in this section will acquaint us with British history from different perspectives.

Reading One is a British scholar's verdicts on British Empire.

Reading Two is a brief introduction to the current situation of this used-to-be superpower.

Before reading the articles, brainstorm with your cohorts on the following questions:
1. Tell us some of your familiar historical stories.
2. Why did Britain cooperate closely with the United States after WWII?

Reading One

For most of the nineteenth and twentieth centuries, the British ruled over a colossal empire that stretched from one end of the map to the other. One cannot contemplate modern history without considering the role of the British Empire. In the following article, a British scholar gives his verdicts on the British Empire.

The World Shaped by Empire
P. J. Marshall

For most of the 19th and 20th centuries the British ruled over a colossal territorial empire, extending over a large part of North America, much of the Caribbean region, great tracts of Africa south of the Sahara, the whole of the Indian subcontinent and **Australasia**①, territories in South East Asia and the Pacific, and even for a time much of the Middle East.

The British Empire has profoundly shaped the modern world. Most present-day countries outside Europe owe their existence to empires, especially to the British Empire. The British fixed boundaries by conquest and partition treaties. Huge movements of people took place within the empire, determining the ethnic composition of many countries. It was British people under British rule who were responsible for ensuring that, once indigenous peoples has been displaced, North American and Australasian societies would be overwhelmingly European in character. The British were also the major carries of the estimated eleven million Africans shifted to the Americas as slaves. Most of those carried by the British went to Britain's own colonies in the Caribbean, whose present population are for the most part the consequence of that forced migration. From the middle of the 19th century large numbers of Indian and Chinese people went to labor in colonies ruled by Britain. Their descendants make up a large part of the population of many countries from Guyana and Trinidad to Fiji, Mauritius, Malaysia, and Singapore.

Through their empire the British disseminated their institutions, culture, and

---

① Australasia: 澳大拉西亚、指澳大利亚,新西兰及附近南太平洋诸岛,有时也泛指大洋洲和太平洋岛屿。

language. Every country in the present-day world can be regarded as anything approaching a carbon copy of what Britain was or is: national identities evolve by very complex processes of interaction between a society's own traditions and external influences. Occupation by an imperial power is, nevertheless, likely to have been a very potent external influence, especially when the imperial power was as self-confident in its values and institutions as Britain has been for most of its history. In varying degrees British influences can be detected in systems of government, religious adherence, patterns of education, the layout of towns and cities, cultural tastes, sports, and pastimes throughout the world. The claim of English to be a virtually universal language in the contemporary world is no doubt partly a reflection of the power of the United States. But the United States is of course an English-speaking society as a consequence of the British Empire; so are very many other countries.

The British Empire changed not only people but the land in which they lived. New patterns of farming, mining, or manufacturing all meant that the land and its resources were used in new ways. Sometimes environmental change was rapid and spectacular, as prairies were ploughed up or previously forested islands were turned into sugar plantations; the full effects of other changes that began in the colonial period have only become apparent in modern times with an increase in pressure to use the land and its resources to the full.

The contemporary world is sharply divided between rich and poor. The legacy of empire has played a part in bringing about this divide, although it is not a part that is easy to interpret. Some ex-imperial countries are rich; some are very poor. Does this simply indicate that, regardless of what the British did or did not do, some countries have favorable endowments of land, people, and resources, which have made economic growth possible, while others lack such endowment? Or does it mean that the experience of imperial rule by Britain was very different—enabling, for instance, white immigrant communities in Australia and Canada to improve their lot, while impoverishing Asians or Africans? Answers to such questions are rarely simple: economic change, like the evolution of cultures, involves a process of interaction. Colonial economies were shaped by the enterprise of the colonial people, as well as by the intervention of the British.

The history of the empire as a whole is indeed the study of interactions between the British and other people rather than of the British "impact" on them. Interaction supposes that the peoples over whom the British ruled were not merely hapless "natives" to whom the British brought blessings or misfortune. Before colonial rule, the people of Asia, Africa, the Americas, and the Pacific of course made their own history. Under British rule they continued to do so, as well as having it made for them by British power. The history of slavery, for instance, is the history of how the slaves developed their own culture and resisted their masters, as well as being the history of their oppression.

References
P. J. Marshall. 1996. *The Cambridge Illustrated History of the British Empire*. Cambridge: Cambridge University Press.

About the Author
P. J. Marshall is Emeritus Professor of History at King's College, London, where he taught the history of empire. He was born in Calcutta, educated at Oxford, and is a Fellow of the British Academy.

Discussions
1. What is the author's tone towards British Empire?
2. Why was Britain once called "the empire on which the sun never sets"? What led to the fall of the British Empire? Do you know any other empires which used to be powerful but eventually declined? How do they remind you of the decline of China after Qing Dynasty?
3. The author said, "Every country in the present-day world can be regarded as anything approaching a carbon copy of what Britain was or is." Do you agree with him? If you do, can you find out the similarity between Britain and other commonwealth members in political system?

Reading Two

Post-1945, Britain quickly relinquished its status as the world's largest imperial power, but it was the massive cultural and social changes at home that truly transformed British society.

Britain from 1945 Onwards
Jeremy Black

Changing population
Britain and the British have changed profoundly since 1945. A principal driver of change has been a major growth in population, matched by rapidly rising expectations about lifestyle.

Large-scale immigration has made the population ethnically far more diverse, with important cultural consequences.

The composition of the population has undergone a marked transformation, due primarily to advances in medicine. In line with a general trend around the developed world, life expectancy has risen greatly for both men and women. This has meant that the average age has risen, a process accentuated by the extent to which the birth rate has remained static.

Furthermore, large-scale immigration, particularly from the West Indies and South Asia, but also from other areas such as Eastern Europe, has made the population ethnically far more diverse, with important cultural consequences. In 1970 there were about 375,000 Hindus, Muslims and Sikhs in Britain. By 1993 the figure was about 1,620,000, with the rise in the number of Muslims being particularly pronounced.

Moral codes

Social and cultural change has also reflected the extent to which the population has become more individualistic and less deferential.

The moral code that prevailed in 1945 broke down, a process formalised by legal changes in the 1960s. Abortion and homosexuality became legal, capital punishment was abolished, and measures were taken to improve the position of women.

These changes were linked to shifts in religious practice. By the 1990s, only one in seven Britons was an active member of a Christian church, although more claimed to be believers. But for most believers, formal expressions of faith became less important. The failure in the 1990s of the heavily church-backed "Keep Sunday Special" campaign (to prevent shops from opening on the sabbath) confirmed the general trend.

More generally, the authority of age and experience were overthrown and, in their place, came an emphasis on youth and novelty.

Domestic policies

In contrast to the situation in Northern Ireland, Welsh and Scottish nationalism remained essentially non-violent, and in 1997 each gained a devolved assembly exercising a considerable amount of local control.

At times, Britain itself appeared to be going the same way, as entry into the European Economic Community (EEC) – later European Union (EU) – in 1973 led to a marked erosion of national sovereignty and to a transfer of powers to Europe.

At the national level, government was controlled by the Labour Party (1945—1951, 1964—1970, 1974—1979 and 1997 onwards) and its Conservative rival (1951—1964, 1970—1974, 1979—1997), with no coalition ministries. The Labour and Conservative parties shared major overlaps in policy throughout the post-war period, for example in maintaining free health care at the point of delivery – the basis of the National Health Service.

The Conservatives tended to favour individual liberties and low taxation, while Labour preferred collectivist solutions and were therefore happier to advocate a major role for the state.

This was particularly evident in Labour's support for the nationalisation of major parts of the economy during their pre-1979 governments. Most, in turn, were denationalised again under the Conservatives between 1979 and 1997.

References

Jeremy Black. 2011. *Overview: Britain from 1945 onwards*.
http://www.bbc.co.uk/history/british/modern/overview_1945_present_01.shtml

About the author

Jeremy Black is Professor of History at the University of Exeter. He works on post-1500 military history, 18th-century British history, international relations, cartographic history and newspaper history. His recent publications include *The European Question and the National Interest* (Social Affairs Unit, 2006) and *War and the New Disorder in the 21st-century* (Continuum, 2005).

Discussions

1. Large-scale immigration has made the British population ethnically far more diverse, with important cultural consequences. Can you give us some examples of the immigrants' cultural impact on Britain?
2. In July, 2013, England and Wales legalized homosexual marriage. Some took it as a sign of political liberalism, while some argued that it was moral breakdown, how do you see this incident?
3. Nowadays, the British economy relies heavily on services, like traveling, education, music and so on. Can you give us some specific examples of the services provided in Britain?

Chapter 3

Government and Politics

Section One: A Brief Introduction

1. Constitution

A constitution is a set of laws on how a country is governed. The British Constitution is unwritten in one single document, unlike the constitution in America or the proposed European Constitution, and as such, is referred to as an uncodified or "unwritten" constitution in the sense that there is no single document that can be classed as Britain's constitution. The British Constitution can be found in a variety of documents. Supporters of British Constitution believe that the current way allows for flexibility and change to occur without too many problems. Those who want a written constitution believe that it should be codified so that the public as a whole has access to it — as opposed to just constitutional experts who know where to look and how to interpret it. Amendments to Britain's unwritten constitution are made the same way — by simply a majority support in both Houses of Parliament to be followed by the Royal Assent.

The British Constitution comes from a variety of sources. The main ones are: Statutes, Common Law and Conventions. Statutes are those that have been passed by Parliament, such as the *Magna Carta* (1215), *the Bill of Rights* (1689), the *Act of Settlement* (1701), the *Reform Act* (1832) and the *European Communities Act* (1972). Common law is also called case law, which is law developed by judges through decisions of courts and similar tribunals. Conventions are accepted ways in which things are done; they are not written down in law but tend to be old, established practices.

A historic feature of the UK constitution, the Royal Prerogative gives the Crown (the monarch) special powers, including the power to declare war, to make treaties, to pardon criminals, and to dissolve Parliament. Today the role of the monarch in such matters is largely ceremonial, but the Royal Prerogative gives considerable powers to government ministers acting on the Queen's behalf.

The single most important principle of the UK constitution is that of **Parliamentary sovereignty**①. Under this principle, Parliament can make or unmake any law on any subject whatsoever. No one Parliament is bound by the decisions of its predecessors, nor can it bind its successors. There is no higher body, such as a supreme court, that constrains the legal authority of Parliament.

2. Separation of Power

"Separation of powers" refers to the idea that the major institutions of state should be functionally independent and that no individual should have powers that span these offices. The principal institutions are usually taken to be the executive, the legislature and the judiciary.

In America all three branches are systematically split between the Executive (the president), the legislative (Congress) and the Judiciary (the Supreme Court). The president cannot serve in Congress when president and serving Congressmen cannot be a Supreme Court judge. In theory, no branch becomes more powerful than the other two so that a balance occurs. The American Constitution clearly states what the executive, the legislative and the judiciary can do.

In Britain, the legislative is Parliament where laws are passed; the executive (which plans prospective laws and formulates policy) is the cabinet of the government and the judiciary is the Law Lords and the Judicial Committee of the Privy Council who have a final say on legal issues (the European Court excluded).

However, whereas the American model has separation as part of the American Constitution, this is less clear in Britain.

The Prime Minister is an active member of the legislative and can vote in Parliament, yet he is also the leading member of the executive. Also the **Lord Chancellor**② is a member of the cabinet and therefore of the executive as well as being head of the judiciary. The House of Lords also has a right to vote on bills so they are part of the legislative but the Lords also contains the Law Lords who are an important part of the judiciary. As with the PM, the members of the Cabinet are also members of the legislative who have the right, as a Member of Parliament, to vote on issues.

Therefore, there is a merging of roles in the British model. Some have argued

---

① Parliamentary sovereignty：议会至上是英国宪法的根基，它指法案一旦获议会通过，便具有不可动摇的权威。从理论上讲，议会有权制定和废除宪法以下的任何一项法律；此外，英国法律不承认任何个人和单位有权推翻或废弃议会所通过的法律。

② Lord Chancellor：大法官，英国上议院院长及内阁成员。

that this is needed for flexibility in a modern society. Supporters of the American model claim that a written constitution restricts each section's powers and avoids crossover between the three sectors of politics.

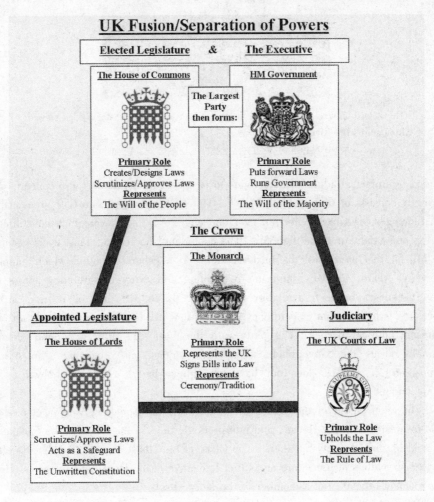

Separation of powers
From: http://en.wikipedia.org/wiki/Separation_of_powers

2.1 The Legislature

Parliament is the law-making body of Britain, and is separate from government. It is made up of the King or Queen, the House of Lords and the House of Commons, its role is to: 1) look at what the government is doing; 2) debate issues and pass new laws; 3) set taxes.

The House of Commons is the lower house of the UK bicameral Parliament. It is

The Palace of Westminster with Elizabeth Tower and Westminster Bridge viewed from across the River Thames
From: http://en.wikipedia.org/wiki/Palace_of_Westminster

elected by universal adult suffrage voters to represent their interests and concerns and currently consists of **650 elected MPs**①. The UK is divided into 650 areas called constituencies. During an election everyone eligible to cast a vote in a constituency selects one candidate to be their MP. The candidate who gets the most votes becomes the MP for that area until the next election. At a general election which happens every five years, all MPs stand for re-election and every constituency across the country chooses between available candidates. If an MP dies or retires, a **by-election**② is held in that constituency to find a new MP for that area. Nearly all MPs represent political parties. The party with the most MPs after a general election normally forms the Government. The next largest party becomes the official Opposition. If an MP does not have a political party, they are known as an "Independent".

The chief officer of the House of Commons is the Speaker, who is elected by MPs to preside over the House, and interprets the rules of the House. The Speaker is assisted by three Deputy Speakers. The Clerk of the House is both the House's chief adviser on matters of procedure and Chief Executive of the House of Commons. He is a permanent official, not a member of the House itself.

MPs are involved in attending debates and voting on new laws, and can use their position to ask government ministers questions about current issues. MPs split their time between working in Parliament itself, working in the constituency that elected them and working for their political party. Some MPs from the governing party (or parties) become government ministers with specific responsibilities in certain areas,

---

① MP: Member of Parliament, 英国下议院议员。英国大选之前会先根据人口稠密程度划分选区,因人口分布不断变化,每次选区的划分都会略有不同,下议院议员人数也有所增减,现有650名议员(2010年至今)。

② by-election: 缺补选举指组织中席位出现空缺时进行选举。

such as Health or Defence.

The House of Lords is the second chamber of the UK Parliament. It is independent from, and complements the work of, the elected House of Commons. The Lords shares the task of making and shaping laws and checking and challenging the work of the government. The Lords has three main roles: making laws; in-depth consideration of public policy; holding government to account.

Members of the House of Lords are appointed by the Queen on the advice of the Prime Minister. Some non-party-political members are recommended by an independent body—the House of Lords Appointments Commission. Many members continue to be active in their fields and have successful careers in business, culture, science, sports, academia, law, education, health and public service. They bring this knowledge to their role of examining matters of public interest that affect all UK citizens. Currently, there are about 760 members who are eligible to take part in the work of the House of Lords. The House of Lords is presided over by the Lord Chancellor, who is a political appointee of the government. The majority are life peers. Most members of the Lords do not receive a salary for their parliamentary duties but are eligible to receive allowances and, within certain limits, the travel expenses they incur in fulfilling their parliamentary duties.

Members of the House of Lords are organized on a party basis in much the same way as the House of Commons but with important differences: Members of the Lords do not represent constituencies and many are not members of a political party. Lords who do not support one of the three main parties are known as Crossbenchers or Independent Peers.

The meeting place in House of Commons chamber
From: http://en.wikipedia.org/wiki/House_of_Commons_of_the_United_Kingdom

2.2 The Executive

Whereas Parliament is the focus of the legislative process, the formulation and execution of policy is the responsibility of the government.

As head of the executive branch of government the prime minister enjoys considerable power. He (or she) hires and fires cabinet ministers and directs, presents and co-ordinates the work of the government. He also has the power to decide when to hold the next election (within the maximum five-year term), enhancing his power over his political opponents. In his role as national leader the prime minister represents the country in international relations and enjoys extensive prerogative powers in international negotiations and crises.

Surrounding the prime minister is a cabinet, usually of around 20 to 23 ministers. Each is appointed by the prime minister from the members of the House of Commons and House of Lords and is given responsibility for directing the work of a government department. The cabinet coordinates government business, including the legislative programme, constitutional issues, and public expenditure decisions. Every Tuesday during Parliament, members of the Cabinet (Secretaries of State from all departments and some other ministers) meet to discuss the most important issues for the government.

In practice the business of government more commonly takes place in smaller cabinet committees. There are 25 ~ 30 standing committees, covering permanent policy areas in domestic and international affairs. Much work is also carried out within a range of temporary, ad hoc committees, set up to tackle issues of the day. The most important committees are chaired by the prime minister and senior ministers. Cabinet ministers and committees are bound by **the convention of collective responsibility**①. As such, once a decision is made, all ministers are bound by it and must support it publicly. If they cannot do so, they are expected to resign their ministerial post.

10 Downing Street
From: http://en.wikipedia.org/wiki/10_Downing_Street

---

① the convention of collective responsibility: 责任内阁制指内阁整体需对议会负责。如果议会对某位阁员或整体内阁不信任,个别阁员或整体内阁便需要辞职以示负责。

2.3 The Judiciary

Under the doctrine of the separation of powers, the judiciary generally does not make law (that is, in a plenary fashion, which is the responsibility of the legislature) or enforce law (which is the responsibility of the executive), but rather interprets law and applies it to the facts of each case. This branch of the state is often tasked with ensuring equal justice under law. It usually consists of a court of final appeal (called the "Supreme Court" or "Constitutional Court"), together with lower courts.

The judges of the Supreme Court of the United Kingdom are known as Justices of the Supreme Court, and they are also Privy Counsellors. Justices of the Supreme Court are granted the courtesy title Lord or Lady for life.

The Supreme Court is a relatively new Court being established in October 2009 following the Constitutional Reform Act 2005. Formerly, the Highest Court of Appeal in the United Kingdom was the House of Lords Appellate Committee made up of **Lords of Appeal in Ordinary**[①], also known as Law Lords, which with other Lord Justices now form the Supreme Court. Such Law Lords were allowed to sit in the House of Lords and were members for life.

The Supreme Court is headed by the President and Deputy President of the Supreme Court and is composed of a further ten Justices of the Supreme Court. The Justices do not wear any gowns or wigs in court, but on ceremonial occasions they wear black damask gowns with gold lace without a wig.

3. Political Parties

There are many political parties in Britain but throughout the whole of England, there are three dominant political parties: Labor, Conservatives and Liberal Democrats.

3.1 Conservative Party

The Conservative Party, officially the "Conservative & Unionist Party", and commonly known as "The Tory Party" or "the Tories" is one of the two largest political parties in the United Kingdom. Since World War Two, every Prime Minister has come from the Conservative Party or the Labour Party. Generally standing for lower taxation, a smaller state and lower welfare, the Conservative Party is the traditional right-wing party in the UK. Given that the Conservative Party vehemently

---

① Lords of Appeal in Ordinary：常任上诉法官，简称上院法官（英语：Law Lords），是指根据《1876年上诉司法权法令》任命，负责在英国上议院行使其司法职能的法官，对本土绝大部分案件扮演终审法院法官的角色。

opposed almost all of **Blair's**[①] early manifesto promises and that the party leadership has now accepted many of them (minimum wage, Bank of England independence, civil partnerships, various anti-discrimination laws), the party can be quite fractured at times, with a significant minority being very much opposed to membership of the European Union. Notable figures include Winston Churchill, Margaret Thatcher and David Cameron.

David Cameron
From: http://en.wikipedia.org/wiki/David_Cameron

3.2 Labour Party

The Labour Party is the other main party. Founded as a socialist party, the Labour Party had a huge role in the creation of the Welfare State and the National Health Service. After nearly two decades of Conservative rule, the Labour Party moved much closed to the centre, stepping away from its socialist roots and becoming a "**big tent**"[②] centrist party. This step clearly made them an electable opposition, as they won in a massive landslide in 1997, but it's now somewhat unclear exactly what they stand for other than "we're nicer and more left-wing than those bastard Tories". Notable figures include Clement Attlee, Tony Blair and Gordon Brown.

3.3 Liberal Democrats

The Liberal Democrats are traditionally the third party in the United Kingdom. The Liberal Party declined severely before World War Two as the Labour Party took over as the main left-wing party. The Liberals were less of a serious force in British

---

① Tony Blair: 英国历史上首位三次连任的工党首相，帮助伦敦赢得申奥主办权。继位者为工党的戈登·布朗。

② big tent: 包容各种不同的政治和社会观点的大帐篷政策，对各种不同观点的宽容政策。

politics, but they merged with the Social Democrat Party (a splinter group of the Labour Party) in 1988 to form the Liberal Democrats. The Liberal Democrats are hugely popular among students and are often the go-to "protest vote" of the middle classes. Advocating progressive taxation, nuclear disarmament and electoral reform, the Liberal Democrats saw a large surge in support as they were the only major party to seriously oppose the Iraq War. In a weird twist, they formed a coalition government with the Conservative Party in 2010, with the idea of taking the edge off the Tory spending cuts and making them fairer for the poor. Their complete failure to do this has severely damaged their support among students, public sector workers. All those affected by the budget cuts, and lost them a lot of support at local government level, losing them control of many local councils. Notable figures include Nick Clegg, Charles Kennedy (the UK's favourite alcoholic), Vince Cable, and former leader Paddy Ashdown, who effectively ran Bosnia for a four year period.

4. General Election

The British general election is based on the first-past-the-post system and the simple criterion for victory is that the party that wins an overall majority of seats in the Commons forms the next government. Britain's last general election was on 6 May 2010. The Conservative/Liberal Democrat coalition government was formed on 10 May 2010. The coalition agreement sets out a joint programme for government to rebuild the economy, unlock social mobility, mend the political system and give people the power to call the shots over the decisions that affect their lives.

When Parliament is dissolved every seat in the House of Commons becomes vacant and a general election is held. Each constituency in the UK elects one MP (Member of Parliament) to a seat in the House of Commons. The political party that wins a majority of seats in the House of Commons usually forms the Government.

The duration of a Parliament was set at five years, although many were dissolved before that, at the request of the Prime Minister to the Queen. Candidates may be from a political party registered with the Electoral Commission or they may stand as an Independent rather than represent a registered party.

British citizens living overseas are entitled to be registered to vote in UK Parliamentary elections for up to 15 years in the constituency they were registered in before leaving the UK. They are not entitled to vote in UK local elections or elections to the devolved assemblies. After a general election has taken place and the vote has been counted, the Returning Officer for that constituency declares the result. He or she also sends the name of the elected candidate to the Clerk of the Crown at the Ministry of Justice. The Ministry produces the White Book, a list of all Members of the new Parliament, which is brought to the Chamber on the first day the Parliament sits. The election results then appear in the London Gazette.

References

https://www.gov.uk/government/how-government-works

www.gov.uk consists of the websites of all government departments and many other agencies and public bodies. On this website, you can see all policies, announcements, publications, statistics and consultations. It is the best place to find government services and information, simpler, clearer and faster.

http://www.parliament.uk/about/how/elections-and-voting/general/

www.parliament.uk is the official website of UK parliament. It is accessible to everyone, regardless of nationality. It includes five parts: Parliamentary business, MPs, Lords & Offices, About Parliament, Visiting and Education.

Political parties of the United Kingdom, edited on 3 May 2014. From:
http://rationalwiki.org/wiki/Political_parties_of_the_United_Kingdom#Conservative_Party

rationalwiki.org is a wiki full of rational articles, which are partly truth and partly copied from Wikipedia. A majority of the userbase on RationalWiki are established by liberal thinkers who liberally interpret everything. Usually the first paragraph of each section is copied from Wikipedia and the second part is not.

McEwen, Nicola. *Power within the Executive*, 2004. From:
http://news.bbc.co.uk/2/hi/programmes/bbc_parliament/2561931.stm

Exercises

I. Choose the one that best completes each of the following statements.

1. The Prime Minister in Britain is head of _____.
   A. the Shadow Cabinet   B. the Parliament
   C. the Opposition   D. the Cabinet
2. In the United Kingdom, ministers are appointed by the Queen on the recommendation of _____.
   A. the Lord Chancellor   B. the Monarch
   C. the Prime Minister   D. the King
3. In the United Kingdom, the party which wins the _____ number of seats in the House of Commons becomes the official Opposition.
   A. largest   B. second largest
   C. third largest   D. fourth largest
4. Which of the following statement is NOT correct?
   A. There are no legal restraints upon Parliament.
   B. Strictly speaking, the Queen is part of the Parliament.
   C. Parliament has the supreme power of passing laws.

D. Parliament has no power to change the terms of the Constitution.
5. Which of the following is NOT a characteristic of British government?
   A. It offers the Queen high political status and supreme power.
   B. It is both a parliamentary democracy and a constitutional monarchy.
   C. It is the oldest representative democracy in the world.
   D. It has no written form of Constitution.
6. On accepting _____, the age of constitutional monarchy, of a monarchy with powers limited by Parliament, began.
   A. Constitutional Law   B. Bill of Rights
   C. Civil Law   D. The Declaration of Independence
7. The general election in Britain is held every _____ years.
   A. four   B. three   C. six   D. five
8. Westminster Palace is the _____.
   A. site of British House of Parliament   B. site of English church
   C. residence of king of queen   D. residence of Prime Minister
9. The president of the Lords in Britain is called _____.
   A. Lord Chancellor   B. speaker
   C. Prime Minister   D. President
10. The real centre of power in the British Parliament is _____.
    A. the King or the Queen   B. the House of Commons
    C. the House of Lords   D. the Cabinet
11. The oldest part of British Parliament is the _____.
    A. House of Lords   B. House of Commons
    C. Shadow Cabinet   D. Chamber
12. The Prime Minister has the following power except _____.
    A. appointing government officials   B. commanding the armed forces
    C. making foreign policies   D. interpreting the Constitution
13. The United Kingdom is a constitutional monarchy. The head of State is the _____.
    A. Prime Minister   B. monarchy
    C. Lord Chancellor   D. governor-general
14. The head of the executive branch in UK is the _____.
    A. President   B. Governor-General
    C. monarch   D. Prime Minister

II. Read the following statements carefully and decide whether they are TRUE or FALSE.

1. The main sources of British Constitution are Statutes, Common Law and Conventions.
2. Conventions are regarded less important than common law in the working of the

British government.
3. Today, the Queen has special powers, including the power to declare war, to make treaties, to pardon criminals, and to dissolve Parliament.
4. Under the "separation of powers" the major institutions of state are functionally divided into the executive, the legislature and the judiciary.
5. Lord Chancellor is the president of the House of Commons.
6. The members in the House of Commons are elected, while the members in the House of Lords are appointed.
7. Cabinet members are appointed by the Prime Minister from his own political party in Parliament.
8. The legal system in England, Wales, Scotland and Northern Ireland are much similar in terms of law, organization and practice.
9. The Conservative Party is commonly known as "The Tory Party".
10. The Supreme Court is headed by the President and Deputy President of the Supreme Court and is composed of a further ten Justices of the Supreme Court.

III. **Give brief answers to the following questions.**
1. Give a brief account of the differences between UK and USA in terms of the "Separation of Power".
2. Give a brief account of the UK parliament and the function of each part.

Section Two: In-depth Reading

The United Kingdom is a constitutional monarchy and parliamentary democracy, with a monarch and a parliament that has two houses: the House of Lords and the House of Commons. The British political system is the basis of that of its former colonists—America, New Zealand, Canada, Australia and so on. That's why once you get yourself acquainted with the British political system; you can easily understand the political system of the above mentioned countries. The two articles in this section will acquaint us with British political system from different perspectives.

Reading One is an introduction to some interesting conventions.

Reading Two shows us the differences between UK and USA in terms of general election.

Before reading the articles, brainstorm with your cohorts on the following questions:
1. What are conventions? Why do conventions exist?
2. How a Prime Minister is elected in UK?

Reading One

A constitutional convention is an informal and uncodified procedural agreement.

Though these conventions have no legal status, their very existence over the years has invariably ensured the smooth operation of government. What are conventions? Why do conventions exist? This passage will introduce some interesting conventions in Great Britain.

Some Interesting Conventions

A convention is an accepted way in which things are done. They are not written down in law but tend to be old, established practices—the way they have always been done. Though these conventions are not set in legal stone, their very existence over the years has invariably led to the smooth operation of government. This, again, is an argument for an unwritten, uncodified constitution. If the ways of governmental working were set in stone and had been for years (through a codified constitution), could government evolve and develop and mould to society's change if the way government works was rigidly stated in a written constitution?

It is accepted that a departmental minister will resign if he/she loses the confidence of the House of Commons (i.e. within their own party). Usually, pressure is put on the person concerned to resign, as a sacking looks bad. In recent weeks, pressure from non-governmental sources (though primarily the media) has tried to tarnish the name of Stephen Byers, the Transport Minister, claiming that he has lost the confidence of the House. However, the simple fact is that Byers has kept his place simply because there has been no public party revolt against him—hence, why he has not resigned. A future Cabinet reshuffle would spare blushes all round as he was appointed by Tony Blair and it would look bad if Blair had to sack him if he did not resign.

It is a convention that the queen will accept the legislation passed by the government. In the past, the fear of what happened to Charles I has usually ensured a harmonious relationship between monarch and Parliament! When Charles II became king in 1660, the rule of thumb was for Parliament to give the king enough money per year to maintain a royal lifestyle but for him not to get involved in politics. This worked tolerably well and monarchs and Parliament had usually worked well since then especially as Parliament held the monarch's purse. Now in the 21st century, it is just accepted that the queen will give parliamentary legislation the Royal Assent. It is almost beyond belief that she would not do so—the constitutional crisis this would create would be huge. The public backlash against an unelected person rejecting what a democratically elected government has pushed through would almost certainly be massive.

It is a convention that if something in government goes wrong, the cabinet will all sing the same song and support the minister who may be receiving all manner of criticism from the media. This has been very apparent with the recent history of Stephen Byers—all his cabinet colleagues have leapt to his defense over the problems he has recently faced.

Conventions can be changed, as they have no legal status. But they tend to be tolerated as they allow the system to work. Any reform to a convention has one major problem: how do you know that it will work as well as before it was reformed? It is does not work as well, do you admit defeat and go back or stubbornly proceed and make out all is well?

References

http://www.historylearningsite.co.uk/conventions_ of_ a_ constitution.htm

Chris Trueman, a BA (Honours) in History from Aberystwyth University, set up www.historylearningsite.co.uk in 2000 to offer accessible and comprehensive website on World History on the web. The site has grown in popularity and is now viewed by hundreds of thousands of people each month from around the world. In May 2013, Chris Trueman sadly died of cancer. Chris was extremely passionate about the History Learning Site and what it can offer its readers and it was his intention to continue to expand the depth and breadth of topics on the site.

Discussions

1. Why do conventions exist?
2. What do you think are the advantages and disadvantages of conventions?

Reading Two

This passage will show us the differences between the Great Britain and the United States in General Election, including such aspects as time, duration, budget, electoral process and so on. The readers are expected to grasp both election systems after reading this article.

GB vs. USA General Elections

A British Prime Minister can call an election at any time in his 5-year term. In theory, he can use good economic news, for example, to boost his party's representation in Parliament by calling a snap general election hoping that voters will be swept along by such good news. It is said that Harold Wilson, the Labour Prime Minister in the 1960's—1970's used this good factor after England won the World Cup in 1966. The US President has no such flexibility. The date of each US national election is set in stone and the President goes into it on the back of whatever news is around at the time—be it good or bad. He cannot call an election—as it has to take place in the first week on November. The next US national election is on the first Tuesday in November 2008 and there is nothing the Republicans or G. W. Bush can do about this.

The US has an election every 4 years—the UK every 5 years maximum. The UK's Prime Minister can serve any number of years. The US President is limited via the Constitution to two four-year terms—a maximum of 8 years. Though the Constitution can be amended, there has been no evidence in recent years that there will be any such change to this part of the Constitution.

Even if the two countries populations are made into a comparable proportion, the amount of money spent during an American national election dwarfs the money spent during a UK general election. For the UK 2001 general election, political pundits spoke in terms of tens of millions being spent in total by all parties. In the 2004 American election, pundits spoke in terms of hundreds of million of dollars being spent—possibly even a billion dollars.

One of the main reasons for the above is the difference in duration of the two campaigns. In the UK, Tony Blair announced on April 5th the date for the 2005 general election – May 5th—leaving just one month for campaigning. In America, the election campaign starts in January in the year of the election with primaries and caucuses, leaving 10 months until the actual election.

In America, the national election is between two candidates—a Republican one and a Democrat one. (Other candidates do stand but they have no chance of being elected) Voters vote for a presidential candidate. In the UK there is a totally different approach. There is a vote for all 646 constituencies (2005 figure) and voters will probably vote for a party rather than for a candidate.

In America, the opportunity for a protest vote barely exists—unless you deliberately abstain and count this as a protest vote. The Reform Party and **Green Party**[①] do exist but the Electoral College system means that they have no chance of getting any form of power. In the UK, there are plenty of opportunities to have a protest vote against the standing party/Prime Minister. The election of Michael Bell as an Independent anti-corruption MP in 1997 showed this. In 2001 an Independent candidate won Wyre Forest as the Kidderminster Hospital and Health Concern MP—his manifesto was based primarily on keeping open the local hospital whatever the cost. He received the support of the local populace and became that constituency's MP. The system in America does not allow for this at presidential level—though it does happen at Congressional level, especially in the mid-term elections.

---

① Green party：绿党是一个在1991年由美国众多州的绿党自愿结合形成的全国性政党。绿党目前在美国参众两院中都没有代表，同时也没有获得任何州级的可通过选举获得的席位。在州级的立法机构中，绿党也仅仅在阿肯色州的众议院中获得一个席位。

Turnout at both national (USA) /general (UK) elections is poor. In both 2001 (UK) and 2004 (US), 1/3rd of those who could have voted did not. The announcement of an election in the UK on April 5th 2005 was described in one broadsheet as "the lull before the lull."

The UK's electoral system is based on the first-past-the-post system. All the winning party needs is a majority of MP's elected to Westminster to win a general election. For 2005, all the winning party will need is 324 MP's to have an overall majority in Parliament.

In America, some say that there are 50 elections as opposed to just one. Whoever wins a state gets all of that state's Electoral College votes and the loser gets none. Once a presidential candidate gets a majority of Electoral College votes, he is declared the winner even if some states have yet to declare. In 2000, Bush won with fewer public votes but with a majority of Electoral College votes. The same oddity has happened in the UK. In 1951, the Conservatives won the general election with 11.62 million votes (including National Liberal and Conservative MP's) while the Labour Party got 11.63 million votes. However, the Conservatives won 259 seats in Westminster to Labour's 233.

In the UK an election manifesto is traditionally considered to be binding. It is not uncommon during Commons Question Time for Opposition MP's to state: "In your manifesto you said... why hasn't this happened?" In America, an election platform (the equivalent of a manifesto) is not considered to be binding. It is what would be done given the perfect opportunity to do so.

References

http://www.historylearningsite.co.uk/gb_v_usa_general_elections.htm

Discussions

Try to state the differences between the Great Britain and the United States in General Election in your own words.

Chapter 4

Economy

Section One: A Brief Introduction

1. Economy of the United Kingdom

The United Kingdom has the 6th-largest national economy in the world (and 3rd-largest in Europe) measured by nominal **GDP**① and 8th-largest in the world (and 2nd-largest in Europe) measured by **Purchasing Power Parity (PPP)**②. The UK's GDP per capita is the 22nd-highest in the world in nominal terms and 22nd-highest measured by PPP. In 2012, the UK was the 10th-largest exporter in the world and the 6th-largest importer. In 2012, the UK had the 3rd-largest stock of inward foreign direct investment and the 2nd-largest stock of outward foreign direct investment. The British economy comprises (in descending order of size) the economies of England, Scotland, Wales and Northern Ireland. The UK has one of the world's most globalised economies. One-sixth of the tax revenue comes from **VAT**③ from the consumer market of the British Economy.

The service sector dominates the UK economy, contributing around 78% of GDP, with the financial services industry particularly important. London is the world's largest financial centre, and has the largest city GDP in Europe. The UK aerospace industry is the second – or third-largest national aerospace industry depending on the method of measurement. The pharmaceutical industry plays an important role in the economy and the UK has the third-highest share of global

---

① GDP：国内生产总值（Gross Domestic Product）。
② Purchasing Power Parity（简称PPP）：购买力平价。在经济学上，是一种根据各国不同的价格水平计算出来的货币之间的等值系数，以对各国的国内生产总值进行合理比较。但是，这种理论汇率与实际汇率可能有很大的差距。
③ VAT（value added tax）：增值税。

Canary Wharf business district in London
From: http://en.wikipedia.org/wiki/Economy_of_the_United_Kingdom

pharmaceutical R&D. The automotive industry is also a major employer and exporter. The British economy is boosted by North Sea oil and gas production; its reserves were valued at an estimated £ 250 billion in 2007. There are significant regional variations in prosperity, with the South East of England and southern Scotland the richest areas per capita.

In the 18th century, the UK was the first country to industrialise and during the 19th century had a dominant role in the global economy. From the late-19th century the **Second Industrial Revolution**[1] in the United States and Germany presented an increasing economic challenge, and the costs of fighting World War I and World War II further weakened the UK's relative position. However it still maintains a significant role in the world economy, such as in financial services, and the knowledge economy. The UK economy is currently recovering from a recession arising from the financial crisis of 2007/08, and GDP remains 1.3% below its pre-recession peak as of Q4 2013; the UK experienced a deeper downturn than all of the **G7**[2] except Japan, and has experienced a slower recovery than all but Italy. In 2013, the UK experienced its fastest growth since 2007; it is now the fastest growing major European economy.

Government involvement in the British economy is primarily exercised by **HM Treasury**[3], headed by the Chancellor of the Exchequer, and the Department for Business, Innovation and Skills. Since 1979 management of the UK economy has

---

[1] Second Industrial Revolution：第二次工业革命。1870年以后，科学技术的发展突飞猛进，各种新技术、新发明层出不穷，并被迅速应用于工业生产，大大促进了经济的发展。这就是第二次工业革命。当时，科学技术的突出发展主要表现在四个方面，即电力的广泛应用、内燃机和新交通工具的创制、新通讯手段的发明和化学工业的建立。

[2] G7：七国集团（Group of Seven）。

[3] HM Treasury：英国财政部。

followed a broadly **laissez-faire**①approach. The Bank of England is the UK's central bank and its Monetary Policy Committee is responsible for setting interest rates. The currency of the UK is the pound sterling, which is also the world's third-largest reserve currency after the US dollar and the euro. The UK is a member of **the Commonwealth of Nations**②, the European Union, the G7, the G8, the G20, the International Monetary Fund, **the Organisation for Economic Co-operation and Development**,③ the World Bank, the World Trade Organisation and the United Nations.

2. Economic History of the United Kingdom

2.1　1945 to 1979

Following the end of the Second World War, the United Kingdom enjoyed a long period without a major recession (from 1945 to 1973) and a rapid growth in prosperity in the 1950s and 1960s, with unemployment staying low and not exceeding 500,000 until the second half of the 1960s. According to the OECD, the annual rate of growth (percentage change) between 1960 and 1973 averaged 2.9%, although this figure was far behind the rates of other European countries such as France, West Germany and Italy.

However, following the 1973 oil crisis and the 1973—1974 stock market crash, the British economy fell into recession and the government of Edward Heath was ousted by the Labour Party under **Harold Wilson**④, which had previously ruled from 1964 to 1970. Wilson formed a minority government on 4 March 1974 after the general election on 28 February ended in **a hung parliament**⑤. Wilson subsequently secured a three seat majority in a second election in October that year.

The UK recorded weaker growth than many other European nations in the 1970s; even after the early 1970s recession ended, the economy was still blighted by rising unemployment and double-digit inflation, which exceeded 20% more than once after 1973 and was rarely below 10% after this date.

In 1976, the UK was forced to request a loan of £2.3 billion from the International Monetary Fund. The then Chancellor of the Exchequer Denis Healey

---

①　laissez-faire：不干涉主义。
②　The Commonwealth of Nations：英联邦（等于 British Commonwealth）。
③　The Organisation for Economic Co-operation and Development：经济合作与发展组织（OECD）。
④　Harold Wilson：哈罗德·威尔逊（James Harold Wilson, 1916 年 3 月 11 日—1995 年 5 月 24 日），是 20 世纪其中一位最重要的英国政治家。曾分别在 1964 年、1966 年、1974 年 2 月和 1974 年 6 月的大选中胜出，虽然他每次大选只是险胜，但综合而言，他在大选赢出的次数，冠绝所有 20 世纪的英国首相。另外，比较其他同时代的政治人物，他被普遍认为是一位智慧型的政治家。
⑤　a hung parliament：一个无任何党派占明显多数的议会。

was required to implement public spending cuts and other economic reforms in order to secure the loan, and for a while the British economy improved. However, following the Winter of Discontent, when Britain was hit by numerous public sector strikes, the government of James Callaghan lost a vote of no confidence in March 1979. This triggered the May 1979 general election which resulted in Margaret Thatcher's Conservative Party forming a new government.

2.2　1979 to 1997

A new period of neo-liberal economics began in 1979 with the election of Margaret Thatcher who won the general election on 3 May that year to return the Conservative Party to government after five years of Labour government.

During the 1980s most state-owned enterprises were privatised, taxes cut, union reforms passed and markets deregulated. GDP fell 5.9% initially but growth subsequently returned and rose to 5% at its peak in 1988, one of the highest rates of any European nation.

However, Thatcher's modernisation of the British economy was far from trouble free; her battle against inflation resulted in a substantial increase in unemployment from 1.5 million in 1979 to over 3 million by the start of 1982, peaking at nearly 3.3 million in 1984. In spite of this, Thatcher was re-elected in June 1983 with a landslide majority, as the Labour Party suffered its worst general election result in decades and the recently formed SDP-Liberal Alliance almost matched Labour in terms of votes, if not seats.

The increase in unemployment was substantially due to government economic policy which resulted in the closure of outdated factories and coalpits which were no longer economically viable; this process continued for most of the 1980s, with newer industries and the service sector enjoying significant growth. Unemployment had fallen below 3 million by the time of Thatcher's third successive election victory in June 1987 and by the end of 1989 it was down to 1.6 million. However, the British economy slid into another recession in late 1990, concurrently with a global recession, and this caused the economy to shrink by a total of 8% from peak to trough and unemployment to increase from around 1.6million in the spring of 1990 to nearly 3 million by the end of 1992. The subsequent economic recovery was extremely strong, and unlike after the early 1980s recession, the recovery saw a rapid and substantial fall in unemployment, which was down to 1.7 million by 1997, although the popularity of the Conservative government failed to improve with the economic upturn.

2.3　1997 to 2008

The Labour Party, led by Tony Blair since the death of his predecessor John

Smith three years earlier, returned to power in May 1997 after 18 years in opposition. During Blair's 10 years in office there were 40 successive quarters of economic growth, lasting until the second quarter of 2008, helped by Blair's decision to keep taxes relatively low and abandon traditional Labour policies including public ownership of industries and utilities. The previous 15 years had seen one of the highest economic growth rates of major developed economies during that time and certainly the strongest of any European nation. GDP growth had briefly reached 4% per year in the early 1990s, gently declining thereafter. Peak growth was relatively anaemic compared to prior decades, such as the 6.5% p.a. peak in the early 1970s, although growth was smoother and more consistent. Annual growth rates averaged 2.68% between 1992—2007 according to the IMF, with the finance sector accounting for a greater part than previously.

This extended period of growth ended in 2008 when the United Kingdom suddenly entered a recession—its first for nearly two decades—brought about by the global financial crisis. Beginning with the collapse of Northern Rock, which was taken into public ownership in February 2008, other banks had to be partly nationalised. **The Royal Bank of Scotland Group**[①], which at its peak was the fifth-largest in the world by market capitalisation, was effectively nationalised on 13 October 2008. By mid-2009, HM Treasury had a 70.33% controlling shareholding in RBS, and a 43% shareholding, through UK Financial Investments Limited, in **Lloyds Banking Group**[②]. The recession saw unemployment rise from just over 1.6 million in January 2008 to nearly 2.5 million by October 2009.

Britain's economy
From: http://www.bdza.cn/bdzaportal/middle.do?act=show&cid=4&mid=183&id=00002459

The UK economy had been one of the strongest economies in terms of inflation, interest rates and unemployment, all of which remained relatively low until the

---

① The Royal Bank of Scotland Group: 苏格兰皇家银行集团（RBS）。
② Lloyds Banking Group: 英国莱斯银行集团。

2008—2009 recession. Unemployment has since reached a peak of just under 2.5 million (7.8%), the highest level since the early 1990s, although still far lower than some other European nations. However, interest rates have reduced to 0.5% p.a. During August 2008 the IMF warned that the UK economic outlook had worsened due to a twin shock: financial turmoil and rising commodity prices. Both developments harm the UK more than most developed countries, as the UK obtains revenue from exporting financial services while recording deficits in finished goods and commodities, including food. In 2007, the UK had the world's third largest current account deficit, due mainly to a large deficit in manufactured goods. During May 2008, the IMF advised the UK government to broaden the scope of fiscal policy to promote external balance. Although the UK's "labour productivity per person employed" has been progressing well over the last two decades and has overtaken productivity in Germany, it still lags around 20% behind France, where workers have a 35-hour working week. The UK's "labour productivity per hour worked" is currently on a par with the average for the "old" EU (15 countries). In 2010, the United Kingdom ranked 26th on the Human Development Index.

2.4 2008 to Present

The UK entered a recession in Q2 of 2008 and exited it in Q4 of 2009, according to figures produced by the Office for National Statistics. The subsequently revised ONS figures show that the UK suffered six consecutive quarters of negative growth, making it the longest recession since records began. As of the end of Q4 2009, revised statistics from the Office for National Statistics demonstrate that the UK economy shrank by 7.2% from peak to trough.

Support for the Labour government (led by Gordon Brown after Tony Blair's resignation in June 2007) slumped during the financial crisis of 2008 and 2009, and the general election of May 2010 ended in a hung parliament. The Conservatives, led by David Cameron since the end of 2005, had the largest number of seats, but came 20 seats short of an overall majority. This resulted in a coalition being formed with the Liberal Democrats in order for the Conservatives to take government within four days of the election results being announced. In order to ease the large deficit created under the previous Labour government, the Conservative-led government has made deep spending cuts since taking office. Within three years, this had led to public sector job losses well into six figures, but the private sector has enjoyed strong job growth and by October 2013 unemployment had fallen back below 2.5 million for the first time in four years.

The Office for National Statistics estimates that UK growth in Q4 of 2013 was 0.7%, and that the volume of GDP remains 1.3% below its pre-recession peak; the UK economy's recovery has thus been more lackluster than previously thought.

Furthermore, *The Blue Book* 2013 demonstrates that the UK experienced a deeper initial downturn than all of the G7 economies save for Japan, and has experienced a slower recovery than all but Italy.

In Q1 of 2012, the UK economy was thought to have entered a double-dip recession by posting two consecutive negative quarters of growth. However, revised figures by the Office for National Statistics show that in fact the UK economy stagnated in Q1 with growth at 0.0%, thereby not fulfilling the technical requirement of two consecutive quarters of negative growth for a recession.

A report released by the Office for National Statistics on 14 May 2013 revealed that over the six-year period between 2005 and 2011, the UK dropped from 5th place to 12th place in terms of household income on an international scale—the drop was partially attributed to the devaluation of sterling over this time frame. However, the report also concluded that, during this period, inflation was relatively less volatile, the UK labour market was more resilient in comparison to other recessions, and household spending and wealth in the UK remained relatively strong in comparison with other OECD countries. According to a report by Moody's Corporation, Britain's debt-to-GDP ratio continues to increase in 2013 and is expected to reach 93% at the end of the year. The UK has lost its triple-A credit rating on the basis of poor economic outlook. 2013 Economic Growth has surprised many Economists, Ministers and the OBR as the 2013 budget projected annual growth of just 0.6%. In 2013 Q1 the economy grew by 0.5%, in Q2 the economy grew by 0.8%, in Q3 the economy grew by 0.8% and in Q4 the economy is estimated to have grown by 0.7%. It is also predicted that the economy will continue to grow in 2014, by as much as 2.8% (up from previous estimates of 2.7%) and surpass the 2008 pre-receccession peak by Q3 of 2014.

References

http://en.wikipedia.org/wiki/Economy_ of_ the_ United_ Kingdom

Wikipedia is a multilingual, web-based, free-content encyclopedia project supported by the Wikimedia Foundation and based on an openly editable model. The name "Wikipedia" is a portmanteau of the words wiki (a technology for creating collaborative websites, from the Hawaiian word wiki, meaning "quick") and encyclopedia. Wikipedia's articles provide links designed to guide the user to related pages with additional information and all the articles are written collaboratively by largely anonymous Internet volunteers who write without pay. Anyone with Internet access can write and make changes to Wikipedia articles, except in limited cases where editing is restricted to prevent disruption or vandalism. Users can contribute anonymously, under a pseudonym, or, if they choose to, with their real identity

Exercises

I. Choose the one that best completes each of the following statements.

1. In January _____ Britain became a member of the European Economic Community.
   A. 1957   B. 1967   C. 1973   D. 1979

2. Soon after _____, Britain not only gave up its economic hegemony but also suffered a deep loss of its position of industrial leadership.
   A. 1900   B. the First World War
   C. the Second World War   D. 1960

3. In the 1970s among the developed countries, Britain maintained the lowest _____ rate and the highest _____ rate.
   A. inflation, growth   B. growth, inflation
   C. growth, divorce   D. growth, birth

4. The following are all reasons of British decline of coal industry except _____.
   A. the exhaustion of old mines   B. costly extraction
   C. little money being invested   D. the labor shortage

5. Britain's foreign trade is mainly with _____.
   A. developing countries   B. other Commonwealth countries
   C. other developed countries   D. EC

6. Britain was the first country to industrialize because of the following factors except _____.
   A. Britain was well placed geographically to participate in European and world trade.
   B. Britain had many rivers, which were useful for transport.
   C. British engineers had sound training and the inventors were respected.
   D. British government was increasingly interested in overseas and colonies after the 17th century.

7. Which party has always had strong links with the trade unions and received financial support from them?
   A. the Labor Party.   B. the Conservative Party.
   C. the Liberal Party.   D. the Social Democratic Party.

8. The term "British disease" is now often used to characterize Britain's _____ decline.
   A. political   B. educational   C. military   D. economic

9. The 1980s was remembered as the decade of _____.
   A. globalization   B. nationalization   C. privatization   D. competition

10. Today, in Britain, _____ is called a "sick" industry.
    A. coal mining   B. iron and steel   C. textiles   D. shipbuilding

11. The first steam engine was devised by Thomas Newcomen at the end of the 17th century, and the Scottish inventor _____ modified and improved the design in 1765.
    A. Abraham Darby   B. James Watt
    C. John Kay   D. Richard Arkwrightthe
12. _____ is the key to Industrial Revolution.
    A. Iron   B. Cotton textile
    C. Coal mining   D. Steam engine
13. Britain is basically an importer of _____.
    A. food   B. raw materials
    C. manufactures   D. both A and B
14. The United Kingdom has the _____ largest national economy in the world (and 3rd-largest in Europe) measured by nominal GDP.
    A. 6th   B. 3rd   C. 8th   D. 2nd
15. During Blair's 10 years in office there were 40 successive quarters of economic growth, lasting until the second quarter of _____.
    A. 2003   B. 2000   C. 2007   D. 2008

II. Read the following statements carefully and decide whether they are TRUE or FALSE.

1. There are steady development in the 50s and 60s, economic recession in the 70s and economic recovery in the 80s as far as the evolution of the British economy is concerned.
2. Before the Industrial Revolution, Britain became the "workshop" of the world.
3. In 1974 and 1977, the two oil shocks caused inflation to rise dramatically.
4. New industries in Britain include microprocessors and computer, biotechnology and other high-tech industries.
5. The British economy comprises the economies of England, Scotland and Wales.
6. The UK has one of the world's most globalised economies.
7. In the 18th century the UK was the first country to industrialize and during the 19th century had a dominant role in the global economy.
8. The UK recorded weaker growth than many other nations in the 1970s.
9. During the 1980s most state-owned enterprises were privatized, taxes cut, union reforms passed and markets deregulated.
10. Thatcher's modernization of the British economy was far from trouble free; her battle against inflation resulted in a substantial increase in unemployment.

III. Give brief answers to the following questions.

1. How did the English Industrial Revolution proceed?
2. What is the status quo of UK's economy?

Section Two: In-depth Reading

There are four regions in the UK and each of them has different paths of economic development. Thus, if you want to know more about the economy of the UK, you should make it clear what economic situations are in different regions. Moreover, as a nation, the UK is a member to some world-class economic organizations. Then, how does UK function in those organizations? In this section, you will get some hints to the answers.

Reading One is about a debate over the economic development of Scotland.

Reading Two talks about the role of Commonwealth in Britain's future.

Before reading the articles, brainstorm with your cohorts on the following questions:

1. Can you name some economic organizations?
2. How many times has China been through economic recession in the history?

Reading One

As Scotland looks to a choice on its future, with the economy a feature of the debate, two academic contributions give us a new take on the past route that got Scottish to where they are now, especially in terms of economy.

Scottish Independence: Has Scotland "de-globalised"?
Douglas Fraser

Two groups of economic historians from Glasgow University, and together, put a new slant on the powerful political narratives, first, that Margaret Thatcher's government was to blame for the demise of heavy industry in Scotland, and second, that Scotland is well adapted to the demands of competing in the globalised economy.

Could it be, on the contrary, that the Thatcher government merely accelerated a trend that was not only already clear, but which had previously been seen positively by Scots?

And it may also be that Scots are far less globalised now than we were a century ago, with far more people now working for the state or selling to other Scots, with possible implications for the way voters approach their nation's future.

Long-term decline

An academic paper by Jim Phillips argues that the old industries had been in long-term decline long before Margaret Thatcher's government accelerated the effect.

He says there had already been a recognition that the old heavy industries were not delivering growth while sustaining employment, which is why the industrial

Prof Jim Tomlinson sees a link between the demise of
traditional industries and the rise of nationalism
From http://www.bbc.com/news/uk-scotland-26815714

policies of the 1950s, 1960s and 1970s tried to find new industries to which people could move, offering higher value jobs, and a route to faster economic growth.

They may not have succeeded, but that was the intention.

That's why the emphasis was on consumer goods, for instance attracting the car plant into Linwood in Renfrewshire, and Burroughs the computer manufacturer into Cumbernauld.

The loss of coal-mining employment was seen as acceptable before the Thatcher era because they were negotiated with the workforce, because there were jobs in more modern, productive pits and because new jobs were becoming available, not least to employ women as they entered the workforce.

Jim Phillips argues that Scotland's heavy industries were in decline
long before Margaret Thatcher arrived in Downing Street
From: http://www.bbc.com/news/uk-scotland-26815714

Through this period, Jim Phillips' academic paper points to the share of industrial employment falling from 42% of Scottish jobs in 1951 to 21% by 1991. It was an even steeper decline for Glasgow, with the figures demonstrating how long-term it had been; 50% industrial jobs in 1951, falling to 39% by 1971, 28% in 1981 as the Thatcher acceleration began to kick in, and 19% by 1991.

Even more marked was the decline in two of the big employing industries. In railways, employment fell from 55,000 in 1951 to 23,000 only 20 years later, and then down to 12,000 by 1991.

In coal, the fall was from 89,000 in 1951, to 34,000 in 1971, 25,000 in 1981, ahead of the miners' strike to stop pit closures, and only 2,400 ten years later.

Jim Phillips' point is that much of this change was intended rather than merely the result of external forces, natural process or accident. The new, more productive industries appeared attractive, at least until they turned out to offer much lower-skilled 'screwdriver' jobs, without negotiating change with workers or unions, and then it turned out the multinational companies moved on when their operating costs looked more attractive elsewhere.

Rising insecurity

What has this got to do with the way Scotland thinks now? Well, Prof Jim Tomlinson, also an economic historian at the University of Glasgow, was presenting a paper at the annual conference of the Economic History Society at Warwick University this past weekend, which takes on Jim Phillips' argument.

Tomlinson sees a link from the demise of the old industries, the rising insecurity of the new ones, and the rise of nationalism since the 1960s.

His argument is that Scotland in 1913 was probably the most globalised economy in the world. It exported to the empire in vast quantities. And while that empire was administered from London, the trade was not mediated through the UK economy.

Dundonians in the jute mills looked to the monsoon in Bengal more than the London stock exchange. Glaswegians looked to the demand for shipping worldwide, and the world market for capital goods.

It's even been suggested that, a century ago, the US provided a larger market for Scottish goods than England and Wales. Now, the rest of the UK accounts for twice as big a market for Scottish goods and services as the rest of the world put together.

State jobs

The state, meanwhile, was very much smaller than we're used to now, with direct employment by the various layers of government coming to around 23% in Scotland, and indirect, state-funded employment putting that figure above 30%. A hundred years ago, the state's share was closer to 4%.

By contrast, it is reckoned that only around 10% of Scottish jobs are now in the manufacturing sector. Whisky, for instance, has been a huge exporting success of late, but as I've noted before, it isn't delivering as impressively on the jobs front.

So the argument is that Scots have ceased to look to a global market for the fruits of their labour. While trade has globalised the economy, Scotland has apparently been heading in the opposite direction. We're now more focused on the national economy, on provision of services for fellow Scots, not least through provision of public services such as health.

With an economy that's been made much less export-oriented, the Tomlinson thesis is that "there is now more of a 'national economy' in Scotland than ever before in its history".

He's implying that fewer people have a personal stake in securing trade routes into export markets. Their focus is much closer to home. And the professor has pointed out that has left Scotland much less vulnerable to shocks from elsewhere, so while it sounds like it may be a retreat from forces playing on the economy around us, it isn't entirely to be regretted.

Does that help explain the rising appeal of nationalism over the past 50 years? Most nationalists, of course, would argue the contrary. As Winnie Ewing put it at her by-election success in 1967, 'stop the world-Scotland wants to get on'.

Growth rate

At least one other consequence may be a tad controversial for some, but here it is anyway. Where a part of the nationalist story is that Scotland had disappointingly low growth at least until the 1990s, that may be because it had slow-growing, old, heavy industries. When they went, growth picked up to the UK levels we've seen more recently.

Yet the demise of these industries, by the 1980s and 1990s, faced a strong consensus of Scottish opposition. The Labour Party, in those decades, was electorally successful at persuading Scots it was protecting them against those forces. The SNP was making similar arguments, though much less successfully at that time. In protecting the British welfare state, it has been much more successful of late.

Here's the question for both parties; had that opposition been more successful in protecting industries, would that growth rate not have been held back for longer?

Referendum message

One final thought from yet another economics paper published this past weekend, this one with a more directly political application.

A study of a referendum campaign on electoral reform in western Canada sought to find out if it is the politician or the message that makes the difference to the campaign, or as these academics from Columbia, the London School of Economics and Ryerson put it; 'content, charisma or cue?'

The outcome of their study was that the personality of the politician doesn't make much difference. Endorsements do, and equally so on the left and right.

The message can also be much more important than the political messenger. "Employing a message-based campaign or an endorsement-based campaign leads to about a 6 percentage point increase in the intention to vote 'yes' in the referendum," the report concludes.

You can interpret that according to taste, but it may have lessons for both sides of Scotland's independence campaign.

References

http://www.bbc.com/news/uk-scotland-26815714

BBC News reaches about 40 million adults in the UK every week-its international services are consumed by an additional 239 million adults around the world. The department is the largest in the BBC in terms of staff, with more than 8,500 people around the UK and the rest of the world. BBC News incorporates network news (the newsroom, news programmes such as Newsnight and Newsbeat, political programmes such as the Daily Politics, and the weather team), English Regions and Global News. Material is brought into the BBC by its newsgathering staff, one of the largest operations of its kind in the world, with more than 40 international bureaux and seven in the UK. It is transmitted to audiences on an increasingly diverse range of platforms including tablet computers and mobile phones.

About the Author

Douglas Fraser is a business and economy editor and mainly covers the news of Scotland in the sector of BBC News.

Discussions

1. Do you think that the independence of Scotland will accelerate its economic growth?
2. Old industries, like coal mining, have ever slowed down the growth of Scottish economy. Similarly, do you think the declining of old industries in China will also drag down the development of Chinese economy?

Reading Two

Most notably, the Commonwealth of Nations, an association primarily of former members of the British Empire, is often referred to as simply "the Commonwealth". Nowadays Britain is still the centre of the Commonwealth, as the head of Commonwealth is the Queen of the UK. But what can Commonwealth do for Britain? Will Britain benefit from it or not? Read the following article, you may get the answer.

The Commonwealth Should Play a Much Bigger Role in Britain's Future
Ruth Lea

An interesting snippet of news slipped out recently that could, given a fair wind, be really rather positive for the future of this country. Foreign Secretary William Hague signed an agreement in Ottawa late last month that will involve Britain and Canada cooperating, albeit in a limited way, to share embassy facilities and provide consular services in third countries.

Apparently, Mr. Hague described the two countries as "first cousins" under one queen and united by a set of values. More generally, he has been instrumental in boosting relations with Commonwealth states to an "unprecedented degree".

Some of us would say "not before time", as we have been dismayed by the FCO's neglect of the Commonwealth and the seemingly obsessive devotion to the EU, dysfunctional, expensive and anachronistic that it is. To use a phrase, the EU may have been the future once (with the emphasis on "may"), but it most certainly is not the future now. Mr. Hague's interest in the Commonwealth reminds us that there is big wide world outside the EU, where we have many strong and deep ties. We should make those ties stronger and deeper. Britain's focus of attention should again be global, as it was for much its history, not European.

My enthusiasm for the Commonwealth has nothing to with a romantic attachment to a fading dream of Imperial glory. In fact nothing could be further from the truth. Commonwealth countries do not have their best years behind them, as I fear many EU countries do, they have their best years ahead of them. And it's worth reminding us Commonwealth nations, taken together and including the UK, are an economic colossus comprising some 15% of world GDP, 54 member states (53 excluding Fiji, which is currently suspended) and two billion citizens. They will inevitably become more influential and powerful. The Commonwealth spans five continents and contains developed, emerging and developing economies. Crucially, the Commonwealth, in its richness and diversity, mirrors today's global economy in a way that the EU simply cannot start to aspire to.

The latest IMF forecasts show that the major Commonwealth countries have healthy growth prospects in the medium-term, significantly better than for major EU economies. And looking to the longer-term, they are blessed with favourable demographics. Their working populations are projected to increase to 2050 and, insofar as economic growth is correlated with growth in the working population, they will represent some of the most important growth markets in the longer-term. Specifically, the Commonwealth's demographics compare very favourably with some major European countries including Germany and Italy, where working populations will age and shrink. It is mistaken and old-fashioned to regard the Commonwealth as the "past", an outmoded relic of Empire. Commonwealth countries are young and dynamic and should play a much bigger part in Britain's future.

It has moreover been estimated that business costs are 10% ~ 15% lower for Commonwealth countries trading with one another compared with Commonwealth countries trading with non-Commonwealth countries of comparable size and GDP. This benefit, the "Commonwealth advantage", reflects shared history and commonalities of language, law and business practice. It should act, other things being equal, as a major incentive to intra-Commonwealth trade.

UK-Commonwealth trade is already significant. Nearly one tenth of total of exports of goods and services went to the major Commonwealth countries in 2011. But it was not just the size of the trade that was important. Significantly Britain had a healthy, GDP-enhancing trade surplus with our Commonwealth partners. Indeed, after the US, the top surplus country was Australia. But more could be done, and more should be done, to stimulate trade with rich, lucrative and growing Commonwealth markets.

In particular, serious consideration needs to be given to the development of mutually beneficial Free Trade Agreements with Commonwealth countries (along with the USA). As one of the world's major trading nations, our future prosperity partly depends on building ties with countries that have bright futures. But we cannot unilaterally pursue these optimal trade policies whilst we are in the EU's Customs Union. This is an inescapable fact. And the EU currently has no trade deals with either the USA or Australia or, indeed, with New Zealand. These are lost opportunities. And, by the way, this country is quite large enough and significant enough to negotiate its own trade deals. Do not believe those people who claim we are "too small".

As I have written before, if Britain were free of the EU we could push ahead and negotiate the right trade deals for this country—with the Commonwealth, with the USA and with other favoured trading partners. And rather than being an "isolated" country without trading partners or friends, we would be far better networked with the world's growing economies than we are now. We would be far better placed to benefit from the inexorable shifts in world economic power.

There is an alternative to EU membership—and it is an attractive one. The alternative is to be free to build mutually beneficial bridges with countries which have rosy futures. It just so happens that many of those countries are in the Commonwealth.

References
http://leablog.dailymail.co.uk/2012/10/the-commonwealth-should-play-a-much-bigger-role-of-britains-future-an-interesting-snippet-of-news-slipped-out-recently-th.html

About the Author
Ruth Lea is currently Economic Adviser to and a non-executive director of the Arbuthnot Banking Group. She is also a member of the IEA's Shadow Monetary Policy Committee. She is the author of many papers on economic matters. Her previous posts include the Director of Global Vision (2007—2010), Director of the Centre for Policy Studies (2004—2007), Head of the Policy Unit at the Institute of Directors (1995—2003) and Economics Editor at ITN (1994—1995). She was also Chief UK Economist at Lehman Brothers and Chief Economist at Mitsubishi Bank; worked for 16 years in the Civil Service (the Treasury, the DTI, the Civil Service College and the Central Statistical Office) and was an economics lecturer at Thames Polytechnic (now the University of Greenwich).

Discussions
1. What is the "Commonwealth advantage" in this article? Which do you think will play a more important role in Britain's economy in the near future, EU or the Commonwealth?
2. To what extent do you agree that cooperation works more efficiently than struggling alone from the perspective of economy development?

Chapter 5

Education

Section One: A Brief Introduction

In terms of education, the UK Government is only responsible for England; the Scottish Government, the Welsh Government and the Northern Ireland Executive are responsible for the education in Scotland, Wales and Northern Ireland, respectively.

1. Overview

There are many commonalities between the education systems of the respective countries within the UK. There are five stages of education: early years, primary, secondary, further education (FE) and higher education (HE). Education is compulsory for all children between the ages of 5 (4 in Northern Ireland) and 16; before this children can be educated at **nursery**①. FE is non-compulsory, and covers non-advanced education which can be taken at further (including tertiary) education colleges and HE institutions (HEIs). The fifth stage, HE, is study beyond GCE A levels (and their equivalent) which, for most full-time students, takes place in universities and other HEIs and colleges.

The "**National Curriculum**②", established in 1988, provides a framework for education in England and Wales between the ages of 5 and 18; in Scotland the nearest equivalent is the 5 – 14 programme, as the common curriculum, in Northern Ireland. The Scottish qualifications the Standard Grades, Highers and Advanced Highers are highly similar to the English Advanced Subsidiary (AS) and Advanced Level (A2) courses.

Traditionally a high-performing country in international rankings of education,

---

① nursery: 幼儿园, 保育学校。
② National Curriculum: 全国教育大纲、全国性课程。

the UK has **stagnated**① in recent years in such rankings as the Programme for International Student Assessment (PISA) tests; in 2013, for reading and maths the country as a whole stood in the middle-rankings, a position that was broadly similar to three years before. Within the UK, Scotland performed marginally better than England; both were slightly ahead of Northern Ireland, and markedly ahead of Wales.

2. Education in England

Education in England is overseen by the Department for Education and the Department for Business, Innovation and Skills. Local authorities (LAs) take responsibility for implementing policy for public education and state schools at a local level.

The education system is divided into early years (ages 3—4), primary education (ages 4—11), secondary education (ages 11—18) and tertiary education (ages 18 +).

Full-time education is compulsory for all children aged between 5 and 17 (from 2013, and up to 18 from 2015), either at school or **otherwise**②, with a child beginning primary education during the school year he or she turns 5. Students may then continue their secondary studies for a further two years (sixth form), leading most typically to **A-level**③ qualifications, although other qualifications and courses exist, including Business and Technology Education Council (BTEC) qualifications, the International Baccalaureate (IB) and the Cambridge Pre-U. The leaving age for compulsory education was raised to 18 by the Education and Skills Act 2008. The change takes effect in 2013 for 16-year-olds and 2015 for 17-year-olds. State-provided schooling and sixth form education is paid for by taxes. England also has a tradition of independent schooling, but parents may choose to educate their children by any suitable means.

Higher education often begins with a **three-year bachelor's degree**④. Postgraduate degrees include master's degrees, either **taught or by research**⑤, and the doctorate, a research degree that usually takes at least three years. Universities

---

① stagnate: 停滞。
② education otherwise: 在家上学；家庭教育。类似的有 home education, unschooling, deschooling etc。
③ A-level: 英国中学高级水平考试，可以视为英国高考。
④ 3-year bachelor's degree: 英国大学的本科学制为三年。
⑤ taught or by research: 英国大学的硕士研究生有两类，授课型硕士学制一年，研究型硕士为两年。

require a **Royal Charter**① in order to issue degrees, and all but one are financed by the state via tuition fees, which cost up to £ 9,000 per academic year for English, Welsh and EU students.

English pupils in school uniform.
From: http://en.wikipedia.org/wiki/File:School_ uniforms_ GBR.jpg

2.1 Private to Public

Until 1870 all schools were charitable or private institutions, but in that year the Elementary Education Act 1870 permitted local governments to complement the existing elementary schools, to fill up any gaps. The Education Act 1902 allowed local authorities to create secondary schools. The Education Act 1918 abolished fees for elementary schools.

2.2 Education to the Age of 18

All children in England must currently receive an effective education (at school or otherwise) from **the first " prescribed day**②**"** which falls on or after their fifth birthday to the last Friday in June of the school year in which they turn 16. This will be raised, in 2013, to the year in which they turn 17 and, in 2015, to their 18th birthday. The prescribed days are 31 August, 31 December and 31 March. The school year begins on 1 September (or 1 August if a term starts in August).

---

① Royal Charter: 皇家特许状,是一种由英国君主签发的正式文书,类似于皇室制诰,专门用于向个人或者法人团体授予特定的权利或者权力,不少英国城市(部分连同都会特许状)和大学等重要机构都是凭借皇家特许状而设立,并得到学位授予权。剑桥大学于1231年获得其皇家特许状。

② the first "prescribed day": 规定入学日,法定的义务教育起始日。

2.3 State-funded Schools

Some 93% of children between the ages of 3 and 18 are in education in state-funded schools without charge (other than for activities such as swimming, theatre visits and **field trips**① for which a voluntary payment can be requested, and limited charges at state-funded boarding schools.

2.4 Independent Schools

Approximately 7% of school children in England attend privately run fee-paying independent schools rising to 18% for sixth form students. Some independent schools for 13—18 year olds are known for historical reasons as "**public schools**②" and for 8—13 year olds as "**prep schools**③". Some schools offer scholarships for those with particular skills or aptitudes, or bursaries to allow students from less financially well-off families to attend. Independent schools do not have to follow the National Curriculum, and their teachers are not required or regulated by law to have official teaching qualifications.

2.5 Sixth Form④ Colleges / Further Education Colleges

Students at both state schools and independent schools typically take **GCSE examinations**⑤, which mark the end of **compulsory education**⑥. Above school-leaving age, the independent and state sectors are similarly structured. In the 16—18 age group, sixth form education is not compulsory at present, although mandatory education until the age of 18 is to be phased in under the Education and Skills Act 2008. This will take effect for 16-year-olds in 2013, and for 17-year-olds in 2015.

Students will typically study in the sixth form of a school, in a separate sixth form college, or in a further education college. These courses can also be studied by adults over 18. This sector is referred to as Further Education. Some 16—18 students will be encouraged to study Key Skills in Communication, Application of Number, and Information Technology at this time.

---

① field trip：一般意为中小学组织的野外郊游，而非实地考察。
② public school：英国的公学，为私立寄宿中学。在美国则为免费的公立学校。
③ prep school：在英国为 11—13 岁的孩子提供教育的私立预备学校。在美国则为私立的大学预科学校。
④ sixth form：在英国指中学的六年级，而中六学院、课程主要面向完成了 GCSE、准备升读大学的中学生，为其准备 A-level 考试，相当于英国的高中教育阶段。
⑤ GCSE：General Certificate of Secondary Education，中文译为普通中等教育证书，是英国学生完成第一阶段中等教育所参加的主要会考。可以视为英国的中学会考。
⑥ compulsory education：义务教育。

2.6 Homeschooling

The 1944 Education Act (Section 36) stated that parents are responsible for the education of their children, "by regular attendance at school or otherwise", which allows children to be educated at home. The legislation places no requirement for parents who choose not to send their children to school to follow the National Curriculum, or to give formal lessons, or to follow school hours and terms, and parents do not need to be qualified teachers. A small but increasing numbers of parents do choose to educate their children outside the conventional school systems.

Officially referred to as "Elective Home Education", teaching ranges from structured homeschooling (using a school-style curriculum) to less-structured unschooling. Education Otherwise has supported parents who wished to educate their children outside school since the 1970s. The state provides no financial support to parents who choose to educate their children outside of school.

3. Further Education[①]

Further education (often abbreviated FE) in the United Kingdom and Ireland, not dissimilar to continuing education in the United States, is a term used to refer to post-compulsory education (in addition to that received at secondary school), that is distinct from the higher education offered in universities. It may be at any level above compulsory secondary education, from basic skills training to higher vocational qualifications such as PGCE, NVQ, City and Guilds, BTEC, HNC, HND or **Foundation Degree**[②].

A distinction is usually made between FE and higher education HE, an education at a higher level than secondary school, usually provided in distinct institutions such as universities. FE in the United Kingdom is usually a means to attain an intermediate or follow up qualification necessary to attend university, or begin a specifie career path, e.g. Quantity Surveyor, Town Planner or Veterinary Surgeon, for anyone over 16, primarily available at Colleges of Further Education, work-based learning, or adult and community learning institutions.

4. Higher Education

Students normally enter university from age 18 onwards, and study for an

---

① further education：指在英国中学毕业后，接受非大学类教育的继续教育。强调教育的职业特性，与各种职业技能证书挂钩。类似于中国的高职以及大专教育阶段，但不尽相同。

② foundation degree：英国的基础学位、副学士学位，全职学制为2年，半脱产学制为3～4年，低于学士、硕士和博士学位。类似于美国的 associate's degree 和中国的大专文凭（全职学制3年）。

academic degree. Historically, all undergraduate education outside the private **Regent's University London**① **University of Buckingham**② and BPP University College was largely state-financed, with a small contribution from **top-up fees**③, however fees of up to £ 9,000 per annum have been charged from October 2012. There is a distinct hierarchy among universities, with the **Russell Group**④ containing most of the country's more prestigious, research-led and research-focused universities. The state does not control university **syllabuses**⑤, but it does influence admission procedures through the Office for Fair Access (OfFA), which approves and monitors access agreements to safeguard and promote fair access to higher education. Unlike most degrees, the state still has control over teacher training courses, and uses its **Ofsted**⑥ inspectors to maintain standards.

University of Buckingham, Chancellors Court.
From: http://en.wikipedia.org/wiki/File:BirminghamUniversityChancellorsCourt.jpg

---

① Regent's University London: 伦敦摄政学院，位于伦敦市中心的 Regent's Park（摄政公园），是一所成立于 1984 年的私立非营利高校，以慈善机构的名义注册。

② University of Buckingham: 白金汉大学，是英国唯一一所私立大学。于 1976 年以白金汉大学学院（University College of Buckingham）的名称创立。1983 年，该学院获得皇家特许状后正式改称大学。白金汉大学坐落于离英格兰米尔顿凯恩斯北部约 15 英里白金汉郡的白金汉（Buckingham）。

③ top-up fees: 附加学费，即学生缴交给大学的学费。英国政府从 2006 年 9 月起允许高校收取每生每年最多 3000 英镑的附加学费，以应对政府的教育经费不足以及通货膨胀。此后，附加学费一再提高，触发社会各界的强烈反响。

④ Russell Group: 罗素大学集团，成立于 1994 年，由 24 四所英国一流的研究型大学组成，被称为"英国的常春藤联盟"，代表着英国最顶尖的大学。与美国的常春藤盟校（Ivy League Universities）不同的是，罗素集团大学皆由国家资助。其目的是要代表这些机构的观点、游说政府国会、提出研究报告来支持集团的立场。罗素集团名称的由来，是因为最初的 20 所院校的校长，每年春季固定于伦敦罗素广场旁的罗素饭店举行研究经费大会而得名。

⑤ syllabuses: 教学大纲。

⑥ Ofsted: Office for Standards in Education:（英国）教育标准办公室。

The typical first degree offered at English universities is the bachelor's degree, and usually lasts for three years. Many institutions now offer an undergraduate master's degree as a first degree, which typically lasts for four years. During a first degree students are known as undergraduates. The difference in fees between undergraduate and traditional postgraduate master's degrees (and the possibility of securing LEA funding for the former) makes taking an undergraduate master's degree as a first degree a more attractive option, although the novelty of undergraduate master's degrees means that the relative educational merit of the two is currently unclear.

Some universities offer a vocationally based foundation degree, typically two years in length for those students who hope to continue on to a first degree but wish to remain in employment.

4.1 Postgraduate Education

Students who have completed a first degree are eligible to undertake a postgraduate degree, which might be: 1) Master's degree (typically taken in one year, though research-based master's degrees may last for two); 2) Doctorate (typically taken in three years). Postgraduate education is not automatically financed by the state.

4.2 Specialist Qualifications

Education: Postgraduate Certificate in Education (PGCE), Certificate in Education (Cert Ed), City and Guilds of London Institute (C&G), or Bachelor of Education (BA or BEd), most of which also incorporate Qualified Teacher Status (QTS).

Law: Bachelor of Laws (LLB).

Medicine: Bachelor of Medicine, Bachelor of Surgery, studied at medical school.

Business: Master of Business Administration (MBA).

Psychology: Doctor of Educational Psychology (D. Ed. Psych) or Clinical Psychology (D. Clin. Psych.).

4.3 Fees

In the academic year 2011—2012, most undergraduates paid fees that were set at a maximum of £ 3,375 per annum. These fees are repayable after graduation, contingent on attaining a certain level of income, with the state paying all fees for students from the poorest backgrounds. UK students are generally entitled to student loans for maintenance. Undergraduates admitted for the academic year 2012—2013 will pay tuition fees set at a maximum of up to £ 9,000 per annum, with most universities charging over £ 6,000 per annum, and other higher education providers charging less.

Postgraduate fees vary but are generally more than undergraduate fees, depending on the degree and university. There are numerous **bursaries**① (awarded to low income applicants) to offset undergraduate fees and, for postgraduates, **full scholarships**② are available for most subjects, and are usually awarded competitively.

Different arrangements will apply to English students studying in Scotland, and to Scottish and Welsh students studying in England. Students from outside the UK and the EU attending English universities are charged differing amounts, often in the region of £ 5,000 ~ £ 20,000 per annum for undergraduate and postgraduate degrees. The actual amount differs by institution and subject, with the lab based subjects charging a greater amount.

University of Cambridge, Clare College (left) and part of King's College, including King's College Chapel (centre), built between 1441 and 1515
From: http://en.wikipedia.org/wiki/File:KingsCollegeChapelWest.jpg

5. Adult Education

Adult education, continuing education or lifelong learning is offered to students of all ages. This can include the vocational qualifications mentioned above, and also:

One or two year access courses, to allow adults without suitable qualifications access to university.

The Open University runs undergraduate and postgraduate distance learning

---

① bursaries: 助学金。
② full scholarship: 全额奖学金。

programmes.

The Workers' Educational Association offers large number of semi-recreational courses, with or without qualifications, made available by Local Education Authorities under the guise of Adult Education. Courses are available in a wide variety of areas, such as holiday languages, crafts and yacht navigation.

6. Criticism

One-half of British universities have lost confidence in the A* or A grades that are awarded by secondary schools, and require many applicants to sit for a competitive entrance examination. According to the Schools Minister, "strong evidence has been emerging of **grade inflation**① across subjects" in recent years.

An analysis of 2010 school data by *The Guardian* found that **state faith schools**② were not taking a fair share of the poorest pupils in their local areas, as indicated by free school meal entitlement. Not only was this so at an overall national level, but also in the postcode areas nearby the schools. This suggested selection by religion was leading to selection of children from more well-off families.

The Moser Group of the Basic Skills Agency has found that one out of five English adults are **functionally illiterate**③, while two out of five are **functionally innumerate**④. The Confederation of British Industry and the British Chambers of Commerce are also complaining of falling academic standards. Employers often experience difficulty in finding young people who have such basic employability skills as literacy, numeracy, problem solving, teamworking and time management. As a result, employers either have to pay for employees' **remedial education**⑤, or they must hire foreign candidates.

Katharine Birbalsingh has written of the problems she perceives in many community schools. She cites the impossibility of effective classroom management, bad teachers who cannot be dismissed, and government policies encouraging "soft" subjects. Birbalsingh has visited schools in Jamaica and India where pupils are desperate to gain the kind of education to which pupils in her own school (and their parents) were indifferent. She was a deputy head teacher in south London until she spoke at a Conservative Party conference in 2010 and was quickly sacked. Frank

---

① grade inflation：分数贬值、分数通胀，指因评分过高，导致得高分者激增而使教学质量下降。
② state faith school：指英国公立的教会学校。
③ functional illiterate：功能性文盲，是联合国于1965年在德黑兰的一次国际性会议上提出的，指的是受过一定传统教育，会基本的读、写、算，却不能识别现代信息符号及图表，无法利用现代化生活设施的人。
④ functional innumerate：功能性数学障碍。
⑤ remedial education：补习教育，此处不是指矫正教育。

Chalk, who taught at an inner-city school for ten years before resigning in frustration, makes similar claims.

A survey of 2000 teachers by *The Guardian* in 2011 cited a recurring reason for not enjoying the job. A lack of trust was referred to by respondents in the survey's "free text" area for extra comments, and related to senior staff, parents and governments. Writing about her own reasons for leaving teaching, a contributing editor to the newspaper's Guardian Teacher Network described the realisation of needing to leave the profession as having slowly crept up on her. Being a mature entrant, she questioned things in her aspiration to improve education and was reluctant to "be moulded into a standard shape".

References

http://en.wikipedia.org/wiki/Education_in_the_United_Kingdom

Exercises

I. Choose the one that best completes each of the following statements.

1. In Britain, children from the age of 5 to 16 _____.
   A. can legally receive completely free education
   B. can legally receive partly free education
   C. cannot receive free education at all
   D. cannot receive free education of their parents are rich

2. Which one of the following Russell Group universities is NOT in Great Britain?
   A. University of Edinburgh.　　B. Cardiff University.
   C. Queen's University Belfast.　　D. Cambridge University.

3. In terms of college education, who is going to pay more for the tuition fees?
   A. Students in England.
   B. students in Scotland.
   C. Students outside the UK but in the EU.
   D. Students outside the UK and the EU.

4. The world-famous Cambridge University is situated in _____.
   A. London　　B. Cambridge　　C. Windsor　　D. Eton

5. Which of the following statements about British education is wrong?
   A. All middle schools are free of charge for the British students.
   B. Public schools in the UK are not funded by the British government.
   C. "Independent school" and "public school" can usually be used interchangeably.
   D. Independent schools do not have to follow the National Curriculum, and their teachers may not have official teaching qualifications.

6. Traditionally, all the following pairs of universities have been rivals in sporting

competitions EXCEPT _____.
   A. Oxford University—Cambridge University
   B. Lancaster University—University of York
   C. Harvard University—Yale University
   D. Princeton University—MIT

II. Give brief answers to the following questions.

1. What are the major periods of schooling and the important exams, if you were to study in the UK between the ages of 5 to 18?
2. How is UK's higher education system similar to or different from that in China, in terms of the years of schooling, degree titles and tuitions?
3. What is the organization for the prestigious universities in the UK? Who are those included? Do you think they are really the best in the UK according to the latest rankings?
4. Can you name some of the major problems facing the education in the UK? Discuss from the perspectives of tuition fees, academic standards and teachers.

Section Two: In-depth Reading

The education system of the United Kingdom is regarded by many as one of the most respectable and highly-acclaimed in the world, but what are the key features that constitute such a prestigious system? What are the challenges that the old system faces? What are the highlights of it? Here we can find out more.

Reading One is about the cradle of education for the elites of Britain-Eton College.

Reading Two is a discussion about the divide between private and public schools in the UK.

Before reading the articles, brainstorm with your cohorts on the following questions:

1. What do you think of the private boarding schools in the UK? What are their advantages and costs?
2. Should public schools learn from private ones? Should they or could they become partners?
3. What are the criteria for a university to become world-famous?

Reading One

In 1440, King Henry VI founded the Eton College as a school that prepared students for enrollment into the King's College of the University of Cambridge. It was built with an intention to provide free education for the poor, but later evolved into an expensive fee-charging public school for the elites. Eton has educated 19 British

Prime Ministers and many other backbones of the UK. What can we learn from such a prestigious school?

Eton: Why the Old Boys' Network Still Flourishes
The Guardian

The new archbishop of Canterbury is the latest Old Etonian to make it to the top of the establishment. But what is it about the school that makes it such a breeding ground for leadership?

In the Porter's Lodge at Eton, a surprisingly small, panelled room that guards the main entrance to probably the world's most famous and self-conscious school, a recent issue of the *Week* magazine lies on a table between two chairs for visitors. On the cover is a cartoon of David Cameron, the 19th Old Etonian to be British prime minister, and a photo of the mayor of London, Boris Johnson, who may become the 20th. The magazine is well-thumbed: outsiders remain as fascinated by Eton's influence as the school is.

On the official Eton website, an elegant sales brochure with pictures of sunlit old school walls and pupils in their ancient, photogenic uniforms, there is an extensive section on "famous Old Etonians". The list of most recent "OEs" is startling, even to anyone well aware that elite Britain can be narrow. There are smooth media grandees (Geordie Greig, Nicholas Coleridge) and prickly dissenters (the New Left Review veteran Perry Anderson); lifestyle-sellers both macho (Bear Grylls) and gentle (Hugh Fearnley-Whittingstall); environmentalists (Jonathon Porritt) and climate change sceptics (Matt Ridley); actors (Hugh Laurie, Dominic West, Damian Lewis) and princes (Harry and William); rising Tory MPs (Rory Stewart, Kwasi Kwarteng) and people who are likely to interview them (BBC deputy political editor James Landale). Reading the long, hypnotic index of Eton eminences, back to the college's foundation in the 15th century, British public life begins to seem little more than Eton—a school of 1,300 13- to 18-year-old boys—talking to itself. And the list is not even comprehensive: at the time of writing, no one has thought to include Justin Welby, the new Archbishop of Canterbury.

But the power of an institution can be more than its people. Under the coalition, the patchy egalitarianism of postwar state schooling is giving way to a more traditional philosophy: stricter uniforms and rules, pupils organised into private school-style "houses", more powerful headteachers, more competition and difference between schools. It is a philosophy increasingly friendly to Eton. The current headmaster, Tony Little, remembers his first headship at another private school in the late 80s: "The local comprehensive wouldn't invite me over the threshold. That has changed massively. The number of phone calls I get from heads of academies has greatly risen in the last two or three years. They want to visit, they want to collaborate." Eton now has state "partner schools" in nearby Slough, and this year joined with seven other private schools to open a free school in Stratford in east London.

Other trends are working in Eton's favour. With annual fees of £ 32,067—more than the average after-tax British household income—Eton is, more than ever, "a luxury brand", as Greig puts it in fellow Old Etonian Nick Fraser's 2006 book *The Importance of Being Eton*. As the super-rich and the wish to imitate them have strengthened, Greig continues, "luxury brands have come back". Like Britain's many other luxury businesses, Eton has improved its product. "When I was there in 1958 to 1963, the bottom 40% of boys did absolutely no work," says Simon Head, fellow of the Rothermere American Institute at Oxford University. "That's gone. Eton has hunkered down. It's mobilised itself for the global economy."

Even the uniform seems more in keeping with the times. In an era of Downton Abbey and dandyish, aristocratic menswear fashions, Eton's waistcoats, tailcoats and stripes look less anachronistic. In the windows of the elderly school outfitters along Eton High Street, the long, theatrical approach to the college through the pretty, prosperous Berkshire town of the same name, there are items you could imagine selling well to east London hipsters.

Last month, a mildly droll Etonian reworking of the international pop hit Gangnam Style by PSY, called Eton Style, was posted by pupils on YouTube. Filmed around the school, it has had more than 2.6m views. Eton is adept at mocking and advertising itself simultaneously.

And yet, aspects of the school's success and longevity remain mysterious. What exactly is the source of its pupils' legendary charm and confidence, their almost as legendary slipperiness? In his book, Fraser interviews the late Anthony Sampson, the famous investigator of Britain's elites. "I'd meet Etonians everywhere I went," says Sampson, not one himself. "I've never understood why they were so good at networking and politics." Fraser speculates: "The Etonian mystique often seems a matter of mirrors, a collusion between those (non-Etonians) hungry for (Eton) notoriety and Etonians who are only too happy to supply it." One afternoon last week, I emailed the school to ask if I could visit. Within less than two hours, Little emailed back and offered to meet the next day.

Like many British centres of power, Eton owes some of its influence to geography. It was founded in 1440 on the orders of Henry VI, frequently in residence with his court nearby at Windsor Castle. Nowadays, the school emphasises its closeness to London, the great global money hub, a dozen miles to the east. "About a third of our boys have London addresses," says Little, leaving open the possibility that they also have others. For the tenth who live abroad—the proportion "has grown a little" since he became head in 2002—Heathrow airport is even closer. Jets

pupils on their way to lessons—known as "divs" or "schools" in the college's arcane slang
From: Christopher Furlong/Getty Images

intermittently moan loud and low over the school's spikes and towers.

But otherwise, for much of the long school day, there is an uncanny hush. As you approach the college, there is no grand announcement of Eton's existence, just small, hand-painted signs, white lettering on black, indicating that an increasing number of the courtyards, alleyways and driveways branching off the High Street are private property. From the open windows of neat classrooms, some late medieval, some Victorian, some Edwardian, some with expensive glass-and-steel modern additions, little of the usual hubbub of secondary school life emerges. Pupils and teachers alike sit upright in the black-and-white uniform, which is somehow both uptight and flamboyant—some might say like Etonians themselves. The uniform was standardised in the 19th century and must be worn for all lessons, AKA "divs" or "schools" in Eton's elaborate private language.

When the lesson ends, the spotless pavements are suddenly flooded with pupils. Some are tall and languid, some are chubby and scurrying, some are black or Asian, most are white. Everyone carries old-fashioned ring-binder files, and no one texts or makes a phone call. But some of the boys greet each other with hugs, or bursts of transatlantic up-talking, or say "like" with a long "i", London-style—for a minute or two, many seem reasonably modern and normal. Then everyone rushes off to the next lesson. "It is possible to be bored at Eton," says the school website, "but it takes a bit of effort!"

"In many ways it is a conservative institution, with lots of tiny rules," says someone who was a pupil from 2002 to 2007. The ambiguous outside status of Eton often makes old boys reluctant to declare themselves. "But Eton is probably more liberal, more permissive than its reputation. There are amazing cultural facilities, to do art and theatre for example. There were so many opportunities, it seemed churlish to focus on how annoying it was to have to wear a gown in the heat of summer." Last month, the History of Art Society, one of dozens of such pupil-run bodies, held a typical extracurricular event, a talk on 20th-century modernism. It was given by the

BBC's arts editor, Will Gompertz.

Some boys are so well-connected when they first arrive at the school, they already have a certain swagger. In focusing on a single institution, Eton's critics are sometimes avoiding the more uncomfortable truth that the roots of Britain's elites go wider and deeper. But for less overwhelmingly privileged boys, says the ex-pupil, Eton can be life-changing: "It's just expected that you will drink from the cup of opportunity. So you become used to being able to do whatever you put your hand to. Or at the least, you learn not to seem fazed by opportunities in the wider world."

Little himself was a pupil from 1967 to 1972, "the first male in my family to be educated past the age of 14". His study is baronial and high-ceilinged, with a window austerely open to the cold evening, but he is less forbidding than you might expect, with a quiet, calm, middle-class voice, like a senior doctor. "Dad worked at Heathrow, security for British Airways," he says. One of the school's main aims, he continues, is to admit a broader mix. But how can it, given the fees, which have raced ahead of earnings and inflation in recent decades? "It's a huge amount of money," he admits—the appearance of candour is one of Little's tactics when he talks to the outside world. "Sometimes I think, short of robbing a bank, what d'you do?"

Currently, by giving out scholarships on academic and musical merit, and bursaries according to "financial need", Eton subsidises the fees of about 20% of its pupils. "Forty-five boys pay nothing at all," says Little. "Our stated aim is 25% on reduced fees, of whom 70 pay nothing." What is the timescale? "Quite deliberately non-specific. But I'll be disappointed if we have not achieved it in 10 years." Not exactly a social revolution. "A long-term goal" is for Eton to become "needs-blind": to admit any boy, regardless of ability to pay, who makes it through the school's selection procedure of an interview, a "reasoning test", and the standard private-school Common Entrance exam. Whether Eton would then become a genuinely inclusive place is open to doubt: one of its selection criteria is an applicant's suitability for boarding, and many people connected with Eton would surely resist its metamorphosis into a meritocracy. Hierarchy is in Eton's bones.

Either way, Little says, the school does not have nearly enough money to become "needs-blind" yet. According to its latest accounts, Eton has an investment portfolio worth £ 200m. The school looks enviously on the wealth of private American universities: Harvard, the richest, has an endowment of more than £ 20bn. Eton seems unlikely to return soon to its core purpose as decreed by Henry VI: the education of poor scholars.

In fact, the school's history has been more erratic than many of its admirers and detractors imagine. Henry VI was deposed when Eton was only 21 years old and its funding was cut off: the college was left with a stunted-looking chapel, built to less than half the intended length. Eton is hardly the oldest British private school—one of its main rivals, Westminster, was founded in 1179. According to Fraser, "Etonmania", like so many supposedly eternal British traditions, only started in the reign of Queen Victoria. From the 1860s to the early 1960s, the school enjoyed a golden age of power and prestige. Then its influence plummeted. The Etonian-packed, slightly drifting Tory administrations of Harold Macmillan and Alec Douglas-Home were blamed for Britain's apparent decline. Within the school itself, as Harold Wilson's 60s Labour government—there has never been an Etonian Labour prime minister—seemed poised to create a fairer Britain, a friend of Fraser's "wasn't alone in his belief that Eton was doomed, and should be forthwith incorporated within the state system ⋯ The Provost and Fellows (the school's governing body) did consider relocating to Ireland or France, but this was never a very serious notion."

A perceived lack of seriousness hampered Eton for decades afterwards. Reforming headmasters struggled against the school establishment, nostalgic Old Etonians, and sometimes the pupils themselves to make Eton more academic and less obsessed by rules and rituals. Margaret Thatcher still had OEs in her 80s cabinets, but she marginalised and often fired them: they seemed too passive and paternalistic for modern Britain.

How different Etonians seem now. Little says the school teaches pupils "how to juggle time, how to work hard", and how to present themselves in public: "One thing I say to them when they leave is, if you choose to behave the way a tabloid would expect ... you deserve everything you get." He downplays Eton slang as "a quirk and an oddity. A lot of words have fallen out of use."

I wonder if he would say quite the same to a *Daily Telegraph* journalist. The classic Etonian skills—Cameron has them—have long included adjusting your message to your audience, defusing the issue of privilege with self-deprecation, and bending to the prevailing social and political winds, but only so far. "Do institutions in England change totally while seeming not to, or do they do the opposite?" asks Fraser. "I think the latter. And Eton has changed far less than Oxbridge."

Rushing between lessons with their old-fashioned files, some boys talk earnestly about their essays and marks. But Eton has not quite become an elite academic school: it is usually high, but rarely top, of the exam league tables. "Eton's view of education encompasses much more than just intellectual achievement," says the school's annual report. Nor does Eton participate unreservedly in the global education marketplace: it restricts its number of foreign pupils. "We are a British school that is cosmopolitan," says Little. "We're not an international school."

Does he think a school can ever be too powerful? For once, his affability gives way to something fiercer: "I'm unashamed that we're aiming for excellence. We want ... people who get on with things. The fact that people who come from here will stand in public life — for me, that is a cause for celebration." If Eton is too influential, he suggests, other schools should try harder. Fraser has another explanation for the success of Old Etonians: "At moments in their lives," he writes, "they are mysteriously available for each other." Subtle networking, a sense of mission, an elite that does not think too hard about its material advantages—Eton's is a very British formula for dominance.

It can be a high-pressure place. For all the Old Etonians who have considered the rest of life an anti-climax, there have been others damaged by the school: by its relentless timetable, by its crueller rituals, such as the "rips" torn by teachers in bad schoolwork, and by Eton's strange combination of worldliness and otherworldliness. Compared to most other boarding schools, Eton seems more eccentric and intense, its mental legacy more lingering. "Eton never left me," writes Fraser. Little says: "I've come across a fair number of casualties who were here [with me] in the 60s." Another more recent ex-pupil describes Eton as "a millstone round my neck every day".

After my interview with Little, I had a parting look inside the grand, domed School Hall. The building was empty except for a single boy, onstage in his stiff uniform at a grand piano, and a watching teacher with a clipboard. Dusk had fallen, and his playing rippled gorgeously through the overheated building. When he finished, the teacher immediately came and stood over him. I couldn't catch what she said, but he touched his face nervously and nodded.

For some people, that is what education should be about. And Eton nowadays works restlessly to satisfy them. Beside its seemingly endless playing fields, the school is building a new quadrangle for 40 more classrooms. Next to the development is a small, bucolic, council-owned park, with litter and rusty goalposts. As Eton flourishes for the next few years at least, the rest of Britain may have to make do.

References

http://www.theguardian.com/education/2012/nov/13/eton-old-boys-network-flourishes

The Guardian is a British national daily newspaper. Founded in 1821, it was known as *The Manchester Guardian* until 1959. From its beginnings as a local paper it has grown into a national paper associated with a complex organisational structure and an international multimedia and web presence. The newspaper's online edition was the third most widely read in the world as of June 2012. Its combined print and online editions reach nearly 9 million readers.

Discussions

1. Regarding the pupils' reworking of the pop hit "Gangnam Style" into Eton Style,

what is the impact and what does it tell us about Eton?
2. For the pupils from a less affluent background, what is the effect of Eton on them?
3. What are the head teacher Tony Little's words in response to Eton's high tuition fees? What is the meaning of "needs-blind", which is a long term goal for Eton?
4. What is one of the classic Eton skills as displayed by the British Prime Minister David Cameron?
5. What does the author mean by saying "Eton's is a very British formula for dominance"?

Reading Two

The inequality of education in the UK is a prominent issue due to the fact that the divide between public schools and state-funded schools is widening. Such a divide tends to separate the British society and affect social mobility in fundamental ways. The public has discussed a number of ways to address this issue.

A Divided Education System Breeds a Divided UK
The Guardian

"The only logical solution is to remove the socially divisive separate development regime which the state/private sector division constitutes." writes David Webster.

Anthony Seldon acknowledges that "Britain has a uniquely divided education system that both reflects and in turn shapes our divided society" (The future for schools is partnership, not apartheid, 27 January). One might have thought that the master of Wellington College would be an apologist for such a divided society which the private education sector is designed to reproduce from one generation to the next. But no. He feigns to want to reduce the polarisation in the education system and society. His proposal is that "both school sectors ... learn from each other, and the closer they bond, the better for all". But no matter how closely they bond, the continuing existence of two sectors makes the reduction of polarisation impossible. The only logical solution is to remove the socially divisive separate development regime which the state/private sector division constitutes.

We will not "reverse our stagnating social mobility" by encouraging the two sectors to work more closely together. The elephant in the room here is the existence of the two sectors, the relationship between which is an engine for protecting and nurturing a privileged group. "Good societies," says Seldon, "build bridges between divides." No, societies which want to end the injustice of privilege work to remove the divides rather than leave them in place. Seldon argues that "divisions are broken down as both sides learn how much they have in common". No, divisions are perpetuated by the continued existence of two sides. Seldon argues that "the potential

Eton pupils sit watching the traditional Wall Game being played
From: Christopher Furlong/Getty Images

benefits of bonding state and independent schools in perpetuity are transformative". No, transformation of a polarised education system and society are precisely what you won't get as long as the two sectors remain. Seldon has the gall to claim that those who argue against greater bonding between the two sectors are guilty of promoting apartheid. No. An apartheid regime is imposed by a dominant group as a way of defending and legitimising its dominance. You would not have accused black South Africans who refused to collaborate with apartheid of creating that apartheid. Calls for greater collaboration between the two sides in Britain's apartheid education system are designed to divert attention away from the gross inequities and injustices the system ensures.

Dr David Webster
Crewe, Cheshire

Anthony Seldon's attack on John Harris's excellent piece about private schools is misplaced. Why must private schools be seen as the model to which state-funded schools should aspire? Despite their lavish resource base, at a level unmatched anywhere in state education, the OECD has found that, once you account for the pupils' different socioeconomic background, private schools are easily outperformed by our publicly funded schools. Over recent decades, our system has been increasingly distorted by futile and pointless attempts to make state schools look more like private schools. The way forward instead should be to provide a strong and consistent infrastructure of support as in the highly successful programmes known as the London Challenge and the Greater Manchester Challenge.

Ron Glatter
Emeritus professor of educational administration and management, the Open University

Rather than uneasy couplings between private and state schools, the most productive partnerships would be between nearby state schools, which can easily share good practice and resources and understand each other's situations. However, Michael's Gove's chaotic, anti-education, anti-teacher and anti-children policies of fragmenting state education into a free-for-all, where any ideological or religious group with an axe to grind can set up a free school with unqualified staff, or else schools are handed over to profit-driven companies whose core business is selling carpets, for example, wrecks collaboration and drives up competitiveness, thus increasing educational apartheid. If private schools genuinely want to work with state schools for the best reasons, perhaps they should review their voting patterns for 2015 to ensure that more policies like Gove's never see the light of day.

Max Fishel
Bromley, Kent

If Anthony Seldon really believes his private-school sector can help state education, he could make a start by doing something practical. Giving private places to the difficult, often-excluded pupils that the state sector has to deal with all the time would actually be of some practical use and would operate as an interesting test case to see how effective private education would be in helping kids who are not keen on learning.

Alistair Richardson
Stirling

Your editorial on social mobility in schools (28 January) painted a bleak picture of educational opportunity in Britain today. However, it would be wrong to suggest schools of all stripes are engaged in some sort of conspiracy to widen social divisions. Within the boarding sector, for instance, efforts have been made to find places for children from some of the most deprived parts of the UK. The SpringBoard Bursary Foundation—of which my school is a member—aims to offer fully funded places to hundreds of disadvantaged pupils over the next decade. In doing so, it will specifically avoid "cherry-picking" students, working with partner organisations to find children with the potential to inspire aspiration within their communities. The only plot we in the boarding sector are complicit in is to break down class barriers.

Patrick Derham
Head master of Rugby school

Demos is right to call the pupil premium "a good policy, in theory" (Pupil premium failing to help poor children prosper, 28 January). Their new research adds to the overwhelming evidence from Ofsted that, in practice, the premium is failing to meet its purpose of raising the educational attainment of disadvantaged pupils. But this will not change as long as schools are allocated this funding regardless of whether they actually succeed in raising attainment or improving long-term outcomes for pupils on free school meals. Currently schools are being rewarded for failing pupils.

This is why we're calling on government to pay a portion of the premium by results, not all upfront. Schools should receive their final payment for eligible pupils 18 months after they leave school, on condition that the child is in education, employment or training at that point. This would build accountability into the premium, and focus schools' attention on the pupils who need most support, and for whom the policy was designed. Payment-by-results is a key principle of public-service funding and can turn a good idea in theory into improved outcomes in practice. The attainment gap isn't closing—we need to act fast to ensure the opportunity offered by the pupil premium isn't wasted.

References

http://www.theguardian.com/education/2014/jan/29/divided-education-system-private-schools

Discussions

1. How did Dr. David Webster argue against Seldon's "bridge theory" and his idea on "the broken of divisions"?
2. According to Ron Glatter, are pupils in private schools doing better than those in state schools or not, if pupils' socioeconomic background was taken into account?
3. What did Alistair Richardson suggest private schools do to practically help education?

Chapter 6

Media

Section One: A Brief Introduction

Media of the United Kingdom consist of several different types of communications media: television, radio, newspapers, magazines, and Web sites. The country also has a strong music industry. The United Kingdom has a diverse range of providers, the most prominent being the state-owned public service broadcaster, the BBC (British Broadcasting Corporation). The BBC's largest competitors are **ITV plc**[①] and **News Corporation**[②]. Regional media is covered by local radio, television and print newspapers.

1. Audiences

In 2009 it was estimated that individuals viewed a mean of 3.75 hours of television per day and listened to 2.81 hours of radio. The main BBC public service broadcasting channels accounted for and estimated 28.4% of all television viewing; the three main independent channels accounted for 29.5% and the increasingly important other satellite and digital channels for the remaining 42.1%. Sales of newspapers have fallen since the 1970s and in 2009 42% of people reported reading a daily national newspaper. In 2010, 82.5% of the United Kingdom population were

---

① ITV plc: 英国独立电视公司, 拥有 12 家电视播出执照持有公司, 在 15 个地区播出。独立电视台是英国历史最长、规模最大的商业电视网。独立电视台（频道）也是英国收视率最高的电视频道之一。独立电视公司是由格拉纳达（Granada）股份和卡尔顿（Carlton）传媒这两家公司合并而成。独立电视公司在伦敦证券交易所上市, 并且是 FTSE 100 指数的构成公司。

② News Corporation: 新闻集团, 是一个庞大传媒帝国的名称。新闻集团涉足所有的媒体领域, 它的首席执行官鲁伯特·默多克用 50 多年的时间将一个普通地方报业公司变成当今世界上规模最大、国际化程度最高的综合性传媒公司之一。在英国, 40% 的报纸都由他控股, 6 张发行量最大的报纸, 其中包括《泰晤士报》《每日电讯》《镜报》《卫报》等日总发行量达到 2500 万份。

BBC Television Centre at White City, West London, which opened in 1960 and closed in 2013
From: http://en.wikipedia.org/wiki/File:BBC_ TV_ Centre.jpg

Internet users, the highest proportion amongst the 20 countries with the largest total number of users in that year.

2. National Media Hubs

London dominates the media sector in the United Kingdom: national newspapers, television and radio are largely based there, notable centres include **Fleet Street**① and BBC Broadcasting House. Greater Manchester is also a significant national media hub. *The Guardian*② national newspaper was founded in Manchester in 1821, and was known as the *Manchester Guardian* until 1959. Edinburgh and Glasgow, and Cardiff, are important centres of newspaper and broadcasting production in Scotland and Wales respectively.

3. National Media Organizations

The BBC, founded in 1922, is the United Kingdom's publicly funded radio, television and Internet broadcasting corporation, and is the oldest and largest broadcaster in the world. It operates numerous television and radio stations in the United Kingdom and abroad and its domestic services are funded by the television

---

① Fleet Street: 舰队街, 是英国伦敦市内一条著名的街道, 以邻近的舰队河命名。一直到 1980 年代, 舰队街都是传统上英国媒体的总部, 因此被称为英国报纸的老家。即使最后一家英国主要媒体路透社的办公室也在 2005 年搬离舰队街。今日舰队街依旧是英国媒体的代名词。

② The Guardian:《卫报》, 是英国的全国性综合日报。创刊于 1959 年, 因总部设于曼彻斯特而称为《曼彻斯特卫报》。总部于 1964 年迁至首都伦敦, 不过曼城和伦敦均设有印刷设施。一般公众视《卫报》的政治观点为中间偏左。《卫报》的排印系统在 1988 年实行电脑化之前, 由于经常出现植字错误, 因此被民众戏称为 *The Grauniad*, 揶揄报章连自己报名也拼错。

licence. Other major players in the United Kingdom media include ITV plc, which operates 11 of the 15 regional television broadcasters that make up the ITV Network, and News Corporation, which owns a number of national newspapers through News International such as the most popular tabloid *The Sun* and the longest-established daily "broadsheet" ***The Times***①, as well as holding a large stake in satellite broadcaster **British Sky Broadcasting**②.

4. Print Media

The United Kingdom print publishing sector, including books, server, directories and databases, journals, magazines and business media, newspapers and news agencies, has a combined turnover of around £ 20 billion and employs around 167,000 people.

Fleet Street in 2008, London.
From: http://en.wikipedia.org/wiki/File:Londres_-_Fleet_Street.JPG

Traditionally British newspapers have been divided into "quality", serious-minded newspapers (usually referred to as "**broadsheets**③" because of their large size) and the more populist, "**tabloid**④" varieties. For convenience of reading,

---

① *The Times*:《泰晤士报》,诞生于 1785 年元旦,创始人是约翰·沃尔特。起初称为《每日环球纪录报》(*The Daily Universal Register*),也有资料翻译为《世鉴日报》。1788 年 1 月 1 日,正式改为如今的名称。然而,正是在约翰·沃尔特职掌时期,《泰晤士报》最先将新闻视角延伸至英国之外的其他欧洲国家,尤其是法国。这为《泰晤士报》在政界和金融界内赢得了很高的声誉。

② British Sky Broadcasting:英国天空广播集团,简称 BSkyB,是一间卫星广播公司,总部设在伦敦。天空广播在英国和爱尔兰均有业务。天空广播于 1990 年由天空电视台和英国卫星广播合并。英国天空广播公司是英国最大收费电视台,在英国拥有超过 1000 万用户。天空广播公司在伦敦证券交易所上市,是富时 100 指数的成分股。新闻集团拥有 39.1% 的股份。

③ broadsheet:大报,大幅面印刷的报纸,内容通常比较严肃。

④ tabloid:小报,小幅面印刷,以通俗内容为主。

many traditional broadsheets have switched to a more compact-sized format, traditionally used by tabloids. In 2008 ***The Sun***① had the highest circulation of any daily newspaper in the United Kingdom at 3.1 million, approximately a quarter of the market. Its sister paper, ***The News of the World***②, had the highest circulation in the Sunday newspaper market, and traditionally focused on celebrity-led stories until its closure in 2011. ***The Daily Telegraph***③, a centre-right broadsheet paper, is the highest-selling of the "quality" newspapers. *The Guardian* is a more liberal "quality" broadsheet and ***The Financial Times***④ is the main business newspaper, printed on distinctive salmon-pink broadsheet paper. Trinity Mirror operates 240 local and regional newspapers in the United Kingdom, as well as national newspapers such as the *Daily Mirror* and the *Sunday Mirror*. Scotland has a distinct tradition of newspaper readership. The tabloid *Daily Record* has the highest circulation of any daily newspaper outselling *The Scottish Sun* by four to one while its sister paper, *the Sunday Mail* similarly leads the Sunday newspaper market. The leading "quality" daily newspaper in Scotland is *The Herald*, though it is the sister paper of *The Scotsman*, and *the Scotland on Sunday* that leads in the Sunday newspaper market.

A large range of magazines are sold in the United Kingdom covering most interests and potential topics. British magazines and journals that have achieved worldwide circulation include ***The Economist***⑤, ***Nature***⑥, and ***New Scientist***⑦,

---

① *The Sun*：《太阳报》，被视为 tabloid 类的典型报纸。

② *The News of the World*：《世界新闻报》，英国星期日版的《太阳报》。这份有 168 年历史的报纸在 2011 年 7 月 10 日停止发行，原因即是该报被揭发卷入多宗窃听丑闻（包括窃听 13 岁凶案受害少女杜勒，窃听伦敦七七爆炸案中死者亲人的手机）而在英国本土声名狼藉。该报曾为最畅销的英文报纸，直至停发时仍为发行量最大的英文报纸之一。

③ *The Daily Telegraph*：《每日电讯报》，是一份英国大开型报章，成立于 1855 年 6 月 29 日，是英国销量最高的报纸之一。

④ *The Financial Times*：《金融时报》，英国 1888 年发行的报刊，具有世界性的影响力。

⑤ *The Economist*：《经济学人》，是一份由伦敦经济学人报纸有限公司出版的杂志，于 1843 年 9 月由詹姆士·威尔逊创办。杂志中所有文章都不署名，而且往往带有鲜明的立场，但又处处用事实说话。它的主编们认为：写出了什么东西，比出自谁的手笔更重要。从 2012 年 1 月 28 日的那一期杂志开始，《经济学人》杂志开辟了中国专栏，为有关中国的文章提供更多的版面。

⑥ *Nature*：《自然》，是世界上最早的科学期刊之一，也是全世界最权威及最有名望的学术杂志之一，首版于 1869 年 11 月 4 日。虽然今天大多数科学期刊都专注于一个特殊的领域，《自然》是少数（其他类似期刊有《科学》和《美国国家科学院院刊》等）依然发表来自多个科学领域的一手研究论文的期刊。在许多科学研究领域中，每年最重要、最前沿的研究结果是在《自然》中以短文章的形式发表的。

⑦ *New Scientist*：《新科学家》，创刊于 1956 年，周刊。它是一个自由的国际化科学杂志，内容关于最近的科技发展，网站开始于 1996 年，每天登载关于科技界的新闻。它虽然并非是一个经过同行评议的科学杂志，但仍被科学家和非科学家们广为传阅，杂志还经常刊登一些评论，比如气候变化等环境问题。该周刊通常被认为是与《科学美国人》（SCIENTIFIC AMERICAN）齐名的大众化高水平学术期刊。

Private Eye, *Hello*!, *The Spectator*, *the Radio Times* and **NME**①.

5. Broadcasting

Radio in the United Kingdom is dominated by the BBC, which operates radio stations both in the United Kingdom and abroad. The **BBC World Service**② radio network is broadcast in 33 languages globally. Domestically the BBC also operates ten national networks and over 40 local radio stations including services in Welsh on BBC Radio Cymru, Gaelic on BBC Radio nan Gàidheal in Scotland and Irish in Northern Ireland. The domestic services of the BBC are funded by the television licence. The internationally targeted BBC World Service Radio is funded by the Foreign and Commonwealth Office, though from 2014 it will be funded by the television licence. The most popular radio station by number of listeners is BBC Radio 2, closely followed by BBC Radio 4. Advances in digital radio technology have enabled the launch of several new stations by the Corporation.

Rather than operating as independent entities, many commercial local radio stations are owned by large radio groups which broadcast a similar format to many areas. The largest operator of radio stations is Global Radio, owner of the major Heart and Galaxy radio brands. It also owns Classic FM and London's most popular commercial radio station, 95.8 CapitalFM. Other owners are UTV Radio, with stations broadcasting in large city areas and Bauer Radio, holding radio in the North of England. There are also regional stations, like Real Radio and *the Century Network*, broadcasting in some main parts of England, Wales and Scotland, and a number of licensed community radio stations which broadcast to local audiences.

Analogue terrestrial television③ in the United Kingdom is made up of two **chartered**④ **public broadcasting companies**, the BBC and Channel 4 and two franchised commercial television companies, (ITV and Channel 5). There are five

---

① NME: *The New Musical Express*，即英国《新音乐快递》杂志，与美国的《滚石》(*The Rolling Stones*) 杂志齐名，它经营杂志、online、音乐新闻多方面，并设有NME音乐奖，该奖立足于非主流音乐的推荐，被称为全英音乐奖的另类版本。NME由于在20世纪70年代之朋克音乐、90年代之另类音乐，以及新世纪之独立音乐传播中所作出的贡献，赢得了相当好的口碑。

② BBC World Service：英国广播公司国际广播频道。

③ analogue terrestrial television：使用模拟信号的地面电视。是利用大气电波收发电视信号的传输方式之一。相对于卫星电视和有线电视，该模拟信号的地面电视又被称为无线电视。在早期没有人造卫星的时代，电视台多以此方式播放节目。另有digital terrestrial television，即使用数字信号的地面电视。

④ chartered public broadcasting company：公共广播又称公共播送服务或公共媒体，指的是由政府编列预算或（及）以其他方式（如向用户收取费用或接受第三方捐助等）获得资金，所成立、运作的非营利性电子媒体。这类媒体多半以制作和播放公共政策的讨论、文教艺术或知识性节目为主，目的是提升国民知识水平、促进民众参与政治决策。

major nationwide television channels: BBC One, BBC Two, ITV, Channel 4 and Channel 5—currently transmitted by analogue and digital terrestrial, **free-to-air**① signals with the latter three channels funded by commercial advertising. The United Kingdom now has a large number of digital terrestrial channels including a further six from the BBC, five from ITV and three from Channel 4, and one from S4C which is solely in Welsh, among a variety of others. The vast majority of digital cable television services are provided by Virgin Media with satellite television available from Freesat or British Sky Broadcasting and free-to-air digital terrestrial television by Freeview. The entire country switched to digital in 2012.

The BBC operates several television channels in the United Kingdom and abroad. The BBC's international television news service, **BBC World News**②, is broadcast throughout the world. The domestic services of the BBC are funded by the television licence. The international television broadcast services are operated by **BBC Worldwide**③ on a **commercial subscription**④ basis over cable and satellite services. This commercial arm of the BBC also forms half of UKTV along with Virgin Media.

Channel 4 is similarly chartered to the BBC, with a remit to provide public service broadcasting and schools programs, however it runs commercial advertisements to provide a revenue stream. It produces an analogue channel branded as Channel 4, as well as digital channels E4, More 4 and Film4.

The commercial operators rely on advertising for their revenue, and are run as commercial ventures, in contrast to the public service operators. The ITV franchise transmits the analogue channel known as ITV1 (in England, Wales, Scottish Borders, Isle of Man and Channel Islands), STV (In Central and Northern Scotland), and UTV in Northern Ireland. Channel 5 transmits one analogue channel.

All the major analogue broadcasters provide additional channels on the free-to-air Freeview digital television service, and all of these channels can be accessed via a cable or satellite provider, such as Virgin Media or BSkyB.

6. Internet

The Internet country code top-level domain (ccTLD) for Internet in the United Kingdom is .uk. The most visited ".uk" websites are the British version of Google followed by BBC Online.

---

① free-to-air: FTA, 用户可以免费接收的卫星电视。
② BBC World News: 英国广播公司国际新闻电视频道。
③ BBC Worldwide: 英国广播公司的商业性分公司,其主要业务是向国际买家贩卖知名节目。
④ commercial subscription: 收取收视费用的经营模式。

References

http://en.wikipedia.org/wiki/UK_media

Exercises

I. Choose the one that best completes each of the following statements.

1. Which of the following is NOT considered a characteristic of London?
   A. The cultural centre.
   B. The business centre.
   C. The financial centre.
   D. The sports centre.
2. Three of the following are characteristics of London, Which of the four is the EXCEPTION?
   A. London is a political, economic and cultural centre of the country.
   B. London has a larger population than all other cities in England.
   C. London is not only the largest city in Britain, but also the largest in the world.
   D. London has played a significant role in the economic construction of the country.
3. Which one of the four is NOT correct?
   A. English-speaking countries are UK, USA, Canada, Barbados, etc.
   B. English-speaking countries are UK, Canada, Australia, New Zealand, etc.
   C. English-speaking countries are USA, Canada, Australia, the Republic of Ireland, etc.
   D. English-speaking countries USA, Canada, Australia, Egypt, etc.
4. Which of the following is the British oldest daily newspaper?
   A. The *Telegraph*.
   B. The *Guardian*.
   C. The *News of the World*.
   D. The *Times*.
5. Which of the following is the oldest national Sunday newspaper in Britain?
   A. The *Times*.
   B. The *Guardian*.
   C. The *Observer*.
   D. The *Financial Times*.
6. The news agency Reuters was founded in _____.
   A. London
   B. Birmingham
   C. Liverpool
   D. Manchester
7. Which is the correct name to use to refer to Britain in a political way?
   A. Great Britain.
   B. The British Isles.
   C. The United Kingdom.
   D. England.
8. The two areas in Britain where a lot of immigrants live are _____.
   A. London and Cambridge
   B. London and heart of England
   C. Manchester and Birmingham
   D. Edinburgh and Nottingham
9. The flag of the United Kingdom, known as the Union Jack, is made up of _____

crosses.

   A. one   B. two   C. three   D. four
10. Which flower is symbol of England?
   A. Thistle.   B. Shamrock.   C. Daffodil.   D. Rose.
11. _____ is the home of golf.
   A. England   B. Scotland   C. Wales   D. Ireland
12. Which of the following languages is NOT spoken in Scotland?
   A. English.   B. Scottish.   C. Gaelic.   D. Danish.
13. The Tower of London, a historical sight, located in the center of London, was built by _____.
   A. King Harold   B. Robin Hood
   C. Oliver Cromwell   D. William the Conqueror
14. There are _____ state churches in Britain.
   A. two   B. three   C. four   D. five
15. _____ birthday is a great event in Britain since it marks the beginning of full manhood or womanhood.
   A. The twenty-first   B. The eighteenth
   C. The nineteenth   D. The twentieth
16. Reuters was founded in _____.
   A. 1715   B. 1751   C. 1851   D. 1815

II. Give brief answers to the following questions.

1. What are the most important broadcasters in the UK, and who are its competitors?
2. What is difference between a broadsheet and a tabloid? Can you name some examples?
3. As audiences from outside the UK, how do we distinguish between BBC World Service, BBC World News and BBC Worldwide?

Section Two: In-depth Reading

Scandals are perhaps one of the most eye-catching elements in a newspaper, but what happens when scandals are surrounding a newspaper itself? The concerning issues are inexhaustible, e. g. underhand practices, black box manipulations, out-of-court settlements, hacking, tapping, compensation, compromises, etc. How would you cope with such a chaos correctly? We will find out the place of justice and integrity in the following articles.

Reading One is a record of a time-honored British newspaper's death.

Reading Two is a statement by James Murdoch who announced the closing of the paper.

Before reading the articles, brainstorm with your cohorts on the following

questions:
1. What are the bottom lines for a free press?
2. What is the correct way to deal with a press scandal?

Reading One

News of the World, a time-honored newspaper which had been on the British newsstands for 168 years, abruptly came to an end and ceased its publication on July 10th, 2011. The sudden collapse is due to its involvement in several phone hacking scandals. In these incidents, we can have a grasp of the untold underhand practices and black box rules existing in the Western media.

News of the World to Cease Publication

No adverts will be placed in the newspaper this weekend and the title will close. The Irish *News of the World* employs 22 full-time staff and around ten people on a part-time basis.

News International announcing that this Sunday's edition of the *News of the World* will be the last
From: http://en.wikipedia.org/wiki/File:Final_NOTW_cover.jpeg

A series of hacking revelations have hit the tabloid in recent months, with parent companies News International and News Corp coming under increasing pressure as a result.

Police said there could be as many as 4,000 victims of phone hacking by the paper, which has been published for 168 years.

Scotland Yard have also confirmed that they are considering the allegation that emails were hacked.

News Corporation chairman James Murdoch issued a statement to staff this afternoon, praising the paper's achievements but condemning the hacking revelations.

"The *News of the World* is in the business of holding others to account, but it failed when it came to itself."

The main accusations are that journalists, or their hired investigators, took advantage of often limited security on mobile phone voicemail boxes to listen in to messages left for celebrities, politicians or people involved in major stories.

Disclosure that the practice involved victims of crime came when police said a private detective working for the *News of the World* in 2002 hacked into messages left on the phone of murdered schoolgirl Milly Dowler while police were still looking for her.

Since that revelation it has also been claimed that the newspaper accessed the phones of the Soham murder victims' parents, the parents of missing child Madeline McCann and the families of victims killed in the 2005 London bombings.

Families of British soldiers killed in Iraq and Afghanistan are also alleged to have been targeted.

It has been widely reported that a number of other papers had also been involved in underhand practices to secure circulation-boosting stories. A lawyer for the Dowler family said *News of the World* was "unlucky" because investigator Glenn Mulcaire had kept copious notes.

In 2007, Mulcaire and the paper's then royal correspondent went to jail for hacking.

Police are mining those notes for clues to possible other victims as part of what is described as the biggest investigation in modern British history.

Rupert Murdoch, chairman and chief executive of News International's parent company, News Corporation, branded claims of phone hacking at the paper "deplorable and unacceptable".

He has backed Rebekah Brooks to continue as chief executive of *News International* however, despite the fact that she was the newspaper's editor while many of the hacks are alleged to have taken place.

Future plans

It remains unclear whether the company will produce a replacement title for the lucrative Sunday market, in which, despite difficult times for newspaper circulations, the *News of the World* is still selling 2.6 million copies a week.

One widely expected option could see sister paper *The Sun* expanding to a seven day publication.

The sunonsunday.co.uk domain name was registered two days ago by a web design company called Mediaspring.

The sunonsunday. com was also registered two days ago.

The British Conservative-led government has already backed a deal for Murdoch's News Corp to buy out the 61% of BSkyB it does not already own, and insists the two cases are not linked.

Formal approval for the deal had been expected within weeks, but it now seems unlikely for months, although officials deny suggestions that they are delaying a decision because of the scandal.

Critics say giving Murdoch full control of Sky television would concentrate too much media power in his hands and risk skewing political debate.

The MP who secured this week's dramatic parliamentary debate into the phone hacking scandal has claimed the closure of the *News of the World* is an attempt to protect News International chief executive Rebekah Brooks.

Chris Bryant, who is taking legal action against the newspaper over claims his phone was hacked, said Ms Brooks should have resigned over the initial allegations murdered schoolgirl Milly Dowler's phone was hacked when she was editor.

"This strategy of chucking first journalists, then executives and now a whole newspaper overboard isn't going to protect the person at the helm of the ship."

Elsewhere, the UK labour leader Ed Miliband has said he will call for the Press Complaints Commission to be scrapped and a new "beefed up" body with effective powers of investigation and enforcement be established instead.

References

http://www.rte.ie/news/2011/0707/303370-hacking/

About the Author

Raidió Teilifís Éireann: Radio (and) Television of Ireland; abbreviated as RTÉ, is a semi-state company and the national public service broadcaster of Ireland. It both produces programmes and broadcasts them on television, radio and the Internet. The radio service began on 1 January 1926, while regular television broadcasts began on 31 December 1961, making it one of the oldest continuously operating public service broadcasters in the world.

Discussions

1. What are the main accusations of the phone hacking scandal of the *News of the World*?
2. Is it common for newspapers to commit underhand practices to gain information? Why someone said *News of the World* was "unlucky"? How did the perpetrators end up?
3. What is the strategy of News Corp in dealing with the hacking scandal?

Reading Two

The century-old newspaper *News of the World* ceased publication, "A newspaper in the business of holding others to account failed when it came to itself", described by James Rupert Jacob Murdoch, the younger son of media mogul Rupert Murdoch and the deputy chief operating officer of News Corporation. What else did he say to bid farewell to this time-honored paper?

Full Statement from James Murdoch

News International chairman James Murdoch announced today that this Sunday's issue of the *News of the World* will be the last edition of the paper.

Private Eye cover satirising the scandal
From: http://en.wikipedia.org/wiki/File:Private_Eye_Cover.jpg

This is how he announced the news to staff:

I have important things to say about the *News of the World* and the steps we are taking to address the very serious problems that have occurred.

It is only right that you as colleagues at *News International* are first to hear what I have to say and that you hear it directly from me. So thank you very much for coming here and listening.

You do not need to be told that the *News of the World* is 168 years old. That it is read by more people than any other English language newspaper. That it has enjoyed support from Britain's largest advertisers. And that it has a proud history of fighting crime, exposing wrong-doing and regularly setting the news agenda for the nation.

When I tell people why I am proud to be part of News Corporation, I say that our commitment to journalism and a free press is one of the things that sets us apart. Your work is a credit to this.

The good things the *News of the World* does, however, have been sullied by behaviour that was wrong. Indeed, if recent allegations were true, it was inhuman and had no place in our company.

The *News of the World* is in the business of holding others to account. But it failed when it came to itself.

In 2006, the police focused their investigations on two men. Both went to jail. But the *News of the World* and *News International* failed to get to the bottom of repeated wrongdoing that occurred without conscience or legitimate purpose.

Wrongdoers turned a good newsroom bad and this was not fully understood or adequately pursued.

As a result, the *News of the World* and *News International* wrongly maintained that these issues were confined to one reporter.

We now have voluntarily given evidence to the police that I believe will prove that this was untrue and those who acted wrongly will have to face the consequences.

This was not the only fault.

The paper made statements to Parliament without being in the full possession of the facts. This was wrong.

The company paid out-of-court settlements approved by me. I now know that I did not have a complete picture when I did so. This was wrong and is a matter of serious regret.

Currently, there are two major and ongoing police investigations. We are co-operating fully and actively with both. You know that it was News International who voluntarily brought evidence that led to opening Operation Weeting and Operation Elveden. This full cooperation will continue until the Police's work is done.

We have also admitted liability in civil cases. Already, we have settled a number of prominent cases and set up a compensation scheme, with cases to be adjudicated by former High Court judge Sir Charles Gray. Apologising and making amends is the right thing to do.

Inside the company, we set up a Management and Standards Committee that is working on these issues and that has hired Olswang to examine past failings and recommend systems and practices that over time should become standards for the industry. We have committed to publishing Olswang's terms of reference and eventual recommendations in a way that is open and transparent.

We have welcomed broad public inquiries into press standards and police practices and will cooperate with them fully.

So, just as I acknowledge we have made mistakes, I hope you and everyone inside and outside the company will acknowledge that we are doing our utmost to fix them, atone for them, and make sure they never happen again.

Having consulted senior colleagues, I have decided that we must take further decisive action with respect to the paper.

This Sunday will be the last issue of the *News of the World*.

Colin Myler will edit the final edition of the paper.

In addition, I have decided that all of the *News of the World*'s revenue this weekend will go to good causes.

While we may never be able to make up for distress that has been caused, the right thing to do is for every penny of the circulation revenue we receive this weekend to go to organisations-many of whom are long-term friends and partners-that improve life in Britain and are devoted to treating others with dignity.

We will run no commercial advertisements this weekend. Any advertising space in this last edition will be donated to causes and charities that wish to expose their good works to our millions of readers.

These are strong measures. They are made humbly and out of respect. I am convinced they are the right thing to do.

Many of you, if not the vast majority of you, are either new to the Company or have had no connection to the *News of the World* during the years when egregious behaviour occurred.

I can understand how unfair these decisions may feel. Particularly, for colleagues who will leave the company. Of course, we will communicate next steps in detail and begin appropriate consultations.

You may see these changes as a price loyal staff at the *News of the World* are paying for the transgressions of others. So please hear me when I say that your good work is a credit to journalism. I do not want the legitimacy of what you do to be compromised by acts of others. I want all journalism at News International to be beyond reproach. I insist that this organisation lives up to the standard of behaviour we expect of others. And, finally, I want you all to know that it is critical that the integrity of every journalist who has played fairly is restored.

Thank you for listening.

References

http://www.rte.ie/news/2011/0707/303416-notwstatement/

About the Author

James Rupert Jacob Murdoch is the younger son of media mogul Rupert Murdoch and the deputy chief operating officer of News Corporation. He is the former chairman and chief executive of News Corp., Europe and Asia, where he oversaw assets such as *News International* (British newspapers), publisher of the *News of the World* newspaper, SKY Italia (satellite television in Italy), Sky Deutschland, and STAR TV (satellite television in Asia).

Discussions
1. What is the glorious history of the *News of the World*?
2. What are the several things that the paper had done wrong in the scandal? What would be the right thing to do?
3. After acknowledging the faults, what does James hope to assure everyone inside the company?

Chapter 7

Holidays

Section One: A Brief Introduction

1. Holidays in the United Kingdom of Great Britain and Northern Ireland

British people celebrate bank holidays and other holidays. There are between eight and ten bank holidays in the UK.

1.1 Bank Holidays in the UK

Public holidays in the UK are commonly referred to as bank holidays. As the UK is a country made of four more or less independent regions, official holidays in the UK are slightly different in the four regions of England, Wales, Scotland, or Northern Ireland.

There are eight bank holidays in England and Wales:
- New Year's Day: January 1
- **Good Friday**[①]: March or April (April 18, 2014 / April 3, 2015)
- **Easter Monday**[②]: March or April (April 21, 2014 / April 6, 2015)
- Early May bank holiday: May (May 5, 2014 / May 4, 2015)
- Spring bank holiday: May (May 26, 2014 / May 25, 2015)
- Summer bank holiday: August (August 25, 2014 / August 31, 2015)
- Christmas Day: December 25
- **Boxing Day**[③]: December 26

---

① Good Friday: 耶稣受难日,复活节前的星期五。
② Easter Monday: 复活节星期一。
③ Boxing Day: 节礼日,圣诞节后的第一个工作日。这一日传统上要向服务业工人赠送圣诞节礼物。

In Scotland, the summer bank holiday is earlier in August. Moreover, Scots celebrate **St. Andrew's Day**① on November 30. The 2nd of January is also a bank holiday in Scotland, but Easter Monday is not. All in all, there are nine bank holidays in Scotland.

In Northern Ireland, **St. Patrick's Day**②, celebrated on March 17, is a bank holiday, as well as Orangemen's Day on July 12, which commemorates the Battle of Boyne. There is a total of ten bank holidays in Northern Ireland, meaning it is the region with the most holidays in the UK.

Although banks in the UK are indeed closed, people do not necessarily have paid leaves on bank holidays. Also, today many shops are still open on holidays in the UK, so not everyone even has these days off.

When bank holidays in the UK fall on a weekend, the following Monday is usually a holiday as well. This is called a "substitute" holiday. For instance, there will be a substitute holiday for Boxing Day on Monday, December 28, 2015.

The UK does not have a **national day**③, making it only one of two countries in the world without one (the other country is Denmark). This is slightly ironic considering that many countries in the world have national days to celebrate independence from British rule.

1.2　Other Holidays in the UK

There are, of course, more celebrations and special occasions than just bank holidays in the UK.

Bonfire Night（Guy Fawkes Night）

"Remember, remember, the fifth of November..." This slightly haunting rhyme introduces **Bonfire Night**④, also known as Guy Fawkes Night. It is one of the most unique holidays in the UK.

Bonfire Night takes a different approach to holidays. Instead of celebrating something that happened, it celebrates something that didn't happen: **the 1605 Gunpowder Plot**⑤. Guy Fawkes and other passionate Roman Catholics were

---

① St. Andrew's Day：圣安德鲁是苏格兰的守护神。在苏格兰，每年的11月30日是圣安德鲁日。这是一个庆祝苏格兰文化、美食和凯利舞的节日。

② St. Patrick's Day：圣帕特里克节是每年的3月17日，是为了纪念爱尔兰守护神圣帕特里克。这一节日5世纪末期起源于爱尔兰，如今已成为爱尔兰的国庆节。

③ national day：国庆节。

④ Bonfire Night：篝火之夜，也叫盖伊·福克斯之夜。

⑤ the 1605 Gunpowder Plot：火药阴谋。反叛者由于詹姆士拒绝给予天主教徒同等权利而大失所望。他们企盼火药阴谋引发叛乱从而使詹姆士的女儿波希米亚的伊丽莎白（Elizabeth of Bohemia）能够成为一个天主教元首。但11月5日的阴谋却在计划发生之前数小时流产了。每年的11月5日，英国人以大篝火之夜（即焰火之夜或盖伊·福克斯之夜）来庆祝阴谋被粉碎。

involved in a conspiracy to blow up parliament and to assassinate King James I. It's hard to imagine the damage that could have been done, considering that much of London was made from wood at the time and the entire royal elite would have been present on the intended day. Instead of celebrating a national hero, Guy Fawkes Night condemns a national villain and, by today's standards, a political terrorist.

British people mark the 5th of November by making bonfires, setting off fireworks, and burning effigies of Guy Fawkes. Today, the popularity of Guy Fawkes Night has somewhat decreased, due to dwindling interest and higher safety regulations. Guy Fawkes Night is not celebrated in Northern Ireland at all. It is very much a British holiday, as opposed to one of the holidays in the UK which are shared between all four regions.

Remembrance Day in the UK

As the name implies, Remembrance Day, which was originally called Armistice Day, is also about remembering. It is observed in the United Kingdom and Commonwealth Countries.

Remembrance Day
From: http://www.douban.com/note/50141630/

Remembrance Day marks the eleventh hour on the eleventh day of the eleventh month in 1918 when the Great War was finally over. It was first commemorated in 1919, and every November it is celebrated to pay tribute to the men and women who have lost their lives in war.

In the United Kingdom, Remembrance Sunday is celebrated on the second Sunday in November, in addition to the actual Remembrance Day. On November 11, there are two minutes of silence across the UK. However, the main ceremony always occurs on Remembrance Sunday. In London, leading politicians, religious leaders and, of course, the Royal Family gather for a service at the **Cenotaph**①. It is

---

① the Cenotaph: 阵亡纪念碑。

common practice to lay a wreath in commemoration.

As Remembrance Day approaches, you might notice people with **felt poppies**① pinned to their autumn coats. The poppy is symbolic of Remembrance Day. These bright red flowers have become emblematic of "Flanders' Fields" and the lives lost in World War One.

Royal Holidays in the UK

Although there isn't a specific bank holiday that celebrates the royal family, there are certainly celebrations. Even though her actual birthday is in April, the Queen officially celebrates her birthday on a Saturday in June. The Trooping, the Colour Parade celebrates her majesty's birthday, and although it is a grand spectacle, a public holiday is not part of the deal.

Queen's diamond jubilee: window display in London
From: http://www.thinkdo3.com/s/3072

Should something monumental, however, take place, the UK might create a public holiday. For example, 2012 marked **the Queen's diamond jubilee**②, i.e. her 60th year on the throne. She was only the second monarch to reach sixty years of rule (other than Queen Victoria). To celebrate, the traditional end of May bank holiday was moved to June 4, 2012, and June 5, 2012 also became a one-off bank holiday, thus creating a four day weekend.

---

① felt poppies: 纸质的罂粟花。在英国，每年11月11日是纪念战争先烈的"荣军日"，届时，上到女王，下至平民，都将佩戴纸质的罂粟花以表哀悼。这项传统来源于一场法国和比利时的战争。"一战"期间，比利时西部和法国北部边境是战斗最为激烈的地区，许多士兵在那里牺牲。1915年5月，一名军医在掩埋战友遗体时看到漫山遍野的罂粟花，于是写下了名作《在弗兰德土地上》。此后，罂粟花就逐渐作为英国纪念阵亡士兵的象征花。

② the Queen's diamond jubilee: 伊丽莎白二世女王钻禧纪念。2012年6月2日至5日，英国耗资13亿，举办了一系列"英女王钻禧庆典"官方活动，纪念英国女王伊丽莎白二世登基60周年。

Interfaith Holidays in the UK

The UK is very much a multicultural society today (though discrimination and racism still exist). With multiculturalism comes a multitude of religious and cultural holidays, such as **Eid-Ul-Fitr**[①], **Diwali**[②] and **Rosh Hashanah**[③]. These holidays have made it onto the annual calendar for holidays in the UK, although they are only celebrated by certain parts of the population.

References

http://www.usa.gov/citizens/holidays.shtml

USA. gov is the U.S. government's official web portal. It makes it easy for the public to get U.S. government information and services on the web.

http://www.internations.org/great-britain-expats/guide/16134-culture-shopping-recreation/public-holidays-in-the-uk-16131

InterNations is the first international online community for people who live and work abroad. As a network based on trust, it enables the members to interact with other global minds in a similar situation, with comparable interests and needs. InterNations users can keep in touch with friends and business contacts; they can exchange reliable information on expat-specific topics, both on a global and a local level.

Exercises

I. Choose the one that best completes each of the following statements.

1. Of all the symbols, _____, which are considered to represent fertility and new life: are those most frequently associated with Easter.
   A. the pumpkin and the turkey   B. the lamb and the beef
   C. the spring peas and the potatoes   D. the egg and the rabbit
2. _____ is basically a home and family festival.
   A. Christmas   B. Boxing Day
   C. Easter Monday   D. Halloween
3. American Independence Day falls on _____.
   A. the 4th of July   B. October 31st
   C. March 20th D. May 1st

[①] Eid-Ul-Fitr: 开斋节。一年一度的穆斯林节日，标志着斋月的结束；在此期间人们互赠礼品，享用美食佳肴。

[②] Diwali: (印度) 排灯节，一个为期五天的灯火的节日，有多个不同的神话学的习俗。耆那教徒、锡克教徒和印度教徒都庆祝这个节日。

[③] Rosh Hashanah: 犹太新年。按照犹太教的传统说法，天地万物的创造就是在秋天里完成的。因此，犹太人的新年——拉什·哈夏那节定在夏末秋初。

4. Christmas is usually connected to _____.
   A. the reunion of a large family   B. the eating of Easter eggs
   C. the resurrection of Christ   D. the forgiving of other's sins
5. In which day is Halloween celebrated?
   A. 5 November.   B. 31 October.
   C. 17 March.   D. 25 December.
6. Americans celebrate Memorial Day on the last Monday in May to honor those who have _____.
   A. given their lives for their country
   B. made great scientific discoveries
   C. won American great reputation in sports
   D. donated large amounts of money to the country
7. "Trick or Treat" is a phrase that children often use when they celebrate _____.
   A. New Year's Day   B. Veteran's Day
   C. Halloween   D. Christmas
8. The Easter egg and the hare, two of the symbols most frequently associated with Easter, are considered to represent _____.
   A. vigor and bravery   B. fertility and new life
   C. originality and speed   D. happiness and fun
9. The first Puritans came to America on the ship _____.
   A. Codpeed   B. Susan Constant
   C. May Flower   D. Discovery
10. Halloween is a _____.
    A. summer festival   B. night-time festival
    C. pilgrims' holiday   D. religious holiday
11. British people do NOT celebrate _____.
    A. Thanksgiving Day   B. Christmas Day
    C. Easter Day   D. National Day
12. _____ is not related to Bonfire Night.
    A. Fireworks   B. Reunion
    C. Guy Fawkes   D. November
13. Labor Day is celebrated on _____.
    A. May 1st B. the first Monday of September
    C. June 1st D. October 1st
14. _____ aims to predict winter weather.
    A. Valentine's Day   B. Earth Day
    C. Arbor Days   D. Groundhog Day
15. _____ is NOT a bank holiday in the UK.
    A. Remembrance Day   B. Boxing Day

C. Good Friday D. New Year's Day

II. Read the following statements carefully and decide whether they are TRUE or FALSE.

1. Few Americans make New Year's resolutions on New Year's Day.
2. Memorial Day originally honored the people killed in World War I.
3. Independence Day honors the nation's birthday.
4. In the fall of 1621, the Pilgrims held a three-day feast to celebrate a bountiful harvest.
5. The first mass-produced valentine cards were sold in the 1940s.
6. The neighbors are expected to respond by giving children in costumes small gifts of candy or money on Halloween.
7. Bank holidays in the UK are only celebrated by employers in the banks.
8. Bonfire Night celebrates something that didn't happen: the 1605 Gunpowder Plot.
9. Remembrance Day is observed in the United Kingdom and Commonwealth Countries.
10. Although there isn't a specific bank holiday that celebrates the royal family, there are certainly celebrations, such as the Queen's birthday.

III. Give brief answers to the following questions.

1. What do American people do on Thanksgiving Day?
2. Thanksgiving Day is an important federal holiday in the United States. Federal law establishes some public holidays for federal employees and those public holidays are federal holidays. Besides Thanksgiving Day, do you know any other federal holidays in the United States?
3. In addition to federal holidays, there are also some popular American celebrations that occur every year, such as Valentine's Day, Mother's Day, etc. Do you know what these celebrations are for? Can you name some other popular celebrations and observances?

Section Two: In-depth Reading

As US and UK are multi-ethnic countries, all the different holidays and observances can perfectly manifest various cultures in both of the two countries. However, there are both similarities and differences. In addition to New Year's Day, which is observed everywhere in the world, among all the holidays and celebrations, Christmas Day is day when people in both the US and the UK celebrate at the same time. In the UK, Bonfire Night may be the most special day, for that is the only moment all over the year people from the four regions will celebrate on the same day. Moreover, Thanksgiving Day is a big day for American people, but not for British people. The following two articles will provide us an opportunity to know more about

Bonfire Night and Thanksgiving Day respectively.

Reading One discusses Bonfire Night and Halloween from a special point of view.

Reading Two tells us Native Americans' view on Thanksgiving Day.

Before reading the articles, brainstorm with your cohorts on the following questions:

1. On which holidays will the Chinese president deliver a speech to our people? What are the differences of style and contents between the Queen's speech and our president's speech?

2. Can you tell us how we Chinese observe our traditional holidays?

Reading One

Halloween and Guy Fawkes Day, both are night celebrations. The difference is Halloween is more popular and not only celebrated by British people but also by American people, especially kids and teenagers, however, Bonfire Night or Guy Fawkes Day is a local observance in Britain and British people have been enjoying burning effigies for a long time. But in some parts of Britain more people celebrate Halloween rather than Bonfire Night. Why? How to explain the change? Historians may know.

Halloween v Guy Fawkes Day: A POINT OF VIEW
David Cannadine

Lament the Americanisation of British culture? Guy Fawkes is your man, says historian David Cannadine in his weekly opinion column.

2005 has been a bumper year for anniversaries, and I've found myself editing a book about one of them, and contributing to another.

In January, it was 40 years since the death of Winston Churchill; and between May and August a series of observances marked the 60th anniversary of the end of World War Two. Forty and 60 are not, perhaps, the roundest of round numbers. But one good reason these events and these endings were being commemorated was for the benefit of those who were alive then, and who can still remember that far back in time.

Once commemoration moves from the realm of remembrance to the province of history, the numbers tend to get much rounder, and it's centenaries or multiple centenaries that are usually marked. And in recent weeks, we've been right in the midst of two of them: the 200th anniversary of the Battle of Trafalgar on 21 October, marking Nelson's great naval triumph in 1805; and the 400th anniversary of Guy Fawkes' abortive attempt to blow up the Houses of Parliament on 5 November 1605.

Guy Fawkes failed in his plot
From: http://news.bbc.co.uk/2/hi/uk_news/magazine/4408078.stm

It's hard to imagine two events more different, both in terms of what went on, and in terms of the people who were at the centre of them. Nelson's annihilating naval victory rendered a French invasion of Britain impossible for the remainder of the Napoleonic Wars; it was the final, supreme triumph of a naval commander of astonishing gifts and undoubted genius; and the manner and the moment of his death assured him a posthumous glory and global fame which continue to this day.

Tourists still visit HMS Victory at Portsmouth, Nelson remains the iconic hero at the National Maritime Museum in Greenwich, and he is always gazing down on us from the top of his column in Trafalgar Square.

But as his statue there reminds us, Nelson lost an arm and an eye in the service of the state, which means he showed that disability was no obstacle to achievement well over 100 years before the wheelchair-bound Franklin Roosevelt became president of the United States and long before David Blunkett was ever even heard of.

How appropriate, then, that he has recently been joined in Trafalgar Square by another statue to another disabled person—Alison Lapper pregnant, who since September has occupied the fourth plinth, in the north-west corner.

Heroes and villains

Trafalgar was a great national victory; and Nelson was (and is) a great national hero. By contrast, the Gunpowder Plot was a non event: the attempt to blow up the Houses of Parliament was foiled, and the plotters were apprehended, tortured and executed.

And Guy Fawkes is not a national hero but a national villain. Like Nelson, he was a professional fighting man, and there was about him a dashing sense of glamour and danger. But he is widely remembered as a sinister and melodramatic figure whose brief and ignominious appearance on the stage of our nation's past has been greeted with collective boos and catcalls ever since. No wonder he is burned in effigy every year.

In fact, the Gunpowder Plot was a close-run thing. The conspirators, who were

Nelson, a national hero
From: http://news.bbc.co.uk/2/hi/uk_news/magazine/4408078.stm

Roman Catholics, wanted to blow up parliament on the day of the state opening, with the aim of assassinating King James I, who'd been less sympathetic to the Catholic cause than they'd expected.

They planned to replace James by his daughter, Princess Elizabeth, who they hoped would be a more malleable and a more Catholic queen. Had they succeeded, England might have become a Catholic nation once more, and members of the Church of England would have been distinctly thin on the ground.

It's not easy to get a sense of the scale of the carnage that would have taken place had they succeeded. On the day of the state opening of parliament, almost the entire elite of the nation would have been there: king, lords and commons, and all the senior officers of the church, the military and the state.

If all of them had gone up in smoke and flames, virtually the whole of the nation's establishment would have been taken out. And since many of the neighbouring buildings were made of wood, a large part of the capital would also have been destroyed in a conflagration that would have anticipated the Great Fire of London that did in fact happen later in the century.

But the conspiracy was detected in advance. Unlike the Battle of Trafalgar, which was a big event, the attempt to blow up the Houses of Parliament was a failure. Put in the Bush-and-Blair language of our own day, the foiling of the Gunpowder Plot was thus an outstandingly successful pre-emptive strike against what would now be described as the forces of organised, fanatical, religiously-motivated terrorism.

Guy Fawkes duly got his comeuppance: illustrated literally in the wrenching contrast between the elegant, confident calligraphy of his signature before torture, and the enfeebled scrawl which was all he could manage after his body had been broken on the rack.

National identity

So what, if anything, unites these two very different figures and these two very different events? And why are they still commemorated centuries later? Both 21 October and 5 November serve to remind us, as they reminded our forbears even more forcefully, that Britain was a Protestant nation.

Burnt in effigy
From: http://news.bbc.co.uk/2/hi/uk_news/magazine/4408078.stm

The Gunpowder Plot was a foiled Catholic conspiracy, and during the 17th Century, it was the pope, rather than Guy Fawkes, who was often burned in effigy. And the Battle of Trafalgar was fought against France and Spain, our nation's two hereditary enemies, which for much of their histories were both despotic and Catholic regimes.

For many Britons, then, both Trafalgar Day and Guy Fawkes Day were national events to celebrate our Protestant patriotism, and it was that re-affirmation of our collective identity which gave them their long-lasting appeal.

Not surprisingly, Catholic Britons have always been uncomfortable with 5 November, and nowadays there are frequent calls to abolish an event which seems to them to be based on little more than religious bigotry and intolerance.

It's possible to be a Catholic Briton and admire Nelson; it's hard to be a Catholic Briton without wincing at the sight of an effigy of Guy Fawkes going up in flames. I'm not a Catholic, but I do rather sympathise.

Americanised festivities

But Catholics take heart: for these days, Bonfire Night is not the event it was when I was young. I can vividly remember that for me 5 November meant street-corner guys in rickety prams; roasted potatoes and chestnuts; and my father in our back garden lighting the blue touch paper on rockets, roman candles and catherine wheels, and then retiring.

Nowadays, family bonfire gatherings are much less popular, and many once-large civic celebrations have been given up because of increasingly intrusive health and safety regulations. But 5 November has also been overtaken by a popular festival that barely existed when I was growing up, and that is Halloween, which takes place on 31 October, the eve of All Saints Day.

Trick or treat!
From: http://news.bbc.co.uk/2/hi/uk_news/magazine/4408078.stm

It's a strange festival, part pagan, part Christian, which can be traced back in these islands to Celtic and medieval times. But in its present-day guise, we associate it with America, with kids dressing up in spooky and lurid costumes, who then go trick or treating—a custom I first encountered when I visited the United States as a graduate student in the early 1970s.

Halloween has long been big business in America, but it's only very recently become big business here in Britain, where it's now much easier for shops and supermarkets to sell pointed hats in garish colours than fireworks.

As long as Britain has a Royal Navy, and as long as people read the novels of authors like CS Forester and Patrick O'Brian, there will always be a cult of Nelson and Trafalgar will retain its devotees.

But although it's been around for much longer, the prospects don't look quite as good for Guy Fawkes and Bonfire Night once this anniversary is past. Britain is not the Protestant nation it was when I was young: it is now a multi-faith society. And the Americanised Halloween is sweeping all before it—a vivid reminder of just how powerfully American culture and American consumerism can be transported across the Atlantic.

But here, perhaps, is an opportunity for the revival of 5 November. For those who wish to protest at the ever increasing Americanisation of our world might take up Bonfire Night as their cause. Guy Fawkes may have been a bad Briton, but in some ways he was a good European, and from there it's only a step to pulling faces at Uncle Sam.

References

http://news.bbc.co.uk/2/hi/uk_news/magazine/4408078.stm

About the Author

David Cannadine is a British historian, known for a number of books, including *The Decline and Fall of the British Aristocracy* and *Ornamentalism*. He is also notable as a commentator and broadcaster on British public life, especially the monarchy. He serves as the general editor of the *Penguin History of Europe* series. He was at the University of London from 1998 to 2003 working at the Institute of Historical Research but is currently a professor at Princeton University. On 1 October 2014, he became the new Editor of the *Oxford Dictionary of National Biography*.

Discussions

1. Gunpowder Plot, as a failed historical event, has been remembered by British people for hundreds of years and the effigies of Guy Fawkes are still being burned every 5th of November. What's the real meaning of Bonfire Night nowadays? Can you explain its long-lasting popularity from a religious perspective?
2. According to David Cannadine, increasing popularity of Halloween means Americanisation of British culture. What do you think of this viewpoint? What about the prevalence of Christmas Day, Halloween, Valentine's Day and other western celebrations in China? Americanisation? Westernisation? Or even culture invasion?

Reading Two

People in the United States often wonder why the country really celebrates Thanksgiving Day. They wonder what the real story behind it is even though most of them are taught the quaint little story of "Pilgrims and Indians" in elementary schools. Thanksgiving has been declared a national holiday in America and it is considered as a day of giving thanks in return for all of the blessings received from the past year. But what about the Native Americans (members of ethnic groups or tribes, who had been living on the land of North America before Europeans arrived)? What's their view on Thanksgiving Day?

Thanksgiving: A Native American View
Jacqueline Keeler

For a Native American, the story of Thanksgiving is not a very happy one. But a member of the Dineh Nation and the Yankton Dakota Sioux finds occasion for hope.

I celebrate the holiday of Thanksgiving. This may surprise those people who wonder what Native Americans think of this official U. S. celebration of the survival of early arrivals in a European invasion that culminated in the death of 10 to 30 million native people.

Thanksgiving to me has never been about Pilgrims. When I was six, my mother, a woman of the Dineh nation, told my sister and me not to sing "Land of the Pilgrim's pride" in "America the Beautiful." Our people, she said, had been here much longer and taken much better care of the land. We were to sing "Land of the Indian's pride" instead. I was proud to sing the new lyrics in school, but I sang softly. It was enough for me to know the difference. At six, I felt I had learned something very important. As a child of a Native American family, you are part of a very select group of survivors, and I learned that my family possessed some "inside" knowledge of what really happened when those poor, tired masses came to our homes.

When the Pilgrims came to Plymouth Rock, they were poor and hungry—half of them died within a few months from disease and hunger. When Squanto, a Wampanoag man, found them, they were in a pitiful state. He spoke English, having traveled to Europe, and took pity on them. Their English crops had failed. The native people fed them through the winter and taught them how to grow their food.

These were not merely "friendly Indians." They had already experienced European slave traders raiding their villages for a hundred years or so, and they were wary—but it was their way to give freely to those who had nothing. Among many of our peoples, showing that you can give without holding back is the way to earn respect. Among the Dakota, my father's people, they say, when asked to give, "Are we not Dakota and alive?" It was believed that by giving there would be enough for all—the exact opposite of the system we live in now, which is based on selling, not giving. To the Pilgrims, and most English and European peoples, the Wampanoags were heathens, and of the Devil. They saw Squanto not as an equal but as an instrument of their God to help his chosen people, themselves.

Since that initial sharing, Native American food has spread around the world. Nearly 70 percent of all crops grown today were originally cultivated by Native American peoples. I sometimes wonder what they ate in Europe before they met us. Spaghetti without tomatoes? Meat and potatoes without potatoes? And at the "first Thanksgiving" the Wampanoags provided most of the food—and signed a treaty granting Pilgrims the right to the land at Plymouth, the real reason for the first Thanksgiving.

What did the Europeans give in return? Within 20 years European disease and treachery had decimated the Wampanoags. Most diseases then came from animals that Europeans had domesticated. Cowpox from cows led to smallpox, one of the great killers of our people, spread through gifts of blankets used by infected Europeans. Some estimate that diseases accounted for a death toll reaching 90 percent in some Native American communities.

By 1623, Mather the elder, a Pilgrim leader, was giving thanks to his God for destroying the heathen savages to make way "for a better growth," meaning his people. In stories told by the Dakota people, an evil person always keeps his or her heart in a secret place separate from the body. The hero must find that secret place and destroy the heart in order to stop the evil. I see, in the "First Thanksgiving" story, a hidden Pilgrim heart. The story of that heart is the real tale than needs to be told. What did it hold? Bigotry, hatred, greed, self-righteousness? We have seen the evil that it caused in the 350 years since. Genocide, environmental devastation, poverty, world wars, racism. Where is the hero who will destroy that heart of evil? I believe it must be each of us. Indeed, when I give thanks this Thursday and I cook my native food, I will be thinking of this hidden heart and how my ancestors survived the evil it caused. Because if we can survive, with our ability to share and to give intact, then the evil and the good will that met that Thanksgiving Day in the land of the Wampanoag will have come full circle. And the healing can begin.

References

http://www.alternet.org/story/4391/thanksgiving%3A_a_native_american_view

AlterNet, a project of the non-profit Independent Media Institute, is a liberal activist news service. Launched in 1998, AlterNet publishes original content as well as journalism from a wide variety of other sources. AlterNet states that its mission is to "inspire citizen action and advocacy on the environment, human rights and civil liberties, social justice, media, and health care issues". AlterNet's tagline is "The Mix is the Message."

About the Author

Jacqueline Keeler is a member of the Dineh Nation and the Yankton Dakota Sioux. Her work has appeared in *Winds of Change*, an American Indian journal.

Discussions

1. What was new to you in Keeler's descriptions of the first Thanksgiving? Why do you think these details are sometimes omitted from popular culture's take on Thanksgiving?
2. Why does Keeler refer to Native Americans as a "very select group of survivors"?
3. For some Native Americans, Thanksgiving is no cause for celebration, but rather serves as a reminder of colonization's devastating impact on indigenous peoples. To what extent do you agree that Pilgrims' settlement in the land of North America is the colonization of the natives?

Chapter 8

Literature

Section One: A Brief Introduction

1. Old British and Late Medieval Literature: 449—1500

Old English literature, or Anglo-Saxon literature, encompasses the literature in the period after the settlement of the Saxons and other Germanic tribes in England. These works include genres such as epic poetry, hagiography, sermons, *Bible* translations, legal works, chronicles, riddles, and others.

The epic poem **Beowulf**① is the most famous work in Old English, and has achieved national epic status in England. It tells a story of Beowulf battling three antagonists: Grendel, Grendel's mother, and a Dragon.

Old English poetry falls broadly into two styles, the heroic Germanic and the Christian. The most popular and well-known understanding of Old English poetry continues to be alliterative verse. The system is based upon accent, alliteration, the quantity of vowels, and patterns of syllabic accentuation. It consists of five permutations on a base verse scheme; any one of the five types can be used in any verse. The system was inherited from and exists in one form or another in all of the older Germanic languages.

Following the Norman Conquest of 1066, the development of Anglo-Norman literature in the Anglo-Norman realm introduced literary trends from Continental Europe. Geoffrey Chaucer (1343—1400), known as the Father of English literature, is widely considered the greatest English poet of the Middle Ages and was

---

① *Beowulf*:《贝奥武夫》,英国古代史诗,公元5世纪时已开始口头传诵,约8世纪时成书。本诗以西撒克斯(Wessex)方言写成,押头韵而不押尾韵,用双字隐喻而不用明喻。是现存古英语文学中最古老的作品,是流传至今的欧洲最完整的一部史诗,也是欧洲最早的方言史诗。在语言学方面也是相当珍贵的文献。

the first poet to have been buried in Poet's Corner of Westminster Abbey. Among his many works, which include *The Book of the Duchess*, *The House of Fame*, *The Legend of Good Women* and *Troilus and Criseyde*, Chaucer is best known today for **The Canterbury Tales**[①], a collection of stories written in Middle English (mostly written in verse although some are in prose), that are presented as part of a story-telling contest by a group of Pilgrims as they travel together on a journey from Southwark to the shrine of Saint Thomas Becket at Canterbury Cathedral. Chaucer is a crucial figure in developing the legitimacy of the vernacular, Middle English, at a time when the dominant literary languages in England were French and Latin.

A woodcut from William Caxton's second edition of *The Canterbury Tales* printed in 1483
From: http://en.wikipedia.org/wiki/The_Canterbury_Tales

Women writers were also active, such as Marie de France in the 12th century and Julian of Norwich in the early 14th century. Julian's *Revelations of Divine Love* (1393) is believed to be the first published book written by a woman in the English language. Margery Kempe (1373—after 1438) is known for writing *The Book of Margery Kempe*, a work considered by some to be the first autobiography in the English language.

2. The Renaissance: 1500—1660

The English Renaissance and the Renaissance in Scotland date from the late 15th century to the early 17th century. Italian literary influences arrived in Britain: the sonnet form was introduced into English by Thomas Wyatt in the early 16th

---

① *The Canterbury Tales*:《坎特伯雷故事集》为诗体短篇小说集。它展现了广阔的社会画面,朝圣者来自社会各个阶层:骑士、僧侣、学者、律师、商人、手工业者、自耕农、磨坊主等。它综合采用了中世纪的各种文学体裁,有骑士传奇、圣徒传、布道文、寓言等。总序和开场白中对人物的描写和故事本身饶有趣味,充满幽默感。语言带上了讲述人自身的特征,每人所讲的故事都体现出讲述人的身份、趣味、爱好、职业和生活。

century, and developed by Henry Howard, Earl of Surrey (1516—1547), who also introduced blank verse into England.

In the later 16th century, English poetry was characterised by elaboration of language and extensive allusion to classical myths. Edmund Spenser (1555—99) was the author of *The Faerie Queene*, an epic poem and fantastical allegory celebrating the Tudor dynasty and Elizabeth I. The works of Sir Philip Sidney (1554—1586), a poet, courtier and soldier, include *Astrophel and Stella*, *The Defence of Poetry*, and *The Countess of Pembroke's Arcadia*. Poems intended to be set to music as songs, such as by Thomas Campion, became popular as printed literature was disseminated more widely in households. Jane Lumley (1537—1578) was the first person to translate **Euripides**① into English. Her translation of *Iphigeneia at Aulis* is the first known dramatic work by a woman in English.

During the reign of Elizabeth I (1558—1603) and then James I (1603—25), in the late 16th and early 17th century, a London-centred culture, that was both courtly and popular, produced great poetry and drama. William Shakespeare stands out in this period as a poet and playwright as yet unsurpassed. Shakespeare wrote plays in a variety of genres, including histories, tragedies, comedies and the late romances, or tragicomedies. His early classical and Italianate comedies, like *A Comedy of Errors*, contain tight double plots and precise comic sequences. *A Midsummer Night's Dream* is a witty mixture of romance, fairy magic, and comic lowlife scenes. Shakespeare's next comedy, the equally romantic *Merchant of Venice*, can be problematic because of how it portrays Shylock, a vengeful Jewish moneylender. The wit and wordplay of *Much Ado About Nothing*, the charming rural setting of *As You Like It*, and the lively merrymaking of *Twelfth Night* complete Shakespeare's sequence of great comedies. After the lyrical *Richard II*, written almost entirely in verse, Shakespeare introduced prose comedy, *Henry IV* and *Henry V*, into the histories of the late 1590s. His characters become more complex and tender as he switches deftly between comic and serious scenes, prose and poetry, and achieves the narrative variety of his mature work. This period begins and ends with two tragedies: *Romeo and Juliet* and *Julius Caesar*. In the early 17th century, Shakespeare wrote the so-called "problem plays", *Measure for Measure*, *Troilus and Cressida*, and *All's Well That Ends Well*, as well as a number of his best known tragedies, including *Hamlet*, *Othello*, *Macbeth*, *King Lear* and *Anthony and Cleopatra*. The plots of Shakespeare's tragedies often hinge on such fatal errors or flaws, which overturn order and destroy the hero and those he loves. In his final period, Shakespeare turned to romance or tragicomedy and completed three more major plays: *Cymbeline*, *The*

---

① Euripides：欧里庇得斯与埃斯库罗斯和索福克勒斯并称为希腊三大悲剧大师，他一生共创作了90多部作品，保留至今的有18部。

Winter's Tale and *The Tempest*, as well as the collaboration, *Pericles*, *Prince of Tyre*. Less bleak than the tragedies, these four plays are graver in tone than the comedies of the 1590s, but they end with reconciliation and the forgiveness of potentially tragic errors. Some commentators have seen this change in mood as evidence of a more serene view of life on Shakespeare's part, but it may merely reflect the theatrical fashion of the day. Shakespeare collaborated on two further surviving plays, *Henry VIII* and *The Two Noble Kinsmen*, probably with John Fletcher.

Shakespeare also popularised the English sonnet. A collection of 154 by sonnets, dealing with themes such as the passage of time, love, beauty and mortality, were first published in a 1609 quarto entitled *SHAKE-SPEARES SONNETS*: *Never before imprinted* (although sonnets 138 and 144 had previously been published in the 1599 miscellany *The Passionate Pilgrim*). The first 17 poems, traditionally called the procreation sonnets, are addressed to a young man, urging him to marry and have children to immortalise his beauty by passing it to the next generation. Other sonnets express the speaker's love for a young man. The final two sonnets are allegorical treatments of Greek epigrams referring to the "little love-god" Cupid.

After Shakespeare's death, the poet and dramatist Ben Jonson (1572—1637) was the leading literary figure of the **Jacobean era**[①]. Jonson's aesthetics hark back to the Middle Ages and his characters embody the theory of humours. He is a master of style, and a brilliant satirist. Jonson's famous comedy *Volpone* (1605 or 1606) shows how a group of scammers are fooled by a top con-artist, vice being punished by vice, virtue meting out its reward. Other major plays by Jonson are *Epicoene* (1609), *The Alchemist* (1610), and *Bartholomew Fair* (1614).

The metaphysical poets John Donne (1572—1631) is also one of the major poets of the early 17th century. Donne's metaphysical poetry uses unconventional or "unpoetic" figures, such as a compass or a mosquito, to reach surprise effects. For example, in *Valediction: Forbidding Mourning*, the points of a compass represent two lovers, the woman who is home, waiting, being the centre, the farther point being her lover sailing away from her. But the larger the distance, the more the hands of the compass lean to each other: separation makes love grow fonder. The paradox or the oxymoron is a constant in this poetry whose fears and anxieties also speak of a world of spiritual certainties shaken by the modern discoveries of geography and science, one that is no longer the centre of the universe.

3. Neoclassicism: 1660—1798

The Restoration of the monarchy in 1660 launched a fresh start for literature,

---

① Jacobean era: 詹姆士一世时代指英王詹姆士一世（同时也是苏格兰王詹姆士四世）统治时期。英王詹姆士一世为伊丽莎白一世的继承人。

both in celebration of the new worldly and playful court of the king, and in reaction to it. Theatres in England reopened after having been closed during the protectorship of Oliver Cromwell. In addition, women were allowed to perform on stage for the first time.

John Dryden (1631—1700) was an English poet, literary critic, translator, and playwright who dominated the literary life of Restoration England to such a point that the period came to be known in literary circles as the Age of Dryden. He established the heroic couplet as a standard form of English poetry by writing successful satires, religious pieces, fables, epigrams, compliments, prologues, and plays with it; he also introduced the **alexandrine**① and triplet into the form. In his poems, translations, and criticism, he established a poetic diction appropriate to the heroic couplet. Dryden's greatest achievements were in satiric verse in works like the mock-heroic *MacFlecknoe* (1682). W. H. Auden referred to him as "the master of the middle style" that was a model for his contemporaries and for much of the 18th century. The considerable loss felt by the English literary community at his death was evident from the elegies that it inspired. Alexander Pope (1688—1744) was heavily influenced by Dryden, and often borrowed from him; other writers in the 18th century were equally influenced by both Dryden and Pope.

The Pilgrim's Progress established John Bunyan (1628—1688) as a notable writer. This book is an allegory of personal salvation and a guide to the Christian life. Bunyan writes about how the individual can prevail against the temptations of mind and body that threaten damnation. The book is written in a straightforward narrative and shows influence from both drama and biography, and yet it also shows an awareness of the grand allegorical tradition found in Edmund Spenser.

The late 17th, early 18th century (1689—1750) in English literature is known as the Augustan Age. Writers at this time greatly admired their Roman counterparts, imitated their works and frequently drew parallels between contemporary world and the age of the Roman emperor Augustus. Some of the major writers in this period were John Dryden (1631—1700), Jonathan Swift (1667—1745), William Congreve (1670—1729), Joseph Addison (1672—1719), Richard Steele (1672—1729), Alexander Pope (1688—1744), Henry Fielding (1707—1754), and Samuel Johnson (1709—1784).

The English novel has generally been seen as beginning with Daniel Defoe's *Robinson Crusoe* (1719) and *Moll Flanders* (1722), though John Bunyan's *The Pilgrim's Progress* (1678) and Aphra Behn's *Oroonoko* (1688) are also contenders. The rise of the novel as an important literary genre is generally associated with the

---

① alexandrine: 亚历山大格是法语诗中最重要的诗格（诗行）。龙沙的爱情诗、古典主义悲剧及喜剧、雨果的重要诗集等大都采用此诗格。每行12音节，抑扬格。

growth of the middle class in England. Other major 18th-century British novelists are Samuel Richardson (1689—1761), author of *Pamela, or Virtue Rewarded* (1740) and *Clarissa* (1747—1748); Henry Fielding (1707—1754), who wrote *Joseph Andrews* (1742) and *The History of Tom Jones, a Foundling* (1749).

Anglo-Irish literature achieved an ambiguous independence in the 18th century with the emergence of writers such as Jonathan Swift, whose important early novel *Gulliver's Travels* (1726, amended 1735) is both a satire of human nature, as well as a parody of travelers' tales like *Robinson Crusoe*.

The most outstanding poet of the age is Alexander Pope (1688—1744), whose major works include: *The Rape of the Lock* (1712; enlarged in 1714), a translation of the *Iliad* (1715—20), a translation of the *Odyssey* (1725—26) and *The Dunciad* (1728; 1743). Since his death, Pope has been in a constant state of re-evaluation. His high artifice, strict prosody, and, at times, the sheer cruelty of his satire were an object of derision for the Romantic poets, and it was not until the 1930s that his reputation was revived. Pope is now considered the dominant poetic voice of his century, a model of prosodic elegance, biting wit, and an enduring, demanding moral force. *The Rape of the Lock* and *The Dunciad* are masterpieces of the **mock-epic**① genre.

4. Romanticism: 1798—1837

Romanticism was an artistic, literary, and intellectual movement that originated in Europe toward the end of the 18th century. Various dates are given for the Romantic period in British literature, but here the publishing of *Lyrical Ballads* in 1798 is taken as the beginning, and the crowning of Queen Victoria in 1837 as its end.

Robert Burns (1759—1796) was a pioneer of the Romantic movement, and after his death he became a cultural icon in Scotland. As well as writing poems, Burns also collected folk songs from across Scotland, often revising or adapting them. His poems, chiefly in the Scottish dialect was published in 1786. Among poems and songs of Burns that remain well known across the world are, *Auld Lang Syne*, *A Red, Red Rose*, *To a Louse*, *To a Mouse*, *The Battle of Sherramuir*, *Tam o' Shanter* and *Ae Fond Kiss*.

The poet, painter, and printmaker William Blake (1757—1827) was one of the first of the English Romantic poets. Largely disconnected from the major streams of the literature of the time, Blake was generally unrecognised during his lifetime, but is now considered a seminal figure in the history of both the poetry and visual arts

---

① mock-epic：模仿史诗，指以史诗的状丽、英雄主义的风格针对一件小事所写的一种诗。

of the Romantic Age. Considered mad by contemporaries for his idiosyncratic views, Blake is held in high regard by later critics for his expressiveness and creativity, and for the philosophical and mystical undercurrents within his work. Among his most important works are *Songs of Innocence* (1789) and *Songs of Experience* (1794) and profound and difficult prophecies such as *Visions of the Daughters of Albion* (1793), *The First Book of Urizen* (1794) and *Milton* (1804).

After Blake, among the earliest Romantics were the Lake Poets, a small group of friends, including William Wordsworth (1770—1850), Samuel Taylor Coleridge (1772—1834), Robert Southey (1774—1843) and journalist Thomas de Quincey (1785—1859).

The second generation of Romantic poets includes Lord Byron (1788—1824), Percy Bysshe Shelley (1792—1822) and John Keats (1795—1821). Byron achieved enormous fame and influence throughout Europe with works exploiting the violence and drama of their exotic and historical settings. However, despite the success of *Childe Harold* and other works, Byron was forced to leave England for good in 1816 and seek asylum on the Continent, because, among other things, of his alleged incestuous affair with his half-sister Augusta Leigh. Between 1819 and 1824 Byron published his unfinished epic satire *Don Juan*, which, though initially condemned by the critics, was much admired by Goethe who translated part of it.

John Keats is especially noted for its sensuous music and imagery, along with a concern with material beauty and the transience of life. Among his most famous works are: *The Eve of St Agnes*, *Ode to Psyche*, *La Belle Dame sans Merci*, *Ode to a Nightingale*, *Ode on a Grecian Urn*, *Ode on Melancholy*, *To Autumn* and the incomplete *Hyperion*, a philosophical poem in blank verse, which was conceived on the model of Milton's *Paradise Lost*. Keats has always been regarded as a major Romantic and his stature as a poet has grown steadily through all changes of fashion.

Percy Shelley, famous for his association with Keats and Byron, was the third major romantic poet of the second generation. Generally regarded as among the finest lyric poets in the English language, Shelley is perhaps best known for poems such as *Ozymandias*, *Ode to the West Wind*, *To a Skylark*, *When Soft Voices Die*, *The Cloud*, *The Masque of Anarchy* and *Adonaïs*, an elegy written on the death of Keats.

English woman Jane Austen (1775—1817) is one of the major novelists in this period. Austen's works satirise the novels of sensibility of the second half of the 18th century and are part of the transition to 19th-century realism. Her plots, though fundamentally comic, highlight the dependence of women on marriage to secure social standing and economic security. Austen brings to light the hardships women faced, who usually did not inherit money, could not work and where their only chance in life depended on the man they married. She reveals not only the difficulties women faced in her day, but also what was expected of men and of the careers they had to follow.

This she does with wit and humour and with endings where all characters, good or bad, receive exactly what they deserve. Austen's work brought her little personal fame and only a few positive reviews during her lifetime, but the publication in 1869 of her nephew's *A Memoir of Jane Austen* introduced her to a wider public, and by the 1940s she had become accepted as a major writer. The second half of the 20th century saw a proliferation of Austen scholarship and the emergence of a Janeite fan culture. Austen's works include *Pride and Prejudice* (1813), *Sense and Sensibility* (1811), *Mansfield Park* (1814), *Emma* (1815) and *Persuasion* (1818).

5. Victorian Literature: 1837—1901

It was in the Victorian era (1837—1901) that the novel became the leading literary genre in English. Women played an important part in this rising popularity both as authors and as readers. Monthly serialising of fiction encouraged this surge in popularity, due to a combination of the rise of literacy, technological advances in printing, and improved economics of distribution.

Charles Dickens (1812—70) emerged on the literary scene in the late 1830s and soon became probably the most famous novelist in the history of British literature. One of his most popular works to this day is *A Christmas Carol* (1843). Dickens fiercely satirised various aspects of society, including the workhouse in *Oliver Twist*, the failures of the legal system in *Bleak House*, the dehumanising effect of money in *Dombey and Son* and the influence of the philosophy of utilitarianism in factories and education in *Hard Times*. In more recent years Dickens has been most admired for his later novels, such as *Dombey and Son* (1846—48), *Bleak House* (1852—53) and *Little Dorrit* (1855—57), *Great Expectations* (1860—1), and *Our Mutual Friend* (1864—65). An early rival to Dickens was William Makepeace Thackeray (1811—63), who during the Victorian period ranked second only to him, but he is now much less read and is known almost exclusively for *Vanity Fair* (1847). In that novel he satirises whole swaths of humanity while retaining a light touch. It features his most memorable character, the engagingly roguish Becky Sharp.

The Brontë sisters, Emily, Charlotte and Anne, were other significant novelists in the 1840s and 1850s. Their novels caused a sensation when they were first published but were subsequently accepted as classics. They had written compulsively from early childhood and were first published, at their own expense, in 1846 as poets under the pseudonyms Currer, Ellis and Acton Bell. In 1847, the three sisters each published a novel: Charlotte Brontë's (1816—55) *Jane Eyre*, Emily Brontë's (1818—48) *Wuthering Heights*, and Anne Brontë's (1820—49) *Agnes Grey*. Anne Brontë's second novel, *The Tenant of Wildfell Hall* (1848), is perhaps the most shocking of the Brontës' novels. In seeking to present the truth in literature, Anne's depiction of alcoholism and debauchery was profoundly disturbing to 19th-century sensibilities. Charlotte Brontë's *Shirley* was published in 1849, *Villette* in 1853, and *The Professor* in 1857.

Anne, Emily, and Charlotte Brontë
From: http://en.wikipedia.org/wiki/Bront%C3%AB_sisters

George Eliot's (1819—1880) first novel *Adam Bede* was published in 1859, and she was a major novelist of the mid-Victorian period. Her works, especially *Middlemarch* (1871-1872), are important examples of literary realism. While her reputation declined somewhat after her death, in the 20th century she was championed by a new breed of critics, most notably by Virginia Woolf, who called *Middlemarch* one of the few English novels written for grown-up people. Various film and television adaptations of Eliot's books have also introduced her to a wider readership.

An interest in rural matters and the changing social and economic situation of the countryside is seen in the novels of Thomas Hardy (1840—1928). A Victorian realist, in the tradition of George Eliot, he was also influenced both in his novels and poetry by Romanticism, especially by William Wordsworth. While Hardy wrote poetry throughout his life, and regarded himself primarily as a poet, his first collection was not published until 1898, so that initially he gained fame as the author of such novels as, *Far from the Madding Crowd* (1874), *The Mayor of Casterbridge* (1886), *Tess of the d'Urbervilles* (1891), and *Jude the Obscure* (1895). He ceased writing novels following adverse criticism of this last novel. In novels such as *The Mayor of Casterbridge* and *Tess of the d'Urbervilles*, Hardy attempts to create modern works in the genre of tragedy, that are modelled on the Greek drama, especially *Aeschylus and Sophocles*, though in prose, not poetry, fiction, not a play, and with characters of low social standing, not nobility. Another significant late 19th century novelist is George Robert Gissing (1857—1903), who published 23 novels between 1880 and 1903. His best known novel is *New Grub Street* (1891). Also in the late 1890s, the first novel of Polish-born immigrant Joseph Conrad, (1857—1924), an important forerunner of modernist literature, was published. Conrad's *Heart of Darkness* was published in 1899, a symbolic story within a story, or frame narrative, about the journey to the Belgian Congo by an Englishman called Marlow. This was followed by *Lord Jim* in 1900.

Drama did not achieve importance as a genre in the 19th century until the end of the century, and then the main figures were Irish-born. Irish playwright Dion Boucicault (1820—90), was an extremely popular writer of comedies who achieved success on the London stage (*London Assurance*, 1841). In the last decade of the century major playwrights emerged, including George Bernard Shaw (1856—1950) (*Arms and the Man*, 1894) and Oscar Wilde (1854—1900) (*The Importance of Being Earnest*, 1895). Both these writers lived mainly in England and wrote in English, with the exception of some works in French by Wilde.

6. Modernism and Cultural Revivals: 1901—1945

From around 1910 the Modernist movement began to influence British literature. While their Victorian predecessors had usually been happy to cater to mainstream middle-class taste, 20th-century writers often felt alienated from it, so responded by writing more intellectually challenging works or by pushing the boundaries of acceptable content.

6.1 Poetry

Two Victorian poets who published little in the 19th century, Thomas Hardy (1840—1928) and Gerard Manley Hopkins (1844—89), have since come to be regarded as major poets. While Hardy first established his reputation the late 19th century with novels, he also wrote poetry throughout his career. However he did not publish his first collection until 1898, so that he tends to be treated as a 20th-century poet. Hardy lived well into the third decade of the twentieth century, an important transitional figure between the Victorian era and the 20th century, but because of the adverse criticism of his last novel, *Jude the Obscure*, in 1895, from that time Hardy concentrated on publishing poetry. Victorian poet Gerald Manley Hopkins's *Poems* were posthumously published in 1918 by Robert Bridges (1844—1930, Poet Laureate from 1913). Hopkins' poem, *The Wreck of the Deutschland*, written in 1875, first introduced what Hopkins called **sprung rhythm**①. As well as developing new rhythmic effects, Hopkins was also very interested in ways of rejuvenating poetic

---

① sprung rhythm: 弹跳式节拍，是由 19 世纪晚期诗人霍普金斯（Gerard Manley Hopkins）对格律诗体进行的改革创新，指以普通讲话的常规节奏而不以规定音节数为基础的英诗格律，在一定程度上打破了原有格律诗的严格规范。

language and frequently employed compound and unusual word combinations. Several twentieth century poets, including W. H. Auden, Dylan Thomas, and American Charles Wright, turned to his work for its inventiveness and rich aural patterning.

Thomas Hardy
From: http://en.wikipedia.org/wiki/Thomas_Hardy

Free verse and other stylistic innovations came to the forefront in this era, with which T. S. Eliot and Ezra Pound were especially associated. T. S. Eliot (1888—1965) was born American, migrated to England in 1914, at the age of 25, and was naturalised as a British subject in 1927 at the age of 39. He was arguably the most important English-language poet of the 20th century. He produced some of the best-known poems in the English language, including *The Waste Land* (1922) and *Four Quartets* (1935—1942). He is also known for his seven plays, particularly *Murder in the Cathedral* (1935). He was awarded the Nobel Prize in Literature in 1948. Eliot's friend Ezra Pound (1885—1972), an American expatriate, made important contributions of British literature during his residence in London. He was responsible for the publication in 1915 of Eliot's *The Love Song of J. Alfred Prufrock*, but more important was the major editing that he did on the *The Waste Land*.

6.2 Fiction

Writing in the 1920s and 1930s Virginia Woolf was an influential feminist, and a major stylistic innovator associated with the stream-of-consciousness technique. Her novels include *Mrs Dalloway* (1925), *To the Lighthouse* (1927), *Orlando* (1928), *The Waves* (1931), and *A Room of One's Own* (1929). Woolf and E. M. Forster were members of the *Bloomsbury Group*, an enormously influential group of associated English writers, intellectuals, philosophers and artists.

Other early modernists were Dorothy Richardson (1873—1957), whose novel *Pointed Roof* (1915), is one of the earliest example of the stream of consciousness technique and D. H. Lawrence (1885—1930), who wrote with understanding about the social life of the lower and middle classes, and the personal life of those who could not adapt to the social norms of his time. *Sons and Lovers* (1913), is widely regarded as his earliest masterpiece. There followed *The Rainbow* (1915) and its sequel *Women in Love* (1920). Lawrence attempted to explore human emotions more deeply than his contemporaries and challenged the boundaries of the acceptable treatment of sexual issues, most notably in *Lady Chatterley's Lover*, which was privately published in Florence in 1928. However, the unexpurgated version of this novel was not published until 1959.

An essayist and novelist, George Orwell's works are considered important social and political commentaries of the 20th century, dealing with issues such as poverty in *The Road to Wigan Pier* (1937) and *Down and Out in Paris and London* (1933), the exploration of colonialism in *Burmese Days* (1934), and in the 1940s his satires of totalitarianism included *Animal Farm* (1945). Orwell's works were often semi-autobiographical and in the case of *Homage to Catalonia*, wholly. Malcolm Lowry published in the 1930s, but is best known for *Under the Volcano* (1947).

6.3 Drama

Irish playwrights George Bernard Shaw (1856—1950) and J. M. Synge (1871—1909) were influential in British drama. Shaw's career as a playwright began in the last decade of the nineteenth century, while Synge's plays belong to the first decade of the twentieth century. Synge's most famous play, *The Playboy of the Western World*, caused outrage and riots when it was first performed in Dublin in 1907. George Bernard Shaw turned the Edwardian theatre into an arena for debate about important political and social issues, like marriage, class, the morality of armaments and war and the rights of women In the 1920s and later Noël Coward (1899—1973) achieved enduring success as a playwright, publishing more than 50 plays from his teens onwards. Many of his works, such as *Hay Fever* (1925), *Private Lives* (1930), *Design for Living* (1932), *Present Laughter* (1942) and *Blithe Spirit* (1941), have remained in the regular theatre repertoire. In the 1930s, W. H. Auden and Christopher Isherwood co-authored verse dramas, of which *The Ascent of F6* (1936) is the most notable, that owed much to Bertolt Brecht. T. S. Eliot had begun this attempt to revive poetic drama with *Sweeney Agonistes* in 1932, and this was followed by *The Rock* (1934), *Murder in the Cathedral* (1935) and *Family Reunion* (1939). There were three further plays after the war.

References

Beers, Henry A. *Brief History of English and American Literature*. New York: Eaton Publication, 2007.

http://en.wikipedia.org/wiki/British_literature#Old_English_literature:_c.658.E2.80.931100

Exercises

I. Choose the one that best completes each of the following statements.

1. Which of the following are regarded as Shakespeare's four great tragedies?
   A. *Romeo and Juliet*, *Hamlet*, *Othello*, *King Lear*.
   B. *Romeo and Juliet*, *Hamlet*, *Othello*, *Macbeth*.
   C. *Hamlet*, *Othello*, *King Lear*, *Macbeth*.
   D. *Romeo and Juliet*, *Othello*, *Macbeth*, *Timon of Athens*.
2. *The Canterbury Tales*, a collection of stories told by a group of pilgrims on their way to Canterbury, is an important poetic work by _____.
   A. William Langland   B. Geoffrey Chaucer
   C. William Shakespeare   D. Alfred Tennyson
3. _____ refers to a long narrative poem that records the adventures of a hero in a nation's history.
   A. Ballad   B. Romance   C. Epic   D. Elegy
4. Which of the following novels was written by Emily Bronte?
   A. *Oliver Twist*   B. *Middlemarch*   C. *Jane Eyre*   D. *Wuthering Heights*
5. The novel *Sons and Lovers* was written by _____.
   A. Thomas Hardy   B. John Galsworthy
   C. D. H. Lawrence   D. James Joyce
6. Who is referred to as "the father of English poetry"?
   A. Geoffrey Chaucer.   B. Edmund Spenser.
   C. John Donne.   D. Francis Bacon.
7. *Gulliver's Travel* was written by _____.
   A. Daniel Defoe   B. Charles Dickens
   C. Jonathan Swift   D. Joseph Addison
8. _____ is a folk legend brought to England by Anglo-Saxons from their continental homes; it is a long poem of over 3000 lines and the national epic of the English people.
   A. *Beowulf*   B. *Sir Gawain*
   C. *Canterbury Tale*   D. *King Arthur*
9. Which of the following books is not written by Charles Dickens?
   A. *Olive Twist*.   B. *Great Expectations*.
   C. *The Grapes of Wrath*.   D. *A Christmas Carol*.
10. *Auld Lang Syne* was written by the author of _____.
    A. *A Red, Red Rose*   B. *The Sick Rose*
    C. *A Rose for Emily*   D. *Tiger*

II. Read the following statements carefully and decide whether they are TRUE or FALSE.

1. The rhyme scheme of a sonnet is abba abba cde cde.
2. Currer Bell, Ellis Bell and Acton Bell were the men's names under which Charlotte Bronte, Emily Bronte and Anne Bronte first published their works.
3. Bunyan's *The Pilgrim's Progress* is the first important novel in British literature.
4. In the 14th century, the most important writer (poet) is Chaucer.
5. Alexander Pope was a great English Poet who translated Homer's *Iliad*.
6. Jonathan Swift is probably the foremost prose satirist in the English language, and *Robinson Crusoe* is his masterpiece.
7. Virginia Woolf was a well-known novelist of the stream of consciousness school.
8. *Hamlet* depicts the hero's struggle with two opposing forces: moral integrity and the need to revenge his father's murder.
9. William Makepeace Thackeray is known almost exclusively for *Vanity Fair*.
10. Percy Shelley is perhaps best known for poems such *Ode to the West Wind*.

III. Give brief answers to the following questions.

1. What is stream-of-consciousness?
2. What are the three main categories of Shakespeare's plays and their representatives?

Section Two: In-depth Reading

Literature is a very powerful expression tool that offers insight into the building elements of a culture, the particular characteristics of a society or social group in terms of spirituality, intellect, emotion and physical environment. It is without doubt that literature is one of the strongest transmission channels of the cultural heritage of a society and helps understand the drivers and mechanisms of the culture in question. The two passages in this section concentrate on the lingering effect of two of the greatest writers in British history.

Reading one is a brief analysis of William Shakespeare's influence on modern English.

Reading two is Charles Dickens' timeless effect in the eye of an actor and theater director.

Before reading these articles, brainstorm with your cohorts on the following questions:

1. Who is your favorite British writer? What is your favorite book? Why?
2. Are you familiar with any story written by William Shakespeare? Why is Shakespeare still popular around the whole world?

Reading One

The English language has been in constant transition throughout its history, but the most significant transformation in modern English can be credited to William Shakespeare. His influence on modern English is not only visible in everyday speech, but also in the fact that his work has survived over four hundred years and it continues to be performed and read worldwide. The following passage will show us one of the aspects of Shakespeare's influence on modern English.

Shakespeare & the Development of Early Modern English

Shakespeare is probably the most famous of all Englishmen. One of the things he is famous for is the effect he had on the development of the Early Modern English language. For example, without even realising it, our everyday speech is full of words and phrases invented by Shakespeare. He was able to do that because English was changing as people modernised it in their normal workaday speech.

William Shakespeare
From: http://en.wikipedia.org/wiki/Shakespeare

One of the ways the grammar was changing was that inflectional endings (suffixes that indicated the word's grammatical functions in the way that many modern languages still have) had largely disappeared. Modern English was becoming wonderfully flexible and that was the background to the Renaissance explosion of the inventive language we see when we look at the poetry of the time. Shakespeare was a leading figure in that.

Writers were able to invent new uses for words with great freedom. For example, Caesar is able to say: "The wild disguise has almost anticked us all." An antic is a fool, which is a noun. Shakespeare turns it into a verb "to make a fool of". English was being set free to go where writers wanted to take it in their poetry. Shakespeare takes it where he likes throughout his texts, transforming the English language, pointing to the way we use it today. Modern English is still changing and developing, of course, and you are playing a vital role in that as you pick up and use new phrases, borrow foreign words, incorporate other dialects into your speech and so on.

There was a huge inflow of other European vocabulary into the English language as a result of Renaissance cross-pollination. That created new variations for English words. It allowed endless possibilities for Shakespeare. In *Love's Labours Lost* he is able to exploit multiple meanings of one word to create a sentence like "Light, seeking light, doth light of light beguile—intellect, wisdom, eyesight and daylight."

Generally speaking, the grammar of Early Modern English is identical to that of Modern English so there is little difficulty in that regard. There is one issue that seems to bother newcomers to Shakespeare, however. Teachers will often find students complaining: "All those thees and thous. It's soooo old-fashioned and I can't be bothered with it." Once again, this usage was in a state of transition and, as always, Shakespeare exploits that.

In Modern English we use the word "you" as both the singular and the plural form. In Old English, "thou" was used for addressing one person; ye for more than one. "You" was around then, and while "thou" and "ye" were used as a subject of a clause, "you" was used as the object. By the time of Early Modern English, the distinction between subject and object uses of "ye" and "you" had virtually disappeared, and "you" became the norm in all grammatical functions and social situations. "Ye" had become old-fashioned and so, when we see it in the *Authorised Bible* ("Oh ye of little faith") we are seeing that, in spite of the fact that you may think you understand the language in the *Bible* better than you do Shakespeare, Shakespeare is more modern!

By Shakespeare's time in Early Modern English "you" was being used for both singular and plural, but in the singular it also had a role as an alternative to "thou and thee". "You" was used by people of lower status to those above them (such as ordinary people to nobles, children to parents, servants to masters), and was also the formal way for the upper classes to talk to each other. By contrast, "thou" and "thee" were used by people of higher rank to those beneath them, and by the lower classes to each other; also, strangely enough, in addressing God, and in talking to witches, ghosts, and other supernatural beings. As a reflection of the higher status of males in the male/female context a husband might address his wife as "thou", and she might reply respectfully with you.

The use of "thou" and "you" also had an emotional dimension. Thou commonly expressed special intimacy or affection; you, formality, politeness, and distance.

That form is still used in French today in the use of "vous" and "tu". "Thou" might also be used by an inferior to a superior, to express such feelings as anger and contempt or to be insulting and this is one of the areas where Shakespeare is able to get extra levels of meaning by showing disrespect by one character for another's status. The use of "thou" to a person of equal rank could be used as an insult. Sir Toby Belch advises Sir Andrew Aguecheek on how to write a challenge to the Count's youth, Viola: "if thou thou'st him some thrice, it shall not be amiss" (*Twelfth Night*).

Shakespeare was acutely aware of the way the Early Modern English language that he grew up with was changing and it is yet another way that he was able to create the levels of meaning that made him such an enduring writer. When students take the trouble to understand the use of the "these" and "thous" they are able to appreciate the additional meaning rather than seeing them as a difficulty.

References

http://www.nosweatshakespeare.com/resources/shakespeare-early-modern-english/

www.nosweatshakespeare.com is the home of modern Shakespeare ebooks, Shakespeare quotes, Shakespeare sonnets, Shakespeare resources and Shakespeare facts. It aims to help students of all ages understand Shakespeare's language, and to providing in-depth articles on Shakespeare's life and times and Shakespeare essays.

Discussions

It is believed that much of common English speech can be traced back to idioms used in Shakespeare's writing, please find some examples.

Reading Two

Charles Dickens is dead, but remains so irrepressibly alive to us. Today, Dickens' legacy is still legible in the work of contemporary novelists on both sides of the Atlantic. His works are still sold and adapted into movies or dramas. The following passage is an actor and theater director's account of Charles Dickens.

An Actor's Take on World of Dickens
Simon Callow

When he was already well established as the most prosperous and famous novelist of his day —not just in England—Charles Dickens was to be found stalking the streets of London at dead of night, witnessing for himself the atrocious conditions under which labored the wretched of the earth.

Charles Dickens
From: http://en.wikipedia.org/wiki/Charles_Dickens

"There lay, in an old egg-box, which the mother had begged from a shop, a feeble, wasted, wan, sick child. With his little wasted face, and his little hot worn hands folded over his breast, and his little bright attentive eyes, I can see him now, as I have seen him for several years, looking steadily at us. There he lay in his little frail box, which was not at all a bad emblem of the little body from which he was slowly parting—there he lay quite quiet, quite patient, saying never a word. He seldom cried, the mother said, he seldom complained. He lay there, seeming to wonder what it was all about. God knows, I thought, as I stood looking at him, he had his reasons for wondering—and why, in the name of a gracious God, such things should be."

His anger thus fueled, Dickens turned it into incandescent words—hundreds and hundreds of pages of journalism, speeches up and down the country, and, of course, the great novels of his maturity, *Bleak House*, *Hard Times*, *Little Dorrit*, in which he puts Britain at its industrial zenith in the dock, prosecuting with savage ferocity those whom he held responsible for the iniquities he had witnessed.

With *The Christmas Carol* and its explicit attacks on the disparity between those who have and those who do not, he had given the conscience of the age a powerful jolt, but that was just a beginning. From his early 40s until his death some 15 years later, he never ceased to engage with the howling injustice he saw all around him. This is not in itself, of course, enough to make a great novelist. But when this sort of active, practical, radical determination to reform the system under which he lived is allied to a genius for storytelling and an incomparable imagination in the creation or character, you have a pretty potent combination.

There is nothing distant or cool about Dickens, nothing formal or academic. His structures are big and unwieldy. He seems to be making it up as he goes along, which, of course, is exactly what he did, writing in episodes, sometimes knocking off three or four at a time for weekly or monthly publications, as he pursued his active, not to say frantic, other life—corresponding, speechifying, editing (weekly journals and even, for a time, a crusading daily newspaper), partying, breeding (10 children by the time he was 40), performing conjuring tricks with nonchalant ease (the fruit of much serious rehearsal).

Need to communicate

The thing that pulses through his work like an electric current is his almost carnal need to communicate with his readers. His relationship with them far exceeds in intensity any other relationship in his life: those with his children (devoted but formal), his wife (initially affectionate, ultimately disgusted), his friends (passionate but erratic), or even his hidden mistress Ellen Ternan.

His relationship with his public was something quite different, altogether more real. Simply put, he needed their love in order to exist. Like a lover, he responded instantly to their moods and to their wants; they, for their part, expected him to speak for them, to express their joys and their miseries, to create for them their monsters and their comic heroes. In almost shamanic fashion, he was possessed by their spirit, the great popular Carnival spirit.

His playful, metamorphosing language—distorting, personifying, now engorging, now withering, transforming a city into a single breathing organism or an individual into a swarming mass of grotesque features—is the vernacular mode at its most extended and its most exuberant. He embodies appetite, glories in extremes. This is where he can most be compared to Shakespeare, his immediate superior in the pantheon of English literature—in this and in his matchless creation of character. In every other area, his inventiveness is almost surreal, which is why adaptations of his books, attempting to treat him as a social realist, or a psychological realist, are so rarely successful. The screen and even the stage have a confining effect on the psychedelic fantasies of Dickens' pen.

In true Carnival spirit, Dickens' work is a performance, generous and unstinting, for his audience of readers. We never forget that it is he that is doing it, and doing it for us. And, on cue, we laugh, we cry, we moan, we applaud.

The performer

Dickens is the writer as actor. In life, of course, he acted whenever he had the opportunity, finally, triumphantly, taking to the boards with great tours of England and America in which he "read" his own work. In fact, his readings were memorized and meticulously rehearsed and performed with a degree of histrionic energy that even drew the stunned admiration of the theatrical profession. His audiences (who also knew his books by heart and who were more or less chanting the words in unison with him) were in ecstasy; they thronged to him in their thousands and the performances became cathartic experiences, both comic and tragic, on a grand scale. They were unprecedented events, only to be compared today in their emotional fervor to rock concerts.

Dickens wrote fiercely and pertinently about the abuses of his day, which are not, alas, so different from the abuses of ours. He attacked imbalances in income, indifference to mental suffering, the venality of lawyers, the heartlessness of capitalists, the death of the soul and the rape of the child.

But it is not for this alone that we read him now—not even for the great generous heart, or for the unique literary voice. It is for his huge populist energy that we love him and need him, for his assertion of the glorious vitality of human life and the united diversity of society, for his denial of uniformity and his exploration of the unbounded manifestations of man and woman, both peccable and sublime. Dickens, the hero of his own age, reaches out to a tradition and a culture which long precedes it, which even ante-dates the Elizabethan period, and asserts, for our own age in which the twin horrors of globalization and fundamentalism—both tending towards the standardization of human experience—threaten to overwhelm us, the glorious, contradictory and insuppressible bounteousness of the human experience.

References

http://articles.chicagotribune.com/2001-12-02/news/0112020369_1_pickwick-papers-lay-oliver-twist

The Chicago Tribune is a major daily newspaper based in Chicago, Illinois, United States. Founded in 1847, and formerly self-styled as the "World's Greatest Newspaper", it remains the most-read daily newspaper of the Chicago metropolitan area and the Great Lakes region and is currently the eighth-largest newspaper in the United States by circulation.

About the Author

Simon Callow is an English actor, musician, writer and theatre director. Callow was successful both as a director and as a writer. His *Being An Actor* (1984) was a critique of director dominated theater.

Discussions

Read at least one of the books written by Charles Dickens and write a summary of it. Share your summary and your comments on the book with your classmates.

Part B
The United States of America

Chapter 9

Geography

Section One: A Brief Introduction

The United States of America is the third largest country in the world based on population of 318,662,000 (September, 2014 estimate) and land area of 3,794,100 square miles (9,826,675 sq km). With a coastline of 12,380 miles (19,924 km), the United States establishes its capital in Washington D. C. (District of Colombia). And the United States also has the world's largest economy and is one of the most influential nations in the world. In this section, the geography of the United States will be introduced with great details of physical and human geography facts.

Map of the United States
From: http://www.nanzhao1.com/bencandy.php?fid=32&id=279845

1. The Geography of America

1.1 Physical Geography
Topography

Although the northern New England coast is rocky, along the rest of the eastern seaboard the Atlantic Coastal Plain rises gradually from the shoreline. Narrow in the north, the plain widens to about 320 km (200 mi) in the south and in Georgia merges with the Gulf Coastal Plain that borders the Gulf of Mexico and extends through Mexico as far as the Yucatán. West of the Atlantic Coastal Plain is the Piedmont Plateau, bounded by the Appalachian Mountains. The Appalachians, which extend from southwest Maine into central Alabama—with special names in some areas—are old mountains, largely eroded away, with rounded contours and forested, as a rule, to the top. Few of their summits rise much above 1,100 m (3,500 ft), although the highest, Mt. Mitchell in North Carolina, reaches 2,037 m (6,684 ft).

Between the Appalachians and the Rocky Mountains, more than 1,600 km (1,000 mi) to the west, lies the vast interior plain of the United States. Running south through the center of this plain and draining almost two-thirds of the area of the continental United States is the Mississippi River. Waters starting from the source of the Missouri, the longest of its tributaries, travel almost 6,450 km (4,000 mi) to the Gulf of Mexico. The eastern reaches of the great interior plain are bounded on the north by the Great Lakes, which are thought to contain about half the world's total supply of fresh water. Under US jurisdiction are 57,441 sq km (22,178 sq mi) of Lake Michigan, 54,696 sq km (21,118 sq mi) of Lake Superior, 23,245 sq km (8,975 sq mi) of Lake Huron, 12,955 sq km (5,002 sq mi) of Lake Erie, and 7,855 sq km (3,033 sq mi) of Lake Ontario. The five lakes are now accessible to oceangoing vessels from the Atlantic via the St. Lawrence Seaway. The basins of the Great Lakes were formed by the glacial ice cap that moved down over large parts of North America some 25,000 years ago. The glaciers also determined the direction of flow of the Missouri River and, it is believed, were responsible for carrying soil from what is now Canada down into the central agricultural basin of the United States. The great interior plain consists of two major subregions: the fertile Central Plains, extending from the Appalachian highlands to a line drawn approximately 480 km (300 mi) west of the Mississippi, broken by the Ozark Plateau; and the more arid Great Plains, extending from that line to the foothills of the Rocky Mountains. Although they appear flat, the Great Plains rise gradually from about 460 m (1,500 ft) to more than 1,500 m (5,000 ft) at their western extremity.

The Continental Divide, the Atlantic-Pacific watershed, runs along the crest of the Rocky Mountains. The Rockies and the ranges to the west are parts of the great system of young, rugged mountains, shaped like a gigantic spinal column, that runs along western North, Central, and South America from Alaska to Tierra del Fuego, Chile. In the continental United States, the series of western ranges, most of them paralleling the Pacific coast, are the Sierra Nevada, the Coast Ranges, the Cascade Range, and the Tehachapi and San Bernardino mountains. Between the Rockies and the Sierra Nevada—Cascade mountain barrier to the west lies the Great Basin, a group of vast arid plateaus containing most of the desert areas of the United States, in the south eroded by deep canyons. The coastal plains along the Pacific are narrow, and in many places the mountains plunge directly into the sea. The most extensive lowland near the west coast is the Great Valley of California, lying between the Sierra Nevada and the Coast Ranges. There are 71 peaks in these western ranges of the continental United States that rise to an altitude of 4,267 m (14,000 ft) or more, Mt. Whitney in California at 4,418 m (14,494 ft) being the highest. The greatest rivers of the Far West are the Colorado in the south, flowing into the Gulf of California, and the Columbia in the northwest, flowing to the Pacific. Each is more than 1,900 km (1,200 mi) long; both have been intensively developed to generate electric power, and both are important sources of irrigation.

Separated from the continental United States by Canadian territory, the state of Alaska occupies the extreme northwest portion of the North American continent. A series of precipitous mountain ranges separates the heavily indented Pacific coast on the south from Alaska's broad central basin, through which the Yukon River flows from Canada in the east to the Bering Sea in the west. The central basin is bounded on the north by the Brooks Range, which slopes down gradually to the Arctic Ocean. The Alaskan Peninsula and the Aleutian Islands, sweeping west far out to sea, consist of a chain of volcanoes, many still active. The state of Hawaii consists of a group of Pacific islands formed by volcanoes rising sharply from the ocean floor. The highest of these volcanoes, Mauna Loa, at 4,168 m (13,675 ft), is located on the largest of the islands, Hawaii, and is still active.

The lowest point in the United States is Death Valley in California, 86 m (282 ft) below sea level. At 6,194 m (20,320 ft), Mt. McKinley in Alaska is the highest peak in North America. These topographic extremes suggest the geological instability of the Pacific Coast region. Major earthquakes destroyed San Francisco in 1906 and Anchorage, Alaska, in 1964, and the San Andreas Fault in California still causes frequent earth tremors. Washington State's Mt. St. Helens erupted in 1980, spewing volcanic ash over much of the Northwest.

USA Geography Facts

The third largest country in the world, the United States, spans the North American continent from the Atlantic to the Pacific, covering a huge range of

Chapter 9　Geography　　147

Topographical map of the USA
From: https://images.search.yahoo.com/images/view

ecosystems and some of the world's most extreme geographic features.

The lowest point of elevation in North America is Badwater Basin, in Death Valley, California, at 282 **ft**① (86 m) below sea level. Death Valley also holds the record for the highest recorded air temperature on Earth, 134 °**F**② (57°C), recorded on July 10, 1913.

The highest point in the United States and the North American continent is Mount McKinley (Denali) at 20,320 ft (6,190 m) in Alaska.

The geographic center of all 50 states is 20 miles (32 km) north of Belle Fourche, South Dakota, while the geographic center of the of the 48 contiguous states is 4 miles (6.4 km) west of Lebanon, Kansas.

The most remote part in the United States is the Ipnavik River in Alaska, located 120 miles (190 km) from the nearest settlement. The point further from the ocean (the continental pole of inaccessibility) is located in the Pine Ridge Indian

---

① ft: foot, 简称 ft, 英尺, 1 英尺 = 0.3048 米。古英国时期因为没有国际公认的度量单位, 所以人们往往使用自己的脚来测量实地的面积, 久而久之, 一种基于成年男子单脚的长度就被公认为英国等国家认可的标准度量衡。

② ℉: 华氏温标: 是德国华伦海脱于 1714 年创立的温标。它以水银作测温物质, 规定水的融点为 32 度, 沸点为 212 度, 中间分为 180 度, 以℉表示。0°C = 32°F。

Reservation in South Dakota, 1,025 (1,650 km) from the nearest coastline.

The longest river is the Mississippi, flowing 2,530 miles (4,070 km) from the northern Minnesota to the Mississippi River Delta at the Gulf of Mexico. The Mississippi River is the fourth longest river on Earth and the tenth largest river by water flow.

The largest lake is **Lake Superior**①, bordering Minnesota, Wisconsin, Michigan, and Canada. It is the largest freshwater lake in the world by surface area.

The northernmost point in the 50 states is Point Barrow, Alaska; the southernmost, Ka Lae, Hawaii; the westernmost, Cape Wrangell, Alaska; and the easternmost, West Quoddy Head, Maine (although some of Alaska's Aleutian Islands cross the 180th median and are technically further east, although they are west of the **International Dateline**②).

Mauna Kea③ in Hawaii reaches only 13,796 ft (4,205 m) above sea level but when measured from the seafloor it is over 32,000 ft (10,000 m), making it taller than Mount Everest and the tallest mountain in the world.

Yellowstone National Park④ sits on top of a vast volcanic caldera that last erupted 640,000 years ago. Geologists closely monitor the rise and fall of the Yellowstone Plateau to track changes in the magna chamber pressure and don't expect an explosion within the foreseeable future.

1.2　Human Geography
Population

As of September 1, 2014, the United States has a total resident population of 318,662,000, making it the third-most populous country in the world. It is very urbanized, with 81% residing in cities and suburbs as of 2014 (the worldwide urban rate is 54%). California and Texas are the most populous states, as the mean center of U.S. population has consistently shifted westward and southward. New York City

---

① Lake Superior：苏必利尔湖，是世界上最大的淡水湖，1622 年为法国探险家所发现，湖名取自法语，意为"上湖"。该湖为美国和加拿大共有，被加拿大的安大略省与美国的明尼苏达州、威斯康星州和密歇根州所环绕。苏必利尔湖是五大湖之一。五大湖（the Great Lakes）是位于加拿大与美国交界处的几座大型淡水湖泊，按面积从大到小分别为苏必利尔湖（Lake Superior）、休伦湖（Lake Huron）、密歇根湖（Lake Michigan）、伊利湖（Lake Erie）和安大略湖（Lake Ontario）。除密歇根湖属于美国之外，其他四湖为加拿大和美国共有。

② International Dateline：国际日期变更线。

③ Mauna Kea：莫纳克亚山，坐落在夏威夷岛上，是一座死火山，是世界上总高度最高的山（包括海平面以下部分）。

④ Yellowstone National Park：黄石国家公园（简称黄石公园,）是一个主要位于美国怀俄明州境内并部分位于蒙大拿州和爱达荷州的国家公园，于 1872 年 3 月 1 日美国总统尤利西斯·辛普森·格兰特签署国会通过的法案后建立，是世界上第一个国家公园。

is the most populous city in the United States.

There were over 158.6 million females in the United States in 2009. The number of males was 151.4 million. At age 85 and older, there were more than twice as many women as men. People under 20 years of age made up over a quarter of the U.S. population (27.3%), and people age 65 and over made up one-eighth (12.8%) in 2009. The national median age was 36.8 years.

The United States Census Bureau defines White people as those "having origins in any of the original peoples of Europe, the Middle East, or North Africa. It includes people who reported 'White' or wrote in entries such as Irish, German, Italian, Lebanese, Near Easterner, Arab, or Polish." Whites constitute the majority of the U.S. population, with a total of 223,553,265 or 72.4% of the population in the 2010 United States Census. There are 63.7% Whites when Hispanics who describe themselves as "white" are taken out of the calculation. Despite major changes due to illegal and legal immigration since the 1960s and the higher birth-rates of nonwhites, the overall current majority of American citizens are still white, and English-speaking, though regional differences exist.

The American population almost quadrupled during the 20th century—at a growth rate of about 1.3% a year—from about 76 million in 1900 to 281 million in 2000. It reached the 200 million mark in 1968, and the 300 million mark on October 17, 2006. Population growth is fastest among minorities as a whole, and according to the Census Bureau's estimation for 2012, 50.4% of American children under the age of 1 belonged to minority groups.

Hispanic and Latino Americans accounted for 48% of the national population growth of 2.9 million between July 1, 2005, and July 1, 2006. Immigrants and their U.S.-born descendants are expected to provide most of the U.S. population gains in the decades ahead.

The Census Bureau projects a U.S. population of 439 million in 2050, which is a 46% increase from 2007 (301.3 million). However, the United Nations projects a U.S. population of 402 million in 2050, an increase of 32% from 2007. In either case, such growth is unlike most European countries, especially Germany, and Greece, or Asian countries such as Japan or South Korea, whose populations are slowly declining, and whose fertility rates are below replacement. Official census report, reported that 54.4% (2,150,926 out of 3,953,593) of births in 2010, were non-Hispanic white. This represents an increase of 0.34% compared to the previous year, which was 54.06%.

USA Climate Facts

The U.S. borders both the North Atlantic and North Pacific Oceans and is bordered by Canada and Mexico. It is the third largest country in the world by area and has a varied topography. The eastern regions consist of hills and low mountains while the central interior is a vast plain (called the Great Plains region) and the west has high rugged mountain ranges (some of which are volcanic in the Pacific Northwest). **Alaska**① also features rugged mountains as well as river valleys. **Hawaii**②'s landscape varies but is dominated by volcanic topography.

Like its topography, the climate of the U. S. also varies depending on location. It is considered mostly temperate but is tropical in Hawaii and Florida, arctic in Alaska, semiarid in the plains west of the Mississippi River and arid in the Great Basin of the southwest.

The United States has climate zones ranging from semi-arid steppe (the Great Plains) to frozen tundra (Alaska), humid subtropics (the Southeast) to deserts and highlands. With this much diversity, it's little wonder that the US witnesses some of the world's most dramatic weather and natural disasters, including hurricanes, tornados, wildfires, and floods.

The lowest temperature ever recorded in the United States was −80 °F (−62 ℃) on January 23, 1971 in Prospect Creek, Alaska. The highest temperature ever recorded in the U. S. —and the world—was 134 °F (56.7 ℃) in Death Valley, California on July, 10, 1913.

The Pacific Northwest is the wettest place in the continental United States: Quinalt Ranger station in Washington receives an average of 137 inches of rainfall, but Hawaii well exceeds that, receiving a drenching average of 460 inches annually. The Mojave Desert is the driest place in the U. S. Yuma, Arizona averages only 2.63 inches of precipitation each year.

Devastating hurricanes regularly batter the eastern seaboard and the Gulf of Mexico. Among them Hurricane Katrina, striking the Gulf of Mexico and particularly New Orleans in 2005, and Hurricane Sandy, ravaging the Mid-Atlantic and New England in 2012, have been the costliest. Among other notorious storms are the Galveston Hurricane, demolishing an entire town and killing between 6,000 and 12,000 people in 1900 (still the deadliest natural disaster in North American history), and Hurricane Andrew, a 1992 storm that held the record for the costliest hurricane in U. S. history until being overtaken by a rush of superstorms in the past decade.

Tornados are more common in the United States than in any other country. The Tri-State tornado, sweeping a path of destruction across Missouri, Illinois, and

---

① Alaska：阿拉斯加州（Alaska State）是美国西北一个北临北冰洋，南临太平洋，西隔白令海峡和俄罗斯隔海相望，东部和加拿大接壤。是美国面积最大的州，同时也是一个世界上最大的飞地地区。

② Hawaii：夏威夷州（Hawaii State）美国唯一的群岛州，由太平洋中部的132个岛屿组成。陆地面积1.67万平方千米。城市人口占86.5%。全州约80%的人口聚集在瓦胡岛上。首府位于瓦胡岛上的檀香山（Honolulu）。夏威夷属于海岛型气候，终年有季风调节，每年温度约在摄氏26度至31度。

Indiana on March 18, 1925, was the deadliest single tornado, claiming 695 lives. The largest tornado outbreak (occurrence of multiple tornados spawned by the same weather system) occurred April 25—28, 2011, when as many as 358 tornados tore through 21 states, striking Alabama, Georgia, Mississippi, Tennessee, and Virginia hardest, causing 11 billion dollars in damage and killing 324 people.

Notable floods in United States include the Great Dayton Flood, which killed 360 people in Ohio in 1913, and the Great Mississippi Floor of 1927, the most destructive flood in the nation's history, flooding 27,000 square miles to a depth of up to 30 ft (10 m).

Blizzards have also wreaked significant destruction in the U. S. Notoriously, the Great Blizzard of 1888 blanketed the Eastern seaboard with 20—60 inches of snow, created snowdrifts over 50 ft high, and killed more than 400 people. The 1993 "Storm of the Century" devastated the entire Eastern United states, killing 310 people and causing $6.65 billion in damage.

2. Geographic Regions of the United States

Americans often speak of their country as one of several large regions. These regions are cultural units rather than governmental units—formed by history and geography and shaped by the economics, literature and folkways that all the parts of a region share. What makes one region different from another? A region's multicultural

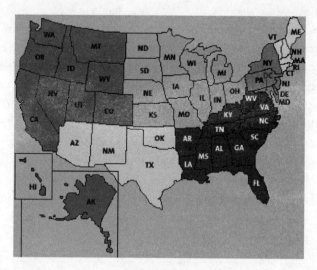

Map of regions division
Upper left to right: the West, Midwest, Mid-Atlantic, New England
Lower left to right: the Southwest, the South
From http://usa.usembassy.de/travel-regions.htm#west

heritage as well as distinct demographic characteristics like age and occupation make regions different and special. Within several regions, language is used differently and there are strong dialects. There are also differences in outlook and attitude based on geography. The following part is about details of the six regions in America: New England, Mid-Atlantic, the South, Midwest, the West, and the Southwest.

2.1 New England

New England has played a dominant role in American history. Until well into the 19th century, New England was the country's cultural and economic center. The earliest European settlers of New England were English Protestants who came in search of religious liberty. They gave the region its distinctive political format—town meetings (an outgrowth of meetings held by church elders) in which citizens gathered to discuss issues of the day. Town meetings still function in many New England communities today and have been revived as a form of dialogue in the national political arena. New England is also important for the cultural contribution it has made to the nation. The critic Van Wyck Brooks called the creation of a distinctive American literature, in the first half of the 19th century, "the flowering of New England." Education is another of the region's strongest legacies. The cluster of top-ranking universities and colleges in New England-including Harvard, Yale, Brown, Dartmouth, Wellesley, Smith, Williams, Amherst, and Wesleyan-is unequaled by any other region. America's first college, Harvard, was founded at Cambridge, Massachusetts in 1636. Without, however, large expanses of rich farmland or a mild climate, generations of exasperated New England farmers declared that the chief product of their land was stones. By 1750, many settlers had turned from farming to other pursuits. In their business dealings, New Englanders gained a reputation for hard work, shrewdness, thrift, and ingenuity.

2.2 Mid-Atlantic

If New England provided the brains and dollars for 19th century American expansion, the Mid-Atlantic states provided the muscle. The region's largest states, New York and Pennsylvania, became centers of heavy industry (iron, glass, and steel). The Mid-Atlantic region was settled by a wider range of people than New England. Into this area of industry, came millions of Europeans who made of it what became known as the "melting pot." As heavy industry spread throughout the region, rivers such as the Hudson and Delaware were transformed into vital shipping lanes. Cities on waterways—New York on the Hudson, Philadelphia on the Delaware, Baltimore on Chesapeake Bay—grew dramatically. New York is still the nation's largest city, its financial hub, and its cultural center. But even today, the visitor who expects only factories and crowded cities is surprised. In the Mid-

Atlantic, there are more wooded hills than factory chimneys, more fields than concrete roads, and more farmhouses than office buildings.

2.3 The South

The South is perhaps the most distinctive region of the United States region. The American Civil War (1861—1865) devastated the Old South socially and economically. Slavery was the issue that divided North and South. To northerners, it was immoral; to southerners, it was integral to their way of life and their plantation system of agriculture. The scars left by the war took decades to heal. The abolition of slavery failed to provide African Americans with political or economic equality; and it took a long, concerted effort to end segregation. The "New South" has evolved into a manufacturing region and high-rise buildings crowd the skylines of such cities as Atlanta and Little Rock. The region however still has many landscapes to delight the human sense of poetry and wonder. The region is blessed with plentiful rainfall and a mild climate. Crops grow easily in its soil and can be grown without frost for at least six months of the year. Owing to its mild weather, the South has become a Mecca for retirees from other regions.

2.4 Midwest

The Midwest is known as the nation's "breadbasket." The fertile soil of the region makes it possible for farmers to produce abundant harvests of cereal crops such as wheat, oats, and corn. Corn is the most important of all American crops, as basic to American agriculture as iron is to American industry. The annual crop is greater than the nation's yield of wheat, rice and other grains combined. On hot, still midsummer nights in the Corn Belt, farmers insist they can hear the corn growing.

Farms are normally located separate from each other, close to the fields, and often beyond the sight of its neighbors. The village or town is principally a place where the farm family travels to buy supplies, to attend church and to go for entertainment or political, social or business meetings. Midwesterners are praised as being open, friendly, and straightforward. Their politics tend to be cautious, but the caution is sometimes peppered with protest.

2.5 The Southwest

The Southwest is drier than the adjoining Midwest in weather. The population is less dense and, with strong Spanish-American and Native-American components, more ethnically varied than neighboring areas. Outside the cities, the region is a land of open spaces, much of which is desert. The magnificent Grand Canyon is located in this region, as is Monument Valley, the starkly beautiful backdrop for many western movies. Monument Valley is within the Navajo Reservation, home of the most populous American Indian tribe. To the south and east, lie dozens of other Indian reservations, including those of the Hopi, Zuni, and Apache tribes. Parts of the Southwest once belonged to Mexico. The United States obtained this land following the Mexican-American War of 1846—1848.

The population in the region is growing rapidly. Arizona, for example, now rivals the southern states as a destination for retired Americans in search of a warm climate. Since the last third of the 19th century, the immense stretch of barren American desert has been growing smaller. In the 1860s, the wasteland extended from the Mississippi Valley almost to the Pacific Coast. But settlers learned that the prairies could grow corn and that the grasslands could feed cattle and sheep or yield wheat. As they continued to cultivate the desert, its size decreased. Dams on the Colorado and other rivers and aqueducts have brought water to the once small towns of Las Vegas, Nevada, Phoenix, Arizona, and Albuquerque, New Mexico, allowing them to become metropolises.

2.6 The West

Americans have long regarded the West as the last frontier. Yet California has a history of European settlement older than that of most midwestern states. Spanish priests founded missions along the California coast a few years before the outbreak of the American Revolution. In the 19th century, California and Oregon entered the Union ahead of many states to the east. The West is a region of scenic beauty on a grand scale. In much of the West, the population is sparse and the federal government owns and manages millions of hectares of undeveloped land. Americans use these areas for recreational and commercial activities, such as fishing, camping, hiking, boating, grazing, lumbering, and mining. In recent years, some local residents who earn their livelihoods on federal property have come into conflict with the government agencies, which are charged with keeping land use within environmentally acceptable limits.

Hawaii is the only state in the union in which Asian Americans are the largest ethnic group. Beginning in the 1980s, large numbers of Asians have also settled in California. Los Angeles—and Southern California as a whole—bears the stamp of its large Mexican-American population. Now the second largest city in the nation, Los Angeles is best known as the home of the Hollywood film industry. Fueled by the growth of Los Angeles and the "Silicon Valley" area near San Jose, California has become the most populous of all the states. Perhaps because so many westerners have moved there from other regions to make a new start, Western cities are known for their tolerance and a very strong "live-and-let-live" attitude.

References

http://geography.about.com/od/unitedstatesofamerica/a/unitedstatesgeography.htm

About.com (an IAC Company) is one of the largest sites on the Internet that helps nearly 90 million people each month discover, learn about, and be inspired by topics ranging from parenting and healthcare to cooking to travel. About.com is for anyone who has a question, a problem, a passion or just wants to learn something new.

http://usa-facts.com/climate
http://usa-facts.com/geography

usa-facts.com, originally started in 2000 to help local businesses get an online presence, they traded on the name SeanJones.co.uk winning an award from Lord Sugar for Excellence in Enterprise for delivering sites for a monthly fee rather than an up front build cost. In 2006 one of their personal sites had grown to the point that their focus had moved away from taking on clients and instead to working on their own portfolio. They no longer do web design or development for clients.

http://www.nationsencyclopedia.com/Americas/United-States-TOPOGRAPHY.html

The Encyclopedia of the Nations is a complete source for detailed information about one hundred ninety three countries in the world, information about the United Nations and the associated agencies, and World Leaders. There is detailed information about physical geography of all countries: Afghanistan to Comoros, Congo to India, Indonesia to Mongolia, Morocco to Slovakia, Slovenia to Zimbabwe.

http://en.wikipedia.org/wiki/Demographics_of_the_United_States
http://usa.usembassy.de/travel-regions.htm#west

Exercises

I. Choose the one that best completes each of the following statements.

1. The cultivated land in the U.S. makes up _____ of the total land, and people who are engaged in farming make up only 2.7% of the total population.
   A. 21%   B. 31%   C. 41%   D. 51%
2. The term "Father of Waters" is used to refer to _____.
   A. the Amazon River   B. the Mississippi River
   C. the Nile River   D. the Hudson River
3. With regard to its size, the USA is the _____ country in the world.
   A. largest   B. second largest
   C. third largest   D. fourth largest

4. In the following rivers, _____ has been called the American Ruhr.
   A. the Mississippi   B. the Missouri
   C. the Hudson   D. the Ohio
5. Among the following rivers, _____ forms a natural boundary between Mexico and the U.S.
   A. the Potomac   B. the Columbia
   C. the Rio Grande River D. the Colorado
6. The nation's capital city Washington D.C. and New York are located in _____.
   A. the American West   B. the Great Plains
   C. the Midwest   D. the Middle Atlantic States
7. The Midwest is America's most important _____ area.
   A. agricultural   B. industrial
   C. manufacturing   D. mining industry
8. The _____ part of America consists of high plateaus and mountains formed by the Great Cordillera Range.
   A. eastern   B. western   C. northeastern   D. southern
9. In eastern _____ lies Death Valley, 85 meters below sea level.
   A. California   B. Utah   C. Arizona   D. Hawaii
10. In the west of the _____ lie the Colorado Plateaus and the Columbia Plateaus.
    A. Rocky Mountain   B. Coast Range
    C. Cascades Mountains   D. Great Plains
11. The _____ lies between the Colorado Plateaus and Columbia Plateaus
    A. Great Basin   B. Colorado Valley
    C. Great Plains   D. Cascades Mountains
12. The famous Yellowstone National Park is situated in northwestern part of _____.
    A. California   B. Arizona   C. Wyoming   D. Utah
13. The world-known Colorado Valley lies in northern _____, which is cut by the Colorado River.
    A. Arizona   B. Utah   C. Montana   D. Texas
14. Among the five Great Lakes, only _____ is wholly within the United States.
    A. Erie   B. Superior   C. Michigan   D. Huron
15. Only the climate in the southern part of _____ is tropical.
    A. Florida   B. Georgia   C. Virginia   D. New England

II. Read the following statements carefully and decide whether they are TRUE or FALSE.

1. Washington, the capital of the US, is on the Potomac River.
2. The width of the Niagara Fall is about 1240 meters and the drop average 49 meters.

3. The southern part is the most densely populated region in America.
4. The Great Salt Lake lies in northern Utah.
5. Philadelphia has been called the "cradle of American Liberty".
6. Almost all of the world's annual agricultural products come from the United States.
7. The highest mountain in the U. S. is Mount Mekinley.
8. Mount Mekinley lies in the Cascades Range.
9. The world's largest freshwater lake is Lake Superior.
10. 1/4 of the America's territory is covered with forests.

III. Give brief answers to the following questions.
1. Give a brief account of the topography of the U. S.
2. Why does the climate in the U. S. vary so much?

Section Two: In-depth Reading

Founded in 1776, the United States of America was not then what it is today. The almost 250-year-history has witnessed a surprisingly quick development of this young nation. When it comes to geography, people may be curious about how the United States expands to be such a large country in area and how the United States, the strongest power in the world, looks like. Bearing these questions in mind, people from other places are attracted to the United States to find out the answers.

Reading One is about the history of US expansion and boundary change.

Reading Two is about some useful tips when travelling in America.

Before reading the articles, brainstorm with your cohorts on the following questions:

1. Do you know how the U. S. developed into so spacious a country?
2. Do you have any travel tips for foreigners coming to China?

Reading One

In 1776 when it was founded, the United States consisted of thirteen states and territory that extended west to the Mississippi River. Since then, after a variety of treaties, purchases, wars, and Acts of Congress, the United States has expanded itself to what it is today. So this article tells us how the boundary of United States changed.

History of U. S. Expansion and Boundary Changes Since 1776
Matt Rosenberg

The United States of America was founded in 1776 along the east coast of North America, wedged between British Canada and Spanish Mexico. The original country consisted of thirteen states and territory that extended west to the Mississippi River. Since 1776, a variety of treaties, purchases, wars, and Acts of Congress have extended the territory of the United States to what we know today.

The U. S. Senate (the upper house of Congress) approves treaties between the United States and other countries. However, boundary changes of states that lie on international borders require the approval of the state legislature in that state. Boundary changes between states require the approval of each state's legislature and the approval of Congress. The U. S. Supreme Court settles boundary disputes between states.

1782—1783: Treaties with the United Kingdom establish the U. S. as an independent country and establish the boundary of the United States as being bound on the north by Canada, on the south by Spanish Florida, on the west by the Mississippi River, and on the east by the Atlantic Ocean.

1803: The Louisiana Purchase extends the western boundary of the United States to the Rocky Mountains, occupying the drainage area of the Mississippi River, as estimated by the French explorer Robert La Salle. The Purchase doubled the territory of the United States.

1818: A convention with the United Kingdom established the northern boundary of the Louisiana Purchase at 49 degrees north.

1819: Florida was ceded to the United States and purchased from Spain.

1820: Maine became a state, carved out of the state of Massachusetts. The northern boundary of Maine was disputed between the U. S. and Canada so the King of the Netherlands was brought in as an arbiter and he settled the dispute in 1829. However, Maine refused the deal and since Congress requires the approval of a state legislature for boundary changes, the Senate could not approve a treaty over the border. Ultimately, in 1842 a treaty established the Maine-Canada border of today although it provided Maine with less territory than the King's plan would have.

1845: The independent Republic of Texas (1836—1845) is annexed to the United States. The territory of Texas extended north to 42 degrees north (into modern Wyoming) due to a secret treaty between Mexico and Texas.

1846: Oregon Territory is ceded to the U. S. from Britain following an 1818 joint claim on the territory (which resulted in the phrase "**Fifty-Four Forty or Fight!**"). *The Treaty of Oregon* establishes the boundary at 49 degrees north.

1848: *The Treaty of Guadalupe Hidalgo* following the Mexican War between the U. S. and Mexico resulted in the purchase of Arizona, California, Nevada, New Mexico, Texas, Utah, and western Colorado.

1853: With the Gadsden Purchase of 1853, the land acquisition that resulted in the area of the 48 contiguous states today was completed. Southern Arizona and southern New Mexico were purchased for $10 million and named for the U. S.

minister to Mexico, James Gadsden.

1862—1863: When Virginia decided to secede from the Union at the start of the Civil War (1861—1865), the western counties of Virginia voted against the secession and decided to form their own state. West Virginia was established with help from Congress, who approved of the new state on December 31, 1862 and West Virginia was admitted to the Union on June 19, 1863. West Virginia was originally going to be called Kanawha.

1867: Alaska was purchased from Russia for $7.2 million in gold. Some thought the idea was ridiculous and the purchase became known as Seward's Folly, after Secretary of State William Henry Seward. The boundary between Russia and Canada was established by treaty in 1825.

1898: Hawaii was annexed into the United States.

1925: The final treaty with the United Kingdom clarifies the boundary through the Lake of the Woods (Minnesota), resulting in the transfer of a few acres between the two countries

References

http://geography.about.com/od/politicalgeography/a/usboundary.htm

About.com (an IAC Company) is one of the largest sites on the Internet that helps nearly 90 million people each month discover, learn about, and be inspired by topics ranging from parenting and healthcare to cooking to travel. About.com is for anyone who has a question, a problem, a passion or just wants to learn something new.

About the Author

Matt Rosenberg is an award-winning professional geographer who has covered the field of geography on **About.com** for more than fifteen years.

Discussions

1. What is the meaning of "Fifty-Four Forty or Fight!"? Why is it important in the history of US expansion?
2. What can you learn from The Louisiana Purchase? Is it still possible for a country to "buy" land from another country? Why or why not?

Reading Two

People are attracted to travel in America to see what on earth the super country and American people look like. However, travelers with different cultural backgrounds find out characteristics of American people from various perspectives.

Don't Drink the Water:
Translated Travel Tips for Coming to America
Christy Karras

Travelers love coming to America, a land many of them have seen via exports from Hollywood. They rave about the landscapes, the recreational opportunities, the vibrant cities and the culture.

Travelers are taking photoes with the Statue of Liberty
From: https://travel.yahoo.com/blogs/compass/don-t-drink-water-visitors-travel-tips-coming-194949993.html

But like international travelers anywhere, foreigners visiting the United States from other countries can be flummoxed by some of what they encounter. Fortunately, their fellow travelers have plenty of advice. The picture they paint portrays Americans as relentlessly cheerful yet sensitive folks who just might raid your fridge.

What outsiders say about the U.S. will strike an American as very true, very strange, or both. Here (with some help from Google Translate) are some travel advice gems from around the world.

From Latin America:
It's probably best not to drink the water. "There are strict laws regarding Hygiene eating places that must be met, so that restaurants and even street stalls are safe. In some areas you can take the tap water. Bottled water is available everywhere and is most recommended."

From Germany:
Americans' social boundaries are very inconsistent. "Things like 'We should get together sometime' doesn't really mean anything, unless the same people keep mentioning it to you."

"During a party at your house, don't be surprised if Americans will just walk up to your fridge and help themselves."

From Switzerland:

Forget public nudity, intoxication or urination. "The legal system can be very different from one state to another and is often inspired by moral principles stiffer than in Switzerland. For example it is forbidden to bathe topless or without shirt (kids), urinate on public roads or photograph partially unclothed children (even at home). It is forbidden for people under 21 to drink alcohol. Similarly, people who drink alcohol in public or carry alcoholic beverages without concealing from the eyes are guilty of an offense."

From France:

Do take a road trip across the West, but don't be weird about American Indians or cops. "Do not miss and be certain to visit driving in a country that venerates it, but scrupulously respect the speed limits, the constabulary of the United States not kidding... Remember that Indian reserves in the western United States are economic and human realities, not museums."

From Italy:

Tipping is fraught with misunderstanding. Is it true that I have to "force" to tip at all? It is not mandatory to tip, however, it is strongly recommended, because in many cases it is the only entry of workers. Generally in a restaurant, in the cab, and in many places where there is a service gratuity is 15%. Since the bill that will take you specify the city tax of 8.875%, is sufficient to double that sum, without bothering to do the calculations. In the hotel you leave two dollars per day per person cleaning. Obviously you do not leave tips in places like McDonalds or Starbucks.

From Australia:

You will probably get sucked into a political discussion. "Americans are REALLY opinionated. And they want to know what you think about the government, about politics, about current issues. A typical conversation might go like this: 'Hi I'm Matt. Nice to meet you.' 'The name's Bob. Where you from, Matt?' 'Sydney, Australia.' 'Oh I see. You've come a long way. So what's your take on Obama Care?'"

Did we mention the violence of U. S. toilets? "A veritable swimming pool of water greets you when you open the toilet lid and when you flush, it all goes down the drain in a huge rotating whirlpool."

From the UK:

America might give you fever. "There are occasional outbreaks of mosquito-borne diseases, including West Nile virus, eastern equine encephalitis and dengue fever."

Americans are proud of their Old World connections, no matter how

tenuous. "When an American announces that they're part Irish, part Polish and part Moldovan because their great-great-grandparents hailed from these far-off lands, you might find yourself snorting dismissively. Try to hold off until they're out of earshot."

From India:

The U. S. doesn't offer much in terms of shopping. "Based on my experience everyone need to bring almost every basic thing you need on a daily basis."

From China:

Americans love to follow rules, even when no one is looking. "Americans are such strict rule followers. I witnessed this once sitting on the sidelines of a high school dodge ball game. To me, it was goofy, a little violent, and very American. It struck me that my classmates followed the rules of the game so strictly. Even when no one noticed that a person had been hit and he could have kept playing, he voluntarily gave himself up and left the game. I was deeply impressed by how much people honored the rules even when they are not seen."

From Russia:

Gifts are not a big deal. And did you know bribery was illegal? "Gifts: Americans do not expect them. On the contrary, an unexpected gift while conducting business can put an American in an awkward position. Such things for Americans suggest reciprocity."

"Business gifts in the U. S. are not acceptable. Moreover, they often cause suspicion. Americans fear that they could be construed as a bribe, and in the United States that is strictly punishable by law."

Socializing with Americans can be tricky. Sports help. "Showing up at a business associate's home uninvited in the United States is not acceptable. You may be invited to a picnic — if you've known each other for several years and are social outside the office."

"As a rule, the invitation will be only on a weekend, and you don't have to prepare for something extravagant. Everything is the same as ours, only with far less booze. Bring something sporty — ball, badminton; Americans are certainly fervent fans of these things."

"Phone etiquette in America usually involves the gradual end of the conversation, confirmation agreements and standard closing remarks. By the way, 'see you later' should not be taken literally. That is a courtesy, and no more... Russian conversational patterns often sound harsh to Americans. Statements such as, 'You're wrong,' can be offensive. This can be interpreted as 'You are telling lies!' Therefore it is better to say, 'I do not think I can agree with this.'"

Americans really are as cheerful as they seem. "Americans and Russians say different things when faced with the same situation. Seeing the man who had fallen in the street, an American asks, 'Are you all right?' Russians will inquire: 'Are you ill?' We see a victim of the incident; they see survivors. Survivors are perceived as heroes. Where we 'aren't sick,' they 'stay well.' We discuss the problem. They discuss issues and items on the agenda."

"Americans: they are a nation that truly feels happy. These people get used to smiling from the cradle onwards, so they do not pretend to be cheerful. The desire for a successful happy life is inculcated from childhood."

The women are a little uptight, and they don't appreciate chivalry. "US etiquette prohibits flirting with a woman who is not your girlfriend or wife. If you are not acquainted with a woman, whether she be in a restaurant, on the street, or on the subway, do not look at her legs, etc. Americans could easily call the police on you, even for just ogling her."

"Welcome and introductions: men and women tend to shake hands. Mutual kissing and kissing ladies' hands is not accepted. Also, women play a greater role in business. Often they insist to be treated exactly as an equal and not as a lady. In this regard, it is not acceptable to be excessively gallant, and you should avoid personal questions (do not find out whether she is married)."

From Japan:

American food is not subtle. "American food is about big, bold taste, and is indifferent to subtleties. Hence 'hidden ingredients' are seldom seen. Sugar, salt, pepper, oils, and routine spices are used for family meals. There is no such thing as purely U.S. cuisine, except for maybe the hamburger, which isn't made at home so much, and not many varieties that can be cooked at home. There's not much emphasis on seasonal foods. Basically, they like sweet tasting foods, as well as foods that are high in fat and calories."

Watch out where you wear hip-hop clothes. "In Japan, hip-hop clothes are considered stylish. But in the United States, it is wise to avoid them, as you might be mistaken for a member of a street gang."

Nobody is impressed by how much you can drink. "In the U.S., they do not have a sense of pride if they drink a large amount. Rather, if you drink a lot, there is a sense that you cannot manage yourself, and you can lose respect from those around you. Being drunk doesn't excuse your actions, and to drink alcohol habitually is a sign of alcoholism. Alcoholics are seen as mentally weak, and are ostracized by society due to their inability to have self control."

They tend to laugh out loud, even the women. It's how they show they're honest. "In Japan, when most women laugh, they place their hand over their lips so it does not show their mouth. It is disgraceful to laugh by loudly opening the mouth. In reality, many adult males do not laugh. There is the saying, 'A man should not show his teeth so much when laughing.'"

"In America, when men or women laugh, they do not turn away. In general, they face front, open the mouth, and laugh in a loud voice. This is because in America if you muffle your laugh or turn away while laughing, you give the impression that you are talking about a secret or name-calling. It comes across as vulgar and insidious."

References

https://travel.yahoo.com/blogs/compass/don-t-drink-water-visitors-travel-tips-coming-194949993.html

Yahoo! Travel is the Yahoo!'s travel research site. Yahoo! Travel offers travel guides, booking and reservation services.

About the Author

Christy Karras is a writer of Yahoo! Travel. Most of her writings are travel diaries or travel tips.

Discussions

1. What is your impression on the American people in addition to those mentioned in this article?
2. What do you think of the different comments on America/the American people?

Chapter 10

History

Section One: A Brief Introduction

The United States of America has been a democracy for more than 200 years. The U.S. tries to be a fair and just society, and much of the time it succeeds. Through compromise and change, the country has grown, prospered, and made progress toward its ideals.

1. Early America

The most recent Ice Age was about 35,000 years ago. Much of the world's water was frozen into big sheets of ice. A land bridge—as wide as 1,500 kilometers—joined Asia and North America. By 12,000 years ago, humans lived throughout much of what now are the Americas.

The first "Americans" crossed the land bridge from Asia. Historians believe that they lived in what now is **Alaska**① for thousands of years. They moved south into today's mainland United States. No one knows why, but these groups disappeared. Other groups, Hopi and Zuni, later came to this land and prospered. By the time the first Europeans arrived, about two million native people lived in what now is the United States.

Historians believe that the Norse may have been the first Europeans to arrive. They came from Greenland. It took almost 500 years for other Europeans to reach North America, and another 100 for them to build permanent settlements. The first

---

① Alaska：阿拉斯加州，名称源于阿留申语"Alyeska"，意为"很大的陆地"，位于北美大陆西北端，东与加拿大接壤，另三面环北冰洋、白令海和北太平洋。该州拥有全美20座最高山脉中的17座，6194米的麦金利峰是北美最高峰。州面积1,717,854平方公里，占全国面积的1/5，是美国面积最大的州。在1867年被美国用720万美元从俄国购买，每英亩地仅两分钱。《华盛顿邮报》曾建议美国将其卖给中国，用来抵消16万亿债务。

explorers did not know about America. They were looking for a way to go to Asia from Europe by sea. Other Europeans who arrived later—mostly Spanish and Portuguese, but also Dutch, French, and British—came for land and the riches of the "New World."

The most famous explorer was **Christopher Columbus**①. He was Italian, but Queen Isabella of Spain paid for his trips. Columbus landed on islands in the Caribbean Sea in 1492. He never reached what is now the United States. In 1497, John Cabot, an explorer sailing for England, landed in eastern Canada. His arrival established a British claim to land in North America. During the 1500s, Spain explored and claimed more land in the Americas than did any other country. In 1513, Juan Ponce de Léon landed in Florida. Hernando De Soto landed in Florida in 1539 and then explored all the way to the Mississippi River.

Spain conquered Mexico in 1522. Other Europeans, such as Giovanni da Verrazano, Jacques Cartier, and **Amerigo Vespucci**②, explored further north. The two American continents were named after Amerigo Vespucci.

The first permanent European settlement in North America was Spanish. It was built in St. Augustine in Florida. Thirteen British colonies to the north would later form the United States. Virginia and Massachusetts were the two earliest. It wasn't just explorers who settled in the New World. People started to come to the New World to live. These people were immigrants from Europe.

2. Colonial Period

Most people who came to the British colonies in the 1600s were English. Others came from the Netherlands, Sweden, Germany, France, Scotland, and Northern Ireland. By 1690, 250,000 people lived in the New World. By 1790, there were 2.5 million people. People came for different reasons. Some left their homes to escape war. Others sought political or religious freedom. Some had to work as servants to pay back the cost of their trip before gaining their freedom. Some, like black Africans, arrived as slaves.

In time, the 13 colonies developed within three distinct regions. The North-east

---

① Christopher Columbus：克里斯托弗·哥伦布，意大利航海家、探险家。在西班牙女皇鼎力支持下，先后 4 次出海远航。开辟了横渡大西洋到美洲的航路。在帕里亚湾南岸首次登上美洲大陆，考察了中美洲洪都拉斯到达连湾 2000 多千米的海岸线；认识了巴拿马地峡；发现和利用了大西洋低纬度吹东风，较高纬度吹西风的风向变化。

② Amerigo Vespucci：阿美利哥·韦斯普奇，意大利航海家、商人，美洲新大陆以其命名为 America。

The Mayflower, which transported Pilgrims to the New World
From: http://en.wikipedia.org/wiki/File:MayflowerHarbor.jpg

was called **New England**①, and it included Massachusetts, Connecticut, and Rhode Island. The economy was based on timber, fishing, ship-building, and trade.

The middle colonies included New York, New Jersey, Pennsylvania, Delaware, and Maryland. The weather was milder and the countryside was more varied. People worked in industry and agriculture. The society was more diverse and sophisticated. People living in New York came from all over Europe.

The Southern colonies included Virginia, Georgia, and North Carolina and South Carolina. The growing season was long and the soil was fertile. Most people were farmers. Some owned small farms that they worked themselves. The wealthy farmers owned large plantations and used African slaves as workers.

The relationships between settlers and Native Americans (also called **Indians**②) were good and bad. In some areas, the two groups traded and were friendly. In most cases, as the settlements grew bigger, the settlers forced the Indians to move.

As time went on, all the colonies developed governments based on the British tradition of citizen participation. In Britain, the Glorious Revolution of 1688—1689 limited the power of the king and gave more power to the people. The American

---

① New England：新英格兰，当地华人常称之为"纽英仑"，是位于美国大陆东北角、濒临大西洋、毗邻加拿大的区域。新英格兰地区包括美国的6个州，由北至南分别为缅因州、新罕布什尔州、佛蒙特州、马萨诸塞州（麻省）、罗得岛州、康涅狄格州。马萨诸塞州（麻省）首府波士顿是该地区的最大城市以及经济与文化中心。

② Indians：即北美土著的印第安人。根据当时兴起的地圆说，哥伦布自欧洲向西航行的动机之一是到达印度，所以对于新大陆上的土著人，其误以为是印度人。后来亦有人称美洲为"西印度"，而亚洲的印度则为"东印度"。

colonists closely observed these changes. **Colonial assemblies**① claimed the right to act as local parliaments. They passed laws that limited the power of the **royal governor**② and increased their own authority.

3. The Road to Independence

The ideas of **liberalism**③ and democracy are the basis of the U. S. political system. As the colonists built their new society, they believed more strongly in these ideas. After Britain won a costly war with France in the 1750s, the colonists were asked to help pay for the war, and for Britain's large empire. These policies restricted the colonists' way of life. For example, the Royal Proclamation of 1763 restricted the colonists from settling new land.

The Currency Act of 1764 made it illegal to print paper money in the colonies. The Quartering Act of 1765 forced the colonists to provide food and housing for the royal soldiers. The Stamp Act of 1765 taxed all legal papers, licenses, newspapers, and leases. The Stamp Act united the colonists in an organized resistance. The main problem was that they weren't allowed to participate in the government that taxed them.

In October 1765, 27 delegates from nine colonies met in New York. They passed resolutions saying that the individual colonies should have the right to impose their own taxes. By 1773, colonial traders, who were angry with British regulation of the tea trade, were interested in Sam Adams's ideas. In December 1773, a group of men sneaked on three British ships in Boston harbor and threw the cargo of tea overboard. This event became known as the **Boston Tea Party**④.

The British Parliament punished Massachusetts by closing Boston's port and by restricting local authority. Colonists called these new laws the Intolerable Acts and united to oppose them. All the colonies except Georgia sent representatives to Philadelphia in September 1774 to talk about their "present unhappy state." It was the First Continental Congress.

Colonists were angry with the British for taking away their rights, but not everyone agreed on the solution. **Loyalists**⑤ wanted to stay **subjects**⑥ under the

---

① colonial assembly：殖民地议会。
② royal governor：总督，即在英国海外殖民地代表英国君主的最高行政长官。
③ liberalism：自由主义、改良主义，主张个体拥有广泛的政治和个人自由，通过渐进地改善法治，而非通过暴力革命来推动社会进步。
④ Boston Tea Party：波士顿倾茶事件。1773 年，为了抵制茶税和反抗东印度公司对茶叶交易的垄断，扮作印第安人的波士顿居民在港口对 3 艘英国船只进行了突然袭击，将数百箱茶叶倾倒在海内。
⑤ loyalist：保皇党人、保皇派，反对独立者。
⑥ subjects：臣民、子民。

1846 painting of the 1773 Boston Tea Party
From: http://en.wikipedia.org/wiki/File:Boston_Tea_Party_Currier_colored.jpg

king. Moderates wanted to compromise and build a better relationship with the British government. The revolutionaries wanted complete independence.

4. Revolution

The American Revolution and the war for independence from Britain began with a small fight between British troops and colonists on April 19, 1775. The British troops left Boston, Massachusetts, planning to take weapons and ammunition from revolutionary colonists. At Lexington, they met armed colonists who were called **Minutemen**① because they could be ready to fight in a minute. The Minutemen planned to protest silently and not shoot unless the British shot first.

The British ordered the Minutemen to leave. The colonists obeyed, but as they left, someone fired a shot. The British troops attacked the Minutemen with guns and bayonets. Fighting broke out in other places along the way as the British soldiers in their bright red uniforms returned to Boston. More than 250 "**redcoats**②" were killed or wounded. The Americans lost 93 men.

Colonial representatives hurried to Philadelphia for the Second Continental Congress. More than half voted to go to war against Britain. They decided to form one army from the colonial forces. George Washington of Virginia became the

---

① Minutemen: "一分钟人"是美国独立战争中的民兵。独立战争期间,"一分钟人"在北美享有盛誉,它指的是反抗英军、追求自治的民兵。

② redcoats: 美国独立战争时期的英国军人,因英军穿着红色军装而得名。

commander-in-chief①. At the same time, they sent King George III a peace resolution to try to avoid a war. The king rejected it. On August 23, 1775, the king said the American colonies were in rebellion.

The Second Continental Congress② created a committee to write a document that outlined the colonies' complaints against the king and explained their decision to separate from Britain. The reasons were based on French and British ideas. **Thomas Jefferson**③ was the main writer of the Declaration of Independence.

The Site for Declaration of Independence
From: http://en.wikipedia.org/wiki/File:Declaration_independence.jpg

The Declaration of Independence told the world of a new nation and its beliefs about human freedom. It argued that political rights are basic human rights and are universal. The Second Continental Congress accepted this document on July 4, 1776. The Fourth of July became **Independence Day**④ in the United States.

The colonies and Britain went to war. British soldiers defeated General

---

① Commander-in-chief：美国武装部队的总司令，现由美国总统兼任。

② Continental Congress：大陆会议是 1774 年至 1789 年英属北美 13 个殖民地以及后来美利坚合众国的立法机构，共举办了两届，期间宣布了独立宣言。

③ Thomas Jefferson：托马斯·杰斐逊（1743—1826），美国政治家、思想家、哲学家、科学家、教育家，第三任美国总统。他是美国独立战争期间的主要领导人之一，1776 年，作为包括约翰·亚当斯和本杰明·富兰克林在内的起草委员会的成员之一，起草了美国《独立宣言》。此后，他先后担任了美国第一任国务卿，第二任副总统和第三任总统。他在任期间保护农业，发展民族资本主义工业。从法国手中购买路易斯安那州，使美国领土近乎增加了一倍。他被普遍视为美国历史上最杰出的总统之一，同华盛顿、林肯和罗斯福齐名。最新版美元 5 分的头像就是托马斯·杰斐逊。

④ Independence Day：美国独立纪念日，即美国国庆节，现为每年的 7 月 4 日。

Washington's forces in New York and took control of **Philadelphia**①, forcing the Second Continental Congress to flee. The Continental Army won at Saratoga in New York and at Princeton and Trenton in New Jersey. George Washington had problems getting the men and materials he needed to fight the war.

In 1778, France recognized the United States as an independent country and signed a treaty of alliance. France helped the United States as a way to weaken Britain, its long-time enemy. The war ended when a peace treaty was signed in Paris on April 15, 1783. In this treaty, Britain and other nations recognized the United States as an independent nation.

The Revolution affected more than North America. The idea of natural rights became stronger through-out the Western world. Famous men, such as Thaddeus Kosciusko (Poland), Friedrich von Steuben (Prussia), and the Marquis de Lafayette (France) took the ideas of freedom to their own countries. *The Treaty of Paris* turned the 13 colonies into states, but the job of becoming one nation remained.

5. Forming a National Government

In 1783, the 13 colonies became the United States. Before the war ended, the colonies had developed the Articles of Confederation, a plan to work together as one nation, but the connections among the 13 states were loose. Each state had its own money, army, and navy. Each state traded and worked directly with other countries. Each state collected taxes in its own way. Each state believed its way was the right way. It was a nation of 13 countries.

Alexander Hamilton from New York believed that the 13 states needed to rethink the Confederation. He and others suggested a large meeting to do this. In May 1787, 55 delegates met in Philadelphia. They proposed a constitution describing a new form of government based on separate legislative, executive, and judicial authorities.

The delegates did not agree on all the details. Many delegates wanted a strong national government that would limit a state's rights. Others believed that a weak national government was better. They wanted the states to have more power. Some delegates wanted fewer people to have the right to vote; they believed that most people lacked the education to make good decisions. Some delegates from states where slavery was illegal or not widely used wanted slavery to be unlawful throughout the nation. Delegates from states where slave labor was important refused.

The Constitution provided the framework for the new government. The national government could create money, impose taxes, deal with foreign countries, keep an

---

① Philadelphia: 费城，美国第五大城市，1790—1800 年曾是美国首都。

army, create a postal system, and wage war. To keep the government from becoming too strong, the U. S. Constitution divided it into three equal parts—a legislature (Congress), an executive (president), and a judicial system (Supreme Court). Each part worked to make sure the other parts did not take power that belonged to the others.

On September 17, 1787, most of the delegates signed the new Constitution. It took about a year to ratify the Constitution. When the first U. S. Congress met in New York City in September 1789, the delegates proposed a number of amendments to the Constitution to list these rights. They added 10 amendments, known as **the Bill of Rights**①.

The First Amendment② promises freedom of speech, press, and religion, and the right to protest, meet peacefully, and demand changes. The Fourth Amendment protects against unreasonable searches and arrest. The Fifth Amendment promises due process of law in criminal cases. Since the Bill of Rights, only 17 amendments have been added to the Constitution in more than 200 years.

6. Early Years, Westward Expansion, and Regional Differences

George Washington became the first president of the United States on April 30, 1789. He had been in charge of the army. As president, his job was to create a working government. With Congress, he created the Treasury, Justice, and War departments. Together, the leaders of these departments and the others that were founded in later years are called the cabinet.

One chief justice and five (today eight) associate justices made up the Supreme Court. Three **circuit courts**③ and 13 **district courts**④ were created. Policies were developed for governing the western territories and bringing them into the Union as new states.

George Washington served two four-year terms as president before leaving office. (Only one U. S. president, **Franklin D. Roosevelt**⑤, has served more than two terms. Today, the Constitution says that no one may be elected president more than

---

① Bill of Rights：美国《人权法案》。
② The First Amendment：美国宪法第一修正案，保证公民言论自由及宗教信仰、集会结社等自由的宪法条款。
③ US Circuit Court of Appeals：美国联邦上诉法院，上诉法庭。
④ United States district courts：美国联邦地区法院，地区法院，州地方法院。
⑤ Franklin D. Roosevelt：富兰克林·罗斯福，美国第 32 任总统，美国历史上唯一蝉联 4 届的总统，美国迄今为止在任时间最长的总统。美国历史上最伟大的 3 位总统之一，同华盛顿、林肯齐名。

Settlers crossing the Plains of Nebraska
From: http://en.wikipedia.org/wiki/File: Pioneers_ Crossing_ the_ Plains_ of_ Nebraska_ by_ C. C. A. _ Christensen. png

twice.) The next two presidents—**John Adams**① and Thomas Jefferson—had different ideas about the role of government. This led to the creation of political parties.

John Adams and Alexander Hamilton led the **Federalists**②. Their supporters included people in trade and manufacturing. They believed in a strong central government. Most of their support was in the North. Jefferson led the **Republicans**③. Their supporters included many farmers. They did not want a strong central government. They believed in states having more power. They had strong support in the South.

After years of unsuccessful diplomacy, the United States went to war with Britain in 1812. The battles took place mostly in the Northeastern states and along the East Coast. One part of the British army reached Washington, D. C., the new U. S. capital. Soldiers set fire to the president's mansion. President James Madison fled as

---

① John Adams：约翰·亚当斯（1735年10月30日—1826年7月4日）是美国第一任副总统（1789—1797年），其后接替乔治·华盛顿成为美国第二任总统（1797—1801年）。亚当斯亦是《独立宣言》签署者之一，被美国人视为最重要的开国元勋之一，同华盛顿、杰斐逊和富兰克林齐名。他的长子约翰·昆西·亚当斯后当选为美国第六任总统。

② Federalist：联邦党人，支持北部联邦者。联邦党是美国在1801年之前的执政党。主张增强联邦政府的权力。主要的支持者来自新英格兰和一些南方较富有的农民。其竞争对手为民主共和党。

③ Republican：共和党人。

the White House burned.

The U. S. doubled in size when it bought the Louisiana Territory from France in 1803 and Florida from Spain in 1819. From 1816 to 1821, six new states were created. Between 1812 and 1852, the population tripled.

7. Conflict Within the United States

In 1850, the United States was a large country, full of contrasts. New England and the Middle Atlantic states were the centers of finance, trade, shipping, and manufacturing. Southern states had many farms that used slave labor to grow tobacco, sugar, and cotton. The Middle Western states also had farms, but they were worked by free men.

In the following years, each side held its beliefs more strongly. Many Northerners thought slavery was wrong. Others saw it as a threat to free workers. Most white Southerners considered slavery part of their way of life. Thousands of slaves escaped to the North with help from people along secret routes called the **Underground Railroad**①. In 1860, however, one-third of the total population of slave states was not free.

Most Northerners did not care about slavery in the South, but they did not want slavery in the new territories. The Southerners believed that these territories had the right to decide for themselves whether slavery would be allowed. A young politician from Illinois believed that this was not a local issue, but a national one. His name was Abraham Lincoln. He agreed that the South could keep its slaves, but he fought to keep slavery out of the territories. Lincoln thought that over time slavery would end. "A house divided against itself cannot stand," he said. "This government cannot endure permanently half-slave and half-free."

The South threatened to leave the Union if Lincoln became president. After Lincoln won the election, some Southern states began leaving the Union before he started working as president.

8. Civil War and Post-War Reconstruction

The American Civil War started in April 1861. The South claimed the right to leave the United States, also called the Union, and form its own Confederacy. President Lincoln led the Northern states. He was determined to stop the rebellion and keep the country united.

The North had more people, more raw materials for producing war supplies, and a better railway system. The South had more experienced military leaders and better

---

① Underground Railroad：美国内战前，废奴主义者帮助奴隶逃跑用的地下交通网。

knowledge of the battlefields because most of the war was fought in the South.

The war lasted four years. Tens of thousands of soldiers fought on land and sea. September 17, 1862, was the bloodiest day of the war. The two armies met at Antietam Creek in Maryland. Gen. Robert E. Lee and his Confederate Army failed to force back the Union troops led by Gen. George McClellan. Lee escaped with his army. The battle was not decisive, but it was politically important. Britain and France had planned to recognize the Confederacy, but they delayed. The South never received the help it desperately needed.

Later in 1862, President Lincoln issued a preliminary **Emancipation Proclamation**① that freed all slaves in the Confederate states. It also allowed African Americans into the Union Army. The North fought to keep the Union together and to end slavery. The North began winning important battles. In Virginia in April 1865, Gen. Lee surrendered to Union Gen. Ulysses S. Grant. The Civil War was over.

Less than a week after the South surrendered, a Confederate sympathizer killed President Lincoln. By the end of 1865, most of the former Confederate states canceled the acts of secession but refused to abolish slavery. All the Confederate states except Tennessee refused to give full citizenship to African American men.

During the late 1870s, Southern blacks were free, but the local laws denied them their rights. They had the right to vote, but the threat of violence made them afraid to use it. Southern states introduced "**segregation**②," a system that required blacks and whites to use separate public facilities, from schools to drinking fountains. Not surprisingly, the "black" facilities were not as good as the "white" facilities. The races lived separately in the South for the next 100 years. In the 20th century, this would become a national issue.

9. Growth and Transformation

The United States changed after the Civil War. The frontier became less wild. Cities grew in size and number. More factories, steel mills, and railroads were built. Immigrants arrived in the United States with dreams of better lives. This was the age of inventions. Alexander Graham Bell developed the telephone. Thomas Edison invented the light bulb. George Eastman made the moving picture, later called a movie.

Separate companies merged to become larger companies, sometimes called

---

① Emancipation proclamation:《解放黑奴宣言》，美国总统林肯于 1862 年 9 月颁布，规定从 1863 年 1 月 1 日起美国各州奴隶应被视为自由人。

② segregation: 种族隔离政策。

trusts①. This happened especially in the steel, rail, oil, and communications industries. With fewer companies, buyers had fewer choices and businesses had more power. An anti-trust law was passed in 1890 to stop monopolies, but it was not very effective.

Farming was still America's main occupation. Scientists improved seeds. New machines did some of the work that men had done. The Western regions still had room for exploration and for new settlements. The "Wild West" pictured in many cowboy books and movies lasted only about 30 years.

When Europeans first arrived on the East Coast, they pushed the native people west. Each time, the government promised new land for the native people so they would have a home. Each time, the promises were broken while white settlers took the land. In the late 1800s, Sioux tribes in the Northern plains and Apaches in the Southwest fought back. Although they were strong, the U. S. government forces defeated them. Many tribes would live on **reservations**②, which are federal lands administered by Indian tribes. Today there are more than 300 reservations.

After a brief war with Spain in 1898, the U. S. controlled several Spanish colonies—Cuba, Puerto Rico, Guam, and the Philippines. Officially, the United States encouraged them to become self-governing. In reality, the United States kept control.

By the end of the 19th century, the U. S. was beginning to emerge as a growing world power.

10. World War I, 1920s Prosperity and the Great Depression

In 1914, Germany, Austria-Hungary, and Turkey fought Britain, France, Italy, and Russia. Other nations joined the conflict, and the war reached across the Atlantic Ocean to affect the United States. The British and German navies blocked American shipping. In 1915, almost 130 Americans died when a German submarine sank the British ocean liner Lusitania. President Woodrow Wilson demanded an end to the German attacks. They stopped but started again in 1917. The United States declared war.

More than 1,750,000 U. S. soldiers helped to defeat Germany and Austria-Hungary. The war officially ended on November 11, 1918, when a truce was signed at Versailles in France. President Wilson had a 14-point peace plan, including the

---

① Trust：托拉斯，是资本主义垄断组织的一种形式，生产同类商品或在生产上有密切联系的垄断资本企业，为了获取高额利润而从生产到销售全面合作组成的垄断联合。

② reservations：印第安人居住的保留地，所有权属联邦政府，但由印第安人管治。

Mulberry Street, along which Manhattan's Little Italy is centered
From: http://en.wikipedia.org/wiki/File:Mulberry_Street_NYC_c1900_LOC_3g04637u_edit.jpg

creation of a **League of Nations**①. Today, most Americans accept the United States taking an active role in the world, but at that time they believed otherwise.

After Russia's revolution in 1917, Americans feared the spread of communism. This period is often known as the Red Scare. Yet, the United States enjoyed a period of prosperity. Many families purchased their first automobile, radio, and refrigerator. They went to the movies. Women finally won the right to vote in 1920.

In October 1929 the good times ended with the collapse of the stock market and an economic depression. Businesses and factories shut down. Banks failed. Farms suffered. By November 1932, 20 percent of Americans did not have jobs. That year the candidates for president debated over how to reverse the Great Depression. Herbert Hoover, the president during the collapse, lost to Franklin Roosevelt.

11. The New Deal and World War II

In the early 1930s, President Roosevelt proposed a "New Deal" to end the Great Depression. The New Deal included many programs. The government hired people to plant trees, clean up waterways, and fix national parks. Skilled workers

---

① League of Nations: 国际联盟（法文：Société des Nations；简称 LON 或国联）是第一次世界大战后成立的国际组织，宗旨是减少武器数目及平息国际纠纷。但国联却不能有效阻止法西斯的侵略行为，第二次世界大战后被联合国所取代。

helped build dams and bridges. The government provided food control and electric power for poor areas. The Social Security system helped the poor, disabled, and elderly.

These programs helped, but they didn't solve the economic problems. The next world war would do that. The United States remained neutral while Germany, Italy, and Japan attacked other countries.

As Japan conquered territories in China and elsewhere in Asia, it threatened to seize raw materials used by Western industries. In response, the United States refused to sell oil to Japan. Japan received 80 percent of its oil from the United States. On December 7, 1941, Japan attacked the American feet at Pearl Harbor, Hawaii. The United States declared war on Japan. Because Germany and Italy were allies of Japan, they declared war on America.

The United States fought with Britain and the Soviet Union against the German Nazi threat in Europe. Fighting continued in Asia and the Pacific Ocean even after the war ended in Europe. These battles were among the bloodiest for American forces.

Japan refused to surrender even as U.S. forces approached the Japanese home islands. Some Americans thought invading Japan would cause larger numbers of U.S. and Japanese deaths. When the atomic bomb was ready, President Harry S. Truman decided to use it on two Japanese cities—Hiroshima and Nagasaki—to bring the war to an end without an invasion. World War II was finally over in August 1945.

12. The Cold War, Korean Conflict and Vietnam

Russia had been invaded twice in the past 40 years, and the United States twice had been dragged into European wars not of its making. Each believed that its system could best ensure its security, and each believed its ideas produced the most liberty, equality, and prosperity. This period of disagreement between the United States and Russia often is called the Cold War.

After World War II, many empires fell, and many civil wars occurred. The United States wanted stability, democracy, and open trade. By 1952, through a program to rebuild Western Europe (called the **Marshall Plan**[①]), the United States had invested $13.3 billion.

Communist North Korea invaded South Korea with the support of China and the

---

① The Marshall Plan：马歇尔计划，官方名称为欧洲复兴计划（European Recovery Program），是第二次世界大战结束后美国对被战争破坏的西欧各国进行经济援助、协助重建的计划，对欧洲国家的发展和世界政治格局产生了深远的影响。该计划于 1947 年 7 月正式启动，并整整持续了 4 个财政年度之久。在这段时期内，西欧各国通过参加经济合作发展组织（OECD）总共接受了美国包括金融、技术、设备等各种形式的援助合计 130 亿美元。

Soviet Union in 1950. The United States got support from the United Nations, formerly the League of Nations, for military intervention, and a bloody war continued into 1953. Although an armistice eventually was signed, U. S. troops remain in South Korea to this day.

In the 1960s, the United States helped South Vietnam defend itself against communist North Vietnam. All American troops withdrew by 1973. In 1975, North Vietnam conquered South Vietnam. The war cost hundreds of thousands of lives, and many Vietnamese "boat people" fled their nation's new communist rulers. Americans were divided over the war and not eager to get into other foreign conflicts.

13. Cultural Change 1950—1980

At home, some Americans began to have easier lives. Families grew and some moved from the cities into outlying areas where they could purchase larger homes. Not all Americans were so successful. African Americans started a movement to gain fair treatment everywhere.

In 1954, the Supreme Court ruled that separate schools for black children were not equal to those for white children and must be integrated. President Lyndon Johnson supported the Rev. Martin Luther King Jr. in his peaceful fight for civil rights and voting rights for African Americans. New laws ended segregation and guaranteed African Americans the right to vote. Many black Americans worked toward joining the more prosperous middle class. While racial prejudice was not gone, African Americans had a better chance to live freely and well.

During the 1960s and 1970s, many American women grew angry that they did not have the same opportunities as men. A proposed constitutional amendment promising equal rights for women failed when not enough states ratified it, but many new laws did grant equal rights.

Native Americans fought for the government to keep its past promises. They won back control of tribal lands and water rights. They fought for assistance for housing and education. In 1992, Ben Nighthorse Campbell became the first Native American elected to the Senate.

Hispanic Americans from Mexico, Central America, Puerto Rico, and Cuba were politically active too. They fought against discrimination.

Students protested the war in Vietnam, and President Johnson began peace negotiations. Long hair, rock'n'roll music, and illegal drugs were visible symbols of the "counter-culture" thinking of some young people during this time.

Americans became more concerned about pollution. The first Earth Day was designated in 1970. The Environmental Protection Agency was created. New laws cut down on pollution.

American society was changing. Slowly, the United States was embracing its multicultural population.

14. End of the 20th Century

The United States always has been a place where different ideas and views compete to influence law and social change. The liberal activism of the 1960s—1970s gave way to conservatism in the 1980s.

Conservatives wanted limited government, strong national defense, and tax cuts. Supporters of President Ronald Reagan (1981—1989) believe his policies helped to speed the collapse of the Soviet Union and the end of the Cold War. American politics, however, can change quickly: In 1992, Americans elected the more liberal Bill Clinton as president.

In 2000, George W. Bush was elected president, he expected to focus on education, the U.S. economy, and Social Security. On September 11, 2001, everything changed. Foreign terrorists crashed four passenger airplanes into the two World Trade Center towers in New York, the Pentagon in Washington, D. C., and a rural field in Pennsylvania.

Bush declared war on worldwide terrorism and sent U.S. troops into Afghanistan and Iraq. At first, most Americans backed President Bush, but many grew uncomfortable with his policies. In 2008, Americans chose Barack Obama for the presidency. Obama became the first African American to hold the nation's highest office. He faces serious economic difficulties—the worst, many think, since the Great Depression of the 1930s.

It is too early to know how the new president's administration will face the challenges of the 21st century. Regardless, Americans know that theirs will remain a land of freedom and opportunity. The work for the United States is to keep its values of freedom, democracy, and opportunity secure and vital in the 21st century.

References

http://www.america.gov/publications/books/learner_ english.html

U. S. A. History in Brief. Bureau of International Information Programs, U. S. Department of State.

This chapter is adapted from the learner's edition of *U. S. A. History in Brief.* It will teach you about important events in the history of the United States.

Exercises

I. Choose the one that best completes each of the following statements.

1. The Presidents during the American Civil War was _____.
　　A. Andrew Jackson　　　　　　　　B. Abraham Lincoln

C. Thomas Jefferson   D. George Washington

2. Who wrote the *Declaration of Independence* and later became the U. S. President?
    A. Thomas Jefferson.   B. George Washington.
    C. Thomas Paine.   D. John Adams.

3. The Emancipation Proclamation to end the slavery plantation system in the South of the U. S. was issued by _____.
    A. Abraham Lincoln   B. Thomas Paine
    C. George Washington   D. Thomas Jefferson

4. It is generally agreed that _____ were the first Europeans to reach Australia's shores.
    A. the French   B. the Germans
    C. the British   D. the Dutch

5. Who wrote the famous pamphlet, *The Common Sense*, before the American Revolution?
    A. Thomas Jefferson.   B. Thomas Paine.
    C. John Adams.   D. Benjamin Franklin.

6. Americans celebrate Independence Day on _____.
    A. October 11th   B. July 4th
    C. May 31st   D. September 6th

7. The thirteen former British colonies in North America declared independence from Britain in _____.
    A. 1774   B. 1775   C. 1776   D. 1777

8. Which of the following state refused to participate in the constitutional convention?
    A. Virginia.   B. Rhode Island.   C. New York.   D. Maryland.

9. Washington D. C. is named after _____.
    A. the U. S. President George Washington
    B. Christopher Columbus
    C. Both George Washington and Christopher Columbus
    D. None of them

10. The first American president to be elected from the Republican Party was _____.
    A. Thomas Jefferson   B. James Monroe
    C. James Madison   D. Abraham Lincoln

11. The Statue of Liberty was given to American people by _____ as a gift in 1884.
    A. France   B. Spain   C. Italy   D. Britain

12. John Fitzgerald Kennedy is _____ president.
    A. 35th   B. 34th   C. 33rd   D. 32nd

13. In 1837, the first college-level institution for women, Mount Holyoke Female Seminary, opened in _____ to serve the " Muslim sex".

A. New England   B. Virginia
C. Massachusetts   D. New York

14. When did the American Civil War break out?
    A. 1775.   B. 1812.   C. 1861.   D. 1863.
15. Who prepared the draft of the *Declaration of Independence*?
    A. John Adams.   B. Thomas Jefferson.
    C. Benjamin Franklin.   D. John Hancock.
16. The following were the founding fathers of the American Republic except _____.
    A. George Washington   B. Thomas Jefferson
    C. William Penn   D. Benjamin Franklin
17. The New Deal was started by _____.
    A. Franklin Roosevelt   B. J. K. Kennedy
    C. George Washington   D. Thomas Jefferson
18. The theory of American politics and the American Revolution originated mainly from _____.
    A. George Washington   B. Thomas Jefferson
    C. John Adams   D. John Locke
19. The seats in the Senate are allocated to different states _____.
    A. according to their population
    B. according to their size
    C. according to their tax paid to federal government
    D. equally
20. The first Puritans came to America on the ship _____.
    A. Codpeed   B. Susan Constant
    C. May Flower   D. Discovery
21. On the 30th of April 1789, George Washington took the oath of office in _____, which housed the government then.
    A. New York   B. Washington D. C.
    C. Philadelphia   D. Boston
22. Which of the following people was not an American President?
    A. John Hancock.   B. John Adams.
    C. John Q. Adams.   D. Jimmy Carter.
23. Henry Ford was the first man to _____.
    A. design a plane   B. fly an aeroplane
    C. mass-production   D. design and make a car
24. "That government of the people, by the people, for the people, …" were the words by _____.
    A. Thomas Jefferson   B. Abraham Lincoln
    C. Andrew Johnson   D. Theodore Roosevelt

25. The US formally entered the Second World War in _____
    A. 1937   B. 1939   C. 1941   D. 1943

Section Two: In-depth Reading

The history of the United States could not be called a long one, but the U. S. is certainly the longest standing democracy in the world. During its course, there were a number of notable figures arising from different eras; people will never forget those great Americans when they are learning history.

Reading One is an American scholar's reflection on the virtues of George Washington.

Reading Two is an argument about how Americans should view the past.

Before reading thes articles, brainstorm with your cohorts on the following questions:
1. Recall some facts about George Washington and Abraham Lincoln.
2. What makes a great leader and a great nation?
3. What can we learn from the history of the U. S. ?

Reading One

As Commander-in-Chief of the Continental Army, hero of the revolution and the first president of the United States, George Washington's legacy remains among the greatest in American history. Washington set many precedents for the national government, and the presidency in particular, and was called the "Father of His Country" as early as 1778. But what is being considered the most memorable legacy of him?

The Man Who Would Not Be King
David Boaz

George Washington is the face on the one-dollar bill and—these days—the smiling face of Presidents' Day sales. Most of us know he was the first president of the United States. But why is that important? What else do we know about him?

George Washington was the man who established the American republic. He led the revolutionary army against the British Empire, he served as the first president, and most importantly he stepped down from power.

In an era of brilliant men, Washington was not the deepest thinker. He never wrote a book or even a long essay, unlike George Mason, Thomas Jefferson, James Madison, Alexander Hamilton, and John Adams. But Washington made the ideas of the American founding real. He incarnated liberal and republican ideas in his own person, and he gave them effect through the Revolution, the Constitution, his successful presidency, and his departure from office.

What's so great about leaving office? Surely it matters more what a president does in office. But think about other great military commanders and revolutionary leaders before and after Washington—Caesar, Cromwell, Napoleon, Lenin. They all seized the power they had won and held it until death or military defeat.

John Adams said, "He was the best actor of presidency we have ever had." Indeed, Washington was a person very conscious of his reputation, who worked all his life to develop his character and his image.

In our own time Joshua Micah Marshall writes of America's first president, "It was all a put-on, an act." Marshall missed the point. Washington understood that character is something you develop. He learned from Aristotle that good conduct arises from habits that in turn can only be acquired by repeated action and correction— "We are what we repeatedly do." Indeed, the word "ethics" comes from the Greek word for "habit." We say something is "second nature" because it's not actually natural; it's a habit we've developed. From reading the Greek philosophers and the Roman statesmen, Washington developed an understanding of character, in particular the character appropriate to a gentleman in a republic of free citizens.

What values did Washington's character express? He was a farmer, a businessman, an enthusiast for commerce. As a man of the Enlightenment, he was deeply interested in scientific farming. His letters on running Mount Vernon are longer than letters on running the government. (Of course, in 1795 more people worked at Mount Vernon than in the entire executive branch of the federal government.)

He was also a liberal and tolerant man. In a famous letter to the Jewish congregation in Newport, Rhode Island, he hailed the "liberal policy" of the United States on religious freedom as worthy of emulation by other countries. He explained, "It is now no more that toleration is spoken of as if it were the indulgence of one class of people that another enjoyed the exercise of their inherent natural rights, for, happily, the Government of the United States, which gives to bigotry no sanction, to persecution no assistance, requires only that they who live under its protection should demean themselves as good citizens."

And most notably, he held "republican" values—that is, he believed in a republic of free citizens, with a government based on consent and established to protect the rights of life, liberty, and property.

From his republican values Washington derived his abhorrence of kingship, even for himself. The writer Garry Wills called him "a virtuoso of resignations." He gave up power not once but twice—at the end of the revolutionary war, when he resigned his military commission and returned to Mount Vernon, and again at the end of his second term as president, when he refused entreaties to seek a third term. In doing so, he set a standard for American presidents that lasted until the presidency of Franklin D. Roosevelt, whose taste for power was stronger than the 150 years of precedent set by Washington.

Give the last word to Washington's great adversary, King George III. The king asked his American painter, Benjamin West, what Washington would do after winning independence. West replied, "They say he will return to his farm."

"If he does that," the incredulous monarch said, "he will be the greatest man in the world."

References
http://www.cato.org/publications/commentary/man-who-would-not-be-king

About the Author
David Boaz (born August 29, 1953, Mayfield, Kentucky) is the executive vice president of the Cato Institute, an American libertarian think tank.

Discussions
1. What were the notable achievements of George Washington? Which do you think would be the most important one?
2. How did some great military commanders and revolutionary leaders mentioned above deal with the power they seized?
3. What were the liberal and republican values that Washington upheld, or incarnated in his own person?

Reading Two

In the history classes of its public schools, a nation retells its own story and instills a national identity in the minds of young citizens. In today's America, where competing racial, cultural and linguistic claims make it nearly impossible even to speak of national identity, questions about history have become a struggle for the possession of America's past.

The Challenge of "Multiculturalism" in How Americans View the Past and the Future
Samuel Taylor

The multicultural, multiperspective history that has arisen from this struggle is not merely a departure from the history America has always taught its children. It may be the first time that a nation has abandoned the single identity of its origins and set out deliberately to adopt multiple national identities.

Significantly, the understanding by many non-whites of multicultural history is entirely different from that of whites. For whites, the central concepts are "inclusion" and "pluralism." American history is to be rewritten so that racial and cultural perspectives that were once "ignored" or "neglected" will get equal treatment. For many non-whites, however, multicultural history is merely a step on the way to an explicitly racial, Afrocentric or Hispanic history. Their goal is separation rather than inclusion.

The "conservative" view is that explicitly racial histories are illegitimate. America, it is argued, must be united by a common history, and exclusionist histories will disunite us. This position is logically correct; exclusionist histories are divisive. But as we shall see, the "conservative" position is wrong—practically, emotionally, and even morally. America is already disunited by race, and no approach to history can change that. Just as it would be impossible to use the same history book in both France and England, it is impossible to write a single American history that satisfies, white, black, Indian, Hispanic, and Asian.

Schooling as Assimilation

The purpose of American public education has never been simply to impart knowledge. One of its central goals has been to make children into Americans. American schools fly the American flag and students pledge allegiance to it. The central events of history are from the American past. The most glorious achievements are American achievements. There is nothing odd about that. Every nation gives its children a national education.

Nevertheless, American schools have had an even more explicitly nation-building purpose than others because of the need to assimilate immigrants. John Quincy Adams wrote that immigrants "must cast off their European skin, never to resume it." Horace Mann argued that "a foreign people—cannot be transformed into the full stature of American citizens merely by a voyage across the Atlantic." One of the strongest motives for building public schools was, therefore, the need to make *Americans* out of Europeans.

Europeans weren't going to be made into Americans by teaching them about the contributions of Africans, Mexicans and Indians. The old, standard history united Americans because it has a coherent purpose and a single voice. It emphasized one point of view and ignored others. To put it bluntly, it was history about white people for white people.

This history served the country well, so long as the population was overwhelmingly white, and the two traditional minorities-blacks and Indians—did not have voices. All this changed, beginning in the 1960s. The civil rights movement gave voices to blacks and Indians, and changes in immigration laws brought a massive influx of non-whites. It was the end of a certain kind of America.

Non-whites began to complain about a version of history that left them out. The nation-building history that has bound Europeans into a single people had not bound whites and non-whites into a single people. "Multicultural" history was therefore to be a broader, more inclusive history that would give every American his rightful share of America's past. At the same time, "culturally relevant" history would keep blacks and Hispanics in school and stop them from dropping out at ever-increasing rates.

Squaring the Circle

Something that well-meaning whites did not understand is that an "inclusive" history—one that would be all things to all people—is impossible. History has winners and losers, and they see the same events with different eyes. At the same time, virtually every non-white group sees the conflicts of the past as struggles with whites, so multicultural history becomes a collection of perspectives that are often not merely non-white but anti-white.

How, for example, is a multicultural history to treat the discovery and settlement of North America by Europeans? The old history called it a triumphant advance for civilization. But for Indians, the same historical events are an unending sequence of defeats and disaster. Does a multicultural textbook call this a triumph or a disaster or both or neither?

What about the Mexican-American War (1846—1848)? At the time, it was thought a glorious success because it added huge chunks to the American West. But was it, instead, an imperialist atrocity? Are today's school children to rejoice that California is part of America or are they to weep over the stolen birthright of their Hispanic brothers?

Slavery poses a similar riddle. Blacks want to make it the centerpiece of their history, and in many ways it is. For nearly 300 years, most American blacks were slaves, and virtually everything that blacks did or thought was circumscribed by slavery. Today, it is still the centerpiece of black history, because it excuses failure and can be used to extract benefits from whites.

For whites, though, slavery is a minor historical event. Except for the Civil War (which was set in motion and fought by whites) the course of the nation's history would hardly have been different if there had been no slavery. To give it a prominent place in white history is a transparent effort to manipulate the way that whites think about the present.

Once slavery is promoted to the status of unparalleled evil, much of the past becomes incomprehensible. Is George Washington *both* the Father of his Country *and* a wicked man because he owned slaves? Is Abraham Lincoln the storied savior of the

Union or is he a fiend because he thought blacks were inferior and should be sent back to Africa?

Those of us who went to school when American history still had coherence are likely to learn about the new, multicultural history only by accident. One such accident is that this year is the 500th anniversary of the discovery of America. A typical multicultural problem has thus spilled out of the classroom and gotten wider notice: Was Columbus a great explorer or was he a genocidal tyrant? Are we to celebrate half a millennium of European America or are we to hang our heads in shame? Or are we to do both?

Problems and Uncertainties

Multicultural histories, by their very nature, cannot answer these questions. And because they cannot, they present American history as a bundle of uncertainties, as a series of unsolved "problems." Unlike the old history, which viewed the past with pride and the future with confidence, multicultural histories are diffident and perplexed. Unlike the old history, which at least gave white children a firm foundation for national identity, multicultural history says, in effect, that America has no identity. The only thing left to unite a multicultural America is geography.

One way to understand the impossible task that multicultural history has set itself is to imagine how one would write a school history book to be used in both France and Britain. How would it treat Napoleon? The very geography of London—Waterloo Station, Trafalgar Square—is a monument to Englishmen who killed Frenchmen. Napoleon's tomb, Austerlitz station, and street names like Jena and Ulm all mark the pride the French take in their ancestors' readiness to slaughter foreigners. A "multicultural" history book of the Napoleonic wars would be an absurdity, and everyone knows it. And yet, it would be no more absurd than the history books American children use today.

Non-whites have a much keener sense of their group interests than whites. They see very clearly that the future will have its winners and losers, just as history has had them. Thus, while virtually every school district with a white majority is trying to square the circle by teaching a history that is everything to everyone, school districts with black majorities are beginning to replace the old "Euro-centric" curriculum with one that is openly "Afro-centric." They are not interested in supplementing the traditional history with different points of view. They want a single, African point of view.

In Atlanta, where 92 percent of the public school students are black, history and social studies courses have been rewritten from an "African-American" perspective. New York's public schools recently authorized a curriculum revision based on an openly anti-white position paper drafted, in part, by the black-supremacist professor, Leonard Jeffries. In California, school districts in heavily-black Oakland and East Palo Alto started the 1991/1992 school year without *social studies textbooks*. They decided to develop their own black-centered materials because they could find nothing suitable.

Private black schools have gone the farthest. Some reject America, and teach their pupils that they are the African diasporas. Many teach patent nonsense, claiming that the ancient Egyptians and even King Solomon were black. Nevertheless, even if some of their material is ridiculous, Afro-centric teachers have recognized something that white teachers have forgotten: History has a point of view; it cannot be all things to all people.

Building a Nation

Blacks, then, are learning the kind of history that whites once learned—a history that builds identity and certitude. White children are learning that every interpretation is valid, that nothing is certain, that their nation's past is all paradoxes and unsolved problems. Patriotism will not grow in the heart of a child who cannot look back with pride upon his nation's past. We have come a long way from schooling that made Europeans into Americans. We now make Americans into nothing at all.

Multicultural history is like Affirmative Action. Just as whites are to step aside to give hiring preferences to minorities, whites are to set aside their own point of view and study those of others. Non-whites, on the other hand, are free to promote their own interests and exclusionist histories.

Like Affirmative Action, multicultural history is possible only because the majority has abandoned its position at the center. If whites insisted on their own history as strongly as non-whites insist on theirs, the inevitability of separate histories would have been recognized long ago. Nor will whites be willing to forego their own history forever. They will eventually realize that only they are studying a past with no answers and no certainties. They will eventually see that there *cannot* be one history that satisfies all. And they will begin to wonder whether there can be one nation that satisfies all.

References

http://www.ihr.org/jhr/v12/v12p159_ Taylor.html
The Journal of Historical Review, vol. 12, no. 2, pp. 159-164.

About *The Journal of Historical Review*

The Institute for Historical Review is an independent educational research and publishing center that works to promote peace, understanding and justice through greater public awareness of the past, and especially socially-politically relevant aspects of twentieth-century history. Founded in 1978, the IHR is a non-partisan, non-ideological, and non-sectarian institute located in Orange County, southern

California. *The Journal of Historical Review*—published by the IHR, 1980—2002—cover a wide range of historical, political, current affairs and cultural topics.

Discussions

1. What are the characteristics of the old standard history of the U. S. ?
2. How did the change from the one-voiced, white majority America to the multicultural America take place?
3. What happened in the public schools of Atlanta and New York, where black students are the majority?
4. How did the author picture the "disaster" that a multicultural history might bring?

Chapter 11

American Government and Politics

Section One: A Brief Introduction

1. Constitution

The United States Constitution was groundbreaking in numerous ways, establishing a new government. Indeed, the very features which made it unique have also contributed to its longevity. These features also define the framework of American government and politics, establishing the United States of America, its national government and outlining the relationships between that government, the people and the states.

The most significant features of the U.S. Constitution are the establishment of the rule of law, the creation of a federal system with a supreme national government, the separation of governmental powers into three branches that check and balance each other, its flexibility and the establishment of a republican form of government.

The Constitution of the United States of America is the **supreme law**① of the United States. Empowered with the sovereign authority of the people by the framers and the consent of the legislatures of the states, it is the source of all government powers, and also provides important limitations on the government that protect the fundamental rights of United States citizens.

While the Constitution is the supreme law of the land, most of the specific, day-to-day rules and regulations that bring order to American society are not included in the Constitution itself. These ordinary laws are creations of the Congress, state legislatures and city councils. But the notion that laws are more important than the opinions of individual people—even important people—applies to these laws as well.

---

① supreme law: 当国会或者州的立法机关制定的法律与美国宪法有所冲突的话，这些法律将被宣布无效。两个多世纪以来，美国联邦最高法院通过众多判例不断地强化美国宪法的权威性。

In America, no one is considered to be above the law. In fact, deliberately trying to avoid the law through deception or bribery are crimes in and of themselves. Even a president who violates the law can be held accountable for doing so.

James Madison introduced 12 amendments to the First Congress in 1789. Ten of these would go on to become what we now consider to be the **Bill of Rights**①. Based on the *Virginia Declaration of Rights*, the *English Bill of Rights*, the writings of the Enlightenment, and the rights defined in the *Magna Carta*, the *Bill of Rights* contains rights that many today consider to be fundamental to America.

2. Separation of Power

2.1 The Legislature

Established by **Article I**② of the Constitution, the Legislative Branch consists of the House of Representatives and the Senate, which together form the United States Congress. The Constitution grants Congress the sole authority to enact legislation and declare war, the right to confirm or reject many Presidential appointments, and substantial investigative powers.

The House of Representatives is made up of 435 elected members, divided among the 50 states in proportion to their total population. In addition, there are 6 non-voting members, representing the District of Columbia, the Commonwealth of Puerto Rico, and four other territories of the United States. The presiding officer of the chamber is the Speaker of the House, elected by the Representatives. He or she is third in the line of succession to the Presidency.

Members of the House are elected every two years and must be 25 years of age, a U.S. citizen for at least seven years, and a resident of the state (but not necessarily the district) they represent. The House has several powers assigned exclusively to it, including the power to initiate revenue bills, impeach federal officials, and elect the President in the case of an electoral college **tie**③.

The Senate is composed of 100 Senators, 2 for each state. Until the ratification of the 17th Amendment in 1913, Senators were chosen by state legislatures, not by popular vote. Since then, they have been elected to six-year terms by the people of each state. Senator's terms are staggered so that about one-third of the Senate is up for reelection every two years. Senators must be 30 years of age, U.S. citizens for at

---

① Bill of Rights: 此处提及的《权利法案》并非英国 1689 年的《权利法案》。1789 年，12 条修正案被提出。1791 年 12 月 15 日，10 条修正案获得通过，成为现在所称的美国《权利法案》，为美国宪法的一部分。

② Article I:《美国宪法》第一条确立了国会的立法权。

③ tie: 在美国总统大选中，若选举人团投票出现了平局，则众议院中的议员也参与投票。

least nine years, and residents of the state they represent. The Vice President of the United States serves as President of the Senate and may cast the decisive vote in the event of a tie in the Senate.

The Senate has the sole power to confirm those of the President's appointments that require consent, and to ratify treaties. There are, however, two exceptions to this rule: the House must also approve appointments to the Vice Presidency and any treaty that involves foreign trade. The Senate also tries impeachment cases for federal officials referred to it by the House.

In order to pass legislation and send it to the President for his signature, both the House and the Senate must pass the same bill by majority vote. If the President vetoes a bill, they may override his veto by passing the bill again in each chamber with at least two-thirds of each body voting in favor.

2.2 The Executive

The power of the Executive Branch is vested in the President of the United States, who also acts as head of state and Commander-in-Chief of the armed forces. The President is responsible for implementing and enforcing the laws written by Congress and, to that end, appoints the heads of the federal agencies, including the Cabinet. The Vice President is also part of the Executive Branch, ready to assume the Presidency should the need arise. Including members of the armed forces, the Executive Branch employs more than 4 million Americans.

The Cabinet is an advisory body made up of the heads of the 15 executive departments. Appointed by the President and confirmed by the Senate, the members of the Cabinet are often the President's closest confidants. In addition to running major federal agencies, they play an important role in the Presidential line of succession — after the Vice President, Speaker of the House, and **Senate President pro tempore**[①], the line of succession continues with the Cabinet offices in the order in which the departments were created. All the members of the Cabinet take the title Secretary, excepting the head of the Justice Department, who is styled Attorney General.

The Constitution lists only three qualifications for the Presidency — the President must be 35 years of age, a natural born citizen, and must have lived in the United States for at least 14 years. And though millions of Americans vote in a presidential election every four years, the President is not, in fact, directly elected

---

① President pro tempore of the United States Senate: 美国参议院临时议长是美国参议院地位第二高的成员和地位最高的参议员。美国参议院地位最高的成员是美国副总统，副总统虽然是参议院的议长，但并非参议员（不通过参议员选举产生）。当美国副总统不在场时，参议院临时议长就是参议院中地位最高的人，并临时执行议长职。

by the people. Instead, on the first Tuesday in November of every fourth year, the people elect the members of the Electoral College. Apportioned by population to the 50 states — one for each member of their congressional delegation (with the District of Columbia receiving 3 votes) — these Electors then cast the votes for President. There are currently 538 electors in the Electoral College.

By tradition, the President and the First Family live in the White House in Washington, D. C., also the location of the President's Oval Office and the offices of the his senior staff. When the President travels by plane, his aircraft is designated Air Force One; he may also use a Marine Corps helicopter, known as Marine One while the President is on board. For ground travel, the President uses an armored Presidential limousine.

The southern facade of the White House
From: http://en.wikipedia.org/wiki/The_ White_ House

2.3 The Judiciary

Where the Executive and Legislative branches are elected by the people, members of the Judicial Branch are appointed by the President and confirmed by the Senate. Article III of the Constitution establishes the Judicial Branch, and leaves the Congress significant discretion to determine the shape and structure of the federal judiciary. Even the number of Supreme Court Justices is left to Congress — at times there have been as few as six, while the current number (nine, with one Chief Justice and eight Associate Justices) has only been in place since 1869. The Constitution also grants Congress the power to establish courts inferior to the Supreme

Court, and to that end Congress has established the **United States district courts**①, which try most federal cases, and 13 **United States courts of appeals**②, which review appealed district court cases.

Federal judges can only be removed through impeachment by the House of Representatives and conviction in the Senate. Judges and justices serve no fixed term — they serve until their death, retirement, or conviction by the Senate. By design, this insulates them from the temporary passions of the public, and allows them to apply the law with only justice in mind, and not electoral or political concerns.

Generally, Congress determines the jurisdiction of the federal courts. In some cases, however — such as in the example of a dispute between two or more U.S. states — the Constitution grants the Supreme Court original jurisdiction, an authority that cannot be stripped by Congress.

The courts only try actual cases and controversies — a party must show that it has been harmed in order to bring suit in court. This means that the courts do not issue advisory opinions on the constitutionality of laws or the legality of actions if the ruling would have no practical effect. Cases brought before the judiciary typically proceed from district court to appellate court and may even end at the Supreme Court, although the Supreme Court hears comparatively few cases each year.

Federal courts enjoy the sole power to interpret the law, determine the constitutionality of the law, and apply it to individual cases. The courts, like Congress, can compel the production of evidence and testimony through the use of a subpoena. The inferior courts are constrained by the decisions of the Supreme Court — once the Supreme Court interprets a law, inferior courts must apply the Supreme Court's interpretation to the facts of a particular case.

3. Political Parties

The modern political party system in the U.S. is a two-party system dominated by the Democratic Party and the Republican Party. These two parties have won every United States presidential election since 1852 and have controlled the United States Congress to some extent since at least 1856. The symbol of the Republican Party is an elephant. The symbol of the Democratic Party used to be a donkey. In

---

① United States district courts: 美国联邦地区法院是美国联邦法院系统中的普通初审法院，处理民事和刑事案件。目前在美国领地中一共有 94 个联邦地区法院。50 个州中共有 89 个，首都哥伦比亚特区和波多黎各各有一个，这 91 个联邦地区法院都只拥有联邦管辖权；另外在关岛、维京群岛和北马里亚纳群岛也各有一个联邦地区法院，这 3 个法院则同时拥有联邦和地方管辖权。

② United States courts of appeals: 美国联邦上诉法院，又名巡回上诉法院（circuit courts），是美国联邦司法系统中的中级上诉法院。联邦上诉法院主要裁定来自于其联邦司法管辖区内对于地方法院判决的上诉。

September, 2010, the Democratic Party unveiled its new logo, which featured a blue D inside a blue circle. It was the party's first official logo, as the donkey logo had only been semi-official.

The official logo of the Democratic Party
From: http://en.wikipedia.org/wiki/Democratic_Party_(United_States)

The official logo of the Republican Party
From: http://en.wikipedia.org/wiki/Republican_Party_(United_States)

3.1 Democratic Party

The Democratic Party is one of two major political parties in the U.S. It is arguably oldest political party in the world. The Democratic Party, since the division of the Republican Party in the election of 1912, has positioned itself as the party of labor on economic issues. The economic philosophy of Franklin D. Roosevelt, which has strongly influenced American liberalism, has shaped much of the party's agenda since 1932. Roosevelt's New Deal coalition had controlled the White House until 1968 with the exception of Eisenhower 1953—1961.

In 2004, it was the largest political party, with 72 million voters (42.6% of 169 million registered) claiming affiliation. The president of the United States, Barack Obama, is the 15th Democrat to hold the office, and since the 2006 midterm elections, the Democratic Party is the majority party for the United States Senate.

Obama in front of the Resolute desk in the Oval Office of the White House
From: http://en.wikipedia.org/wiki/Barack_Obama

A 2011 *USA Today* review of state voter rolls indicates that registered Democrats declined in 25 of 28 states (some states do not register voters by party). Democrats were still the largest political party with more than 42 million voters (compared with 30 million Republicans and 24 million independents). But in 2011 Democrats numbers shrank 800,000, and from 2008 they were down by 1.7 million, or 3.9%.

3.2 Republican Party

The Republican Party is one of the two major contemporary political parties in the United States of America. Since the 1880s it has been nicknamed (by the media) the "Grand Old Party" or GOP.

Founded in 1854 by Northern anti-slavery activists and modernizers, the Republican Party rose to prominence in 1860 with the election of Abraham Lincoln, who used the party machinery to support victory in the American Civil War. The GOP dominated national politics during the Third Party System, from 1854 to 1896, and the Fourth Party System from 1896 to 1932. Today, the Republican Party supports an American conservative platform, with further foundations in economic liberalism, fiscal conservatism, and social conservatism.

Abraham Lincoln
From: http://en.wikipedia.org/wiki/Abraham_Lincoln

Former President George W. Bush is the 19th Republican to hold that office. The party's nominee for President of the United States in the 2012 presidential election was Mitt Romney, former Governor of Massachusetts. Since the 2010 midterm elections, the Republicans have held a majority in the United States House of Representatives.

USA Today's review of state voter rolls indicates that registered Republicans declined in 21 of 28 states (not all states register voters by party) and that Republican registrations were down 350,000 in 2011. The number of independents rose in 18 states, increasing by 325,000 in 2011, and was up more than 400,000 from 2008, or 1.7%.

4. General Election

Every four years, the general election for U. S. president takes place on the Tuesday after the first Monday of November. Every two years, Americans elect all 435 members of the U. S. House of Representatives and approximately one-third of the 100 members of the U. S. Senate. Senators serve staggered terms of six years each.

There are two basic types of elections: primary and general. Primary elections are held prior to a general election to determine party candidates for the general election. The winning candidates in the primary go on to represent that party in the general election.

The Electoral College method of choosing presidents reinforces the two-party system. Under the Electoral College system, Americans, technically, do not vote directly for the president and vice president. Instead, they vote within each state for a group of "electors" who are pledged to one or another presidential candidate. The number of electors corresponds to the number in a state's congressional delegation, i. e. , the number of representatives and senators from that state. Election to the presidency requires an absolute majority of the 538 electoral votes. (That figure includes three electoral votes from the national capital city of Washington, the District of Columbia, which is not a state and which does not have voting representation in Congress.)

The absolute majority requirement makes it extremely difficult for a third-party candidate to win the presidency because the individual states' electoral votes are allocated under a winner-take-all arrangement (with two exceptions). That is, whichever candidate receives a plurality of the popular vote in a state—even if it is just a narrow plurality—wins all of that state's electoral votes. The Electoral College works to the disadvantage of third parties, which have little chance of winning any state's electoral votes, let alone carrying enough states to elect a president.

5. Federalism

Federalism is a system of government in which a written constitution divides power between a central government and regional or sub-divisional governments. Both types of government act directly upon the people through their officials and laws. What's more, both types of government are supreme within their proper sphere of authority. Both have to consent (agree) to any changes to the constitution.

In America the term "federal government" is usually understood to refer exclusively to the national government based in Washington. This, however, is not an accurate interpretation of the term as it excludes the role played by other aspects of government concerned with the federalist structure.

Federalism can be seen a compromise between the extreme concentration of power and a loose confederation of independent states for governing a variety of people usually in a large expanse of territory. Federalism has the virtue of retaining local pride, traditions and power, while allowing a central government that can handle common problems. The basic principle of American federalism is fixed in the Tenth Amendment (ratified in 1791) to the Constitution which states: "The powers not delegated to the United States by the Constitution, nor prohibited by it to the States, are reserved to the States respectively, or to the people."

In America each state has its own position of legal autonomy and political significance. Though a state is not a sovereign body, it does exercise power and can carry out functions that would be carried out by the central authority in other governmental set-ups.

The Constitution set up a division of power between the federal and state governments which initially limited the federal unit to the fields of defense, foreign affairs, the control of the currency and the control of commerce between the states. This division of power has been eroded over the years so that today the federal government has functions that have been greatly extended and touch on nearly all aspects of life for American citizens.

References

http://www.whitehouse.gov/our-government

www.whitehouse.gov is the official website of the White House. In this website, you can find the latest news, the information about the White House and the US Government.

http://en.wikipedia.org/wiki/Political_parties_in_the_United_States

Political Parties in the United States. Modified on 2 May 2014.

Exercises

I. Choose the one that best completes each of the following statements.

1. U. S. presidents normally serve a (an) _____ term.
   A. eight-year   B. four-year   C. six-year   D. two-year
2. Richard Nixon resigned in 1974 because of _____.
   A. the Great Depression   B. the Black Power Movement
   C. the Watergate Scandal   D. the Isolation policy
3. The emblem of the Democratic Party is _____.

A. elephant   B. donkey   C. bear   D. capital D
4. The number of the House of Representatives from each American state depends on the _____.
   A. contribution a state has made to the nation
   B. population
   C. size
   D. none of the above
5. According to the United States Constitution, the legislative power is invested in _____.
   A. the Supreme Court   B. the Cabinet
   C. the Congress   D. the Federal Government
6. The Constitution of the United States _____.
   A. gives the most power to Congress
   B. gives the most power to the President
   C. makes each branch balance the others
   D. gives the most power to the Supreme Court
7. The *Bill of Rights* _____.
   A. defines the rights of Congress and the rights of the President
   B. guarantees citizens of the United States specific individual rights and freedoms
   C. is part of the Declaration of Independence
   D. has no relationship with the Constitution
8. The following except _____ are guaranteed in the *Bill of Rights*.
   A. freedom of religion
   B. the right to get into people's house by police
   C. freedom of speech and of press
   D. the right to own one's weapon if one wishes
9. All the following except _____ cannot make legislative proposal.
   A. the Senator   B. the Representative
   C. the Secretary of State   D. the President
10. According to the Constitution, a candidate for President must be _____.
    A. at least 35 years old   B. at least a 14 years' resident of America
    C. born in America   D. all of the above
11. The terms for a Senator and Representative are _____ and _____ years respectively.
    A. two, four   B. two, three   C. two, six   D. six, two

II. Read the following statements carefully and decide whether they are TRUE or FALSE.

1. The Bill of Rights is part of the Constitution.
2. The form of American government is based on three main principles: federalism,

the separation of powers, and respect for the Constitution and the rule of law.
3. The US Congress is composed of two houses: the House of Commons and the House of Lords.
4. The Vice President of the United States serves as President of the Senate.
5. Members of the Judicial Branch are elected by the people.
6. The term for a federal judge is 6 years.
7. Every four years, the general election for U. S. president takes place on the Tuesday after the first Monday of November.
8. Under the Electoral College system, it's extremely difficult for a third-party candidate to win the presidency.
9. Like Britain, America has a two-party system.
10. Abraham Lincoln is the first American president elected from the Republican Party.

III. Give brief answers to the following questions.
1. What are the qualifications for a Senator and a Representative respectively?
2. Why does a third party candidate have no chance of getting any form of power under the Electoral College system?

Section Two: In-depth Reading

Since America declared independence from Great Britain on July 4, 1776, the United States government has sought to realize the fundamental principle on which the whole nation was founded: that all people have the right to life, liberty, and the pursuit of happiness. The government of the United States of America is the federal government of the republic of fifty states that constitute the United States, as well as one capital district, and several other territories. The two articles in this section will acquaint us with American political system from different angles.

Reading One shows us how America's federal, state and local governments work to enact the will of the people.

Reading Two presents us a special voting system of American Presidential Election—Electoral College.

Before reading the articles, brainstorm with your cohorts on the following questions:

1. Do you know how the local government operates in the US? Try to compare the civil service in your country with that in the US.

2. How is a President voted into office in America? What are your ideas about the American election?

Reading One

In the United States, the Constitution grants certain powers to both the U. S. government and the state governments. As for the American citizens, they have easier access to their state or local government than the federal government. The following passage is a brief introduction of the State and Local government in America.

State and Local Governments

Most Americans have more daily contact with their state and local governments than with the federal government. Police departments, libraries, and schools — not to mention driver's licenses and parking tickets — usually fall under the oversight of state and local governments. Each state has its own written constitution, and these documents are often far more elaborate than their federal counterpart. The Alabama Constitution, for example, contains 310,296 words — more than 40 times as many as the U. S. Constitution.

State Government

Under the Tenth Amendment to the U. S. Constitution, all powers not granted to the federal government are reserved for the states and the people. All state governments are modeled after the federal government and consist of three branches: executive, legislative, and judicial. The U. S. Constitution mandates that all states uphold a "republican form" of government, although the three-branch structure is not required.

Executive Branch: In every state, the executive branch is headed by a governor who is directly elected by the people. In most states, the other leaders in the executive branch are also directly elected, including the lieutenant governor, the attorney general, the secretary of state, and auditors and commissioners. States reserve the right to organize in any way, so they often vary greatly with regard to executive structure. No two state executive organizations are identical.

Legislative Branch: All 50 states have legislatures made up of elected representatives, who consider matters brought forth by the governor or introduced by its members to create legislation that becomes law. The legislature also approves a state's budget and initiates tax legislation and articles of impeachment. The latter is part of a system of checks and balances among the three branches of government that mirrors the federal system and prevents any branch from abusing its power.

Except for one state, Nebraska, all states have a bicameral legislature made up of two chambers: a smaller upper house and a larger lower house. Together the two chambers make state laws and fulfill other governing responsibilities. (Nebraska is the lone state that has just one chamber in its legislature.) The smaller upper chamber is always called the Senate, and its members generally serve longer terms, usually four years. The larger lower chamber is most often called the House of Representatives, but some states call it the Assembly or the House of Delegates. Its members usually serve shorter terms, often two years.

Judicial Branch: State judicial branches are usually led by the state supreme court, which hears appeals from lower-level state courts. Court structures and judicial appointments/elections are determined either by legislation or the state constitution. The Supreme Court focuses on correcting errors made in lower courts and therefore holds no trials. Rulings made in state supreme courts are normally binding; however, when questions are raised regarding consistency with the U. S. Constitution, matters may be appealed directly to the United States Supreme Court.

Local Government

Local governments generally include two tiers: counties, also known as boroughs in Alaska and parishes in Louisiana, and municipalities, or cities/towns. In some states, counties are divided into townships. Municipalities can be structured in many ways, as defined by state constitutions, and are called, variously, townships, villages, boroughs, cities, or towns. Various kinds of districts also provide functions in local government outside county or municipal boundaries, such as school districts or fire protection districts.

Municipal governments—those defined as cities, towns, boroughs (except in Alaska), villages, and townships—are generally organized around a population center and in most cases correspond to the geographical designations used by the United States Census Bureau for reporting of housing and population statistics. Municipalities vary greatly in size, from the millions of residents of New York City and Los Angeles to the 287 people who live in Jenkins, Minnesota.

Municipalities generally take responsibility for parks and recreation services, police and fire departments, housing services, emergency medical services, municipal courts, transportation services (including public transportation), and public works (streets, sewers, snow removal, signage, and so forth).

Whereas the federal government and state governments share power in countless ways, a local government must be granted power by the state. In general, mayors, city councils, and other governing bodies are directly elected by the people.

References

http://www.whitehouse.gov/our-government/state-and-local-government

Discussions
1. What is federalism? What are the differences between federalism and centralism?
2. Please state your own understanding of the advantages and disadvantages of

federalism.

Reading Two

The Electoral College dominates the airwaves and the headlines on Election Day Tuesday. But what exactly is the Electoral College? Below is a quick guide on what it does and why it matters.

What Is the Electoral College?

The Electoral College is a process, not a place. The founding fathers established it in the Constitution as a compromise between election of the President by a vote in Congress and election of the President by a popular vote of qualified citizens.

The Electoral College process consists of the selection of the electors, the meeting of the electors where they vote for President and Vice President, and the counting of the electoral votes by Congress.

The Electoral College consists of 538 electors. A majority of 270 electoral votes is required to elect the President. Your state's entitled allotment of electors equals the number of members in its Congressional delegation: one for each member in the House of Representatives plus two for your Senators.

Under the 23rd Amendment of the Constitution, the District of Columbia is allocated 3 electors and treated like a state for purposes of the Electoral College. For this reason, in the following discussion, the word "state" also refers to the District of Columbia.

Each candidate running for President in your state has his or her own group of electors. The electors are generally chosen by the candidate's political party, but state laws vary on how the electors are selected and what their responsibilities are. Read more about the qualifications of the Electors and restrictions on who the Electors may vote for.

The presidential election is held every four years on the Tuesday after the first Monday in November. You help choose your state's electors when you vote for President because when you vote for your candidate you are actually voting for your candidate's electors.

Most states have a "winner-take-all" system that awards all electors to the winning presidential candidate. However, Maine and Nebraska each have a variation of "proportional representation". Read more about the allocation of Electors among the states and try to predict the outcome of the Electoral College vote.

After the presidential election, your governor prepares a "Certificate of Ascertainment" listing all of the candidates who ran for President in your state along with the names of their respective electors. The Certificate of Ascertainment also declares the winning presidential candidate in your state and shows which electors will represent your state at the meeting of the electors in December of the election year. Your state's Certificates of Ascertainments are sent to the Congress and the National Archives as part of the official records of the presidential election. See the key dates for the 2012 election and information about the roles and responsibilities of state officials, the Office of the Federal Register and the National Archives and Records Administration (NARA), and the Congress in the Electoral College process.

The meeting of the electors takes place on the first Monday after the second Wednesday in December after the presidential election. The electors meet in their respective states, where they cast their votes for President and Vice President on separate ballots. Your state's electors' votes are recorded on a "Certificate of Vote", which is prepared at the meeting by the electors. Your state's Certificates of Votes are sent to the Congress and the National Archives as part of the official records of the presidential election. See the key dates for the 2012 election and information about the roles and responsibilities of state officials and the Congress in the Electoral College process.

Each state's electoral votes are counted in a joint session of Congress on the 6th of January in the year following the meeting of the electors. Members of the House and Senate meet in the House chamber to conduct the official tally of electoral votes. (On December 28, 2012, President Obama signed Pub. L. 112—228, as passed by both houses of Congress, moving the day of the vote count from January 6, 2013 (a Sunday) to January 4, 2013.) See the key dates for the 2012 election and information about the role and responsibilities of Congress in the Electoral College process.

The Vice President, as President of the Senate, presides over the count and announces the results of the vote. The President of the Senate then declares which persons, if any, have been elected President and Vice President of the United States.

The President-Elect takes the oath of office and is sworn in as President of the United States on January 20th in the year following the Presidential election.

References

http://www. archives. gov/federal-register/electoral-college/about. html

The National Archives and Records Administration (NARA) is the nation's record keeper. Of all documents and materials created in the course of business conducted by the United States Federal government, only 1%～3% are so important for legal or historical reasons that they are kept by us forever.

Discussions
1. Who selects the Electors?
2. What are the qualifications to be an Elector?
3. Are there restrictions on who the Electors can vote for?

Chapter 12

Economy

Section One: A Brief Introduction

1. Economy of the United States

The economy of the United States is the world's largest single national economy. The United States' nominal GDP was estimated to be $17.4 trillion in January 2014, approximately a quarter of nominal global GDP. Its GDP at purchasing power parity is also the largest of any single country in the world, approximately a fifth of the global total. The United States has a mixed economy and has maintained a stable overall GDP growth rate, a moderate unemployment rate, and high levels of research and capital investment. Its five largest trading partners are Canada, China, Mexico, Japan, and Germany.

The US has abundant natural resources, a well-developed infrastructure, and high productivity. It has the world's seventh-highest per capita GDP (PPP). The U.S. is the world's third-largest producer of oil and largest producer of natural gas. It is the second-largest trading nation in the world behind China. It has been the world's largest national economy (not including colonial empires) since at least the 1890s. As of 2010, the country remains the world's largest manufacturer, representing a fifth of the global manufacturing output. Of the world's 500 largest companies, 132 are headquartered in the US, twice that of any other country. The country has one of the world's largest and most influential financial markets. The **New York Stock Exchange**[①] is by far the world's largest stock exchange by market capitalization.

---

① New York Stock Exchange, NYSE, 纽约证券交易所, 是上市公司总市值第一、IPO 数量及市值第一、交易量第二的交易所, 有大约 2,800 间公司在此上市, 全球市值 15 万亿美元。至 2004 年 7 月, 30 间处于道·琼斯工业平均指数中的公司除了英特尔和微软之外都在 NYSE 上市。2005 年 4 月末, NYSE 和全电子证券交易所（Archipelago）合并, 成为一个盈利性机构。纽约证券交易所有限公司的总部位于美国纽约州纽约市百老汇大街 11 号, 在华尔街的拐角南侧。2006 年 6 月 1 日, 纽约证券交易所宣布与泛欧证券交易所合并组成纽约泛欧证交所（NYSE Euronext）。

Foreign investments made in the US total almost $2.4 trillion, while American investments in foreign countries total over $3.3 trillion. Consumer spending comprises 71% of the US economy in 2013. The labor market has attracted immigrants from all over the world and its net migration rate is among the highest in the world. The U.S. is one of the top-performing economies in studies such as **the Ease of Doing Business Index**①, **the Global Competitiveness Report**②, and others.

The US economy is currently embroiled in the economic downturn which followed the financial crisis of 2007—2008, with output still below potential according to the **Congressional Budget Office**③ and unemployment still above historic trends while household incomes have stagnated. As of September 2013, the **unemployment rate**④ was 7.2% (11.26 million people), while the government's broader U-6 unemployment rate, which includes the part-time underemployed, was 13.1%. At 11.3%, the U.S. has one of the lowest labor union participation rates in the **OECD**⑤. Households living on less than $2 per day before government benefits, doubled from 1996 levels to 1.5 million households in 2011, including 2.8 million children. The wealthiest 10% of the population possess 80% of all financial assets. Total public and private debt was $50.2 trillion at the end of the first quarter of 2010, or 3.5 times GDP. In December 2013, the total of the public debt was about 1.015 times GDP. Domestic financial assets totaled $131 trillion and domestic financial liabilities totaled $106 trillion.

---

① the Ease of Doing Business Index：营商便利指数（1 = 最有利于营商的法规）。营商便利指数从1 到 189 为经济体排名，第一位为最佳。排名越高，表示法规环境越有利于营商。该指数对世界银行营商环境项目所涉及的 10 个专题中的国家百分比排名的简单平均值进行排名

② the Global Competitiveness Report：全球竞争力报告的竞争力排名以全球竞争力指数为基础。这一指数包括制度、基础设施和宏观经济稳定性等 12 个竞争力因素。自 1979 年以来，总部设在瑞士日内瓦的世界经济论坛每年发布一份全球竞争力报告。

③ Congressional Budget Office：国会预算办公室是美国国会下设的一个专业的、非党派的机构，成立于 1975 年，没有审批权。其职责是为国会两院提供客观、专业、及时、非政治化的分析，这些分析有助于经济和预算决策。国会预算办公室对经济与预算有独立的分析与预计，并独立地编制一整套预算，供国会参考。简单地说，国会预算办公室的任务，主要是为参、众两院的预算委员会、筹款委员会、拨款委员会提供辅助性服务，给总统的预算挑毛病，另外也应国会的要求研究预算和经济方面的有关政策。近些年来，CBO 的规模逐步扩大，现在已经有工作人员 300 多人。

④ unemployment rate：失业率是指一定时期满足全部就业条件的就业人口中仍未有工作的劳动力数字，旨在衡量闲置中的劳动产能，是反映一个国家或地区失业状况的主要指标。失业数据的月份变动可适当反映经济发展。失业率与经济增长率具有反向的对应变动关系。

⑤ Organization for Economic Co-operation and Development：经济合作与发展组织，简称经合组织（OECD），是由 30 多个市场经济国家组成的政府间国际经济组织，旨在共同应对全球化带来的经济、社会和政府治理等方面的挑战，并把握全球化带来的机遇，被称为是智囊团、富人俱乐部或者非学术性大学。成立于 1961 年，目前成员国总数 34 个，总部设在巴黎。

2. Economic History of the United States

The economic history of the United States has its roots in European settlements in the 16th, 17th, and 18th centuries. The American colonies went from marginally successful colonial economies to a small, independent farming economy, which in 1776 became the United States of America. In 180 years the US grew to a huge, integrated, industrialized economy that still makes up around one fifth of the world economy. As a result, the US GDP per capita converged on and eventually surpassed that of the U. K. , as well as other nations that it previously trailed economically. The economy has maintained high wages, attracting immigrants by the millions from all over the world.

In the 19th century, recessions frequently coincided with financial crises. The **Panic of 1837**① was followed by a five-year depression, with the failure of banks and then-record-high unemployment levels. Because of the great changes in the economy over the centuries, it is difficult to compare the severity of modern recessions to early recessions. Recessions after World War II appear to have been less severe than earlier recessions, but the reasons for this are unclear.

2.1 World's Largest Economy

The United States has been the world's largest national economy since at least the 1920s. For many years following the **Great Depression**② of the 1930s, when danger of recession appeared most serious, the government strengthened the economy by spending heavily itself or cutting taxes so that consumers would spend more, and by fostering rapid growth in the money supply, which also encouraged more spending. Ideas about the best tools for stabilizing the economy changed substantially

---

① The Panic of 1837：1834—1836年，土地、棉花、黑奴价格上涨，大量银币涌入美国，美国经济一派繁荣。1836年，英格兰银行提高利率，抑制贷款，减少了对美国的投资。与此同时，美国第二合众国银行被关闭，其持有的政府资产被转移到各地方银行。美国西部开发的土地买卖又被强行要求以贵金属支付。一时间，各银行贵金属存量不足，各地出现挤兑风潮，货币流通量巨幅紧缩，发生了1937年的经济大恐慌。股票疯狂下跌，失业率高涨。

② Great Depression：经济大萧条，是指1929年至1933年之间全球性的经济大衰退，是第二次世界大战前最为严重的世界性经济衰退。大萧条的开始时间依国家的不同而不同，但绝大多数在1930年起，持续到30年代末，甚至是40年代末。大萧条是20世纪持续时间最长、影响最广、强度最大的经济衰退。大萧条从美国开始，以1929年10月24日的股市下跌开始，到10月29日成为1929年华尔街股灾，并席卷了全世界。大萧条对发达国家和发展中国家都带来了毁灭性打击。人均收入、税收、盈利、价格全面下挫，国际贸易锐减50%，美国失业率飙升到25%，有的国家甚至达到了33%。全世界各大主要城市全部遭到重创，特别是依赖重工业的地区。许多国家的建筑工程在实际上无法进行。农产品价格下降约60%，重击农业。由于没有可替代的工种，第一产业中的经济作物、采矿、伐木等部门受到的打击最为沉重。

between the 1930s and the 1980s. From the **New Deal**① era that began in 1933, to the **Great Society**② initiatives of the 1960s, national policy makers relied principally on fiscal policy to influence the economy.

US dollar influences the world's economy
From: http://www.cngold.com.cn/zjsd/20140806d1861n32481772.html

The approach, advanced by British economist **John Maynard Keynes**③, gave elected officials a leading role in directing the economy, since spending and taxes are controlled by the U.S. President and the Congress. The "**Baby Boom**" ④ saw a

---

① the New Deal: 罗斯福新政,是指 1933 年富兰克林·罗斯福就任美国总统后所实行的一系列经济政策,其核心是三个 R: 救济 (Relief)、复兴 (Recovery) 和改革 (Reform),因此有时也被称为三 R 新政。新政以增加政府对经济直接或间接干预的方式,大大缓解了大萧条所带来的经济危机与社会矛盾。通过国会制定了《紧急银行法令》《国家工业复兴法》《农业调整法》《社会保障法案》等法案。第二次世界大战爆发后,新政基本结束,但罗斯福新政时期产生的一些制度或机构,如社会安全保障基金、美国证券交易委员会、美国联邦存款保险公司、美国联邦住房管理局、田纳西河谷管理局等至今仍产生着影响。

② Great Society: 伟大社会,指的是 1964 年美国总统约翰逊发表演说宣称: "美国不仅有机会走向一个富裕和强大的社会,而且有机会走向一个伟大的社会。" 由此所提出的施政目标,便是"伟大社会"。为实现这一目标,国会通过了包括"向贫困宣战""保障民权"及医疗卫生等方面的立法 400 多项,将战后美国的社会改革推到了新的高峰。约翰逊的"伟大社会"纲领和肯尼迪的"新边疆"政策都是资产阶级自由主义改革,把罗斯福新政式的国家垄断资本主义发展到了一个新的高度。

③ John Maynard Keynes (1883—1946)(约翰·梅纳德·凯恩斯),英国经济学家,现代西方经济学最有影响的经济学家之一,他创立的宏观经济学与弗洛伊德所创的精神分析法和爱因斯坦发现的相对论一起并称为 20 世纪人类知识界的三大革命。因开创了经济学的"凯恩斯革命"而称著于世,被后人称为"宏观经济学之父""资本主义的救世主"。

④ "Baby Boom": "婴儿潮",特指美国第二次世界大战后的"4664"现象。即从 1946 年至 1964 年,这 18 年间"婴儿潮"人口高达 7600 万人,这个人群被通称为"婴儿潮一代"。1945 年"二战"结束后,大批军人返回美国,从而使 1946 年成为美国"婴儿潮"的开始。1946 年,美国出生了 340 万个婴儿。在此后的 1946—1964 年间,美国共有 7590 多万婴儿出生,约占美国目前总人口的 1/3,他们是当今美国社会的中坚力量。

dramatic increase in fertility in the period 1942—1957; it was caused by delayed marriages and childbearing during depression years, a surge in prosperity, a demand for suburban single-family homes (as opposed to inner city apartments) and new optimism about the future. The boom crested about 1957, then slowly declined. A period of high inflation, interest rates and unemployment after 1973 weakened confidence in fiscal policy as a tool for regulating the overall pace of economic activity.

The US economy grew by an average of 3.8% from 1946 to 1973, while real median household income surged 74% (or 2.1% a year). The economy since 1973, however, has been characterized by both slower growth (averaging 2.7%), and nearly stagnant living standards, with household incomes increasing by 10%, or only 0.3% annually.

The worst recession in recent decades, in terms of lost output, occurred during the financial crisis of 2007—2008, when GDP fell by 5.0% from the spring of 2008 to the spring of 2009. Other significant recessions took place in 1957—1958, when GDP fell 3.7%, following **the 1973 oil crisis**①, with a 3.1% fall from late 1973 to early 1975, and in the 1981—1982 recession, when GDP dropped by 2.9%. Recent, mild recessions have included the 1990—1991 downturn, when output fell by 1.3%, and the 2001 recession, in which GDP slid by 0.3%; the 2001 downturn lasted just eight months. The most vigorous, sustained periods of growth, on the other hand, took place from early 1961 to mid-1969, with an expansion of 53% (5.1% a year), from mid-1991 to late in 2000, at 43% (3.8% a year), and from late 1982 to mid-1990, at 37% (4% a year).

In the 1970s and 1980s, it was popular in the U.S. to believe that Japan's economy would surpass that of the United States, but this did not happen.

2.2 Slower Growth Since the Early 1970s

Since the 1970s, several emerging countries have begun to close the economic gap with the United States. In most cases, this has been due to moving the manufacture of goods formerly made in the U.S. to countries where they could be made for sufficiently less money to cover the cost of shipping plus a higher profit.

In other cases, some countries have gradually learned to produce the same products and services that previously only the U.S. and a few other countries could produce. Real income growth in the U.S. has slowed down.

---

① the 1973 oil crisis: 1973 年石油危机是由于 1973 年 10 月第四次中东战争爆发，石油输出国组织（OPEC）为了打击对手以色列及支持以色列的国家，宣布石油禁运，暂停出口，造成油价上涨。当时原油价格曾从 1973 年的每桶不到 3 美元涨到超过 13 美元，是 20 世纪下半叶三大石油危机之一。

The **North American Free Trade Agreement, or NAFTA**①, created the largest trade bloc in the world in 1994.

Since 1976, the US has sustained merchandise trade deficits with other nations, and since 1982, current account deficits. The nation's long-standing surplus in its trade in services was maintained, however, and reached a record US $231 billion in 2013. In recent years, the primary economic concerns have centered on: high household debt ($11 trillion, including $2.5 trillion in revolving debt, high net national debt ($9 trillion), high corporate debt ($9 trillion), high mortgage debt (over $15 trillion as of 2005 year-end), high external debt (amount owed to foreign lenders), high trade deficits, a serious deterioration in the United States net international investment position (NIIP) (-24% of GDP), and high unemployment. In 2006, the U.S. economy had its lowest saving rate since 1933. These issues have raised concerns among economists and national politicians.

The United States economy experienced a crisis in 2008 led by a **derivatives market**② and **subprime mortgage crisis**③, and a declining dollar value. On December 1, 2008, the **NBER**④ declared that the United States entered a recession in December 2007, citing employment and production figures as well as the third quarter decline in GDP. The recession did, however, lead to a reduction in record trade deficits, which fell from $840 billion annually during the 2006—2008 period, to $500 billion in 2009, as well as to higher personal savings rates, which jumped from a historic low of 1% in early 2008, to nearly 5% in late 2009. The merchandise trade deficit rose to $670 billion in 2010; savings rates, however, remained at around 5%.

The U.S. public debt was $909 billion in 1980, an amount equal to 33.3% of America's gross domestic product (GDP); by 1990, that number had more than

---

① The North American Free Trade Agreement, or NAFTA: 北美自由贸易协议是美国、加拿大及墨西哥在1992年8月12日签署的关于三国间全面贸易的协议。与欧盟性质不一样，北美自由贸易协议不是凌驾于国家政府和国家法律上的一项协议。该协议于1994年1月1日正式生效。北美自由贸易区拥有3.6亿人口，国民生产总值约6.45万亿美元，年贸易总额1.37亿美元，其经济实力和市场规模都超过欧洲联盟，成为当时世界上最大的区域经济一体化组织。

② derivatives market: 衍生产品市场，是指以杠杆或信用交易为特征，以在传统的金融产品如货币、债券、股票等的基础上派生出来的具有新的价值的金融工具，如期货合同、期权合同、互换及远期协议合同等。

③ subprime mortgage crisis: 次信贷危机，是指一场发生在美国，因次级抵押贷款机构破产、投资基金被迫关闭、股市剧烈震荡引起的风暴。它致使全球主要金融市场隐约出现流动性不足的危机。美国次信贷危机是从2006年春季开始逐步显现的，2007年8月席卷美国、欧盟和日本等世界主要金融市场。

④ NBER: 美国国家经济研究局，全称是 National Bureau of Economic Research。建立于1920年，是一个私人的、非营利、无党派分歧的研究机构，专注于更好地理解经济运行状态。NBER决心致力于在经济政策制定者、商业专家和科研院所之间传播无偏的经济研究。

tripled to $3.2 trillion—or 55.9% of GDP. In 2001 the national debt was $5.7 trillion; however, the debt-to-GDP ratio remained at 1990 levels. Debt levels rose quickly in the following decade, and on January 28, 2010, the US debt ceiling was raised to $14.3 trillion. Based on the 2010 United States federal budget, total national debt will grow to nearly 100% of GDP, versus a level of approximately 80% in early 2009. The White House estimates that the government's tab for servicing the debt will exceed $700 billion a year in 2019, up from $202 billion in 2009.

The **U.S. Treasury**[①] statistics indicate that, at the end of 2006, non-US citizens and institutions held 44% of federal debt held by the public. China, holding $801.5 billion in **treasury bonds**[②], is the largest foreign financier of the record U.S. public debt.

US share of world GDP (nominal) peaked in 1985 with 32.74% of global GDP (nominal). Its second highest share was 32.24% in 2001.

US share of world GDP (**PPP**[③]) peaked in 1999 with 23.78% of global GDP (PPP). While its share has been declining each year since 1999, it is still the highest in the world.

References

http://en.wikipedia.org/wiki/Economy_ of_ the_ United_ States

Wikipedia is a multilingual, web-based, free-content encyclopedia project supported by the Wikimedia Foundation and based on an openly editable model. The name "Wikipedia" is a portmanteau of the words wiki (a technology for creating collaborative websites, from the Hawaiian word wiki, meaning "quick") and encyclopedia. Wikipedia's articles provide links designed to guide the user to related pages with additional information and all the articles are written collaboratively by largely anonymous Internet volunteers who write without pay. Anyone with Internet

---

① the U.S. Treasury：美国政府债券是由美国财政部发行的国家债券，但在现代，尤其是近年来的国际金融运作中，常常被用作一种比货币更安全、更方便的支付手段。

② treasury bonds：国债，又称国家公债，是国家以其信用为基础，按照债的一般原则，通过向社会筹集资金所形成的债权债务关系。国债是由国家发行的债券，是中央政府为筹集财政资金而发行的一种政府债券，是中央政府向投资者出具的、承诺在一定时期支付利息和到期偿还本金的债权债务凭证。由于国债的发行主体是国家，所以它具有最高的信用度，被公认为是最安全的投资工具。

③ PPP：公私合作关系（Public-Private-Partnership）也称3P模式，是公共基础设施的一种项目融资模式。是指政府公共部门与民营部门合作过程中，让非公共部门所掌握的资源参与提供公共产品和服务，从而实现政府公共部门的职能并同时也为民营部门带来利益。其管理模式包含与此相符的诸多具体形式。通过这种合作和管理过程，可以在不排除和适当满足私人部门的投资营利目标的同时，为社会更有效率地提供公共产品和服务，使有限的资源发挥更大的作用。狭义的PPP是指政府与私人部门组成特殊目的的机构（SPV），引入社会资本，共同设计开发，共同承担风险，全过程合作，期满后再移交给政府的公共服务开发运营方式。

access can write and make changes to Wikipedia articles, except in limited cases where editing is restricted to prevent disruption or vandalism. Users can contribute anonymously, under a pseudonym, or, if they choose to, with their real identity.

Exercises

I. Choose the one that best completes each of the following statements.

1. The economy of the United States is the world's _____ single national economy.
   A. 2nd   B. 4th   C. 6th   D. largest
2. The U. S. is the world's third-largest producer of _____ and largest producer of _____.
   A. natural gas; oil   B. oil; natural gas
   C. oil; coal   D. natural gas; coal
3. The American colonies went from marginally successful colonial economies to a small, independent farming economy, which in _____ became the United States of America.
   A. 1861   B. 1741   C. 1776   D. 1882
4. In 1932, in the depth of the depression, the American people chose _____ as their next president who promised a "New Deal" to get America out of depression.
   A. Theodore   B. Franklin D. Roosevelt
   C. Woodrow Wilson   D. Herbert Hoover
5. _____ is famous for many stores and shops.
   A. Wall Street B. Broadway   C. Fifth Avenue   D. New York
6. The United States produces as much as half of the world's _____.
   A. wheat and rice B. cotton   C. tobacco   D. soybeans and corn
7. The "Baby Boom" in the period from 1942 to 1957 was caused by several reasons EXCEPT _____.
   A. delayed marriages and childbearing during depression years
   B. a demand for suburban single-family homes
   C. a surge in prosperity
   D. high technology
8. In the 1970s and 1980s, it was popular in the U. S. to believe that _____ economy would surpass that of the United States, but this did not happen.
   A. Canada's   B. UK's   C. Japan's   D. China's
9. Since the _____, several emerging countries have begun to close the economic gap with the United States.
   A. 1970s   B. 1980s   C. 1960s   D. 1950s
10. The North American Free Trade Agreement, or NAFTA, created the largest trade bloc in the world in _____.

A. 1994   B. 1995   C. 2001   D. 2003
11. The United States has been the world's largest national economy _____.
    A. before World War I   B. since World War I
    C. before World War II   D. since World War II
12. Recession in 1973 was mainly caused by _____.
    A. oil crisis   B. increasing trade deficit
    C. declining gold reserve   D. labor shortage
13. The United States completed technical transformation of traditional industries in _____.
    A. 1960s   B. 1970s   C. 1980s   D. 1990s
14. The United States economy experienced a crisis in 2008 led by several reasons EXCEPT _____.
    A. a derivatives market   B. subprime mortgage crisis
    C. a declining dollar value D. oil crisis
15. The United States has a vast land and rich mineral resources. Approximately _____ of its land can be farming.
    A. 90%   B. 80%   C. 70%   D. 60%

II. Read the following statements carefully and decide whether they are TRUE or FALSE.

1. The U. S. A. is the world's biggest producer and user of tobacco.
2. Omaha is known as the agricultural capital of the U. S. A.
3. The United States is the world's leading exporter of industrial products.
4. The South is the headquarters of a large segment of the rocket and missile industry.
5. The economic problem caused by the depression in 1929 was eventually solved by Roosevelt's New Deal.
6. The US has abundant natural resources, a well-developed infrastructure, and high productivity.
7. The New York Stock Exchange is by far the world's second stock exchange by market capitalization.
8. The economic history of the United States has its roots in European settlements in the 16th, 17th, and 18th centuries.
9. The Panic of 1837 was followed by a three-year depression, with the failure of banks and then-record-high unemployment levels.
10. In other cases, some countries have gradually learned to produce the same products and services that previously only the U. S. and a few other countries could produce.

III. Give brief answers to the following questions.

1. What were the contents of Roosevelt's New Deal? Why is it so important in

American history?
2. What does "Baby Boom" refer to?

Section Two: In-depth Reading

The world's super power, the United States cannot stay away from the recent financial crisis. But how does it recover from the crisis? What influence has it brought to the life of Americans? All these are questions worth discussing. If you want to learn more, you may find some answers from the following articles.

Reading One discusses whether there will be a spring of US economy.

Reading Two is about some measures to deal with the crisis.

Before reading the articles, brainstorm with your cohorts on the following questions:

1. How much do you know about the recent financial crisis?
2. What is the influence of the crisis on China's economy?
3. How has it affected our life?

Reading One

Just like the harsh weather in early 2014, the overall picture of US economy is not very good, either. Now, it seems everybody in America is waiting for a spring of economy. However, if waiting is the hardest part, investors are not going to have an easy time. The News Report below tells us more about it.

U. S. Economy Not Springing Ahead—Just Yet Investors Antsy for Signs of Faster Growth, but Evidence Still Unclear
Jeffry Bartash

A flurry of new reports ranging from new home sales to business investment to consumer spending are on the docket and the portrait they'll draw is the same one Wall Street has been staring at for a while: slower growth in early 2014 owing to harsh weather. What investors are itching to see is if the economy began to bounce back in March, but they'll have to cool their heels until the monthly employment report that will be unveiled in the first week of April.

"None of the reports is going to alter the overall picture of the economy," said Scott Brown, chief economist of Raymond James.

That's not to say these reports won't offer any hints. A drumbeat of surprisingly negative numbers, for instance, could inject more uncertainty into financial markets by suggesting the economy has slowed for reasons unrelated to the weather. Or a

US economy may be "tired".
From: http://forex.jrj.com.cn/2011/04/2211309803098.shtml

cascade of upbeat results would nourish the prevailing perception that the economy is about to grow like a lawn laced with an extra springtime feeding.

What Goes Up...

Sales of new homes are supposed to keep rising in 2014 to help support a stronger economic recovery, but there are obstacles standing in the way.

One is rising home prices: two indexes released on Tuesday, Case-Shiller and FHFA, are expected once again to show big increases in the cost of buying a home compared to a year earlier. The other problem is higher mortgage rates that have pushed some prospective buyers to the sidelines.

Despite those obstacles, sales actually surged in January to a five-and-a-half year high, but the monthly numbers are jumpy and prone to big swings. Economists predict new home sales will fall sharply in February, based on a roughly 10% drop in mortgage applications last month.

Orders for durable goods, according to a report that offers a good window on business investment, has also been erratic lately. Order has dropped two straight months and could dip again in February.

Bad weather gets some blame as does weaker demand for expensive commercial jets. Fitting a typical pattern, Boeing has taken fewer orders in early 2014 after a big surge in the waning months of 2013. That's what often happens at the end of one year and the start of the next.

More worrisome, business investment excluding the military and commercial aircraft has declined in three of the past five months. Another drop in that closely followed category would raise a red flag since other indicators imply a small though hardly robust acceleration in demand.

"All in all, manufacturing remains tepid," economists at IHS Global Insight wrote in a report.

Health Care Boosts GDP?

On Thursday, the government is likely to raise its estimate of how fast the U. S. grew in the fourth quarter, but the report will shed little light on the current health of the economy. The source of the expected upward revision to gross domestic product was a big spike in spending on health-care services.

Whether that's actually a good thing for the economy or a quirk somehow related in part to Obamacare is unclear. The law that revamps the U. S. health-care industry took effect in January and there have been anecdotes of higher spending related to its implementation.

Jobless claims, also due Thursday, might draw more attention than GDP because it's more current. The number of people applying for new unemployment benefits has been trending lower lately and that's usually — but not always — a sign of an improving labor market.

Yet consumer spending, normally one of the biggest reports each month, might not offer any tantalizing clues on how Americans are doing. Wall Street expects a modest 0.2% in consumer spending — the fulcrum of U. S. economic growth — and a similar gain in worker incomes.

Purchases at auto dealerships perked up in February, but people probably drove less and energy bills may have fallen after a January spike to keep consumer spending on the milder side.

References

http://www. marketwatch. com/story/us-economy-not-springing-ahead-just-yet-2014-03-23

MarketWatch runs a financial information website that provides business news, analysis, and stock market data. It offers personal finance news and advice, tools for investors and access to industry research. Along with its flagship website, the company runs BigCharts. com and the stock market simulation site VirtualStock-Exchange. com.

About the Author

Jeffry Bartash is a reporter for MarketWatch in Washington.

Discussions

1. What obstacles may prevent the sales of new homes from rising in 2014?
2. Which one, home price or health care, do you think is more crucial to economy

growth in America?

Reading Two

The US financial crisis beginning in 2006 was very impressive and also influential to the world economy. But how did it begin? How did the United States react? Yes, Americans and the government have taken measures trying to boost the economy. However, some policies can avert disaster only if they interrupt the cascading threats to the U. S. economy. So how to fix the US financial crisis? Here are some ideas from Jeffrey D. Sachs.

How to Fix the U. S. Financial Crisis
Jeffrey D. Sachs

The origin of the U. S. financial crisis is that commercial banks and investment banks lent vast sums—trillions of dollars—for housing purchases and consumer loans to borrowers ill-equipped to repay. The easy lending pushed up housing prices around the U. S. , which then ratcheted still higher when speculators bought houses on the expectation of yet further price increases. When the easy lending slowed and then stopped during 2006—2007, the housing prices peaked and began to fall. The housing boom began to unravel and now threatens an economy-wide bust.

US will survive the financial crisis?
From: http://finance.ifeng.com/a/20140514/12331408_ 0. shtml

The U. S. economy faces four cascading threats: First, the sharp decline in consumer spending on houses, autos and other durables, following the sharp decline in lending to households, will cause a recession as construction of new houses and production of consumer durables nosedive. Second, many homeowners will default on their mortgage payments and consumer loans, especially as house values fall below the mortgage values. Third, the banking sector will cut back sharply on its lending in line with the fall in its capital following the write-off of bad mortgage and consumer loans. Those capital losses will push still more financial institutions into bankruptcy or forced mergers with stronger banks. Fourth, the retrenchment of lending now threatens even the shortest-term loans, which banks and other institutions lend to each other for working capital. Interbank loans and other commercial paper are extremely hard to place.

The gravest risks to the economy come back to front. The fourth threat is by far the worst. If the short-term commercial paper and money markets were to break down, the economy could go into a severe collapse because solvent and profitable businesses would be unable to attract working capital. Unemployment, now at 6 percent of the labor force, could soar to more than 10 percent. That kind of liquidity collapse was the basic reason why Asian national incomes declined by around 10 percent between 1997 and 1998, and why the U. S. economy fell by around 25 percent during the Great Depression.

The third threat, the serious impairment of bank capital as banks write off their bad loans, could cause a severe recession, but not a depression. Unemployment might rise, for example, up to 10 percent, which would create enormous social hardships. The ongoing fall in bank capital as the housing boom turns to bust is already forcing banks to cut back their outstanding loans significantly, because they must keep the lending in proportion to their now-shrunken capital base. Major investment projects, such as acquisition of new buildings and major machinery, are being scaled back. Some major nonfinancial companies will likely go bankrupt as well.

The second threat, the financial distress of homeowners, will certainly be painful for millions of households, especially the ones that borrowed heavily in recent years. Many will lose their homes; some will be pushed into bankruptcy. Some may see their credit terms eased in renegotiations with their banks. Consumers as a group will start to become net savers again after years of heavy net borrowing. That trend will not be bad in the long term but will be painful in the short run.

The first threat, the cutback in sales of housing and other consumer durables, is the Humpty-Dumpty of the economy that cannot be put back together. The inventory of unsold homes is now large; housing demand and new construction will be low for many years. Consumer spending on appliances and autos is also plummeting. All these consequences are largely unavoidable and will force the U. S. into at least a modest recession, with unemployment likely to rise temporarily to perhaps 8 percent.

The goal of any new policy cannot be to prevent a recession. It's too late to stop such a downturn. The goal cannot be to save every bank. The U.S. economy has built up too many imbalances—consumer debt, overextended construction, impaired capital of banks—to avoid an economic downturn and a major retrenchment of the banking sector. The goal must be to avoid an outright collapse or deep recession. Two actions are therefore critical, and two more are subsidiary but still important.

Most important, the government and Federal Reserve Board must prevent the collapse of working capital by supplying short-term loans and taking other measures to sustain the commercial paper market, interbank lending and the smooth functioning of money market funds. They have the instruments to do so, and should use them aggressively. The government should also aggressively promote a recapitalization of the banking system so that bank lending is not squeezed for years to come. It can directly inject some public capital into banks, and can both pressure and entice the banks to raise additional private capital. Unfortunately, the $700-billion bailout nearing approval in Congress does not focus adequately on those liquidity or recapitalization challenges. The legislation is better than nothing (to help forestall panic) but the real work of stabilizing and recapitalizing the banking system will now await the next administration, and the Federal Reserve will need to stay aggressive in preventing a liquidity collapse."

Two additional steps will be useful. The first will be to ease the repayment terms on existing mortgage holders, to reduce the flood of defaults and foreclosures that will otherwise occur. The second is to encourage expansionary monetary and fiscal policies abroad (most notably in cash-rich Asia), so that the decline in U.S. consumer spending is smoothly offset by a rise in spending in other countries. This overseas expansion would allow the U.S. to offset the fall in housing construction by a rise in exports, and would allow other countries to offset the fall in their exports to the U.S. by a rise in their internal demand. All these steps will have to await the next administration.

References

http://www.scientificamerican.com/article/fixing-financial-crisis

Scientific American (informally abbreviated SciAm) is an American popular science magazine. It has a long history of presenting scientific information on a monthly basis to the general educated public, with careful attention to the clarity of its text and the quality of its specially commissioned color graphics. Many famous scientists, including Albert Einstein, have contributed articles in the past 168 years. It is the oldest continuously published monthly magazine in the United States.

About the Author

Jeffrey David Sachs (/'sæks/; born November 5, 1954) is an American economist and Director of the Earth Institute at Columbia University. One of the youngest tenured economics professors in the history of Harvard University (at age 28), Sachs became known for his role as an advisor to Eastern European and developing country governments during the transition from communism to a market system or during periods of economic crisis. Subsequently he has been known for his work on the challenges of economic development, environmental sustainability, poverty alleviation, debt cancellation, and globalization.

Discussions
1. What threats may the U.S. economy face and what is its impact on the U.S. economy?
2. What measures should the U.S. government take to avoid or prevent the threats?
3. Do you think the economy in China is facing some similar threats? What measures can the Chinese government learn from the U.S. government to avoid or prevent the threats?

Chapter 13

Education

Section One: A Brief Introduction

All societies must wrestle with fundamental questions about the nature and purpose of their educational system, but the United States was the first nation to face these questions as a democracy. From a broad perspective, the American educational system can be characterized by its large size, organizational structure, marked decentralization, and increasing diversity.

Early on, Americans understood that their future as a free people rested upon their own wisdom and judgment, and not that of some distant ruler. For this reason, the quality, character, and costs of education have remained among the country's central preoccupations since its founding.

Educational institutions of all types and sizes, from **nursery schools**① to advanced research institutions, populate the American landscape. Public schools have been described as the nation's most familiar government institutions. Whether communities are poor or affluent, urban or rural, public schools are a **common denominator**② throughout the United States.

From their origins two centuries ago through today, America's public and private schools have served to define the American identity. Every national experience shaping the American character has been **played out**③ in its classrooms: race and treatment of minorities, immigration and growth of cities, westward expansion and economic growth, individual freedom and the nature of community.

Fundamental questions about the purpose and methods of education have resonated in public debates in the United States from the "common school" movement

---

① nursery school: 幼儿园,保育学校。
② common denominator: 公分母;共同点。
③ play out: 扮演(角色)。

of the early 19th century to debates over academic standards and testing today.

Should schools emphasize basic skills — reading, writing, and mathematics — or provide a broad education in the **liberal arts**① and sciences? How can schools provide equal access to all yet maintain high academic standards? Who should pay for schools — parents or the public? Should schools focus on practical, job-oriented skills, or give all children the academic courses necessary to succeed in college? How should teachers impart moral and spiritual values to the children of different cultural, ethnic, and religious backgrounds? What criteria should be used for selecting secondary school students for admission to prestigious colleges and universities?

The answers to these questions are not easy, and, in fact, schools in the United States have answered them in very different ways at different times in the nation's history. Today, as in the past, education remains a topic of vigorous debate, rapid change, and enduring values.

For someone from another country, the U. S. educational system understandably appears large and varied, even chaotic. Within this complexity, however, American education reflects the history, culture, and values of the changing country itself.

1. Size, Structure and K-12 of U. S. Education

Schools in the United States — public and private, elementary and secondary, state universities and private colleges — can be found everywhere, and the United States continues to operate one of the largest **universal education**② systems in the world. By the mid-20th century, the ideal of universal education from kindergarten through high school had become a reality for substantial numbers of Americans. But certainly not for all, especially the nation's racial minorities. More than 75 million children and adults were enrolled in U. S. schools and colleges in the 2005—2006 academic year, according to the National Center for Education Statistics. Another 6.8 million were employed as teachers, teaching kindergarten through college.

In addition, more than a million preschool children from low-income families, usually ages three and four, attend **Head Start programs**③ designed to provide learning, social development, and nutrition programs to ensure that these preschoolers will be ready for school at age five or six.

Public school enrollments grew exponentially during the post-World War II "Baby Boom" generation (usually defined as those born from 1946 to 1964). After a drop-off in the 1980s, enrollments have rebounded strongly, largely as a result of growing Hispanic populations, according to the latest U. S. Census Bureau reports.

---

① liberal arts (humanities): 人文科学、博雅学科。
② universal education: 普及教育, 全民教育。
③ Head Start Program: 启智计划; 美国启蒙教育方案。

A teacher and her students in an elementary school classroom
From: http://en.wikipedia.org/wiki/File:School-education-learning-1750587-h.jpg

The U. S. educational system today comprises almost 96,000 public elementary and secondary schools, plus more than 4,200 institutions of higher learning, ranging from small, two-year community colleges to massive state universities with undergraduate and graduate programs in excess of 30,000 students. The nation's total expenditures for education stand at approximately $878 billion a year.

School attendance is compulsory for students through age 16 in most states. Children generally begin elementary school with kindergarten (K) at age five and continue through secondary school (grade 12) to age 18. Typically, the elementary school years include kindergarten through grades five or six, and at some schools through grade eight. Secondary schools — known as high schools in the United States — generally include grades nine through 12.

Fifty years ago, elementary school students typically moved immediately to high school, or they attended **junior high school**① for grades seven and eight or grades seven, eight, and nine. During the past 30 years, however, junior high schools have been largely replaced with middle schools configured for grades six through eight, or roughly for the same grades as junior high. Estimates are that 20 million young people, ages 10 to 15, attend middle schools today.

As Minnesota principal Mark Ziebarth described the difference between the two approaches, "A junior high school program is designed to mirror a traditional high school program for students at a younger age. It has a similar schedule to the high school and classes are arranged by departments. Middle schools are designed to provide a forum to meet the special needs of adolescents."

Team teaching and flexible block scheduling, rather than set 45-or 50-minute

---

① junior high school: A school for students from 7th through 9th or 10th grade.

classes, are characteristic of middle schools. These schools also place emphasis on small groups, on an **interdisciplinary**① approach to subject matter, and on special projects that can engage 10-to 15-year-olds, who, says the National Middle School Association, "are undergoing the most rapid intellectual and developmental changes of their lives."

A high-school senior (twelfth grade) classroom in Calhan, Colorado
From: http://en.wikipedia.org/wiki/File: Calhan_ High_ School_ Senior_ Classroom_ by_ David_ Shankbone.jpg

The large contemporary high school, offering a broad menu of academic and **elective**② courses for students age 14 to 18, became a fixture in American education by the mid-20th century. High school students also can choose from a host of clubs, activities, athletics, work-study arrangements, and other extracurricular activities. Based on grades and tests, students can take advanced academic courses or more general or vocational classwork.

Through most of the 20th century, high schools were consolidated into larger units to offer wider class choices to more and more students. The rural country school almost disappeared, replaced by countywide high schools. In cities, it was not uncommon for large school campuses to hold as many as 5,000 students with both college-oriented and **vocational**③ courses that could appeal to just about everyone.

More recently, concerns over the caliber of education in such large schools has led to a call for the establishment of smaller schools with lower student-teacher ratios. The contemporary American high school has long loomed large in the public culture. The popular musical Grease, the television series Happy Days, and movies like

---

① interdisciplinary: 跨学科的；多元学科的。
② elective: 选修课。
③ vocational: 职业的、专科的。

Blackboard Jungle depicted the light and dark sides of schools in the 1950s. Recent popular entertainments with high school settings range from films like Mean Girls, Juno, Election, and High School Musical to such hit TV shows as Beverly Hills 90210 and Saved by the Bell.

2. Decentralization and Diversity

Unlike most other nations, the United States does not operate a national education system—with only a few exceptions, notably the nation's military academies and Native American schools. Neither does the federal government approve nor administer a **national curriculum**①.

Public education constitutes the single largest expenditure or almost every U. S. city and county, which receive the bulk of their funding from local property taxes. Local boards of education, most of which are elected, administer the nation's nearly 15,500 school districts, ranging from small rural schools in states like Kansas and Nebraska to the New York City system, which educates more than a million children annually.

State boards of education, along with a **state superintendent**② or commissioner, oversee local education districts, set student and teacher standards, approve the classroom curriculum, and often review textbook selections. The state's chief power, however, is increasingly financial: Most states now provide substantial aid to schools to supplement local tax revenues.

President George W. Bush signing the *No Child Left Behind Act*
From: http://en.wikipedia.org/wiki/File:No_ Child_ Left_ Behind_ Act.jpg

---

① national curriculum: 全国统一的教学大纲。
② state superintendent: 美国各州教育部门的负责人,类似于中国各省教育厅的厅长。

One consequence of local control and financing of public schools has been disparities between affluent and poor school districts. In recent years, under pressure from state courts and public advocacy groups, many states have taken steps to ensure more equitable funding of school districts regardless of income levels.

The federal government provides research and support to ensure equal access and excellence in education, along with funding student loan programs and assistance to lower-income students. Nevertheless, responsibility for education remains primarily a state and local enterprise. According to the U. S. Department of Education, about 90 percent of the annual expenditures for education at all levels comes from state, local, and private sources.

In the early 20th century, children of immigrant families — most from southern and eastern Europe — flooded public school systems in the Northeast and Midwest. Today new immigrants continue to change the ethnic composition of student populations, although the largest numbers now come from Latin America and Asia.

African Americans constitute about 17 percent of the K-12 student population; Hispanics, however, are becoming the largest single minority group in public schools. It is not uncommon to find schools, especially along the East and West Coasts, where more than a dozen different languages, from Arabic to Vietnamese, are spoken at home by students of foreign-born parents. As a result, the teaching of English as a second language remains one of education's most important responsibilities.

Despite their decentralization and diversity, public schools remain remarkably cohesive in the ways they are run. A student transferring from a school in California to one in Pennsylvania or Georgia will find differences no doubt, but the mix of academic subjects will be largely familiar, despite the fact that the federal government does not mandate a national curriculum.

3. Changing Face of Higher Education in the U. S.

Students can receive higher education from more than 4,000 very different institutions. They can attend two-year community colleges or more specialized technical training institutes. Traditional four-year institutions range from small liberal arts colleges to massive state universities in places like California, Arizona, Ohio, and New York, each with multiple campuses and student populations exceeding 30,000.

3.1 Costs and Competition

Higher education in the United States is an enormous enterprise, costing almost $373 billion and consuming nearly 3 percent of the nation's gross domestic product. College costs for students can be high, especially for private institutions, which do

Massachusetts Institute of Technology (MIT) main campus, seen from Vassar Street
From: http://en.wikipedia.org/wiki/File:MIT_2012-07-18.jpg

not receive general subsidies from either state or federal governments. To ensure equal access to education for all, the United States administers an extensive financial aid program for students. Seven out of 10 students receive some form of financial aid, which typically combines grants, loans, and work opportunities to enable full-time students to meet their living costs and tuition.

Colleges and universities also began opening their doors wider to minorities and women. In recent years, more women than men have been attending colleges and universities and earning more bachelor's and master's degrees — a pattern that shows no signs of changing, according to the National Center for Education Statistics.

The proportion of minority students attending college has increased as well — from 1 percent in 1981 to 27 percent in 2005. Much of the change can be attributed to growing numbers of Hispanic and Asian students. African American enrollments rose from 9 percent to 12 percent in the same period.

Recently, several of the nation's wealthiest and most prestigious universities — schools like Harvard, Princeton, Yale, Columbia, and Dartmouth, among others — announced plans to substantially increase their financial aid for low-and middle-income families.

Students compete for openings in the nation's better colleges and universities. At the same time, American institutions of higher learning of all types must broadly compete for the nation's top students and to admit sufficient numbers to maintain their **enrollments**[①].

The most prestigious American universities — public and private — receive hundreds of applications for each opening. At the same time, it is true that most

---

① Enrollment: 此为招生数量。

Harvard Yard, in Cambridge, Massachusetts. It is the oldest part of the Harvard University campus
From: http://en.wikipedia.org/wiki/File:Harvard_ square_ harvard_ yard. JPG

secondary school graduates with good grades and strong scores on college entrance exams receive hundreds of **solicitations**① from institutions of higher learning.

Reflecting the decentralized nature of American education, state governments may license institutions of higher learning, but **accreditation**②, which grants academic standing to the college or university, is accorded by nongovernmental associations, not by states or the federal government.

3.2 Community Colleges

For an American high school graduate with a modest academic record and limited funds, enrolling in a community college may be a better option than attending a four-year college or university. Two-year, associate-degree programs in such growing professional fields as health, business, and computer technology can be found at most of the nation's roughly 1,200 community colleges.

Community colleges are also gateways to four-year undergraduate institutions for students who need to bolster mediocre high school grades with stronger college credits. Taking advantage of low fees and liberal admissions policies, more than 11 million American and an estimated 100,000 international students now attend community colleges.

---

① solicitation：此为邀请，或作录取通知书。
② accreditation：此为针对高校的评估、认定合格等工作。

3.3 Black Colleges and Universities

Most Historically Black Colleges and Universities (HBCUs) were founded at times when either slavery or segregation ruled the South, and higher education for African Americans elsewhere was ignored or marginalized. Although the first college for African Americans — now Cheney University of Pennsylvania — was established in 1837, many of today's most prestigious black schools were established immediately after the Civil War, including Fisk University in Nashville, Tennessee; Howard University in Washington, D. C. ; and Morehouse College in Atlanta, Georgia.

Nineteen public HBCUs were founded with passage of the Second Morrill (Land Grant) Act in 1890 — many in the then firmly segregated South. Today the White House Initiative on HBCUs counts 40 four-year public colleges and universities, 50 four-year private colleges, and 13 two-year community and business schools.

3.4 Foreign Students Study in the U. S.

Foreign students have long been a familiar and vital element of American higher education. In the 2006-2007 academic year, according to the publication Open Doors, almost 583,000 international students were enrolled in many of America's 4,000 colleges and universities, an increase of 3 percent over the previous year. India remains the largest single source of foreign students, followed by China, Korea, and Japan.

The top five areas of study for international students are business and management, engineering, physical and life sciences, social sciences, and mathematics and computer science. International students attend U. S. colleges and institutions for the same reasons that Americans do: academic excellence, unparalleled choices in types of institutions and academic programs, and great flexibility in designing courses of study and even in transferring between different institutions.

With a wide range of tuition and living costs, plus opportunities for financial aid, foreign students find that a U. S. education can be affordable as well. Most large schools have international student advisers, and a worldwide network of student-advising centers, along with a variety of publications, can guide prospective students through the sometimes complicated process of finding, applying, and being accepted by an American college or university.

References

http://www.america.gov/publications/books/learner_ english.html

U. S. A. Education in Brief. Bureau of International Information Programs, U. S. Department of State.

Exercises

I. Choose the one that best completes each of the following statements.

1. In the United States community colleges offer _____.
   A. two-year programmes
   B. four-year programmes
   C. postgraduate studies
   D. B. A. or B. S. degrees
2. Which one of the following Ivy League Schools is situated in Connecticut?
   A. Yale University.
   B. Harvard.
   C. Princeton.
   D. Columbia.
3. The expenditure in American public schools is guided or decided by _____.
   A. Teachers
   B. students
   C. headmaster
   D. boards of education
4. The world-famous Harvard University is in _____.
   A. Massachusetts
   B. New York
   C. Washington D. C.
   D. Maine
5. Which of the following statements about American education is wrong?
   A. Elementary and secondary education in America is free and compulsory.
   B. Private schools are financially supported by religious or nonreligious private organizations or individuals.
   C. There are more public colleges and universities than the private ones.
   D. Credits taken at community colleges are normally applicable to requirement for a four-year bachelor's degree.
6. All the following universities are located in New England EXCEPT _____.
   A. Yale   B. Harvard   C. MIT   D. Berkeley

II. Give brief answers to the following questions.

1. What do you think of the size of U. S. education when compared to that of China?
2. Why junior high schools are replaced by middle schools in the U. S. ? What are the latter's advantages?
3. What were U. S. high schools in the 20th century like? What are the most recent trends for such schools?

Section Two: In-depth Reading

The education system of the United States is perhaps the most innovative and reputable in the world, but what are the key elements and problems that surround such a prestigious system? What about the important features in different education levels? Here we can find out more about the essence of the American education.

Reading One is on the challenges facing American higher education.

Reading Two is a survey about education from American teachers' perspectives.

Before reading the articles, brainstorm with your cohorts on the following questions:

1. Reflect and conduct a piece of research on the characteristics of education in China.

2. How much do you know about the American colleges and their advantages?

Reading One

On the face of it, American higher education is still in rude health. In worldwide rankings more than half of the top 100 universities, and eight of the top ten, are American. The scientific output of American institutions is unparalleled. They produce most of the world's Nobel laureates and scientific papers. But why is there growing anxiety in America about higher education?

Higher Education: Not What It Used to Be
American Universities Represent Declining Value for
Money to Their Students
The Economist

In the U.S., college graduates, on average, still earn far more and receive better benefits than those who do not have a degree. A degree has always been considered the key to a good job. But rising fees and increasing student debt, combined with shrinking financial and educational returns, are undermining at least the perception that university is a good investment.

Concern springs from a number of things: steep rises in fees, increases in the levels of debt of both students and universities, and the declining quality of graduates. Start with the fees. The cost of university per student has risen by almost five times the rate of inflation since 1983 (see chart 1), making it less affordable and increasing the amount of debt a student must take on. Between 2001 and 2010 the cost of a university education soared from 23% of median annual earnings to 38%; in consequence, debt per student has doubled in the past 15 years. Two-thirds of graduates now take out loans. Those who earned bachelor's degrees in 2011 graduated with an average of $26,000 in debt, according to the Project on Student Debt, a non-profit group.

More debt means more risk, and graduation is far from certain; the chances of an American student completing a four-year degree within six years stand at only around 57%. This is poor by international standards: Australia and Britain, for instance, both do much better.

At the same time, universities have been spending beyond their means. Many

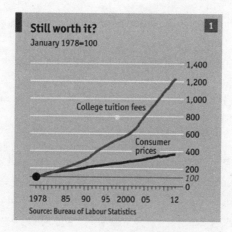

Chart 1

have taken on too much debt and have seen a decline in the health of their balance-sheets. Moreover, the securitisation of student loans led to a rush of unwise private lending. This, at least, has now been curbed by regulation. In 2008 private lenders disbursed $20 billion; last year they shelled out only $6 billion.

Despite so many fat years, universities have done little until recently to improve the courses they offer. University spending is driven by the need to compete in university league tables that tend to rank almost everything about a university except the (hard-to-measure) quality of the graduates it produces. Roger Geiger of Pennsylvania State University and Donald Heller of Michigan State University say that since 1990, in both public and private colleges, expenditures on instruction have risen more slowly than in any other category of spending, even as student numbers have risen. Universities are, however, spending plenty more on administration and support services (see chart 2).

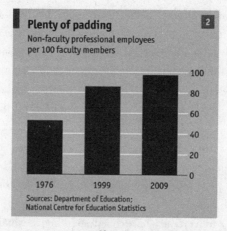

Chart 2

Universities cannot look to government to come to the rescue. States have already cut back dramatically on the amount of financial aid they give universities. Barack Obama has made it clear that he is unhappy about rising tuition fees, and threatens universities with aid cuts if they rise any further. Roger Brinner from the Parthenon Group, a consultancy, predicts that enrolment rates will stay flat for the next five to seven years even as the economy picks up. The party may be well and truly over.

Balloon debate

In 1962 one cent of every dollar spent in America went on higher education; today this figure has tripled. Yet despite spending a greater proportion of its GDP on universities than any other country, America has only the 15th-largest proportion of young people with a university education. Wherever the money is coming from, and however it is being spent, the root of the crisis in higher education (and the evidence that investment in universities may amount to a bubble) comes down to the fact that additional value has not been created to match this extra spending. Indeed, evidence from declines in the quality of students and graduates suggests that a degree may now mean less than it once did.

For example, a federal survey showed that the literacy of college-educated citizens declined between 1992 and 2003. Only a quarter were deemed proficient, defined as "using printed and written information to function in society, to achieve one's goals and to develop one's knowledge and potential". Almost a third of students these days do not take any courses that involve more than 40 pages of reading over an entire term. Moreover, students are spending measurably less time studying and more on recreation. "Workload management", however, is studied with enthusiasm—students share online tips about "blow off" classes (those which can be avoided with no damage to grades) and which teachers are the easiest-going.

Yet neither the lack of investment in teaching nor the deficit of attention appears to have had a negative impact on grades. A remarkable 43% of all grades at four-year universities are As, an increase of 28 percentage points since 1960. Grade point averages rose from about 2.52 in the 1950s to 3.11 in 2006.

At this point a sceptic could argue that none of this matters much, since students are paid a handsome premium for their degree and on the whole earn back their investment over a lifetime. While this is still broadly true, there are a number of important caveats. One is that it is easily possible to overspend on one's education: just ask the hundreds of thousands of law graduates who have not found work as lawyers. And this premium is of little comfort to the 9.1% of borrowers who in 2011 had defaulted on their federal student loans within two years of graduating. There are 200 colleges and universities where the three-year default rate is 30% or more.

Another issue is that the salary gap between those with only a high-school diploma and those with a university degree is created by the plummeting value of the diploma, rather than by soaring graduate salaries. After adjusting for inflation, graduates earned no more in 2007 than they did in 1979. Young graduates facing a decline in earnings over the past decade (16% for women, 19% for men), and a lot more debt, are unlikely to feel particularly cheered by the argument that, over a lifetime, they would be even worse off without a degree than with one.

Moreover, the promise that an expensive degree at a traditional university will pay off rests on some questionable assumptions; for example, that no cheaper way of attaining this educational premium will emerge. Yet there is a tornado of change in education that might challenge this, either through technology or through attempts to improve the two-year community college degree and render it more economically valuable. Another assumption, which is proved wrong in the case of 40% of students, is that they will graduate at all. Indeed, nearly 30% of college students who took out loans eventually dropped out (up from 25% a decade ago). These students are saddled with a debt they have no realistic means of paying off.

Some argue that universities are clinging to a medieval concept of education in an age of mass enrolment. In a recent book, "Reinventing Higher Education", Ben Wildavsky and his colleagues at the Kauffman Foundation, which focuses on entrepreneurship, add that there has been a failure to innovate. Declining productivity and stiff economic headwinds mean that change is coming in a trickle of online learning inside universities, and a rush of "massive open online courses" (MOOCs) outside them. Some universities see online learning as a way of continuing to grow while facing harsh budget cuts. The University of California borrowed $6.9m to do this in the midst of a budget crisis. In 2011 about 6m American students took at least one online course in the autumn term. Around 30% of all college students are learning online—up from less than 10% in 2002.

Digital dilemmas

To see how efficient higher education can be, look at the new online Western Governors University (WGU). Tuition costs less than $6,000 a year, compared with around $54,000 at Harvard. Students can study and take their exams when they want, not when the sabbaticals, holidays and scheduling of teaching staff allow. The average time to completion is just two-and-a-half years.

MOOCs have also now arrived with great fanfare. These offer free college-level classes taught by renowned lecturers to all-comers. Two companies, Coursera and Udacity, and one non-profit enterprise, edX, are leading the charge. At some point these outfits will need to generate some revenue, probably through certification.

The broader significance of MOOCs is that they are part of a trend towards the unbundling of higher education. This will shake many institutions whose business model is based on a set fee for a four-year campus-based degree course. As online education spreads, universities will come under pressure to move to something more like a "buffet" arrangement, under which they will accept credits from each other—and from students who take courses at home or even at high school, spending much less time on campus. StraighterLine, a start-up based in Baltimore, is already selling courses that gain students credits for a few hundred dollars.

Some signs suggest that universities are facing up to their inefficiencies. Indiana University has just announced innovations aimed at lowering the cost and reducing the time it takes to earn a degree. More of this is needed. Universities owe it to the students who have racked up $1 trillion in debt, and to the graduate students who are taking second degrees because their first one was so worthless. They also bear some responsibility for the 17m who are overqualified for their jobs, and for the 3m unfilled positions for which skilled workers cannot be found. They even owe it to the 37m who went to college, dropped out and ended up with nothing: many left for economic reasons.

Universities may counter that the value of a degree cannot be reduced to a simple economic number. That, though, sounds increasingly cynical, when the main reason universities have been able to increase their revenue so much is because of loans given to students on the basis of what they are told they will one day earn.

Correction: Donald Heller is at Michigan State University, not Pennsylvania State University as this article originally suggested. This was corrected on December 17th 2012.

References

http://www.economist.com/news/united-states/21567373-american-universities-represent-declining-value-money-their-students-not-what-it

The Economist is an English-language weekly newspaper owned by The Economist Newspaper Ltd and edited in offices in London, it offers authoritative insight and opinion on international news, politics, business, finance, science and technology. Continuous publication began under founder James Wilson in September 1843.

Discussions

1. What areas do the concerns about American higher education mainly come from?
2. What is the relationship between Universities and the U.S. government in terms of finance?
3. What are the examples that show the declines in the quality of students or a degree?
4. After adjusting for inflation, do students now earn more than their college graduate

fathers in the late 1970s?
5. What is the significance of MOOCs for traditional universities?

Reading Two

Seeking and respecting teacher opinions is a crucial part of shaping education policies. Teaching Ambassador Fellows was a mission to learn from a wide range of stakeholders from across the U. S. A. It is a prime opportunity to probe into American education from the educators' perspectives as well as knowing American teachers' concerns and aspirations.

What Teachers Told the U. S. Department of Education
Dan Brown

Over eighty meetings with teachers and school leaders in a two-week cross-country blitz—not bad work for a team of twelve Teaching Ambassador Fellows (TAFs) working for a year with the U. S. Department of Education.

The Department of Education's third annual back-to-school bus tour kicked off at Sequoia High School in Redwood City, California on September 12 and culminates with rally at the Department's plaza on September 21, with nearly a hundred events in between featuring Secretary Arne Duncan and top federal officials. While Secretary Duncan's appearances have naturally soaked up most of the attention—whether he is dancing at a Denver elementary school for "Let's Move" or honoring the Topeka, Kansas site of the Brown vs. Board of Education case—TAFs have been hosting intimate events to ensure that educators' voices are heard.

The Teaching Ambassador Fellowship, now in its fifth year, includes six teachers from across the country on leave from their schools to work full-time for a year with the U. S. Department of Education, and six who remain teaching in their local districts while consulting and conducting outreach part-time with ED. The September bus tour has been a prime opportunity for TAFs to lead important discussions on how to improve student outcomes. As a TAF just six weeks into the fellowship, it was refreshing for me to hear from folks around the country.

The outreach extravaganza started in California as ten current and former Teaching Ambassador Fellows fanned out across the Bay Area to talk with educators. In one memorable event, Seattle-based TAF Kareen Borders hosted a discussion with current and future science teachers at the NASA Ames Research Center. Locales for TAF-led discussions in California included district and charter schools, where teachers weighed in on the Obama Administration's education agenda, the RESPECT Project for transforming the teaching profession, and their own thoughts on how to increase student learning.

Travelling to over 30 communities in 11 states, TAFs convened teachers in Silicon Valley, Las Vegas and across Wyoming through Louisville, St. Louis and Richmond and many rural communities in between. At Salt Lake City Community College in Sandy, Utah, Arizona-based TAF Cheryl Redfield and I recruited local National Board Certified Teachers to facilitate breakout sessions at a 200-person educational technology summit. At Emporia State University in Kansas, TAF Cindy Apalinski from Linden, New Jersey met with teachers-in-training and introduced Secretary Duncan at a town hall attended by approximately 400 future educators.

Seeking and respecting teacher perspectives must be a crucial part of shaping policies that teachers ultimately implement. Over the past two weeks, Teaching Ambassador Fellows have been on a mission to learn from a wide range of stakeholders from across the country. The next step after the bus tour dust settles is to report back to senior staff and Secretary Duncan.

Here is a sampling of what TAFs heard along the way:

On the importance of great teaching:

"Technology won't save education; great teachers with great tools will save education."

"All you need is a teacher and a program to open students' hearts and minds to help them become global citizens."

"Never forget how complex the teaching profession is. Great teachers have to make high stakes decisions almost every minute of their day. Any policy changes that try to teacher-proof the curriculum are bound to fail."

"Middle school STEM is so important because that's when they are trying to figure out who they are."

"We can teach students about heroes, or we can create our own heroes."

On professional development and career paths:

"I love the classroom, but I need opportunities to advance that aren't taking me away from being in the classroom."

"We need to be in an ongoing process of growth, professionally, not just stuck as either a 'new' educator or an 'experienced' one."

"I would love to stay in the classroom, but can I afford to stay in this pay grade forever? No. So, unfortunately, I will have to leave. I need the opportunity to stay."

"We want to better ourselves. Let us. Offer teachers the opportunities to advance, not just by seniority or maxing out by credits."

"Teachers want to be in positions that allow them to learn while they still teach. They want to learn their subject and their craft."

"Merit pay is okay as long as teachers are evaluated on what we value."

"Ideally leaders would move into a leadership role, and eventually return to the classroom. However, returning to the classroom would mean a pay cut, and it's difficult for someone who has 'lived the life' to then go back to their old salary."

"After five years of teaching, I moved into a mentorship role. From there I could really study the profession and study it from an academic standpoint, rather than an emotional one. I really grew from that. We have term limits for mentors to allow more people to do it and to stay in touch with the profession."

"We don't just need mentors at the beginning of our careers-we need them throughout."

"So much that I've learned about good teaching has been by watching great teachers."

On the future of education:

"The achievement gap won't be closed by one person working in isolation; we need to work together... a group of teachers together is a real impetus for change."

"We need to demystify the definition of college and career readiness so that every student can actually attain it."

"In our work, it's not that good things aren't happening; it's that we aren't doing the good things enough."

"Not all education happens in the classroom."

"We can't continue to fund schools the way we do and hope to be successful. There's a possibility of three weeks being cut off our schedule if a sales tax initiative does not pass is November (in California)."

"A huge recruitment issue is respectability—we're just not respected as teachers, so we need to better educate the public."

"If we want to improve our schools we need to get back to basics and build relationships in our schools and communities."

"The idea of a 'full teaching load' needs to change. If you asked me what I would ideally be doing, I would teach a 3/5 load full-time, and spend the extra energy on those classes. Class sizes do matter. To think about doing anything else in addition to our full-time load is impossible."

"It is up to our current and future educators now to lead the country in the direction we need to go."

On teachers' realities:

"To go to these meetings where every trainer and attendee has an iPad, but not one of my students does, that's an issue."

"I see teachers working their hearts out, one kid at a time."

"Data doesn't say what relationships make happen."

"Our country's acceptance of mathematics illiteracy is appalling."

"We have too many things to do, so we can't do any of them well, and especially not with a 32 minute planning period."

"We need leaders who make us feel wanted, valued. We need to know our input is valued... we also need this among ourselves, letting each other know that we're valued and respected."

"Collaboration is about trust."

"Teachers don't operate in a vacuum and kids need lots of other support service to survive. From psychological help, to breakfast programs, to extra support for struggling students, to basic health needs. If that's not available, no matter how good of a teacher you are you are not able to get the best from students."

"At one point my contract said that I taught 20% mentored 80%, but in reality the teaching part actually took 75% of my time and 90% of my emotional space. Serving as a leader and a teacher I asked myself the following question, 'If you're teaching, can you do anything else well at the same time?'"

References

http://www.huffingtonpost.com/dan-brown/what-teachers-told-the-us_b_1903193.html

About the Author

Dan Brown is a National Board Certified Teacher at The SEED Public Charter School of Washington, D. C. For the 2012—2013 school year, he is serving as a Teaching Ambassador Fellow at the U. S. Department of Education. He is the author of *The Great Expectations School: A Rookie Year in the New Blackboard Jungle*. Dan's writing has appeared in *the Boston Globe*, *the New York Daily News*, *the New York Post*, and *Education Week*. Dan Brown did not write *The Da Vinci Code*, and he is okay with that. He can be reached at danbrownteacher@gmail.com.

Discussions

1. During TAF's nationwide surveys, what are their ways to ensure they can hear the teachers' true voices?
2. Who are in the Teacher Ambassador Fellowship and how do they work in this program?
3. There are more than one teacher's opinions about work-load, what can we learn from them?

Chapter 14

Media

Section One: A Brief Introduction

Media of the United States consist of several different types of communications: television, radio, cinema, newspapers, magazines, and Internet-based Web sites. The U. S. also has a strong music industry.

Many of the media are controlled by large for-profit corporations who reap revenue from advertising, **subscriptions**①, and sale of copyrighted material. American media conglomerates tend to be leading global players, generating large revenues as well as large opposition in many parts of the world.

With the **passage**② of the *Telecommunications Act* of 1996, further deregulation and convergence are under way, leading to mega-mergers, further concentration of media ownership, and the emergence of multinational media conglomerates. These mergers enable tighter control of information. Currently, six corporations control roughly 90% of the media. Critics allege that localism, local news and other content at the community level, media spending and coverage of news, and diversity of ownership and views have suffered as a result of these processes of media concentration.

The organisation Reporters Without Borders compiles and publishes an annual ranking of countries based upon the organisation's assessment of their **press freedom**

---

① subscription: A subscription is an amount of money that you pay regularly in order to belong to an organization, to help a charity or campaign, or to receive copies of a magazine or newspaper. 订阅报刊的费用。

② passage: the passing of a law by a legislative body (法律) 通过。

records①. In 2013-14 United States was ranked 46th out of 180 countries, a drop of thirteen points from the preceding year.

1. Radio

American radio broadcasts in two bands: FM and AM. Some stations are only talk radio—featuring interviews and discussions—while music radio stations broadcast one particular type of music: Top 40, hip-hop, country, etc. Radio broadcast companies have become increasingly consolidated in recent years. National Public Radio is the nation's primary public radio network, but most radio stations are commercial and profit-oriented.

Talk radio as a political medium has also exploded in popularity during the 1990s, due to the 1987 repeal of the Fairness Doctrine, which meant that stations no longer had to "balance" their day by programming alternative points of view.

The Federal Communications Commission (FCC) in 1970 had limited the number of radio station one person or company could own to 1 AM and 1 FM locally and 7 AM and 7 FM stations nationally.

A new form of radio that is gaining popularity is satellite radio. The two biggest subscriptions based radio services are Sirius Satellite Radio and XM Satellite Radio, which have recently merged to form Sirius XM Radio. Unlike terrestrial radio music channels are commercial free and other channels feature minimal commercials. Satellite radio also is not regulated by the FCC.

2. Television

Ninety-nine percent of American households have at least one television and the majority of households have more than one. The four major broadcasters in the U.S. are the National Broadcasting Company (NBC), Columbia Broadcasting System (CBS), the American Broadcasting Company (ABC) and Fox.

Public television has a far smaller role than in most other countries. However, a number of states, including West Virginia, Maryland, Kentucky, and South Carolina, among others, do have state-owned public broadcasting authorities which operate and fund all public television stations in their respective states. The income

---

① press freedom records: 又称 press freedom index, 即新闻自由指数或全球新闻自由指数, 是无国界记者组织根据各国新闻自由状况, 每年都编译出版大部分国家的排名情况。这个名单是根据一份问卷调查而来, 该调查对象来自世界各地, 包括100多位无国界记者及其伙伴组织的成员, 还有相关的专家, 比如研究员、法学家以及人权活动家。在问卷调查中, 会涉及针对记者和媒体的直接攻击情况, 以及间接地针对出版自由的各种压力。无国界记者特别指出, 这个指数仅关于新闻自由, 而不衡量新闻工作的质量。这个排名还考虑非政府组织给记者带来的压力, 比如西班牙的巴斯克军事组织埃塔。2012年全球新闻自由度排名第一的是芬兰, 中国排第174位, 位居倒数第六。

received from the government is insufficient to cover expenses and stations also rely on corporate sponsorships and viewer contributions.

DirecTV and Dish Network are the major satellite television providers, with 20 and 14 million customers respectively as of February 2014. Meanwhile, the major cable television providers are Comcast with 22 million customers, Time Warner Cable with 11 million, and Cox Communications, Charter Communications, AT&T U-Verse and Verizon FiOS with 5-6 million each.

3. Motion Pictures

In the 20th century, the motion picture industry rose to become one of the most successful and powerful industries in the U.S. Along with other intellectual property industries, its relative importance to the American economy has strengthened as the importance of manufacturing and agriculture has decreased due to globalization.

The cinema of the United States, often generally referred to as Hollywood, has had a profound effect on cinema across the world since the early 20th century. Its history is sometimes separated into four main periods: the silent film era, classical Hollywood cinema, New Hollywood, and the contemporary period. While the French Lumière Brothers are generally credited with the birth of modern cinema, it is indisputably American cinema that soon became the most dominant force in an emerging industry. Since the 1920s, the American film industry has **grossed**① more money every year than that of any other country.

In 1878, Eadweard Muybridge demonstrated the power of photography to capture motion. In 1894, the world's first commercial motion picture exhibition was given in New York City, using Thomas Edison's **Kinetoscope**②. The United States was in the forefront of sound film development in the following decades. Since the early 20th century, the U.S. film industry has largely been based in and around Hollywood, Los Angeles, California. Picture City, FL was also a planned site for a movie picture production center in the 1920s, but due to the 1928 Okeechobee hurricane, the idea collapsed and Picture City returned to its original name of Hobe Sound. Director D. W. Griffith was central to the development of film grammar. Orson Welles's *Citizen Kane* (1941) is frequently cited in critics' polls as the greatest film of all time.

American screen actors like John Wayne and Marilyn Monroe have become iconic figures, while producer/entrepreneur Walt Disney was a leader in both

---

① gross: earn before taxes, expenses, etc. （在扣除税项、费用等之前的）总收入。

② Kinetoscope: a device invented by Edison that gave an impression of movement as an endless loop of film moved continuously over a light source with a rapid shutter; precursor of the modern motion picture. 活动电影放映机。

animated film and movie **merchandising**①. The major film studios of Hollywood are the primary source of the most commercially successful movies in the world, such as *Gone with the Wind* (1939), *Star Wars* (1977), *Titanic* (1997), and *Avatar* (2009). Today, American film studios collectively generate several hundred movies every year, making the United States the third most **prolific**② producer of films in the world, after Indian cinema and Nigerian cinema

4. Newspapers

Newspapers have declined in their influence and penetration into American households over the years. The U. S. does not have a national paper. *The New York Times* and *The Wall Street Journal* are sold in most U. S. cities.

Although *The Times'* primary audience has always been the people of New York City, *The New York Times* has gradually become the dominant national "newspaper of record." Apart from its daily nationwide distribution, the term means that **back issues**③ are archived on microfilm by every decent-sized public library in the nation, and the Times' articles are often cited by both historians and judges as evidence that a major historical event occurred on a certain date. *The Los Angeles Times* and *The Wall Street Journal* are also newspapers of record to a lesser extent. Although *USA Today* has tried to establish itself as a national paper, it has been widely derided by the academic world as the "McPaper" and is not subscribed to (let alone archived) by most libraries.

Apart from the newspapers just mentioned, all major metropolitan areas have their own local newspapers. Typically, a metropolitan area will support at most one or two major newspapers, with many smaller publications targeted towards particular audiences. Although the cost of publishing has increased over the years, the price of newspapers has generally remained low, forcing newspapers to rely more on advertising revenue and on articles provided by a major **wire service**④, such as the Associated Press or Reuters, for their national and world coverage.

With very few exceptions, all the newspapers in the U. S. are privately owned, either by large chains such as Gannett or McClatchy, which own dozens or even hundreds of newspapers; by small chains that own a handful of papers; or in a

---

① merchandising: it consists of goods such as toys and clothes that are linked with something such as a film, sports team, or pop group. 附带商品。

② prolific: intellectually productive 富于创造力的。

③ back issue: or a back copy, means a magazine or newspaper is that was published some time ago and is not the most recent 过期刊物。

④ wire service: an agency supplying news, etc, to newspapers, radio and television stations, etc. 新闻社、通讯社,为报纸、无线电台和电视台提供新闻等的机构。

situation that is increasingly rare, by individuals or families.

Most general-purpose newspapers are either being printed one time a week, usually on Thursday or Friday, or are printed daily. Weekly newspapers tend to have much smaller **circulation**① and are more prevalent in rural communities or small towns. Major cities often have "alternative weeklies" to complement the mainstream daily paper (s), for example, New York City's *Village Voice* or Los Angeles' *L. A. Weekly*, to name two of the best-known. Major cities may also support a local business journal, trade papers relating to local industries, and papers for local ethnic and social groups.

Probably due to competition from other media, the number of daily newspapers in the U.S. has declined over the past half-century, according to *Editor & Publisher*, the trade journal of American newspapers. In particular, the number of evening newspapers has fallen by almost one-half since 1970, while the number of morning editions and Sunday editions has grown.

For comparison, in 1950, there were 1,772 daily papers (and 1,450—or about 70 percent—of them were evening papers) while in 2000, there were 1,480 daily papers (and 766—or about half—of them were evening papers.)

Daily newspaper circulation is also slowly declining in America, partly due to the near-demise of two-newspaper towns, as the weaker newspapers in most cities have folded:

1960	58.8 million
1970	62.1 million
1980	62.2 million
1990	62.3 million
2000	55.8 million

The primary source of newspaper income is advertising—in the form of "**classifieds**②" or inserted advertising circulars—rather than circulation income. However, since the late 1990s, this revenue source has been directly challenged by Web sites like eBay (for sales of secondhand items), Monster.com (jobs), and Craigslist (everything).

Additionally, as investigative journalism declined at major daily newspapers in the 2000s, many reporters formed their own non-profit investigative newsrooms. Examples include ProPublica on the national level, Texas Tribune at the state level

---

① circulation: The number of copies of a newspaper or magazine that are sold. 发行量。

② classifieds: A short advertisement in a newspaper or magazine (usually in small print) and appearing along with other ads of the same type. 分类广告。

and Voice of OC at the local level.

The largest newspapers (by circulation) in the United States are *USA Today*, *The Wall Street Journal*, *The New York Times* and *The Los Angeles Times*.

5. Magazines

Thanks to the huge size of the English-speaking North American media market, the United States has a large magazine industry with hundreds of magazines serving almost every interest, as can be determined by glancing at any **newsstand**① in any large American city. Most magazines are owned by one of the large media conglomerates or by one of their smaller regional brethren.

The U. S. has three leading weekly newsmagazines: *Time*, *Newsweek* and *U. S. News and World Report*. *Time* and *Newsweek* are center-left while *U. S. News and World Report* tends to be center-right. *Time* is well known for naming a "Person of the Year" each year, while *U. S. News* publishes annual ratings of American colleges and universities.

The U. S. also has over a dozen major political magazines. Finally, besides the hundreds of specialized magazines that serve the diverse interests and hobbies of the American people, there are also dozens of magazines published by professional organizations for their members, such as *Communications of the ACM* (for computer science specialists) and the *ABA Journal* (for lawyers).

6. Internet

The Internet has provided a means for newspapers and other media organizations to deliver news and, significantly, the means to look up old news. Some organizations only make limited amounts of their output available for free, and charge for access to the rest. Other organizations allow their archives to be freely browsed. It is possible that the latter type obtain more influence, as they are true to the spirit of freedom of information by virtue of making it free. Anyone who has followed external links only to be confronted with a pay to view banner, might attest that the reputations of organizations that charge is not enhanced by their charging policy, particularly when the same information is available from sources that don't charge.

The Internet, by means of making available such constantly growing news archives, is, in effect, writing our history as it happens, at a level of detail never before known. While **proprietary archives**② are slowly exposed to the public after

---

① newsstand: A newsstand is a stall in the street or a public place, which sells newspapers and magazines. 报摊；杂志摊。

② proprietary archives: 私人档案。

many decades, organizations that maintain immediately updating resources have more control over what will be remembered by the general public in the near future.

References

  http://en.wikipedia.org/wiki/US_media

  http://en.wikipedia.org/wiki/Cinema_of_the_United_States

Exercises

I. Choose the one that best completes each of the following statements.

1. Which of the following is an American newspaper?
   - A. *The Guardian.*
   - B. *Newsweek.*
   - C. *The International Herald Tribune.*
   - D. *The Daily Telegraph.*
2. Which of the following is the oldest daily newspaper in the U.S.?
   - A. *The New Hampshire Gazette.*
   - B. *The Hartford Courant.*
   - C. *The New York Post.*
   - D. *The Recorder.*
3. Which of the following has the largest weekday circulation in the U.S. as of 2013?
   - A. *The New York Times.*
   - B. *USA Today.*
   - C. *The Washington Post.*
   - D. *The Wall Street Journal.*
4. The American news agency Associated Press was founded in _____, in 1846.
   - A. Washington D.C.
   - B. Boston
   - C. New York
   - D. Chicago
5. Which is the correct name to use to refer to America in a political way?
   - A. The States.
   - B. The United States.
   - C. The U.S.
   - D. The United States of America.
6. The Associated Press was founded in _____.
   - A. 1846
   - B. 1835
   - C. 1851
   - D. 1931
7. Which of the following is a national newspaper in the U.S.?
   - A. *The New York Times.*
   - B. *Daily News.*
   - C. *Los Angeles Times.*
   - D. *The Wall Street Journal.*
8. Which of the following is not a nickname of the Time Square in New York?
   - A. *The* Crossroads of the World.
   - B. *The* Center of the Universe.
   - C. *The* World Hub.
   - D. *The* Great White Way.

II. Give brief answers to the following questions.

1. What are the major newspapers, newsmagazines and broadcasters in the US?
2. What is the most common type of ownership for American media establishments? How do they reap revenue?
3. Do you agree that the circulation of a newspaper or magazine translates well into its impact on the world? Compare the circulations of key periodicals in China and in

the US and discuss.

Section Two: In-depth Reading

Medium is perhaps the most widely and frequently encountered entity in modern daily life, by which we are surrounded and submerged. However, the issues concerning media from its beginning onto the present day remained relatively unchanged, e. g. What are the worthy periodicals that we should read? What are the ways we acquire information? How can we be an active media receiver or even contributor? Let ws find out the answers in the following passages.

Reading One is a chronicle of technological advances and the press.

Reading Two highlights the fundamental qualities of being an active media reader.

Before reading the articles, brainstorm with your cohorts on the following questions:

1. Is censorship necessary for media?
2. What periodicals should we read? How should we read?

Reading One

"Congress shall make no law... abridging the freedom of speech, or of the press." The First Amendment of the U. S. Constitution enshrines a basic U. S. belief: A free press nurtures democracy. Freedom of the press is essential to democracy because it empowers the citizenry and holds governments accountable. But a free press cannot be effective without efficient mechanisms to deliver the news.

Evolving Media and a Free Press
IIP digital / U. S. Department of State

Introduction

From the earliest printing press to modern-day satellite transmissions, advances in technology have enhanced the power of the press by increasing the speed and reach of information distribution.

1769—The Printing Press

The first printing presses are made in America in 1769. By the Revolutionary War, printing presses will be publishing dozens of weekly newspapers and pamphlets such as Thomas Paine's Common Sense,

Picture 1

which encouraged the revolt against the British. In 1776, more than 20 newspapers will publish the full text of the *Declaration of Independence*.

Picture 1: Robert Hartmann operating a reconstructed version of Johann Gutenberg's printing press in the Gutenberg Museum in Mainz, Germany. (© AP Images)

1846—The Telegraph and Wire Services

The AP was formed in 1846 when newspapers created a new service to supply news via telegraph from around the world for distribution to U.S. newspapers. It will become common to run special telegraph lines to major sporting events, so newspapers can receive up-to-the-minute reports.

Picture 2

The journalist's inverted pyramid—with the main points in the first paragraph following by increasing levels of detail—was developed to ensure the basic news was received even if telegraph service was interrupted.

Picture 2: Senator Estes Kefauver of Tennessee and James Langley (left), publisher of the *Monitor-Patriot* in Concord, New Hampshire, viewing election returns on an Associated Press (AP) teletype on March 11, 1952. (© AP Images)

1861—The Photograph

Picture 3: Wearing a Union Army uniform, a former slave serving as mess corporal for Army at federal headquarters in Belle Plain, Virginia. This undated photograph was taken by photographer Matthew Brady, who was among the hundreds of photo-journalists issuing press credentials in 1861 to cover the Civil War. (© AP Images)

Picture 3

Photographs will not begin to appear regularly in newspapers until the 1880s. In the early 1900s, photographs will be joined in the newspapers by other illustrations—political cartoons.

1873—The Typewriter

In 1873, E. Remington & Sons began manufacture of its first typewriters, which for the first time allowed journalists to generate news stories more quickly than they could write the story by hand. During the late 1800s and early 1900s, typewriters and telephones will bring significant changes to the way work is done in the newsroom.

1893—Color in Publishing

Picture 4: The *New York Journal*'s colored comic supplement was published October 15, 1893, marking one of the earliest uses of color in newspaper comics and parts of the Sunday editions. This development lays the groundwork for later innovations in newspaper and magazine layout and use of color in publishing. (Library of Congress)

Picture 4

1920—Radio

During the 1920s, radio and motion picture newsreels begin to compete with newspapers for audience time and attention. However, newspaper circulation remains high, with approximately 2,600 daily papers and nearly 14,000 weekly papers published in the United States.

1933—Linotype Machines

Picture 5: Albert Einstein sitting at the keyboard of a linotype machine in the composing room of the *Jewish Daily Bulletin*, New York, on January 15, 1933. (© AP Images)

Technical innovations like the linotype machine and larger, faster printing presses allow publishers to print more newspapers in less time to meet ever-tighter deadlines and serve an increasing number of readers.

Picture 5

1939—Television

Television did not become widely used in the United States until the 1950s, but in 1937, nearly 9,000 English households watched the televised coronation of King George VI and the French began construction of a powerful television transmitter in the Eiffel Tower. U.S. networks did not add news to their regular programming until 1948.

1954—Network Television News

20 The medium's importance as a news source was growing: President Harry S. Truman made the first nationwide U.S. telecast on September 4, 1951, and Dwight D. Eisenhower, in his 1952 campaign for the U.S. presidency, used television

advertising. In 1954, some 370 television stations are operating in the United States; another 202 are preparing to go on the air.

1956—Reliable Global Communication

News reporters talk to London as the $42 million trans-Atlantic telephone cable opens officially in New York City on September 25, 1956. In its first 24 hours of operation, the cable carries 588 calls between London and the United States and 119 calls between London and Canada. The increasing reliability of worldwide communication allows reporters access to more sources and increases the speed with which reporters can file stories from around the world.

1980—Cable News Network

Picture 6: Mainstream media were skeptical when broadcast entrepreneur Ted Turner launched a cable television network devoted to 24-hour news coverage. The fledgling news operation would grow steadily and eventually trigger the launch of similar operations by established news networks. (© AP Images)

Within a quarter century, CNN will be available in nearly 90 million U.S. households and almost 1 million American hotel rooms. Globally, CNN will become available in some form to more than 1.5 billion people.

Picture 6

1990s—Satellite Communication

Computers and satellite communication systems allow journalists to file stories from virtually anywhere in the world and have those stories quickly transmitted to newspapers, radio stations and television networks to reach a global audience.

21st Century—Mobile Journalism

Picture 7: Mobile phones allow professional media as well as "citizen journalists" to provide instantaneous reports — via voice, text messaging, still photo and video — at fast-breaking events. Mobile phones with broadband Internet access are promising even more powerful communication possibilities.

Picture 7

References

http://iipdigital.usembassy.gov/st/english/gallery/2012/04/201204023130.html?CP.rss = true#axzz2zPLggBOH

About the Author

The Bureau of International Information Programs (IIP) is the State Department's foreign-facing public diplomacy communications bureau. It provides and supports the places, content, and infrastructure needed for sustained conversations with foreign audiences to build America's reputation abroad. IIP is led by Coordinator Macon Phillips.

Discussions

1. What are the central benefits brought by all these technological advances concerning the media?
2. What is the most powerful means of communication for today's world?

Reading Two

Generally speaking, literacy means a person's basic ability to read and write, but in modern eras, being well-versed in dealing with different printed and online media is another kind of basic skill, that is how the term "media literacy" comes into place. What are the key elements of being a media literate person?

Fundamentals of Media Literacy
Dan Gillmor

The fundamental principles of media literacy provide essential guidelines for being an active media consumer in today's participatory media:

- **Be Skeptical of Everything**: Even the best journalists, not to mention our friends and colleagues, occasionally tell us things that are wrong. We cannot assign absolute trust in anything.
- **Exercise Judgment**: Don't be *equally* skeptical of everything. We give much higher credence to an article from a reputable publication such as the *New York Times* than a random comment on a random blog.
- **Open Your Mind**: We all need to go outside our comfort zones in our media consumption. This means reading and listening to people we disagree with. It also means actively seeking out information about unfamiliar peoples and cultures. And it especially means challenging our own beliefs and biases, no matter how closely held. People who don't occasionally alter their opinions based on new facts are people with closed minds.
- **Ask Questions**: The more important a topic is to our own lives, the more important it is to research it widely. One source is never enough. If the topic is

close to home, we can — and should — ask our own questions of people who may have answers. For example, if a local newspaper's coverage of an issue in our neighborhood is incomplete, we can and should query our local contacts to get the missing information and communicate it to our neighbors who may also be interested or affected.
- **Learn Media Techniques**: More and more people own or have access to computers, and millions more are carrying phones and other mobile devices that can take pictures and videos. These are tools of media creation, and we should learn to use them accurately, productively and credibly. Moreover, we need to understand how media are used to persuade and to manipulate in order to be effective and responsible consumers.

The first four principles of media creation are, for the most part, journalistic: thoroughness, accuracy, fairness and independence. In this new era, we need to add another: transparency. Being transparent can take many forms. For example, we should recognize that everyone, and every organization, has a world view. Explaining that view to one's audience — so all content can be considered in context — is a critical service every responsible media producer should provide.

References

http://iipdigital. usembassy. gov/st/english/publication/2011/09/20110913140304yelhsa0. 6657068. html#ixzz2psqkrdfR

About the Author

Dan Gillmor is a professor of digital media entrepreneurship at Arizona State University's Cronkite School of Journalism & Mass Communication. He is author of *Mediactive*, a book that encourages people to become active media users, and has been a co-founder, investor and adviser in a number of media ventures.

Discussions

1. What do you make of the word "literacy"? How do you understand media literacy?
2. What are the five principles for active media consumer as mentioned by the author?

Chapter 15

Literature

Section One: A Brief Introduction

1. The Colonial and Revolutionary Period: 1607—1790

Owing to the large immigration to Boston in the 1630s, the high articulation of Puritan cultural ideals, and the early establishment of a college and a printing press in Cambridge, the New England colonies have often been regarded as the center of early American literature.

Back then, some of the American literature were pamphlets and writings extolling the benefits of the colonies to both a European and colonist audience. Writers of this manner included Daniel Denton, Thomas Ash, William Penn, George Percy, William Strachey, Daniel Coxe, Gabriel Thomas, and John Lawson.

The religious disputes that prompted settlement in America were also topics of early writing. A journal written by John Winthrop, *The History of New England*, discussed the religious foundations of the Massachusetts Bay Colony. Edward Winslow also recorded a diary of the first years after the **Mayflower's**[①] arrival. *A Model of Christian Charity* by John Winthrop, the first governor of Massachusetts, was a Sermon preached on the Arabela in 1630. This work outlined the ideal society he and his followers of separatists were about to build in an attempt to realize the "Puritan utopia". And still others, like Thomas Morton, cared little for the church; Morton's *The New English Canaan* mocked the religious settlers and declared that the Native Americans were actually better people than the British.

Other writings described conflicts and interaction with the Indians, as seen in writings by Daniel Gookin, Alexander Whitaker, John Mason, Benjamin Church,

---

① Mayflower: 1620年9月6日,"五月花"号载有包括成年男女及儿童在内的102名清教徒,由英国普利茅斯出发,在北美建立了第一块殖民地。

and Mary Rowlandson. John Eliot translated the Bible into the Algonquin language.

Jonathan Edwards and George Whitefield represented **the Great Awakening**①, a religious revival in the early 18th century that asserted strict Calvinism. Other Puritan and religious writers include Thomas Hooker, Thomas Shepard, John Wise, and Samuel Willard. Less strict and serious writers included Samuel Sewall (who wrote a diary revealing the daily life of the late 17th century), and Sarah Kemble Knight.

The revolutionary period also contained political writings, including those by colonists Samuel Adams, Josiah Quincy, John Dickinson, and Joseph Galloway, a loyalist to the crown. Two key figures were Benjamin Franklin and Thomas Paine. Franklin's *Poor Richard's Almanac* and *The Autobiography of Benjamin Franklin* are esteemed works with their wit and influence toward the formation of a budding American identity. Thomas Paine's pamphlet *Common Sense* and *The American Crisis* writings are seen as playing a key role in influencing the political tone of the time.

During the 18th century, writing shifted focus from the Puritanical ideals of Winthrop and Bradford to the power of the human mind and rational thought. The belief that human and natural occurrences were messages from God no longer fit with the new human centered world. Many intellectuals believed that the human mind could comprehend the universe through the laws of physics as described by Isaac Newton. The enormous scientific, economic, social, and philosophical, changes of the 18th century, called **the Enlightenment**②, impacted the authority of clergyman and scripture, making way for democratic principles. The increase in population helped account for the greater diversity of opinion in religious and political life as seen in the literature of this time. The growth of communities and therefore social life led people to become more interested in the progress of individuals and their shared experience on the colonies. These new ideals are accounted for in the widespread popularity of Benjamin Franklin's *Autobiography*.

---

① the Great Awakening:"大觉醒"运动为发生于18世纪30—40年代的美国的一场思想启蒙运动,是反对宗教专制、争取信仰自由的思想解放运动。发起者以宗教复兴为旗帜,把矛头对准宗教压迫的精神支柱——官方教会的要义,以"灵魂自由"为口号,鼓吹民主平等、信仰自由、人民主权和反暴政的革命思想。

② the Enlightenment:启蒙运动,指在17、18世纪的一个新思维不断涌现的时代,与理性主义等一起构成一个较长的文化运动时期。启蒙运动覆盖了各个知识领域,如自然科学、哲学、伦理学、政治学、经济学、历史学、文学、教育学等等。启蒙运动同时为美国独立战争与法国大革命提供了框架,并且导致了资本主义和社会主义的兴起。

2. The Romantic Period

2.1 Fiction

In the post-war period, Thomas Jefferson's *Declaration of Independence*, his influence on the United States Constitution, his autobiography, *The Notes on the State of Virginia*, and his many letters solidify his spot as one of the most talented early American writers. The Federalist essays by Alexander Hamilton, James Madison, and John Jay presented a significant historical discussion of American government organization and republican values. Fisher Ames, James Otis, and Patrick Henry are also valued for their political writings and orations.

Much of the early literature of the new nation struggled to find a uniquely American voice in existing literary genre, and this tendency was also reflected in novels. It was in the late 18th and early 19th centuries that the nation's first novels were published. Among the first American novels are Thomas Attwood Digges' *Adventures of Alonso*, published in London in 1775 and William Hill Brown's *The Power of Sympathy* published in 1791.

The first author to be able to support himself through the income generated by his publications alone was Washington Irving. He completed his first major book in 1809 entitled *A History of New-York* from the Beginning of the World to the End of the Dutch Dynasty.

Washington Irving
From: http://en.wikipedia.org/wiki/Washington_Irving

With the War of 1812 and an increasing desire to produce uniquely American literature and culture, a number of key new literary figures emerged, perhaps most prominently Washington Irving, William Cullen Bryant, James Fenimore Cooper, and Edgar Allan Poe. Irving, often considered the first writer to develop a unique

American style (although this has been debated) wrote humorous works in Salmagundi and the satire *A History of New-York from the Beginning of the World to the End of the Dutch Dynasty* (1809). Bryant wrote early romantic and nature-inspired poetry, which evolved away from their European origins.

In 1832, Edgar Allan Poe began writing short stories—including *The Masque of the Red Death*, *The Pit and the Pendulum*, *The Fall of the House of Usher*, and *The Murders in the Rue Morgue*—that explore previously hidden levels of human psychology and push the boundaries of fiction toward mystery and fantasy. James Fenimore Cooper's *Leatherstocking Tales* about Natty Bumppo were popular both in the new country and abroad.

In 1836, Ralph Waldo Emerson (1803—1882), an ex-minister, published a startling nonfiction work called *Nature*, in which he claimed it was possible to dispense with organized religion and reach a lofty spiritual state by studying and responding to the natural world. His work influenced not only the writers who gathered around him, forming a movement known as **Transcendentalism**①, but also the public, who heard him lecture.

In 1837, the young Nathaniel Hawthorne (1804—1864) collected some of his stories as *Twice-Told Tales*, a volume rich in symbolism and occult incidents. Hawthorne went on to write full-length "romances", quasi-allegorical novels that explore such themes as guilt, pride, and emotional repression in his native New England. His masterpiece, *The Scarlet Letter*, is the stark drama of a woman cast out of her community for committing adultery.

Hawthorne's fiction had a profound impact on his friend Herman Melville (1819—1891), who first made a name for himself by turning material from his seafaring days into exotic and sensational sea narrative novels. Inspired by Hawthorne's focus on allegories and dark psychology, Melville went on to write romances replete with philosophical speculation. In *Moby-Dick*, an adventurous whaling voyage becomes the vehicle for examining such themes as obsession, the nature of evil and human struggle against the elements.

Anti-transcendental works from Melville, Hawthorne, and Poe all comprise the **Dark Romanticism**② subgenre of literature popular during this time.

2.2 Poetry

America's two greatest 19th-century poets could hardly have been more different

---

① Transcendentalism：超验主义，其核心观点是主张人能超越感觉和理性而直接认识真理，强调直觉的重要性，强调万物本质上的统一，万物皆受"超灵"制约，而人类灵魂与"超灵"一致。

② Dark Romanticism：黑色浪漫主义，通常指流行于18世纪末19世纪初的英国哥特小说，它是一种关于过去历史与异域文化的幻想形式，具备浪漫与现实的特征，以荒诞的想象和伤感的情绪来激起读者的兴趣和热情。

in temperament and style. Walt Whitman (1819—1892) was a working man, a traveler, a self-appointed nurse during the American Civil War (1861—1865), and a poetic innovator. His magnum opus was *Leaves of Grass*, in which he uses a free-flowing verse and lines of irregular length to depict the all-inclusiveness of American democracy. Taking that motif one step further, the poet equates the vast range of American experience with himself without being egotistical.

Emily Dickinson (1830—1886), on the other hand, lived the sheltered life of a genteel unmarried woman in small-town Amherst, Massachusetts. Within its formal structure, her poetry is ingenious, witty, exquisitely wrought, and psychologically penetrating. Many of her poems dwell on death, often with a mischievous twist. Her work was unconventional for its day, and little of it was published during her lifetime.

Emily Dickinson
From: http://en.wikipedia.org/wiki/Emily_Dickinson

American poetry arguably reached its peak in the early-to-mid-20th century, with such noted writers as Wallace Stevens and his *Harmonium* (1923) and *The Auroras of Autumn* (1950), T. S. Eliot and his *The Waste Land* (1922), Robert Frost and his *North of Boston* (1914) and *New Hampshire* (1923), Hart Crane and his *White Buildings* (1926) and the epic cycle, *The Bridge* (1930), Ezra Pound, William Carlos Williams and his epic poem about his New Jersey hometown, Paterson, Marianne Moore, E. E. Cummings, Edna St. Vincent Millay and Langston Hughes, in addition to many others.

3. The Realistic Period

Mark Twain (the pen name used by Samuel Langhorne Clemens, 1835—1910) was the first major American writer to be born away from the East Coast—in the border state of Missouri. His regional masterpieces were the memoir *Life on the*

Mississippi and the novels *The Adventures of Tom Sawyer* and *The Adventures of Huckleberry Finn*. Twain's style—influenced by journalism, wedded to the vernacular, direct and unadorned but also highly evocative and irreverently humorous—changed the way Americans write their language. His characters speak like real people and sound distinctively American, using local dialects, newly invented words, and regional accents.

William Dean Howells also represented the realist tradition through his novels, including *The Rise of Silas Lapham* and his work as editor of the *Atlantic Monthly*.

Henry James (1843—1916) confronted the Old World-New World dilemma by writing directly about it. Although born in New York City, he spent most of his adult years in England. Many of his novels center on Americans who live in or travel to Europe. With its intricate, highly qualified sentences and dissection of emotional and psychological nuance, James's fiction can be daunting. Among his more accessible works are the novellas *Daisy Miller*, about an enchanting American girl in Europe, and *The Turn of the Screw*, an enigmatic ghost story.

Realism also influenced American drama of the period, in part through the works of Howells but also through the works of such Europeans as Ibsen and Zola. Although realism was most influential in terms of set design and staging—audiences loved the special effects offered up by the popular melodramas—and in the growth of local color plays, it also showed up in the more subdued, less romantic tone that reflected the effects of the Civil War and continued social turmoil on the American psyche.

The most ambitious attempt at bringing modern realism into the drama was James Herne's *Margaret Fleming*, which addressed issues of social determinism through realistic dialogue, psychological insight and symbolism; the play was not a success, as critics and audiences alike felt it dwelt too much on unseemly topics and included improper scenes, such as the main character nursing her husband's illegitimate child onstage.

4. The Beginning of the 20th Century

At the beginning of the 20th century, American novelists were expanding fiction's social spectrum to encompass both high and low life and sometimes connected to the naturalist school of realism. In her stories and novels, Edith Wharton (1862—1937) scrutinized the upper-class, Eastern-seaboard society in which she had grown up. One of her finest books, *The Age of Innocence*, centers on a man who chooses to marry a conventional, socially acceptable woman rather than a fascinating outsider.

At about the same time, Stephen Crane (1871—1900), best known for his Civil War novel *The Red Badge of Courage*, depicted the life of New York City prostitutes in *Maggie: A Girl of the Streets*. And in *Sister Carrie*, Theodore Dreiser (1871—1945) portrayed a country girl who moves to Chicago and becomes a kept woman. Hamlin Garland and Frank Norris wrote about the problems of American farmers and other social issues from a naturalist perspective.

More directly political writings discussed social issues and power of corporations. Some like Edward Bellamy in *Looking Backward* outlined other possible political and social frameworks. Upton Sinclair, most famous for his muck-raking novel *The Jungle*, advocated socialism. Other political writers of the period included Edwin Markham, William Vaughn Moody. Journalistic critics, including Ida M. Tarbell and Lincoln Steffens were labeled The Muckrakers. Henry Brooks Adams' literate autobiography, *The Education of Henry Adams* also depicted a stinging description of the education system and modern life.

Experimentation in style and form soon joined the new freedom in subject matter. In 1909, Gertrude Stein (1874—1946), by then an expatriate in Paris, published *Three Lives*, an innovative work of fiction influenced by her familiarity with cubism, jazz, and other movements in contemporary art and music. Stein labeled a group of American literary notables who lived in Paris in the 1920s and 1930s as the "Lost Generation".

The poet Ezra Pound (1885—1972) was born in Idaho but spent much of his adult life in Europe. His work is complex, sometimes obscure, with multiple references to other art forms and to a vast range of literature, both Western and Eastern. He influenced many other poets, notably T. S. Eliot (1888—1965), another expatriate. Eliot wrote spare, cerebral poetry, carried by a dense structure of symbols. In *The Waste Land*, he embodied a jaundiced vision of post-World War I society in fragmented, haunted images. Like Pound's, Eliot's poetry could be highly allusive, and some editions of *The Waste Land* come with footnotes supplied by the poet. In 1948, Eliot won the Nobel Prize in Literature.

Ezra Pound
From: http://en.wikipedia.org/wiki/Ezra_Pound

American writers also expressed the disillusionment following upon the war. The stories and novels of F. Scott Fitzgerald (1896—1940) capture the restless, pleasure-hungry, defiant mood of the 1920s. Fitzgerald's characteristic theme, expressed poignantly in *The Great Gatsby*, is the tendency of youth's golden dreams to dissolve in failure and disappointment. Fitzgerald also elucidates the collapse of some key American Ideals, set out in the *Declaration of Independence*, such as liberty, social unity, good governance and peace, features which were severely threatened by the pressures of modern early 20th century society.

Ernest Hemingway (1899—1961) saw violence and death first-hand as an ambulance driver in World War I, and the carnage persuaded him that abstract language was mostly empty and misleading. He cut out unnecessary words from his writing, simplified the sentence structure, and concentrated on concrete objects and actions. He adhered to a moral code that emphasized grace under pressure, and his protagonists were strong, silent men who often dealt awkwardly with women. *The Sun Also Rises* and *A Farewell to Arms* are generally considered his best novels; in 1954, he won the Nobel Prize in Literature.

Five years before Hemingway, another American novelist had won the Nobel Prize: William Faulkner (1897—1962). Faulkner managed to encompass an enormous range of humanity in Yoknapatawpha County, a Mississippian region of his own invention. He recorded his characters' seemingly unedited ramblings in order to represent their inner states, a technique called "stream of consciousness". He also jumbled time sequences to show how the past—especially the slave-holding era of the Deep South—endures in the present. Among his great works are *Absalom, Absalom!*, *As I Lay Dying*, *The Sound and the Fury*, and *Light in August*.

5. Depression-Era Literature

Depression-era literature was blunt and direct in its social criticism. John Steinbeck (1902—1968) was born in Salinas, California, where he set many of his stories. His style was simple and evocative, winning him the favor of the readers but not of the critics. Steinbeck often wrote about poor, working-class people and their struggle to lead a decent and honest life. *The Grapes of Wrath*, considered his masterpiece, is a strong, socially-oriented novel that tells the story of the Joads, a poor family from Oklahoma and their journey to California in search of a better life. Other popular novels include *Tortilla Flat*, *Of Mice and Men*, *Cannery Row*, and *East of Eden*. He was awarded the Nobel Prize in Literature in 1962.

Steinbeck's contemporary, Nathanael West's two most famous short novels, *Miss

Lonelyhearts, which plumbs the life of its eponymous **antihero**①, a reluctant (and, to comic effect, male) advice columnist, and the effects the tragic letters exert on it, and *The Day of the Locust*, which introduces a cast of Hollywood stereotypes and explores the ironies of the movies, have come to be avowed classics of American literature.

Henry Miller assumed a unique place in American Literature in the 1930s when his semi-autobiographical novels, written and published in Paris, were banned from the US. Although his major works, including *Tropic of Cancer* and *Black Spring*, would not be free of the label of obscenity until 1962, their themes and stylistic innovations had already exerted a major influence on succeeding generations of American writers, and paved the way for sexually frank 1960s novels by John Updike, Philip Roth, Gore Vidal, John Rechy and William Styron.

6. Post-World War II

6.1 Fiction

The period in time from the end of World War II up until, roughly, the late 1960s and early 1970s saw the publication of some of the most popular works in American history such as *To Kill a Mockingbird* by Harper Lee. The last few of the more realistic modernists along with the wildly Romantic **beatniks**② largely dominated the period, while the direct respondents to America's involvement in World War II contributed in their notable influence.

Though born in Canada, Chicago-raised Saul Bellow would become one of the most influential novelists in America in the decades directly following World War II. In works like *The Adventures of Augie March* and *Herzog*, Bellow painted vivid portraits of the American city and the distinctive characters that peopled it. Bellow went on to win the Nobel Prize for Literature in 1976.

From J. D. Salinger's *Nine Stories* and *The Catcher in the Rye* to Sylvia Plath's *The Bell Jar*, the perceived madness of the state of affairs in America was brought to the forefront of the nation's literary expression. Immigrant authors such as Vladimir Nabokov, with *Lolita*, forged on with the theme, and, at almost the same time, the beatniks took a concerted step away from their Lost Generation predecessors,

---

① antihero: 反英雄。英雄的特点可以概括为外表俊美、能力强大、行为正确。和英雄相比，反英雄有着面目可憎、行动笨拙、智力愚钝、性格消极被动、处境值得怜悯、行为偏离常规等通常不属于英雄人物的不良特征，他们在某些基本方面是有缺点的或是失败的。反英雄可以和英雄一样有着崇高的理想与强大的力量，也可能在理想与能力方面和普通人接近甚至不如普通人，却不得不完成非凡的举动。

② beatniks:"披头族"一词用于描述"垮掉的一代"的参与者。这些人形象特点是青春四溢、行为举止不合常规，具有反抗气质。

developing a style and tone of their own by drawing on Eastern theology and experimenting with recreational drugs.

Regarding the war novel specifically, there was a literary explosion in America during the post-World War II era. Some of the best known of the works produced included Norman Mailer's *The Naked and the Dead* (1948), Joseph Heller's *Catch-22* (1961) and Kurt Vonnegut Jr.'s *Slaughterhouse-Five* (1969). *The Moviegoer* (1962), by Southern author Walker Percy, winner of the National Book Award, was his attempt at exploring the dislocation of man in the modern age.

In contrast, John Updike approached American life from a more reflective but no less subversive perspective. His 1960 novel *Rabbit, Run*, the first of four chronicling the rising and falling fortunes of Harry "Rabbit" Angstrom over the course of four decades against the backdrop of the major events of the second half of the 20th century, broke new ground on its release in its characterization and detail of the American middle class and frank discussion of taboo topics such as adultery. Notable among Updike's characteristic innovations was his use of present-tense narration, his rich, stylized language, and his attention to sensual detail. His work is also deeply imbued with Christian themes. The two final installments of the Rabbit series, *Rabbit is Rich* (1981) and *Rabbit at Rest* (1990), were both awarded the Pulitzer Prize for Fiction. Other notable works include the Henry Bech novels (1970—98), *The Witches of Eastwick* (1984), *Roger's Version* (1986) and *In the Beauty of the Lilies* (1996).

Perhaps the most ambitious and challenging post-war American novelist was William Gaddis, whose uncompromising, satiric, and gargantuan novels, such as *The Recognitions* (1955) and *JR* (1975) are presented largely in terms of unattributed dialog that requires almost unexampled reader participation. Gaddis's primary themes include forgery, capitalism, religious zealotry, and the legal system, constituting a sustained polyphonic critique of the chaos and chicanery of modern American life. Gaddis's work, though largely ignored for years, anticipated and influenced the development of such ambitious "postmodern" fiction writers as Thomas Pynchon, Joseph McElroy, and Don DeLillo. Another neglected and challenging postwar American novelist, albeit one who wrote much shorter works, was John Hawkes, whose often surreal, visionary fiction addresses themes of violence and eroticism and experiments audaciously with narrative voice and style. Among his most important works is the short nightmarish novel *The Lime Twig* (1961).

6.2 Short Story

In the postwar period, the art of the short story again flourished. Among its most respected practitioners was Flannery O'Connor, who renewed the fascination of such giants as Faulkner and Twain with the American south, developing a distinctive

Southern gothic esthetic wherein characters acted at one level as people and at another as symbols. A devout Catholic, O'Connor often imbued her stories, among them the widely studied *A Good Man Is Hard to Find* and *Everything That Rises Must Converge*, and two novels, *Wise Blood* (1952); *The Violent Bear It Away* (1960), with deeply religious themes, focusing particularly on the search for truth and religious skepticism against the backdrop of the nuclear age. Other important practitioners of the form include Katherine Anne Porter, Eudora Welty, John Cheever, Raymond Carver, Tobias Wolff, and the more experimental Donald Barthelme.

6.3 Poetry

Among the most respected of the postwar American poets are John Ashbery, the key figure of the **surrealistic**① New York School of poetry, and his celebrated *Self-portrait* in a Convex Mirror (Pulitzer Prize for Poetry, 1976); Elizabeth Bishop and her *North & South* (Pulitzer Prize for Poetry, 1956) and *Geography III* (National Book Award, 1970); Richard Wilbur and his *Things of This World*, winner of both the Pulitzer Prize and the National Book Award for Poetry in 1957; John Berryman and his *The Dream Songs*, (Pulitzer Prize for Poetry, 1964, National Book Award, 1968); A. R. Ammons, whose Collected Poems 1951-1971 won a National Book Award in 1973 and whose long poem *Garbage* earned him another in 1993; Theodore Roethke and his *The Waking* (Pulitzer Prize for Poetry, 1954); James Merrill and his epic poem of communication with the dead, *The Changing Light* at Sandover (Pulitzer Prize for Poetry, 1977); Louise Glück for her *The Wild Iris* (Pulitzer Prize for Poetry, 1993); W. S. Merwin for his *The Carrier of Ladders* (Pulitzer Prize for Poetry, 1971) and *The Shadow of Sirius* (Pulitzer Prize for Poetry, 2009); Mark Strand for *Blizzard of One* (Pulitzer Prize for Poetry, 1999); Robert Hass for his *Time and Materials*, which won both the Pulitzer Prize and National Book Award for Poetry in 2008 and 2007 respectively; and Rita Dove for her *Thomas and Beulah* (Pulitzer Prize for Poetry, 1987).

6.4 African-American Literature

In the realm of African-American literature, Ralph Ellison's novel *Invisible Man* (1952) was instantly recognized as among the most powerful and important works of the immediate post-war years. The story of a black underground man in the urban

---

① surrealistic：超现实主义是在法国开始的文学艺术流派，源于达达主义，它的主要特征，是以所谓"超现实""超理智"的梦境、幻觉等作为艺术创作的源泉，认为只有这种超越现实的"无意识"世界才能摆脱一切束缚，最真实地显示客观事实的真面目。超现实主义给传统对艺术的看法有了巨大的影响；它也常被称为超现实主义运动，或简称为超现实。

north, the novel laid bare the often repressed racial tension that still prevailed while also succeeding as an existential character study. Richard Wright was catapulted to fame by the publication in subsequent years of his now widely studied short story, *The Man Who Was Almost a Man* (1939), and his controversial second novel, *Native Son* (1940), and his legacy was cemented by the 1945 publication of *Black Boy*, a work in which Wright drew on his childhood and mostly autodidactic education in the segregated South, fictionalizing and exaggerating some elements as he saw fit. Because of its polemical themes and Wright's involvement with the Communist Party, the novel's final part, "American Hunger", was not published until 1977.

7. Contemporary American Literature

Though its exact parameters remain debatable, from the early 1970s to the present day the most salient literary movement has been postmodernism. Thomas Pynchon, a seminal practitioner of the form, drew in his work on modernist fixtures such as temporal distortion, unreliable narrators, and internal monologue and coupled them with distinctly postmodern techniques such as **metafiction**①, ideogrammatic characterization, unrealistic names (Oedipa Maas, Benny Profane, etc.), absurdist plot elements and hyperbolic humor, deliberate use of **anachronisms**② and archaisms, a strong focus on postcolonial themes, and a subversive commingling of high and low culture. In 1973, he published *Gravity's Rainbow*, a leading work in this genre, which won the National Book Award and was unanimously nominated for the Pulitzer Prize for Fiction that year. His other major works include his debut, *V.* (1963), *The Crying of Lot 49* (1966), *Mason & Dixon* (1997), and *Against the Day* (2006).

Toni Morrison, the most recent American recipient of the Nobel Prize for Literature, writing in a distinctive lyrical prose style, published her controversial debut novel, *The Bluest Eye*, to widespread critical acclaim in 1970. Coming on the heels of the signing of the Civil Rights Act of 1965, the novel, widely studied in American schools, includes an elaborate description of incestuous rape and explores the conventions of beauty established by a historically racist society, painting a portrait of a self-immolating black family in search of beauty in whiteness. Since

---

① metafiction：超小说为现代小说流派或其作品，有意强调作者的媒介作用和写作技巧，忽略传统写作中对真实性的关注。

② anachronisms：时代错误，指把不可能出现于同一时代的事物安排在一起。这些在时间上不一致的可能是物件，也可能是人物、事件、语句、科技、思想、音乐风格、物料、风俗习惯，而把它们放置于同一时空下面在现实上是不正确的。常见的句子"张飞打岳飞"即是一例，只是为了造句顺畅把两个名飞的人拼在一起。各时代也常以当代的时空背景去绘制前代甚至史籍之前的人物社会、服装、建筑、社会习俗等都与考古有相当出入，在文学或艺术的领域中是常有的情况。

then, Morrison has experimented with lyric fantasy, as in her two best-known later works, *Song of Solomon* (1977) and *Beloved* (1987), for which she was awarded the Pulitzer Prize for Fiction; along these lines, critic Harold Bloom has drawn favorable comparisons to Virginia Woolf, and the Nobel committee to Faulkner and to the Latin American tradition. *Beloved* was chosen in a 2006 survey conducted by the *New York Times* as the most important work of fiction of the last 25 years.

Writing in a lyrical, flowing style that eschews excessive use of the comma and semicolon, recalling William Faulkner and Ernest Hemingway in equal measure, Cormac McCarthy's body of work seizes on the literary traditions of several regions of the United States and spans multiple genres. He writes in the Southern Gothic aesthetic in his distinctly Faulknerian 1965 debut, *The Orchard Keeper*, and *Suttree* (1979); in the Epic Western tradition, with grotesquely drawn characters and symbolic narrative turns reminiscent of Melville, in *Blood Meridian* (1985), which Harold Bloom styled the greatest single book since Faulkner's *As I Lay Dying*, in a much more pastoral tone in his celebrated *Border Trilogy* (1992—1998) of bildungsromans, including *All the Pretty Horses* (1992), winner of the National Book Award; and in the post-apocalyptic genre in the Pulitzer Prize-winning *The Road* (2007). His novels are noted for achieving both commercial and critical success, several of his works having been adapted to film.

Don DeLillo, who rose to literary prominence with the publication of his 1985 novel, *White Noise*, a work broaching the subjects of death and consumerism and doubling as a piece of comic social criticism, began his writing career in 1971 with *Americana*. He is listed by Harold Bloom as being among the preeminent contemporary American writers, in the company of such figures as Philip Roth, Cormac McCarthy, and Thomas Pynchon. His 1997 novel *Underworld*, a gargantuan work chronicling American life through and immediately after the "Cold War" and examining with equal depth subjects as various as baseball and nuclear weapons, is generally agreed upon to be his masterpiece and was the runner-up in a survey asking writers to identify the most important work of fiction of the last 25 years. Among his other important novels are *Libra* (1988), *Mao II* (1991) and *Falling Man* (2007).

Stephen King, a noted horror writer and popular novelist of American Contemporary Culture, was awarded the O. Henry Award for a short story he wrote. Harold Bloom was among those who despised King and called his works *Penny Dreadfuls* where other noted American Writers, like Orson Scott Card, lauded the decision and had very high regard for King's ability as a writer.

Other notable writers at the turn of the century include Michael Chabon, whose Pulitzer Prize-winning *The Amazing Adventures of Kavalier & Clay* (2000) tells the story of two friends, Joe Kavalier and Sam Clay, as they rise through the ranks of the comics industry in its heyday; Denis Johnson, whose 2007 novel *Tree of Smoke* about falsified intelligence during Vietnam both won the National Book Award and was a finalist for the Pulitzer Prize for Fiction and was called by critic Michiko Kakutani "one of the classic works of literature produced by (the Vietnam War)"; and Louise Erdrich, whose 2008 novel *The Plague of Doves*, a distinctly Faulknerian, polyphonic examination of the tribal experience set against the backdrop of murder in the fictional town of Pluto, North Dakota, was nominated for the Pulitzer Prize, and her 2012 novel *The Round House*, which builds on the same themes, was awarded the 2012 National Book Award.

References

Bercovitch, Sacvan. ed. *The Cambridge History of American Literature*. Cambridge: Cambridge University Press. 1994.

http://en.wikipedia.org/wiki/American_ literature

Exercises

I. Choose the one that best completes each of the following statements.

1. William Sidney Porter, known as O. Henry, is most famous for _____.
   A. his poems   B. his plays   C. his short stories   D. his novels
2. The author of *The Sound and the Fury* also wrote _____.
   A. *As I Lay Dying*   B. *Penny Dreadfuls*
   C. *The Plague of Doves*   D. *The Road*
3. *Poor Richard's Almanac* was written by _____ who also wrote _____.
   A. Benjamin Franklin; *Autobiography*
   B. Washington Irving; *Autobiography*
   C. Washington Irving; *History of New York*
   D. Benjamin Franklin; *History of New York*
4. *Invisible Man*, the story of a black Underground Man, was written by _____.
   A. Richard Wright   B. Ralph Ellison
   C. Thomas Pynchon   D. Denis Johnson
5. Of the following writers, _____ are from the Colonial and Revolutionary Period.
   A. Benjamin Franklin & Edgar Ellen Poe
   B. Edgar Ellen Poe & Jonathan Edwards
   C. Benjamin Franklin & Jonathan Edwards
   D. Edgar Ellen Poe & Washington Irving
6. Of the following, _____ is considered Herman Melville's masterpiece.
   A. *The Great Gatsby*   B. *Farewell to the Arms*

C. *Moby Dick*   D. *Daisy Miller*
7. F. Scott Firzgerald's finest novel is _____, and its theme is about _____.
   A. *The Great Gatsby*, the American Dream
   B. *Tender is the Night*, love
   C. *Tales of the Jazz Age*, the loss of oneself
   D. *The Sun Also Rises*, cruelty of the war
8. Of the following novels written by John Steinbeck, which is considered his masterpiece?
   A. *Of Mice and Men*   B. *Cannery Row*
   C. *The Grapes of Wrath*   D. *East of Eden*
9. Of the following writers, _____ is NOT included in the group of naturalists.
   A. Stephen Crane   B. Frank Norris
   C. Theodore Dreiser   D. Herman Melville
10. In Nathaniel Hawthorne's novel, *The Scarlet Letter*, letter A stands for _____.
    A. ashamed   B. abandoned
    C. adultery   D. abolished

II. Read the following statements carefully and decide whether they are TRUE or FALSE.

1. Hemingway's style is often simple and almost childlike.
2. Emerson and his young friend Edgar Allan Poe are considered the forerunners of the literary movement of New England Transcendentalism in the 19th century.
3. Emily Dickinson's poems were unconventional for its day, and few of them were published during her lifetime.
4. Walt Whitman introduced great innovations to American literature, and he devised a poetic style, free verse.
5. Thomas Paine's pamphlet *Common Sense* has played a key role in inspiring people in the Thirteen Colonies to declare and fight for independence.
6. Edgar Allan Poe published a startling nonfiction work called *Nature* in 1836.
7. In *The Adventures of Huckleberry Finn*, the characters speak like real people, using local dialects, newly invented words, and regional accents.
8. *A Farewell to Arms* is often considered Ernest Hemingway's autobiographical novel.
9. Ezra Pound led the School of Imagism, which advocates a clear, highly visual presentation.
10. In the postwar period, Flannery O'Connor developed a distinctive Southern gothic esthetic.

III. Give definitions to the following literary terms.
1. allegory
2. alliteration
3. anti-hero

4. ballad
5. epic poetry
6. iambic pentameter
7. lyric
8. Naturalism
9. ode
10. sonnet

Section Two: In-depth Reading

Literature, besides being an art form used for expression, also preserves cultural ideals, customs, and morals. The written words give us a deeper context into the lives and livelihood of people distinct from ourselves. We can learn as much from William Shakespeare's time through his plays as we can from authors from a different mindset or place. All in all, literature is a fascinating discipline, it helps to understand and value the cultural diversity of the human society. The passages in this section focus on the life and work of two great American writers: Ernest Hemingway and Mark Twain.

Reading one provides us with a brief glimpse into the life of Ernest Hemingway and his works.

Reading two leads us into the humorous kingdom built in Mark Twain's works.

Before reading the articles, brainstorm with your cohorts on the following questions:

1. Who is your favorite American writer? What is your favorite book? Why?
2. In which way, do you think, literary work has helped you to understand life or to think better?

Reading One

Nobel Prize winner Ernest Hemingway is seen as one of the greatest American 20th century novelists, and is known for works like *A Farewell to Arms* and *The Old Man and the Sea*. The following passage provides a brief glimpse into the life of Ernest Hemingway and insight as to how he was perceived by those who knew him.

Ernest Hemingway Biography

Synopsis

Born on July 21, 1899, in Cicero (now in Oak Park), Illinois, Ernest Hemingway served in World War I and worked in journalism before publishing his story collection *In Our Time*. He was renowned for novels like *The Sun Also Rises*, *A*

Farewell to Arms, *For Whom the Bell Tolls*, and *The Old Man and the Sea*, which won the 1953 Pulitzer. In 1954, Hemingway won the Nobel Prize. He committed suicide on July 2, 1961, in Ketchum, Idaho.

Hemingway in uniform in Milan, 1918
From: http://en.wikipedia.org/wiki/Ernest_Hemingway

Early Life and Career

Ernest Miller Hemingway was born on July 21, 1899, in Cicero (now in Oak Park), Illinois. Clarence and Grace Hemingway raised their son in this conservative suburb of Chicago, but the family also spent a great deal of time in northern Michigan, where they had a cabin. It was there that the future sportsman learned to hunt, fish and appreciate the outdoors.

In high school, Hemingway worked on his school newspaper, *Trapeze* and *Tabula*, writing primarily about sports. Immediately after graduation, the budding journalist went to work for the *Kansas City Star*, gaining experience that would later influence his distinctively stripped-down prose style.

He once said, "On the *Star* you were forced to learn to write a simple declarative sentence. This is useful to anyone. Newspaper work will not harm a young writer and could help him if he gets out of it in time."

Military Experience

In 1918, Hemingway went overseas to serve in World War I as an ambulance driver in the Italian Army. For his service, he was awarded the Italian Silver Medal of Bravery, but soon sustained injuries that landed him in a hospital in Milan.

There he met a nurse named Agnes von Kurowsky, who soon accepted his proposal of marriage, but later left him for another man. This devastated the young writer but provided fodder for his works *A Very Short Story* and, more famously, *A Farewell to Arms*.

Still nursing his injury and recovering from the brutalities of war at the young age of 20, he returned to the United States and spent time in northern Michigan before taking a job at the *Toronto Star*.

It was in Chicago that Hemingway met Hadley Richardson, the woman who would become his first wife. The couple married and quickly moved to Paris, where Hemingway worked as a foreign correspondent for *the Star*.

Life in Europe

In Paris, Hemingway soon became a key part of what Gertrude Stein would famously call "The Lost Generation". With Stein as his mentor, Hemingway made the acquaintance of many of the great writers and artists of his generation, such as F. Scott Fitzgerald, Ezra Pound, Pablo Picasso and James Joyce. In 1923, Hemingway and Hadley had a son, John Hadley Nicanor Hemingway. By this time the writer had also begun frequenting the famous Festival of San Fermin in Pamplona, Spain.

In 1925, the couple, joining a group of British and American expatriates, took a trip to the festival that would later provided the basis of Hemingway's first novel, *The Sun Also Rises*. The novel is widely considered Hemingway's greatest work, artfully examining the postwar disillusionment of his generation.

Soon after the publication of *The Sun Also Rises*, Hemingway and Hadley divorced, due in part to his affair with a woman named Pauline Pfeiffer, who would become Hemingway's second wife shortly after his divorce from Hadley was finalized. The author continued to work on his book of short stories, *Men Without Women*.

Critical Acclaim

Soon, Pauline became pregnant and the couple decided to move back to America. After the birth of their son Patrick Hemingway in 1928, they settled in Key West, Florida, but summered in Wyoming. During this time, Hemingway finished his celebrated World War I novel *A Farewell to Arms*, securing his lasting place in the literary canon.

When he wasn't writing, Hemingway spent much of the 1930s chasing adventure: big-game hunting in Africa, bullfighting in Spain, deep-sea fishing in Florida. While reporting on the Spanish Civil War in 1937, Hemingway met a fellow war correspondent named Martha Gellhorn (soon to become wife number three) and gathered material for his next novel, *For Whom the Bell Tolls*, which would eventually be nominated for the Pulitzer Prize.

Almost predictably, his marriage to Pauline Pfeiffer deteriorated and the couple divorced. Gellhorn and Hemingway married soon after and purchased a farm near Havana, Cuba, which would serve as their winter residence.

When the United States entered World War II in 1941, Hemingway served as a correspondent and was present at several of the war's key moments, including the D-Day landing. Toward the end of the war, Hemingway met another war correspondent, Mary Welsh, whom he would later marry after divorcing Martha

Gellhorn.

In 1951, Hemingway wrote *The Old Man and the Sea*, which would become perhaps his most famous book, finally winning him the Pulitzer Prize he had long been denied.

Personal Struggles and Suicide

The author continued his forays into Africa and sustained several injuries during his adventures, even surviving multiple plane crashes.

In 1954, he won the Nobel Prize in Literature. Even at this peak of his literary career, though, the burly Hemingway's body and mind were beginning to betray him. Recovering from various old injuries in Cuba, Hemingway suffered from depression and was treated for numerous conditions such as high blood pressure and liver disease.

He wrote *A Moveable Feast*, a memoir of his years in Paris, and retired permanently to Idaho. There he continued to battle with deteriorating mental and physical health.

Early on the morning of July 2, 1961, Ernest Hemingway committed suicide in his Ketchum home.

Legacy

Hemingway left behind an impressive body of work and an iconic style that still influences writers today. His personality and constant pursuit of adventure loomed almost as large as his creative talent.

When asked by George Plimpton about the function of his art, Hemingway proved once again to be a master of the "one true sentence": "From things that have happened and from things as they exist and from all things that you know and all those you cannot know, you make something through your invention that is not a representation but a whole new thing truer than anything true and alive, and you make it alive, and if you make it well enough, you give it immortality."

References

http://www.biography.com/people/ernest-hemingway-9334498 (Accessed 20 May 2014).

Biography.com captures the most gripping, surprising and fascinating stories about famous people. It has over 7,000 biographies and daily features that highlight newsworthy, compelling and surprising points-of-view.

Discussions

Hemingway's life is a legendary one. Full of passion and patriotism, he joined the two world wars and escaped from death's scythe. His wartime experiences formed the basis for his novel *A Farewell to Arms*, and thus some critics called this novel

Hemingway's autobiography. Please read *A Farewell to Arms* and find out the similarity between Hemingway and the hero Frederic Henry.

Reading Two

For nearly fifty years Mark Twain entertained America with his insight as a humorist. It is a tribute to the skill of Mark Twain that his classics are still enjoyed by readers today over 100 years after they were written. His wit and humor are timeless and are able to survive through the ages. The following passage is a professor's account of Mark Twain's wit.

Mark Twain's Humor—With Examples
Robert L. Middlekauff

Rather than speak of the background of Mark Twain's humor, I am simply going to look at it more or less from the inside—what it was, its character and its purposes, in particular as he understood them.

Mark Twain
From: http://en.wikipedia.org/wiki/Mark_Twain

Not surprisingly Mark Twain's maxims are characteristically extravagant, even exuberant, and sometimes sheer burlesque. Here is an array of his sayings:

1. Rise early—it is the early bird that catches the worm. Don't be fooled by this absurd saw. I once knew a man who tried it. He got up at sunrise and a horse bit him.

2. Clothes make the man. Naked people have little or no influence in society.

3. Always acknowledge a fault frankly. This will throw those in authority off their guard and give you opportunity to commit more.

4. Do good when you can, and charge when you think they will stand it.

5. To be good is noble, but to show others how to be good is nobler, and no trouble.

6. It is the foreign element that commits our crimes. There is no native criminal class except Congress.

7. Senator: Person who makes laws in Washington when not doing time.

8. Man is the only animal that blushes. Or needs to.

The best and most amusing of Mark Twain's humor is found in his tales and sketches and stories. Although he was not a conceptual or systematic thinker, he had a theory about such forms that arose from his own practice as a lecturer and storyteller. He argues in "How to Tell a Story" (1895) that the American humorous tale was different from the European comic or witty story. What made a European story funny was its matter, its content; in contrast, the American story depended not on its matter, but on "the manner of the telling." The European story went right to the point—its humor came at the end, with a "nub, point, snapper".

When an American told this story, Mark Twain said, he would "conceal the fact that he even dimly suspects that there is anything funny about it". The European "tells you beforehand that it is one of the funniest things he has ever heard, then tells it with eager delight, and is the first person to laugh when he gets through". The American, on the other hand, tells it in a "rambling and disjointed" fashion and pretends that he does not know that it is funny at all. The European, when he prints it, "italicizes" parts of it, uses "whooping exclamation points liberally", and then sometimes explains it in a parenthesis. "All of which," Mark Twain sadly comments, "is very depressing, and makes one want to renounce joking and lead a better life."

Humor was essential to his very being. He once said, "Against the assault of laughter nothing can stand." He picked his targets carefully—and took pleasure in destroying sham, fraud, and pretense. And when those targets were not available, as they were not in his sketch of Benjamin Franklin, he let his whimsical side express itself. He had fun. He was a playful man, as his friend William Dean Howells said, a man with the "head of a sage and the heart of a boy".

References

Middlekauff, Robert. "Mark Twain's Humor—With Examples." *Proceedings of the American Philosophical Society: Held at Philadelphia for Promoting Useful Knowledge*. Vol. 150. No. 3. American Philosophical Society, 2006.

About the Author

Robert L. Middlekauff (1929—) received his B. A. from University of

Washington and Ph. D from Yale University. Fresh out of graduate school, Middlekauff began his professional teaching career at the University of California, Berkeley in 1962. Middlekauff retired in 2000 and is currently the Preston Hotchkis Professor of American History Emeritus at the University of California, Berkeley. Since his retirement, Professor Middlekauff's scholarly interests have shifted from the colonial era to the nineteenth century and the work of Mark Twain.

Discussions

Times might have changed; examples of the human condition have not. Mark Twain's humor is timeless and even relevant today. The following are some of his most notable quotations:

" 'Classic', a book which people praise and don't read."

"Few things are harder to put up with than the annoyance of a good example."

"One of the most striking differences between a cat and a lie is that a cat has only nine lives."

Discuss with your classmates about how truly contemporary the above quotations are when compared with today's comics, and how universal these themes are.

Appendix
Canada, Australia and New Zealand

Canada

1. Geography

Canada occupies the northern half of the North American continent, with the exception of Greenland, Alaska, and the French islands of St-Pierre and Miquelon. It is the second largest country in the world, with a land mass approaching 10 million square kilometers (over 3.8 million square miles). Canada stretches from the Atlantic Ocean in the east to the Pacific Ocean in the west, and to the Arctic Ocean in the north. The vast majority of Canada's 33 million people live in the southern third of the country. English and French are Canada's official languages, with French predominating in the province of Quebec, and English predominating elsewhere. Many other languages are also spoken, reflecting the vast number of immigrants that the country has attracted, and continues to attract, from every corner of the globe.

Canada's expansive area can be divided into five geographic regions, each with a distinct landscape and climate. These regions are the Atlantic Region, the Central Region, the Prairie Region, the Pacific Region and the Northern Region.

Canada has numerous lakes which cover about 7.6% of its landmass. Among them, the Great Lakes on the border between Canada and the US are the largest group of freshwater lakes in the world. Canada shares with the US Niagara Falls, one of the most spectacular natural wonders on the North American continent.

Ottawa is the capital of Canada, and the fourth largest city in the country. Initially an Irish and French Christian settlement, Ottawa has become a multicultural city with a diverse population. The 2011 census had the city's population as 883,391. The city is known as being among the most educated in Canada, and hosts a number of post-secondary, research, and cultural institutions. Ottawa has a high standard of living and low unemployment.

Map of Canada
From: http://en.wikipedia.org/wiki/Canada

Ottawa
From: http://en.wikipedia.org/wiki/Ottawa,_Ontario

Toronto is the most populous city in Canada and the provincial capital of Ontario. It is located in Southern Ontario on the northwestern shore of Lake Ontario.

According to the 2012 census, the city has 2.8 million residents, making it the forthmost populous city in North America. Its cosmopolitan and international population reflects its role as an important destination for immigrants to Canada. Toronto is one of the world's most diverse cities by percentage of non-native-born residents, with about 49% of the population born outside Canada.

Montreal is a city in the Canadian province of Quebec. It is the largest city in the province and the second-largest in Canada. French is the city's official language, spoken by 56.9% of the population of the city, followed by English at 18.6% and 19.8% other languages (in the 2006 census). 56% of the population are able to speak both English and French, making Montreal one of the most bilingual cities in Quebec and Canada. Montreal is the second largest primarily French-speaking city in the world, after Paris.

Vancouver, officially the City of Vancouver, is a coastal seaport city on the mainland of British Columbia, Canada. Vancouver is one of the most ethnically and linguistically diverse cities in Canada; 52% of its residents have a first language other than English. The City of Vancouver encompasses a land area of about 114 square kilometres. It is the most densely populated Canadian municipality, and the fourth most densely populated city over 250,000 residents in North America, behind New York City, San Francisco, and Mexico City. While forestry remains its largest industry, Vancouver is well known as an urban centre surrounded by nature, making tourism its second-largest industry. Major film production studios in Vancouver and Burnaby have turned **Metro Vancouver**[①] into one of the largest film production centres in North America, earning it the film industry nickname, Hollywood North. Vancouver is consistently named as one of the top five worldwide cities for livability and quality of life, and the Economist Intelligence Unit acknowledged it as the first city to rank among the top-ten of the world's most livable cities for five consecutive years.

2. History

Much of present-day Canada was under the control of France until 1763. Four years earlier, British forces under General James Wolfe had defeated the French under the Marquis de Montcalm at the Plains of Abraham in Quebec City, beginning the end of the period of French rule. The basic duality of Canada—that is, as between English and French speakers—has shaped the country's history, politics and culture ever since. Under the *Quebec Act of* 1774, various rights with respect to language, religion and civil law were granted to the large French-speaking population

---

① Metro Vancouver: 大温哥华区域局是加拿大 BC 省的一个区域局,包含温哥华在内的都会区,又称大温哥华地区,大温地区或温哥华都会区。区域局的最大城市是温哥华,行政中心则在本那比。

of the modern-day province of Quebec. From 1791 to 1841, Ontario (formerly the thinly-populated western frontier of the French territories) and Quebec were separately governed as "Upper Canada" and "Lower Canada", respectively. Pursuant to the 1840 *Act of Union*, however, the two were united as the Province of Canada.

Canada gained its independence from the United Kingdom in stages. The colonial provinces of Canada, Nova Scotia and New Brunswick united to form the self-governing Dominion of Canada in 1867, an event referred to by Canadians as "Confederation". The British North America Act—later renamed the Constitution Act, 1867, but still popularly known as the BNA Act—was the foundational constitutional instrument. (Among other things, the BNA Act once again divided the Province of Canada in two, as "Ontario" and "Quebec".) It was not until the **Statute of Westminster**① of 1931, however, that Canada became fully responsible for its relations with other countries, and only in 1982 did the United Kingdom relinquish its remaining (though long unexercised) jurisdiction over Canadian constitutional law. In the years following Confederation, Canada grew to include ten provinces, including Manitoba (1870), British Columbia (1871), Prince Edward Island (1873), Alberta (1905), Saskatchewan (1905), and Newfoundland & Labrador (1949). In the far north are the Yukon Territory and Northwest Territories, the eastern and northern portion of which became the new territory of Nunavut in 1999.

3. Government

Canada is a parliamentary democracy, a federal state and a constitutional monarchy. The political system under which modern Canada operates is known as the **Westminster system**②. Since Canada's political structure is modeled after those of Britain and the United States, it can be described as both a federation like the US and a constitutional monarchy like Britain.

3.1 Parliamentary Democracy
The Legislature

Canada has a parliamentary form of government. The national Parliament, which sits in Ottawa, includes an upper and a lower chamber—the Senate and the House of

---

① Statute of Westminster: 1931 年 12 月 11 日，英国国会通过了《威斯敏斯特法令》，此法令中订明自治领有权自行制定法律而无需等待英国国会批准，订明加拿大殖民地为自治领。

② Westminster system: 威斯敏斯特体系的特点包括：高级行政官员组成内阁，行政与立法的两权制衡，两党制或多党制，统一的中央集权的国家级政府，两院制，多元的利益集团体系，单一选区多数决制，全国统管的中央银行，宪法弹性。

Commons, respectively. The Senate, whose 105 members are appointed by the Governor General on the advice of the Prime Minister, plays a relatively limited part in the political process. Real legislative power rests almost exclusively in the elected House of Commons, whose 308 members are known as Members of Parliament or MPs. MPs represent single-member geographical constituencies, which Canadians often call ridings.

On average, members of the House of Commons are elected for a maximum of five-year term. If the House of Commons loses confidence in the government, the Prime Minister and his Cabinet are expected either to resign or to ask for Parliament to be dissolved so that a general election can be held.

The Executive

The political party with the largest number of MPs in the House of Commons forms the government. The Prime Minister (the political leader of the country) is the MP whom that party has chosen as its leader. Executive power is concentrated in the federal Cabinet, whose members include the Prime Minister and those other MPs chosen by the Prime Minister to head the various departments of the federal government. Members of the Cabinet are known as Ministers and are usually styled Minister of Finance, Minister of Justice and so forth. Senators may hold Cabinet positions, including the Prime Ministership, but with the exception of the ex officio cabinet position occupied by the Government Leader in the Senate, this is rather unusual.

A significant difference between the Canadian parliamentary system and the congressional system found in the U. S. and other countries is the absence of a strict separation between the executive and the legislature. The Prime Minister and other members of the cabinet are themselves legislators and—significantly—it is the convention in Canada that MPs of the governing party vote in favour of all elements of their party's legislative agenda. Because this convention is only rarely breached, lobbying efforts in Canada tend to be directed toward cabinet and parliamentary committees at the policy formation stage rather than toward legislators at the voting stage.

The Judiciary

Canada's court system is a four-level hierarchy as shown below from highest to lowest in terms of legal authority. Each court is bound by the rulings of the courts above them; however, they are not bound by the rulings of other courts at the same level in the hierarchy.

The Supreme Court of Canada—the country's court of last resort—has nine justices appointed by the governor general on recommendation by the prime minister and led by the Chief Justice of Canada, and hears appeals from decisions rendered by the various appellate courts from the provinces and territories.

Below the Supreme Court is the Federal Court, which hears cases arising under certain areas of federal law. It works in conjunction with the Federal Court of Appeal and Tax Court of Canada.

The next level down consists of the provincial and territorial superior courts of general jurisdiction.

At the bottom of hierarchy are the courts called provincial courts. These courts are generally divided within each province into various divisions defined by the subject matter of their respective jurisdictions.

Political Parties

Canada has several political parties, with some active only in one province or region, while others operate nationally. The principal parties at the federal level, in order of their current representation in the House of Commons, are the Conservative Party of Canada, the Liberal Party of Canada, the Bloc Québécois (BQ) and the New Democratic Party of Canada (NDP). While the NDP and BQ are mildly leftist in their politics and the Conservative Party is somewhat to the right, all of the major Canadian political parties tend to be basically centrist, pragmatic, and open to business investment when actually elected to government.

At the provincial level, wings of the Liberal, Progressive Conservative (PC) and New Democratic Parties dominate political life in most provinces. The NDP is inactive at the provincial level in Quebec, as is the PC Party in Quebec, Saskatchewan and British Columbia. In Quebec, the Liberal Party, Action Démocratique du Québec (ADQ) and the Parti Québécois (PQ) are represented in the National Assembly (Quebec's legislative assembly). In Saskatchewan, the Saskatchewan Party and the New Democratic Party are the principal parties with representation in the Legislative Assembly.

3.2 Federal State

Canada is a federal state in which legislative authority is constitutionally divided between one national and thirteen local jurisdictions. Canada's ten principal local jurisdictions are known as provinces. The governments of the three sparsely populated northern territories exercise many of the powers of provincial governments. In addition, the provinces and territories delegate certain powers to cities, towns, and other municipalities, effectively creating a third level of government. The governments of the provinces are generally similar in form to the federal government, although the provinces have unicameral parliaments—there being no equivalent of the Senate at the provincial level—and generally use different names for their political entities, notably the names "Legislative Assembly", "Premier" and "MLA", which generally take the place, in provincial contexts, of the federal terms "Parliament", "Prime Minister" and "MP", respectively.

The constitutional division of powers in Canada is complex, but as a general rule the federal government has jurisdiction over matters of national and international importance, while the provinces have jurisdiction over matters of local importance. For example, the federal government has authority over trade and commerce, criminal law and intellectual property, while the provinces have authority over property law and, generally speaking, over the law of contract. With respect to property and contract matters, it is important to note that while English common law forms the basis of the private law of most of Canada, the Province of Quebec is a civil law jurisdiction.

3.3 Constitutional Monarchy

Canada is a constitutional monarchy, although Canada's continuing recognition of Queen Elizabeth II as head of state has more symbolic than practical significance. When she is not present in Canada, the Queen's ceremonial functions in Canadian public life are performed by her Canadian representative, the Governor General.

References

http://www.canada.ca/en/index.html

Canada. ca is the new Government of Canada website and it provides easy access to government information online. The launch marks the beginning of a transformation to modernize the website and improve Canadians' online experience.

Exercises

I. Choose the one that best completes each of the following statements.

1. Which of the following about the north region is NOT true?
   A. The north is a scarcely populated area of ice and oceans.
   B. Most of the inhabitants are Aboriginal people.
   C. The north has rich oil and gas deposits.
   D. People in this region depend only on arts and crafts for living.
2. Which of the following provinces is known as "the Land of 100,000 Lakes"?
   A. Nova Scotia.   B. Newfoundland.
   C. Manitoba.   D. British Columbia.
3. Who first came and settled Canada?
   A. British colonists.   B. French colonists.
   C. American colonists.   D. Spanish colonists.
4. Which of the following statements about Central Canada is NOT true?
   A. Early European settlements start from here.
   B. More than half of Canada's population lives here.

C. It has the largest cities like Toronto and Montreal.

   D. It's well-known for its mining and forestry industries.

5. Which of the following provinces are densely populated in Canada?

   A. Saskatchewan and Ontario.   B. Ontario and Quebec.

   C. Manitoba and Saskatchewan.   D. Quebec and Manitoba.

6. Which of the following province is the home of most French-speaking people in Canada?

   A. Manitoba.   B. Ontario.   C. Saskatchewan.   D. Quebec.

7. Who is the most influential person in the Canadian government?

   A. The Queen.   B. The Cabinet Minister.

   C. The Prime Minister.   D. The Governor General.

8. Which of the following about the Queen is true?

   A. She is the official head of state.

   B. She is a member of the Cabinet.

   C. She is a symbol of parliamentary democracy.

   D. She is a symbol of Canada.

9. Which of the following is not correct?

   A. The Senate is controlled by the House of Commons.

   B. The Senate is not elected by Canadian people.

   C. The Senate is recommended by the Prime Minister.

   D. The Senate is appointed by the Governor General.

10. Canada is bounded on the north by _____.

    A. the Great Lakes   B. the Atlantic Ocean

    C. the Pacific Ocean   D. the Arctic Ocean

II. Read the following statements carefully and decide whether they are TRUE or FALSE.

1. Canada is the second largest country in the world in terms of territory.
2. Canada's expansive area can be divided into five geographic regions, each with a distinct landscape and climate.
3. Canada has numerous lakes which cover about 7.6% of its landmass.
4. Canada is a constitutional monarchy and the Queen is member of the Cabinet.

III. Give brief answers to the following questions.

1. Give a brief account of multiculturalism in Canada.
2. What are the similarities between the major cities of Canada?

Australia

1. Geography

Australia, officially **the Commonwealth of Australia**①, is a country comprising the mainland of the Australian continent, the island of **Tasmania**②, and numerous smaller islands. It is the world's sixth-largest country by total area. Neighboring countries include Indonesia, East Timor and Papua New Guinea to the north; the Solomon Islands and Vanuatu to the north-east; and New Zealand to the south-east.

The geography of Australia encompasses a wide variety of biogeographic regions being the world's smallest continent but the sixth-largest country in the world. The population of Australia is concentrated along the eastern and southeastern coasts. The geography of the country is extremely diverse, ranging from the snow-capped mountains of **the Australian Alps**③ and Tasmania to large deserts, tropical and temperate forests.

Australia consists of six states, two major mainland territories, and other minor territories. The states are New South Wales, Queensland, South Australia, Tasmania, Victoria and Western Australia. The two major mainland territories are the Northern Territory and **the Australian Capital Territory**④. Western Australia is the largest state covering just under one third of the Australian landmass, followed by Queensland and New South Wales.

Sydney is the capital of New South Wales, the largest and most modern city in Australia, with a suburb of total area of 4074 square kilometers, a population of nearly 400 million, accounting for the country's population of 1/4. Formerly known as Port Jackson, Sydney is not only Australia's financial center, but also a world famous city. Pleasant local climate, year-round sunny, green grass, verdant trees, and flowers, form a contrast with the blue sky. There are many attractions for visitors

---

① the Commonwealth of Australia：澳大利亚联邦。1901 年，英国殖民统治结束，澳大利亚成为一个独立的联邦国家。

② Tasmania：此处指塔斯马尼亚岛，亦可作塔斯马尼亚州，是澳大利亚最小的一个州。

③ The Australian Alps：澳大利亚阿尔卑斯山脉，位于澳洲东南部，为澳洲大陆最高处，海拔2,228 米，库马（Cooma）和堪培拉为山区主要城市。

④ Australian Capital Territory：澳大利亚首都领地，英文简称 A.C.T.，是澳大利亚联邦政府所在地，是澳大利亚辖区最小但人口最稠密的州层级行政区。它全境位于新南威尔士州境内，面积为2,358 平方公里。澳大利亚首都特区的首府是位于特区北部的堪培拉，亦是澳大利亚联邦的首都。领地的最高行政负责人是行政长官（Chief Administrator）。

Map of Australia

from around the world, such as **Sydney Opera House**①, Harbour Bridge, Sydney Tower, Darling Harbour, China Town, The Rocks, Queen Victoria Building, BONDY beach. Sydney has more than a dozen colleges and universities, the University of New South Wales, University of Sydney, UTS are well-known in the world.

  Melbourne② is the capital of Victoria, Australia's second largest city, with an area of 4,360 square kilometers and a population of 3,000,000. The Melbourne cityscape is beautiful, well-planned and tidy, and was hailed as the "most livable" city. The City is home to Melbourne University and other famous universities, bringing together the world's top multinational foreign students in its rigorous academic atmosphere.

  Canberra is Australia's capital city, a young city, with a total area of 2,395 square kilometers, more than 50% of which are national parks or reserves, Canberra is the national capital and the centre of political and administrative power in Australia, yet it is also a rural city, ringed by gum trees, with the occasional

---

 ① Sydney Opera House：悉尼歌剧院。该歌剧院1973年正式落成，2007年6月28日被联合国教科文组织评为世界文化遗产，该剧院设计者为丹麦设计师约恩·乌松。悉尼歌剧院坐落在悉尼港的便利朗角（Bennelong Point），其特有的帆造型，加上悉尼港湾大桥（Harbor Bridge），与周围景物相映成趣。

 ② Melbourne：墨尔本，在2011、2012和2013年连续3年被联合国人居署评为最适合人类居住的城市。1851年至1860年，由于在墨尔本附近发现金矿，淘金热潮让人口激增，墨尔本迅速成为当时的大英帝国乃至世界上少有的繁华大城市，并因此得到了"新金山"的别称。1901年至1927年，墨尔本曾是澳大利亚的首都。今天的墨尔本有"澳大利亚文化之都"的美誉，是全澳的文化、工业中心。

kangaroo seen hopping down its suburban streets. The city holds the majority of the nation's political, literary and artistic treasures, and contains important national institutions such as the High Court of Australia, the Australian National University and the Australian War Memorial, but it has a population of fewer than 500,000.

Brisbane is the third largest city in Australia with a population of 1.3 million. Brisbane is a safe, clean and welcoming city. Despite its relatively new status as a tourist destination, most of the city's facilities are well established and services are of a high standard.

Adelaide, the country's fifth largest city and the state capital of South Australia, is a vibrant city, whose surrounding hills abound with vineyards from the Barossa Valley to McLaren Vale. To the east, the great Murray River meanders from the Victoria border down to the Southern Ocean. Just off the Fleurieu Peninsula lies Kangaroo Island, a haven for wildlife. The city has a population of 110 million, the machinery manufacturing industry is well developed.

2. History

Prehistoric settlers, the Aborigines arrived on the continent from Southeast Asia at least 40,000 years before the first Europeans began exploration in the 17th century. No formal territorial claims were made until 1770, when **Capt. James Cook**[①] took possession of the east coast in the name of Great Britain (all of Australia was claimed as British territory in 1829 with the creation of the colony of Western Australia). Six colonies were created in the late 18th and 19th centuries; they federated and became the Commonwealth of Australia in 1901.

The new country took advantage of its natural resources to rapidly develop agricultural and manufacturing industries and to make a major contribution to **the Allied effort**[②] in World Wars I and II. In recent decades, Australia has become an internationally competitive, advanced market economy due in large part to economic reforms adopted in the 1980s and its location in one of the fastest growing regions of the world economy. Long-term concerns include aging of the population, pressure on infrastructure, and environmental issues such as floods, droughts, and bushfires.

Australia is the driest inhabited continent on earth, making it particularly vulnerable to the challenges of climate change. Australia is home to 10 per cent of

---

① Capt. James Cook：海军上校詹姆斯·库克（1728年11月7日—1779年2月14日），人称库克船长（Captain Cook），是英国皇家海军军官、航海家、探险家和制图师，他曾经三度奉命出海前往太平洋，带领船员成为首批登陆澳洲东岸和夏威夷群岛的欧洲人，也创下首次有欧洲船只环绕新西兰航行的纪录。

② Allied effort：指澳大利亚在第一、第二次世界大战中均属于跟英、美一致的同盟国一方。

the world's biodiversity, and a great number of its **flora and fauna**① exist nowhere else in the world. In January 2013, Australia assumed a nonpermanent seat on the UN Security Council for the 2013—2014 term.

3. Government

Australia is a developed country and one of the wealthiest in the world, with the world's 12th-largest economy. In 2012 Australia had the world's fifth-highest per capita income, Australia's military expenditure is the world's 13th-largest. With the second-highest human development index globally, Australia ranks highly in many international comparisons of national performance, such as quality of life, health, education, economic freedom, and the protection of civil liberties and political rights. Australia is a member of the United Nations, **G20**②, **Commonwealth of Nations**③, **ANZUS**④, **Organisation for Economic Co-operation and Development (OECD)**⑤, World Trade Organization, Asia-Pacific Economic Cooperation, and the Pacific Islands Forum.

Australia is a constitutional monarchy with a federal division of powers. It uses a parliamentary system of government with Queen Elizabeth II at its apex as the Queen of Australia, a role that is distinct from her position as monarch of the other Commonwealth realms. The Queen resides in the United Kingdom, and she is represented by her **viceroys**⑥ in Australia (the Governor-General at the federal level and by the Governors at the state level), who by convention act on the advice of her ministers. Supreme executive authority is vested by the Constitution of Australia in the sovereign, but the power to exercise it is conferred by the Constitution specifically on the Governor-General. The most notable exercise to date of the Governor-General's reserve powers outside the Prime Minister's request was the dismissal of the Whitlam Government in the constitutional crisis of 1975.

---

① flora and fauna: 拉丁语, 植物和动物, 即动植物之总体。

② G20: 20 国集团, 或者廿国集团, 由 G8 八国集团（美国、日本、德国、法国、英国、意大利、加拿大、俄罗斯）和 11 个重要新兴工业国家（中国、阿根廷、澳大利亚、巴西、印度、印度尼西亚、墨西哥、沙特阿拉伯、南非、韩国和土耳其）以及一个实体（欧盟）组成。按照惯例, 国际货币基金组织与世界银行列席该组织的会议。20 国集团的 GDP 总量约占世界的 85%, 人口约为 40 亿。

③ Commonwealth of Nations: 英联邦, 等于 British Commonwealth。

④ ANZUS: Australia, New Zealand, and the United States, with reference to the security alliance between them 太平洋共同防卫组织。

⑤ OECD: 国际经济合作发展组织, 简称世界经合组织。

⑥ viceroy: 总督, 旧时代表国王、女王或政府统治殖民地的人, 此处指英国君主在澳大利亚联邦的代表。国家级别的总督称为 Governor-General, 州一级的州督为 Governor。

3.1 Division of Powers

The federal government is separated into three branches:

- The legislature: the bicameral Parliament, defined in section 1 of the constitution as comprising the Queen (represented by the Governor-General), the Senate, and the House of Representatives;
- The executive: the Federal Executive Council, in practice the Governor-General as advised by the Prime Minister and Ministers of State;
- The judiciary: the High Court of Australia and other federal courts, whose judges are appointed by the Governor-General on advice of the Council.

3.2 Bicameral Parliament

In the Senate (the upper house), there are 76 senators: twelve each from the states and two each from the mainland territories (the Australian Capital Territory and the Northern Territory). The House of Representatives (the lower house) has 150 members elected from single-member electoral divisions, commonly known as "electorates" or "seats", allocated to states on the basis of population, with each original state guaranteed a minimum of five seats. Elections for both chambers are normally held every three years, simultaneously; senators have overlapping six-year terms except for those from the territories, whose terms are not fixed but are tied to the electoral cycle for the lower house; thus only 40 of the 76 places in the Senate are put to each election unless the cycle is interrupted by a double dissolution.

Australia's electoral system uses preferential voting for all lower house elections with the exception of Tasmania and the ACT which, along with the Senate and most state upper houses, combine it with proportional representation in a system known as the single transferable vote. Voting is compulsory for all enrolled citizens 18 years and over in every jurisdiction, as is enrolment (with the exception of South Australia). The party with majority support in the House of Representatives forms the government and its leader becomes Prime Minister. In cases where no party has majority support, the Governor-General has the constitutional power to appoint the Prime Minister and, if necessary, dismiss one that has lost the confidence of Parliament.

3.3 Political Parties

There are two major political groups that usually form government, federally and in the states: the Australian Labor Party and the Coalition which is a formal grouping of the Liberal Party and its minor partner, the National Party. Independent members and several minor parties have achieved representation in Australian parliaments, mostly in upper houses.

References

http://www.australia.gov.au/about-australia/our-government
https://www.cia.gov/library/publications/the-world-factbook/geos/as.html
http://en.wikipedia.org/wiki/Australia
http://www.australiacitytrip.com/

Exercises

I. Choose the one that best completes each of the following statements.

1. The city of _____, which was formerly known as Port Jackson, is the place of the earliest colonial settlement in Australia.
   A. Melbourne   B. Sydney   C. Perth   D. Darwin
2. The following are products imported by Australia from China EXCEPT _____.
   A. food   B. textiles   C. steel products   D. electronics
3. The republican movement has been gathering momentum in Australia since _____ became Prime Minister in 1992.
   A. John Howard   B. Bob Hawke   C. Malcolm Fraser   D. Paul Keating
4. Who were the natives of Australia before the arrival of the British settlers?
   A. The Aborigines.   B. The Maori.   C. The Indians.   D. The Eskimos.
5. The original inhabitants of Australia were _____.
   A. the Red Indians   B. the Eskimos
   C. the Aborigines   D. the Maoris
6. Which of the following cities is located on the eastern coast of Australia?
   A. Perth.   B. Adelaide.   C. Sydney.   D. Melbourne.
7. When did the Australian Federation officially come into being?
   A. 1770.   B. 1788.   C. 1900.   D. 1901.
8. The Maori people are natives of _____.
   A. New Zealand   B. Australia   C. Ireland   D. Canada
9. The full official name of Australia is _____.
   A. The Republic of Australia   B. The Commonwealth of Australia
   C. The Federation of Australia   D. The Union of Australia
10. _____ is popularly known in the West as the Land Down Under.
    A. Britain   B. Canada   C. Australia   D. New Zealand

II. Read the following statements carefully and decide whether they are TRUE or FALSE.

1. Australia is world's smallest continent but the sixth-largest country in the world.
2. Australia consists of six states, one major mainland territory, and other minor

territories.
3. There are two major political groups in Australia, namely the Liberal Party and the National Party.
4. The Queen resides in the United Kingdom, and she is represented by her viceroys in Australia.

III. Give brief answers to the following questions.
1. Name a few facts about the achievements of Australia as an important global player.

New Zealand

1. Geography

Spectacular glaciers, picturesque fiords, rugged mountains, vast plains, rolling hillsides, subtropical forest, volcanic plateau, and miles of coastline with gorgeous sandy beaches—it's all here. No wonder New Zealand is becoming so popular as a location for movies.

Lying in the south-west Pacific, New Zealand consists of two main islands—the North Island and the South Island. Stewart Island and many smaller islands lie offshore.

Map of New Zealand
From: http://www.qianzhengdaiban.com/gj/xinxilan/map.html

The North Island of New Zealand has a "spine" of mountain ranges running through the middle, with gentle rolling farmland on both sides. The central North Island is dominated by the Volcanic Plateau, an active volcanic and thermal area. The massive Southern Alps form the backbone of the South Island. To the east of the Southern Alps is the rolling farmland of Otago and Southland, and the vast, flat Canterbury Plains.

New Zealand sits on two tectonic plates-the Pacific and the Australian. The North Island and some parts of the South Island sit on the Australian Plate, while the rest of the South Island sits on the Pacific. Because these plates are constantly shifting and grinding into each other, New Zealand gets a lot of geological action.

This subterranean activity blesses New Zealand with some spectacular geothermal areas and relaxing hot springs, as well as providing electricity and heating in some areas. **Rotorua**① is the main hub for geothermal attractions, with plenty of mud pools, geysers, and hot springs in its active thermal areas — not to mention its trademark "Sulphur City" smell. First settled by **Maori**② who used the hot springs for cooking and bathing, Rotorua soon attracted European residents. The reputed health benefits of its hot pools quickly earned the area the name of "Cureland".

New Zealand has over 15,000 kilometres of beautiful and varied coastline. In the Far North and on most of the East Coast of the North Island there are long sandy beaches perfect for swimming, surfing and sunbathing. The North Island's west coast has dark sandy beaches, with sand heavy in iron. The north of the South Island has some beautiful sandy beaches, while the coastline around the rest of the South Island tends to be wilder and more rugged.

About a fifth of the North Island and two-thirds of the South Island are mountains. Stretching from the north of the North Island to the bottom of the South, these mountains are caused by the collision of the Australian and Pacific Plates. New Zealand's Southern Alps have a number of glaciers, the largest being Tasman glacier.

---

① Rotorua: 罗托鲁阿，又译罗托鲁瓦、罗托路亚，是新西兰北岛中北部一座工业城市。位于罗托鲁阿湖南畔，距奥克兰（Auckland）市221公里，多天然温泉，是毛利人聚居区和著名的旅游胜地，人口54700人。"罗托鲁阿"是毛利语，意为"双湖"。罗托鲁阿湖面积为23平方公里。全市遍布热泉，市郊森林密布。湖光潋滟，山色迷离，游禽戏水，海鸥翔空，空气中硫磺弥漫，热泉灰黄泥浆沸腾，加之毛利文化多姿多彩，前来观光的游客终年络绎不绝。

② Maori: 毛利人；毛利语。新西兰的少数民族。属蒙古人种和澳大利亚人种的混合类型。使用毛利语，属南岛语系波利尼西亚语族。有新创拉丁文字母文字。信仰多神，崇拜领袖，有祭司和巫师，禁忌甚多。相传其祖先系10世纪后自波利尼西亚中部的社会群岛迁来。后与当地土著美拉尼西亚人通婚，发生混合，因此在体质特征上与其他波利尼西亚人略有不同。新西兰官方文献证明，毛利人是4,000多年前从台湾迁出的原住民，毛利人参访台湾阿美族太巴塱部落祖祠，发现门窗开的位置、建筑梁柱等结构都和毛利人聚会所相同。

Over thousands of years, the process of **subduction**① has seen parts of the New Zealand landscape become submerged. The Marlborough Sounds and Fiordland are examples of high mountain ranges that have 'sunk' into the sea, creating spectacular sounds and fiords. These areas provide some of New Zealand most picturesque scenery, with steep lush hills plunging down to the deep still bays below. Clear, deep still water surrounded by beautiful bush makes these areas ideal for boating and kayaking.

Auckland is New Zealand's largest city and main transport hub. The region is home to some 1.5 million people and is also the largest **Polynesian**② city in the world. Imagine an urban environment where everyone lives within half an hour of beautiful beaches, hiking trails and a dozen enchanting holiday islands.

Wellington is the capital city and second most populous urban area of New Zealand, with 397,900 residents. It is located at the southwestern tip of the North Island, between Cook Strait and the Rimutaka Range. It is the major population centre of the southern North Island, and is the administrative centre of the Wellington Region, which also includes the Kapiti Coast and Wairarapa. Wellington is the world's southernmost capital city of a sovereign state.

Christchurch is the largest city in the South Island of New Zealand, and the country's third-most populous urban area. It lies one third of the way down the South Island's east coast, just north of Banks Peninsula which itself, since 2006, lies within the formal limits of Christchurch. The population of Christchurch City at the 5 March 2013 census was 341,469.

2. History

New Zealand has a rich and fascinating history, reflecting a unique mix of Maori and European culture.

Maori were the first to arrive in New Zealand, journeying in canoes from **Hawaiki**③ about 1,000 years ago. A Dutchman, Abel Tasman, was the first European to sight the country but it was the British who made New Zealand part of their empire.

In 1840, the ***Treaty of Waitangi***④ was signed, an agreement between the

---

① subduction：潜没，指一个大陆板块降到另一个下面。发生这种情形时，地球内部的高温会产生岩浆，世界上80%的火山都是这样形成的。

② Polynesian：波利尼西亚人。

③ Hawaiki：哈瓦基，传说中是所有毛利人的物质和精神家园。

④ Treaty of Waitangi：《怀唐伊条约》，又译《威坦哲条约》，是1840年时英国王室与毛利人之间签署的一项协议。条约的签订，促使新西兰建立了英国法律体系，同时也确认了毛利人对其土地和文化的拥有权。该条约被公认为新西兰的建国文献，该条约目前仍为现行文件。

British Crown and Maori. It established British law in New Zealand and is considered New Zealand's founding document and an important part of the country's history. The building where the treaty was signed has been preserved and, today, the Waitangi Treaty Grounds are a popular attraction.

3. Government

The politics of New Zealand take place in a framework of a **parliamentary representative democratic monarchy**①. The basic system is closely patterned on that of the **Westminster System**②, although a number of significant modifications have been made. The head of state is Queen Elizabeth II, who is represented by the Governor-General and the head of government is the Prime Minister who chairs the Cabinet drawn from an elected Parliament.

New Zealand has no formal codified constitution; the constitutional framework consists of a mixture of various documents (including certain acts of the United Kingdom and New Zealand Parliaments), the Treaty of Waitangi and constitutional conventions. The Constitution Act in 1852 established the system of government and these were later consolidated in 1986. Constitutional rights are protected under common law and are strengthened by the Bill of Rights Act 1990 and Human Rights Act 1993, although these are not entrenched and can be overturned by Parliament with a simple majority. The Constitution Act describes the three branches of Government in New Zealand: The Executive (the Sovereign and Cabinet), the legislature (Parliament) and the judiciary (Courts).

New Zealand's main legislative body is a unicameral Parliament known as the House of Representatives. Until 1950 there was a second chamber, consisting of an upper house known as the Legislative Council. Suffrage is extended to everyone over the age of 18 years, women having gained the vote in 1893. Parliaments have a maximum term of three years, although an election can be called earlier. The House of Representatives meets in Parliament House.

Several seats are reserved for members elected on a separate Maori roll. However, Maori may choose to vote in and to run for the non-reserved seats and for the party list (since 1996), and as a result many have now entered Parliament outside of the reserved seats.

Almost all parliamentary general elections between 1853 and 1996 were held

---

① parliamentary representative democratic monarchy：议会代表民主君主制。

② Westminster system：威斯敏斯特体系，特点包括：高级行政官员组成内阁，行政与立法的两权制衡，两党制或多党制，统一的中央集权的国家级政府，两院制，多元的利益集团体系，单一选区多数决制，全国统管的中央银行，宪法弹性。

under the **first-past-the-post (FPP) system**①. Under FPP the candidate in a given electorate that received the most votes was elected to parliament. The only deviation from the FPP system during this time occurred in the 1908 election when a second ballot system was tried. Under this system the elections since 1935 have been dominated by two political parties, National and Labour.

Criticism of the FPP system began in the 1950s and intensified after Labour lost the 1978 and 1981 elections despite having more overall votes than National. An indicative (non-binding) referendum to change the voting system was held in 1992, which lead to a binding referendum during the 1993 election. As a result, New Zealand has used the **mixed member proportional (MMP) voting system**② since 1996. Under MMP, each member of Parliament is either elected by voters in a single-member constituency via first-past-the-post or appointed from party lists. Officially, the New Zealand parliament has 120 Seats, however this sometimes differs due to overhangs and underhangs.

References

http://www.newzealand.com/

The Tourism New Zealand website **newzealand.com** is the official tourism website for New Zealand. It features information that is relevant to travellers who are thinking about and actively planning a visit to New Zealand. Through this site, potential visitors will be able to learn about the diversity of what New Zealand has to offer and how to make their visit a fantastic experience. newzealand.com has an open content model and Tourism New Zealand encourages tourism businesses, previous travellers to New Zealand, and Kiwis to contribute content to the website to help future travellers plan their trip.

http://en.wikipedia.org/wiki/

Wikipedia is a multilingual, web-based, free-content encyclopedia project supported by the Wikimedia Foundation and based on an openly editable model.

Exercises

I. Choose the one that best completes each of the following statements.

1. Which of the following island is NOT a part of New Zealand?
   A. North Island.　　　　　　　　B. South Island.
   C. Stewart Island.　　　　　　　D. Isle of Wight.
2. Which of the following tectonic plate(s) does New Zealand sit on?

---

① first-past-the-post (FPP) system: 最高得票者当选的系统。
② mixed member proportional (MMP) voting system: 混合比例成员投票系统。

    A. The Pacific and the Australian.   B. The Pacific.
    C. The Australian.   D. Indo-Australian plate.
3. Which of the following place is called "Cureland"?
    A. Otago.   B. Rotorua.   C. Auckland.   D. Hawaiki.
4. The first European to visit New Zealand was a/an _____, Abel Tasman.
    A. Englishman   B. Dutchman   C. Frenchman   D. German
5. _____ is the capital of New Zealand.
    A. Auckland   B. Wellington   C. Toronto   D. Christchurch
6. The natural disasters in New Zealand may include _____.
    A. earthquakes, volcanoes and flooding
    B. volcanoes, flooding and heavy snows
    C. earthquakes, flooding, and heavy snows
    D. volcanoes, heavy snows and earthquakes
7. _____ is the largest city of New Zealand.
    A. Auckland   B. Wellington   C. Toronto   D. Christchurch
8. In 1840, the Treaty of Waitangi was signed, an agreement between the British Crown and _____.
    A. Polynesian   B. British   C. New Zealanders   D. Maori
9. Who is the head of state in New Zealand?
    A. Prime Minister.   B. President.
    C. Queen Elizabeth II.   D. Parliament Representatives.
10. Officially, how many Seats are there in New Zealand?
    A. 100.   B. 200.   C. 120.   D. 150.

II. Read the following statements carefully and decide whether they are TRUE or FALSE.

1. Maori were the first to arrive in New Zealand, journeying in canoes from Hawaiki about 1,000 years ago.
2. The Governor-General chairs the Cabinet drawn from an elected Parliament in New Zealand.
3. Christchurch is the largest city in the South Island of New Zealand, and the country's third-most populous urban area.
4. Under MMP, each member of Parliament is either elected by voters in a single-member constituency via first-past-the-post or appointed from party lists.

III. Give brief answers to the following question.

What's the role of Maori culture in the culture of New Zealand?

Key to Exercises

Chapter 1 Geography of the U. K.

Section One: A Brief Introduction
I. 1~15   DBCBB   ACACB   CADBB
II. 1~10   TFTTT   FTTTT
III.
1. The British Isles is the geographical term for a group of about 5,000 islands off the north-west coast of mainland Europe between the latitudes 50°N and 61°N. The largest island is Britain or Great Britain, which is also the largest island in Europe. It consists of England Wales and Scotland.
2. New Towns are separated from housing and there are greener, open spaces. However, New Towns have partially failed since many are near enough to conurbations, people to use them as dormitory towns and recent government policy has been to expand existing towns like Telford and Milton Keynes (formed from the amalgamation of a group of villages), which is cheaper than creating an entirely new town.

Section Two: In-depth Reading
Reading One
1. Rye makes an excellent weekend destination or a stop on a cycle or hiking tour of the Romney Marshes. It's also a good place to warm up with tea and a cake after a bracing day on nearby Camber Sands. About 25 antiques stores are scattered around the town, many of them strung along Cinque Ports Street. There are also a good number of tea shops, seafood restaurants and pubs.
2. Omitted.

Reading Two
1. The changeable weather in Britain makes the people love this country deeply.

2. British culture is founded upon politeness and a respect for another's privacy. Asking personal questions was considered impolite and it would be embarrassing to both parties if an emotional response was given to a simple question of "How are you?" Therefore, the easiest topic to discuss that would allow both parties to be friendly and social without any risk of emotional distress is to simply discuss the weather. So, if you are the first time to Britain, you'd better talk about the weather with them who are the native. It's advisable.
3. Omitted.

Chapter 2 History of the U. K.

Section One: A Brief Introduction
I. 1~5 DADAD   6~10 BBAAC   11~15 CCABB
II. 1~5 TTFFF   6~10 TTTTT
III.
1. WWII involved the vast majority of the world's nations, eventually forming two opposing military alliances: the Axis and the Allies, the former included Germany, Austria-Hungary, later joined by the Ottoman Empire and Bulgaria, and the latter were mainly comprised of France, the Russian Empire, the British Empire, Italy and the United States.
2. (1) The use of energy. Coal was the fuel which kick-started the Industrial Revolution, and Britain was very fortunate to have plenty that could be easily mined. Britain had an advantage over other European countries because its mines were near the sea, so ships could carry coal cheaply to the most important market-London.
(2) Intellectual climate. Newcomen and other inventors benefited from the intellectual climate. There was a prolific exchange of scientific and technological ideas. And Britain, unlike many European countries, did not suffer censorship by Church or state. longside the new discoveries was a growing movement of people, trying to find practical applications for these new discoveries. Men of action and men of ideas, industrialists and scientists-often from very different backgrounds-met to share their ideas and observations, in what was to be called the Industrial Enlightenment. They unleashed a wave of free thinking and creativity.
(3) Political liberalism. Britain also had the right political background for free-market capitalism. The system of parliamentary government that followed the Glorious Revolution of 1688-9 provided the background for stable investment and for a basis of taxation favourable to economic expansion. France, by contrast, was home to some of the finest scientific minds, but had an absolute monarchy which

wielded great control over economic and political life.

(4) Naval power. Naval power and imperial possessions enabled Britain to dominate trans-oceanic trade and to profit accordingly. Entrepreneurship was at the heart of economic success in the colonies. There was a considerable human cost to this free trade however, which enabled landowners to buy huge numbers of slaves, transported from Africa. They were treated as a natural resource to be used and exploited in the quest for maximum profit.

Section Two: In-depth Reading
Reading One
1. Proud and a little bit arrogant. See in sentences like: "The British Empire has profoundly shaped the modern world. Most present-day countries outside Europe owe their existence to empires, especially to the British Empire." "Through their empire the British disseminated their institutions, culture, and language. Every country in the present-day world can be regarded as anything approaching a carbon copy of what Britain was or is..."
2. Britain enjoyed a period of almost unchallenged dominance and expanded its territory across the globe. The two world wars drained Britain of its power. As a result, Britain lost the sea supremacy forever to the United States. In addition, the country has exhausted its reserves of gold, dollars and overseas investment, and was deeply in debt to the United States.
3. (1) New Zealand, Australia and Canada also adopted parliamentary system. Note that New Zealand is unicameral (一院制) rather than bicameral (两院制). See the form below:

Parliamentary system	Lower House	Upper House
Britain	House of Commons	House of Lords
Canada	House of Commons	Senate
New Zealand	House of Representatives	
Australia	House of Representatives	Senate

(2) The King or Queen (currently Elizabeth II) acts as the head of state in Commonwealth countries. The monarchy is represented by the governor-general (总督).

(3) The commonwealth countries adopt the separation of powers (executive branch, legislative branch and judicial branch)

Reading Two
1. (1) Language impact. Words from the other languages were and are brought into English vocabulary. For example, shampoo (from Indian), vampire (from Hungarian), kungfu (from China), magazine (from Arabic).

(2) Food impact. It is impossible to walk through any main street in London or

other major British city in the 21st century without encountering fast food outlets for Chinese food (Hong Kong immigrant influence), Indian and Pakistani food, African and Carribean produce.

(3) Religious impact. Immigrants, at first greeted with considerable hostility by white Britons, gradually became accepted, so did their religious institutions, varying widely from the traditional Church of England Christian tradition to Hinduism to Buddhism.

2. omitted
3. Nowadays, the English economy relies heavily on services. The main industries are travel (discount airlines and travel agencies), education (apart from Oxford and Cambridge universities and textbooks, hundreds of language schools for learners of English), music (EMI, HMV, Virgin...), prestige cars (Rolls Royce, Bentley, Jaguar, Lotus, Aston Martin, MG...), fashion (Burberry, Dunhill, Paul Smith, Vivienne Westwood, French Connection...), and surprisingly to some, food (well especially tea, biscuits, chocolates and jam or companies like Unilever and Cadburry-Schweppes)

Chapter 3   British Government and Politics

Section One: A Brief Introduction
I. 1~5 DCBDA   6~10 BDAAB   11~14 ADBD
II. 1~5 TFTTF   6~10 TTTTT
III.
1. American model restricts each section's powers and avoids crossover between the three sectors of politics, while there is a merging of roles in the British mode.

    In America all three branches are systematically split between the Executive (the president), the legislative (Congress) and the Judiciary (the Supreme Court). The president cannot serve in Congress when president and serving Congressmen cannot be a Supreme Court judge. In theory, no branch becomes more powerful than the other two so that a balance occurs. The American Constitution clearly states what the executive, the legislative and the judiciary can do.

    In Britain, the Prime Minister is an active member of the legislative and can vote in Parliament, yet he is also the leading member of the executive. Also the Lord Chancellor is a member of the cabinet and therefore of the executive as well as being head of the judiciary. The House of Lords also has a right to vote on bills so they are part of the legislative but the Lords also contains the Law Lords who are an important part of the judiciary. As with the PM, the members of the

Cabinet are also members of the legislative who have the right, as a Member of Parliament, to vote on issues.
2. Parliament is the law-making body of Britain, and is separate from government. It is made up of the King or Queen, the House of Lords and the House of Commons.

The House of Commons is the lower house of the UK bicameral Parliament. It is elected by universal adult suffrage voters to represent their interests and concerns and currently consists of 650 elected MPs. The chief officer of the House of Commons is the Speaker, who is elected by MPs to preside over the House, and interprets the rules of the House. MPs are involved in attending debates and voting on new laws, and can use their position to ask government ministers questions about current issues.

The House of Lords is the second chamber of the UK Parliament. It is independent from, and complements the work of, the elected House of Commons. Members of the House of Lords are appointed by the Queen on the advice of the Prime Minister. The House of Lords is presided over by the Lord Chancellor, who is a political appointee of the government. The Lords shares the task of making and shaping laws and checking and challenging the work of the government. The Lords has three main roles: making laws; in-depth consideration of public policy; holding government to account.

Section Two: In-depth Reading
Reading One
1. Omitted.
2. An unwritten constitution based on conventions has the advantage of being extremely adaptable or flexible. Since it is unwritten, it can be changed easily to deal with new situations. Old constitutional practices do not become millstones that make it difficult to deal with changed circumstances. Unwritten Constitution changes to reflect the times in which we live. The disadvantage of an unwritten constitution based on conventions is that it carries risks. If a constitution is to place limits on government or to set out the parameters within which governments must operate, then the fact that it can be adapted by government whim can be problematic.

Reading Two

	GB	USA
Time	At any time in the Prime Minister's 5-year term	In the first week on November
Duration of each term	5 years maximum	4 years
Maximum serving terms	No limit	2 terms

	GB	USA
Budget	Tens of millions (£)	A billion ($)
Duration of campaign	No fixed date	10 months
Candidates	a Republican one and a Democrat one	Vote for a party rather than for a candidate
System	First-past-the-post	winner-takes-all

Chapter 4　British Economy

Section One

I. 1～15 CCBDC　　DADCA　　BBDAD
II. 1～10 TFTTF　　TTFTT
III.

1. The Industrial Revolution began with the textile industry. It's characterized by a series of inventions and improvements of machines, such as John Ray's flying shuttle, James Hargreaves' spinning Jenny, Richard Arkwright's waterframe and Samuel Cropton's mule. The Scottish inventor James Watt produced a very efficient steam engine in 1765, which could be applied to textile and other machinery. The most important element in speeding industrialization was the breakthrough in smelting iron with coke instead of charcoal in 1709. Similar developments occurred in the forging side of the iron industry which enabled iron to replace wool and stone in many sectors of the economy. Improved transportation ran parallel with production. As a result of the industrial revolution, Britain was by 1830 the "workshop of the world"; no other country could compete with her in industrial production.

2. After a period of generally disappointing growth in 2011 and 2012, the UK economy showed clear signs of recovery during 2013 and we expect this to continue in 2014-15. All major industry sectors and regions are now showing positive growth trends. Given these projections, the UK could overtake France, to become the fifth largest economy in the world before 2020. Inflation appears to be under control for now, but interest rates are likely to start rising gradually from late 2014 or early 2015 in order to keep inflation around target in the longer term. Higher interest rates will be one factor causing recent rapid rates of house price inflation to moderate later in this decade, as discussed in detail in this report. But the housing market remains an important source of risk for the UK economy, together with possible global shocks and relatively weak productivity growth.

Section Two
Reading One
1. Omitted.
2. Omitted.

Reading Two
1. This benefit, the "Commonwealth advantage", reflects shared history and commonalities of language, law and business practice. It should act, other things being equal, as a major incentive to intra-Commonwealth trade.
2. Omitted.

Chapter 5　Education of the U. K.

Section One: A Brief Introduction
I. 1～6 ACDBAD

II.
1. Major periods between 5～18: primary education (ages 4—11), secondary education (ages 11—18). Important exams: GCSE and A-level.
2. Schooling years and degree titles: Foundation degrees—2 year; Bachelor's degrees—3 year, Master's degrees—1 or 2 year; Doctorate degrees—3 year. Tuitions: up from 3000 GBP in 2006 to 9000 GBP in 2012.
3. The Russell Group, includes 24 universities and their CUG 2014 rankings: 1 Cambridge, 2 Oxford, 3 LSE, 4 Imperial College London, 5 Durham, 7 University College London, 8 Warwick, 10 Exeter, 12 York, 15 Bristol, 17 Birmingham, 18 Edinburgh, 19 King's College London, 20 Southampton, 22 Newcastle, 23 Glasgow, 24 Nottingham, 25 Manchester, 26 Sheffield, 29 Queen's, Belfast, 32 Leeds, 35 Cardiff, 35 Queen Mary, 38 Liverpool. They might not be the top 24 universities in the UK.
4. Incessantly rising top-up fees, falling academic standards, grade inflations, functional illiteracy and innumeracy, a lack of trust for teachers.

Section Two: In-depth Reading
Reading One
1. Etonians reworked the international pop hit Gangnam Style by PSY, called Eton Style, and posted it on YouTube. It has had more than 2.6m views. Eton is adept at mocking and advertising itself simultaneously.
2. For less overwhelmingly privileged boys, says the ex-pupil, Eton can be life-changing: "It's just expected that you will drink from the cup of opportunity. So

you become used to being able to do whatever you put your hand to. Or at the least, you learn not to seem fazed by opportunities in the wider world."
3. "It's a huge amount of money," he admits—the appearance of candour is one of Little's tactics when he talks to the outside world. "Sometimes I think, short of robbing a bank, what d'you do?" A long-term goal is for Eton to become "needs-blind": to admit any boy, regardless of ability to pay,
4. The classic Etonian skills—Cameron has them—have long included adjusting your message to your audience, defusing the issue of privilege with self-deprecation, and bending to the prevailing social and political winds, but only so far.
5. Subtle networking, a sense of mission, an elite that does not think too hard about its material advantages.

Reading Two
1. No, societies which want to end the injustice of privilege work to remove the divides rather than leave them in place. Also, divisions are perpetuated by the continued existence of two sides.
2. Once you account for the pupils' different socioeconomic background, private schools are easily outperformed by our publicly funded schools.
3. Giving private places to the difficult, often-excluded pupils that the state sector has to deal with all the time would actually be of some practical use and would operate as an interesting test case to see how effective private education would be in helping kids who are not keen on learning.

Chapter 6 British Media

Section One: A Brief Introduction
Ⅰ. 1~5 DCDDC   6~10 ACBCD   11~16 BDDAAC
Ⅱ.
1. The most prominent being the state-owned public service broadcaster, the BBC (British Broadcasting Corporation). The BBC's largest competitors are ITV plc and News Corporation.
2. Traditionally British newspapers have been divided into "quality", serious-minded newspapers (usually referred to as "broadsheets" because of their large size—*The Guardian*) and the more populist, "tabloid" varieties—*The Sun*.
3. The BBC World Service is a radio network which broadcast in 33 languages globally. The BBC World News is BBC's international television news service that broadcast throughout the world. BBC Worldwide provides international television broadcast services, and it's operated on a commercial subscription basis over cable and satellite services.

Section Two: In-depth Reading
Reading One
1. The main accusations are that journalists, or their hired investigators, took advantage of often limited security on mobile phone voicemail boxes to listen in to messages left for celebrities, politicians or people involved in major stories.
2. It has been widely reported that a number of other papers had also been involved in underhand practices to secure circulation-boosting stories. A lawyer for the Dowler family said *News of the World* was 'unlucky' because investigator Glenn Mulcaire had kept copious notes. In 2007, Mulcaire and the paper's then royal correspondent went to jail for hacking.
3. The strategy is chucking first journalists, then executives and finally a whole newspaper overboard.

Reading Two
1. *The News of the World* is 168 years old. That it is read by more people than any other English language newspaper. That it has enjoyed support from Britain's largest advertisers. And that it has a proud history of fighting crime, exposing wrong-doing and regularly setting the news agenda for the nation.
2. WRONG: 1) *The News of the World* failed to hold itself to account. 2) The paper made statements to Parliament without being in the full possession of the facts. 3) The company paid out-of-court settlements approved by James Murdoch.
RIGHT: Apologize and make amends.
3. He hopes everyone inside and outside the company will acknowledge that they are doing their utmost to fix the faults, atone for them, and make sure they never happen again.

Chapter 7 Holidays

Section One: A Brief Introduction
I. 1~15 DAAAB   ACDCB   ABBDA
II. 1~10 FFTTF   TFTTT
III.
1. Thanksgiving Day is traditionally a day for families and friends to get together for a special meal. The meal often includes a turkey, stuffing, potatoes, cranberry sauce, gravy, pumpkin pie, and vegetables. Thanksgiving Day is a time for many people to give thanks for what they have.

    Thanksgiving Day parades are held in some cities and towns on or around

Thanksgiving Day. Some parades or festivities also mark the opening of the Christmas shopping season. Some people have a four-day weekend so it is a popular time for trips and to visit family and friends.

2. Federal law establishes the following public holidays for federal employees. If the holiday falls during the weekend, it may be observed on a different day.

Many government offices are closed on federal holidays and some private businesses may close as well. If you plan to visit a government office on or around a federal holiday, you should contact them to determine when they will be open.

New Year's Day is January 1. The celebration of this holiday begins the night before, when Americans gather to wish each other a happy and prosperous coming year. Many Americans make New Year's resolutions.

Birthday of Martin Luther King, Jr. is celebrated on the third Monday in January. The Reverend Martin Luther King, Jr. was an African-American clergyman who is recognized for his tireless efforts to win civil rights for all people through nonviolent means.

Washington's Birthday is observed the third Monday of February in honor George Washington, the first President of the United States. This date is commonly called **Presidents' Day** and many groups honor the legacy of past presidents on this date.

Memorial Day is a observed the last Monday of May. It originally honored the people killed in the American Civil War, but has become a day on which the American dead of all wars are remembered.

Independence Day is July 4. This holiday honors the nation's birthday-the adoption of the Declaration of Independence on July 4, 1776. It is a day of picnics and patriotic parades, a night of concerts, and fireworks.

Labor Day is the first Monday of September. This holiday honors the nation's working people, typically with parades. For most Americans it marks the end of the summer vacation season and the start of the school year.

Columbus Day is a celebrated on the second Monday in October. The day commemorates October 12, 1492, when Italian navigator Christopher Columbus landed in the New World. The holiday was first proclaimed in 1937 by President Franklin D. Roosevelt.

Veterans Day is celebrated on November 11. This holiday was originally called Armistice Day and established to honor Americans who had served in World War I. It now honors veterans of all wars in which the U. S. has fought. Veterans' organizations hold parades, and the president places a wreath on the Tomb of the Unknowns at Arlington National Cemetery in Virginia.

Thanksgiving Day is celebrated on the fourth Thursday in November. In the fall of 1621, the **Pilgrims** held a three-day feast to celebrate a bountiful harvest.

Many regard this event as the nation's first Thanksgiving. The Thanksgiving feast became a national tradition and almost always includes some of the foods served at the first feast: roast turkey, cranberry sauce, potatoes, and pumpkin pie.

Christmas Day is a celebrated on December 25. Christmas is a Christian holiday marking the birth of the Christ Child. Decorating houses and yards with lights, putting up Christmas trees, giving gifts, and sending greeting cards have become holiday traditions even for many non-Christian Americans.

3. There are many commonly observed celebrations in the United States that are not federal holidays. Some of these observances honor groups of people, such as National African American History Month and Women's History Month, or causes, such as National Oceans Month and National Substance Abuse Prevention Month. Many of these holidays and observances are proclaimed by the President ever year. These are some of the most popular American celebrations and observances that occur every year.

Groundhog Day is February 2 and has been celebrated since 1887. On Groundhog Day, crowds gather in Punxsutawney, Pennsylvania, to see if groundhog, Punxsutawney Phil, sees his shadow after emerging from his burrow, thus predicting six more weeks of winter weather.

Valentine's Day is celebrated on February 14. The day was named after an early Christian martyr, and on Valentine's Day, Americans give presents like candy or flowers to the ones they love. The first mass-produced valentine cards were sold in the 1840s.

Earth Day is observed on April 22. First celebrated in 1970 in the United States, it inspired national legislation such as the Clean Air and Clean Water Acts. Earth Day is designed to promote ecology, encourage respect for life on earth, and highlight concern over pollution of the soil, air, and water.

National Arbor Day was proclaimed as the last Friday in April by President Richard Nixon in 1970. A number of state Arbor Days are observed at other times of the year to coincide with the best tree planting weather. The observance began in 1872, when Nebraska settlers and homesteaders were urged to plant trees on the largely treeless plains.

Mother's Day is the second Sunday of May. President Woodrow Wilson issued a proclamation in 1914 that started the holiday. He asked Americans to give a public expression of reverence to mothers on this day. Carnations have come to represent Mother's Day, following President William McKinley's habit of always wearing a white carnation, his mother's favorite flower.

Flag Day, celebrated June 14, has been a presidentially proclaimed observance since 1916. Although Flag Day is not a federal holiday, Americans are encouraged to display the flag outside their homes and businesses on this day to honor the history and heritage the American flag represents.

Father's Day celebrates fathers every third Sunday of June. Father's Day began in 1909 in Spokane, Washington, when a daughter requested a special day to honor her father, a Civil War veteran who raised his children after his wife died. The first presidential proclamation honoring fathers was issued in 1966 by President Lyndon Johnson.

Patriot Day and National Day of Service and Remembrance is observed on September 11 in honor of the victims of these attacks. September 11, 2001, was a defining moment in American history. On that day, terrorists hijacked four commercial airliners to strike targets in the United States. Nearly 3,000 people died as a consequence of the attacks.

Halloween is celebrated on October 31. On Halloween, American children dress up in funny or scary costumes and go "trick or treating" by knocking on doors in their neighborhood. The neighbors are expected to respond by giving them small gifts of candy or money.

Pearl Harbor Remembrance Day is December 7. In 1994, Congress designated this national observance to honor the more than 2,400 military service personnel who died on this date in 1941, during the surprise attack on Pearl Harbor, Hawaii, by Japanese forces. The attack on Pearl Harbor caused the United States to enter World War II.

Section Two: In-depth Reading
Reading One
1. Omitted.
2. Omitted.

Reading Two
1. Omitted.
2. Omitted.

Chapter 8　British Literature

Section One: A Brief Introduction
Ⅰ. 1~5 CBCDC　　6~10 ACACA
Ⅱ. 1~5 FTFTT　　6~10 FTTTT
Ⅲ.
1. In literary criticism, stream of consciousness is a narrative mode that seeks to portray an individual's point of view by giving the written equivalent of the

character's thought processes, either in a loose "interior monologue", or in connection to his or her actions. Stream-of-consciousness writing is usually regarded as a special form of interior monologue and is characterized by associative leaps in thought and lack of punctuation. Stream of consciousness and interior monologue are distinguished from dramatic monologue and soliloquy, where the speaker is addressing an audience or a third person, which are chiefly used in poetry or drama. In stream of consciousness the speaker's thought processes are more often depicted as overheard in the mind (or addressed to oneself); it is primarily a fictional device.

The use of the narrative technique of stream of consciousness is usually associated with modernist novelists in the first part of the twentieth-century. The modernist novelists that are associated with the use of this narrative technique are James Joyce in *Ulysses* (1922), Italo Svevo in *La coscienza di Zeno* (1923), Virginia Woolf in *Mrs Dalloway* (1925) and *To the Lighthouse* (1927) and William Faulkner in *The Sound and the Fury* (1928).

2. The three main categories of Shakespeare's plays are comedy, tragedy and historical play. His major comedies are *A Comedy of Errors*, *A Midsummer Night's Dream*, *Merchant of Venice*, *Much Ado About Nothing*, *As You Like It*, and *Twelfth Night*. His major tragedies are *Hamlet*, *Othello*, *Macbeth*, *King Lear*, *Anthony and Cleopatra*, *Romeo and Juliet* and *Julius Caesar*. His major historical plays are *Richard II*, *Henry IV*, *Henry V* and *Henry VIII*.

Section Two: In-depth Reading
Reading One
Here are some of the most popular Shakespeare phrases in common use today:
(1) A laughing stock (*The Merry Wives of Windsor*): someone who does something very stupid which makes other people laugh at them
(2) A sorry sight (*Macbeth*): a sight that one regrets seeing; someone or something that is unpleasant to look at
(3) As dead as a doornail (*Henry VI*): undoubtedly dead
(4) Eaten out of house and home (*Henry V, Part 2*): to ruin someone, esp. one's parent or one's host, by consuming all his food
(5) Fair play (*The Tempest*): an established standard of decency
(6) Wear one's heart upon/on one's sleeve (*Othello*): to display one's feelings openly and habitually, rather than keep them private
(7) In a pickle (*The Tempest*): in trouble
(8) In stitches (*Twelfth Night*): laughing so hard that it is difficult to control yourself
(9) In the twinkling of an eye (*The Merchant of Venice*): very quickly

(10) Mum's the word (*Henry VI, Part 2*): to keep quiet, to say nothing
(11) Neither here nor there (*Othello*): not of any importance; irrelevant and immaterial
(12) Send him packing (*Henry IV*): to send someone away
(13) Set your teeth on edge (*Henry IV*): to upset someone very much
(14) There's method in my madness (*Hamlet*): although someone seems to be behaving strangely, there is a reason for their behaviour
(15) Too much of a good thing (*As You Like It*): if you have too much of a good thing, something pleasant becomes unpleasant because you have too much of it
(16) Vanish into thin air (*Othello*): to disappear without leaving a trace

Reading Two
omitted

Chapter 9 Geography of the U. S. A.

Section One
Ⅰ. 1～15 ABDDC DABAA ACACA
Ⅱ. 1～10 TTFTT FTFTT
Ⅲ.
1. The U. S. borders both the North Atlantic and North Pacific Oceans and is bordered by Canada and Mexico. It is the third largest country in the world by area and has a varied topography. The eastern regions consist of hills and low mountains while the central interior is a vast plain (called the Great Plains region) and the west has high rugged mountain ranges (some of which are volcanic in the Pacific Northwest). Alaska also features rugged mountains as well as river valleys. Hawaii's landscape varies but is dominated by volcanic topography.
2. Several reasons can explain the various climates in America. Climate changes according to different topography. Like its topography, the climate of the U. S. also varies depending on location. It is considered mostly temperate but is tropical in Hawaii and Florida, arctic in Alaska, semiarid in the plains west of the Mississippi River and arid in the Great Basin of the southwest. As the third largest country by area, America covers broad latitude and, thus, it has climate zones ranging from semi-arid steppe (the Great Plains) to frozen tundra (Alaska), humid subtropics (the Southeast) to deserts and highlands. With this much diversity, it's little wonder that the US witnesses some of the world's most dramatic weather and natural disasters, including hurricanes, tornados, wildfires, and floods.

Key to Exercises   311

Section Two
Reading One
1. It is a famous campaign slogan. In 1818, the United States and the United Kingdom (controlling British Canada) established a joint claim over the Oregon Territory-the region west of the Rocky Mountains and between 42° North and 54° 40' North (the southern boundary of Russia's Alaska territory). Joint control worked for over a decade and a half but ultimately, the parties decided that joint occupancy wasn't working well so they set about to divide Oregon. The 1844 Democratic presidential candidate James K. Polk ran on a platform of taking control over the entire Oregon Territory and used the famous campaign slogan, "Fifty-four Forty or Fight!" (after the line of latitude serving as the northern boundary of Oregon at 54°40'). Polk's plan was to claim and go to war over the entire territory for the United States.
2. Omitted.

Reading Two
1. Omitted.
2. Omitted.

Chapter 10   History of the U. S. A.

Section One: A Brief Introduction
Ⅰ. 1～5 BAADB   6～10 BCBCD   11～15 AACCB
   16～20 CADDC   21～25 AACBC

Section Two: In-depth Reading
Reading One
1. He established the American republic. He led the revolutionary army against the British Empire, he served as the first president, and most importantly he stepped down from power.
2. Caesar, Cromwell, Napoleon, Lenin. They all seized the power they had won and held it until death or military defeat.
3. He hailed the "liberal policy" of the United States on religious freedom as worthy of emulation by other countries. He believed in a republic of free citizens, with a government based on consent and established to protect the rights of life, liberty, and property. He abhorred kingship, even for himself.

Reading Two
1. The old, standard history united Americans because it has a coherent purpose and

a single voice. It emphasized one point of view and ignored others. To put it bluntly, it was history about white people for white people.
2. All this changed, beginning in the 1960s. The civil rights movement gave voices to blacks and Indians, and changes in immigration laws brought a massive influx of non-whites. It was the end of a certain kind of America.
3. In Atlanta, where 92 percent of the public school students are black, history and social studies courses have been rewritten from an "African-American" perspective. New York's public schools recently authorized a curriculum revision based on an openly anti-white position paper drafted, in part, by the black-supremacist professor, Leonard Jeffries.
4. White children are learning that every interpretation is valid, that nothing is certain, that their nation's past is all paradoxes and unsolved problems. Patriotism will not grow in the heart of a child who cannot look back with pride upon his nation's past. We have come a long way from schooling that made Europeans into Americans. We now make Americans into nothing at all.

Chapter 11　U. S. Government and Politics

Section One: A Brief Introduction
I . 1~5 BCBBC　　6~10 CBBCD　　11 D
II . 1~5 TTFTF　　6~10 FTTTT
III.
1. A representative must be 25 years of age, a U. S. citizen for at least seven years, and a resident of the state they represent. A senator must be 30 years of age, U. S. citizens for at least nine years, and residents of the state they represent.
2. Electoral College system is the institution that officially elects the President and Vice President of the United States every four years. The President and Vice President are not elected directly by the voters. Instead, they are elected by "electors" who are chosen by popular vote on a state-by-state basis. Minor parties in America have few electors in the Electoral College and thus are unlikely to win the election.

Section Two: In-depth Reading
Reading One
1. Federalism is a system based upon democratic rules and institutions in which the power to govern is shared between national and provincial/state governments, creating what is often called a federation. In America, federalism is sometimes called "state right".

Centralism refers to the concentration of a government's power—both geographically and politically—into a centralized government.
2. Advantages:
(1) Localized Governance: Every province has political, social and economic problems peculiar to the region itself. Provincial government representatives live in proximity to the people and are most of the time from the same community, so that they are in a better position to understand these problems and offer unique solutions for them.
(2) Local Representation: Federalism offers representation to different populations. Citizens of various provinces may have different aspirations, ethnicity and follow different cultures. The central government can sometimes overlook these differences and adopt policies which cater to the majority. This is where the regional government steps in. While formulating policies, local needs, tastes and opinions are given due consideration by the state governments. Rights of the minorities are protected too.
(3) Freedom to Form Policies: State governments have the freedom to adopt policies which may not be followed nationally or by any other state. For example, same-sex marriages are not recognized by the federal government of USA but they are given legal status within certain states like Connecticut, Iowa, Vermont and Massachusetts.
(4) Optimum Utilization of Resources: Division of work between the central and the regional governments leads to optimum utilization of resources. The central government can concentrate more on international affairs and defense of the country, while the provincial government can cater to the local needs.
(5) Scope for Innovation and Experimentation: Federalism has room for innovation and experimentation. Two local governments can have two different approaches to bring reforms in any area of public domain, be it taxation or education. The comparison of the results of these policies can give a clear idea of which policy is better and thus, can be adopted in the future.
Disadvantages:
(1) Conflict of Authority: Sharing of power between the center and the states includes both advantages and disadvantages of a federal organization. Sometimes there can be overlapping of work and subsequent confusion regarding who is responsible for what. For example, when Hurricane Katrina hit Greater New Orleans, USA, in 2005, there was delay in the rescue work, as there was confusion between the state governments and the federal government on who is responsible for which disaster management work. This resulted in the loss of many lives.
(2) Corruption: Federal system of government is very expensive as more people

are elected to office, both at the state and the center, than necessary. Thus, it is often said that only rich countries can afford it. Too many elected representatives with overlapping roles may also lead to corruption.

(3) Pitches State vs. State: Federalism leads to unnecessary competition between different regions. There can be a rebellion by a regional government against the national government too. Both scenarios pose a threat to the country's integrity.

(4) Uneven Distribution of Wealth: It promotes regional inequalities. Natural resources, industries, employment opportunities differ from region to region. Hence, earnings and wealth are unevenly distributed. Rich states offer more opportunities and benefits to its citizens than poor states. Thus, the gap between rich and poor states widens.

(5) Promotes Regionalism: It can make state governments selfish and concerned only about their own region's progress. They can formulate policies which might be detrimental to other regions. For example, pollution from a province which is promoting industrialization in a big way can affect another region which depends solely on agriculture and cause crop damage.

(6) Framing of Incorrect Policies: Federalism does not eliminate poverty. Even in New York, there are poor neighborhoods like Inwood. The reason for this may be that intellectuals and not the masses are invited by the local government during policy framing. These intellectuals may not understand the local needs properly and thus, policies might not yield good results.

Reading Two

1. The process for selecting Electors varies throughout the United States. Generally, the political parties nominate Electors at their State party conventions or by a vote of the party's central committee in each State. Each candidate will have their own unique slate of potential Electors as a result of this part of the selection process. Electors are often chosen to recognize service and dedication to their political party. They may be State-elected officials, party leaders, or persons who have a personal or political affiliation with the Presidential candidate.

2. The U. S. Constitution contains very few provisions relating to the qualifications of Electors. Article II, section 1, clause 2 provides that no Senator or Representative, or Person holding an Office of Trust or Profit under the United States, shall be appointed an Elector. As a historical matter, the 14th Amendment provides that State officials who have engaged in insurrection or rebellion against the United States or given aid and comfort to its enemies are disqualified from serving as Electors. This prohibition relates to the post-Civil War era. Each state's Certificates of Ascertainment confirms the names of its appointed electors. A state's certification of its electors is generally sufficient to establish the qualifications of electors.

On Election Day, the voters in each State choose the Electors by casting votes for the presidential candidate of their choice. The Electors' names may or may not appear on the ballot below the name of the candidates running for President, depending on the procedure in each State. The winning candidate in each State—except in Nebraska and Maine, which have proportional distribution of the Electors—is awarded all of the State's Electors. In Nebraska and Maine, the state winner receives two Electors and the winner of each congressional district receives one Elector. This system permits the Electors from Nebraska and Maine to be awarded to more than one candidate.

3. There is no Constitutional provision or Federal law that requires Electors to vote according to the results of the popular vote in their States. Some States, however, require Electors to cast their votes according to the popular vote. These pledges fall into two categories—Electors bound by State law and those bound by pledges to political parties.

The U. S. Supreme Court has held that the Constitution does not require that Electors be completely free to act as they choose and therefore, political parties may extract pledges from electors to vote for the parties' nominees. Some State laws provide that so-called "faithless Electors"; may be subject to fines or may be disqualified for casting an invalid vote and be replaced by a substitute elector. The Supreme Court has not specifically ruled on the question of whether pledges and penalties for failure to vote as pledged may be enforced under the Constitution. No Elector has ever been prosecuted for failing to vote as pledged.

Today, it is rare for Electors to disregard the popular vote by casting their electoral vote for someone other than their party's candidate. Electors generally hold a leadership position in their party or were chosen to recognize years of loyal service to the party. Throughout our history as a nation, more than 99 percent of Electors have voted as pledged.

Chapter 12　American Economy

Section One

Ⅰ. 1～15 DBCBC　　DDCAA　　DADDA

Ⅱ. 1～10 TTFTT　　TFTFT

Ⅲ.

1. The New Deal included the following contents;

(1) establishment and strengthening of government regulation and control of banking, credit and currency systems, overcoming the financial crisis and restriction of certain extreme practices of financial capital;

(2) federal government management of relief and establishment of social security system such as the formation of the Civilian Conservation Crops and the setting-up of the Tennessee Valley Authority;

(3) stimulation of the recover of industry and agriculture;

(4) formulation and implementation of federal labour laws to raise the role of labour in the relations of production;

(5) improvement of the situation of minorities and members of certain religious groups.

Franklin D. Roosevelt's program was known as the New Deal. Under it, the federal government took far more responsibility for the economic welfare of the people than it had in any previous administration. There were a series of measures to help the United States economy recover from the Great Depression. In only two New Deal years, 1934 and 1936, the federal deficit, as a percentage of gross national product, exceeded the 4.6 percent of Herbert Hoover's last year in office. So New Deal successfully helped American people get through the Great Depression.

2. 'Baby boom' refers to the great increase of birth rate between 1946 and 1964. People born in this period are called baby bammers. In the United States, approximately 79 million babies were born during the Baby Boom. Much of this cohort of nineteen years (1946-1964) grew up with Woodstock, the Vietnam War, and John F. Kennedy as president. In 2006, the oldest Baby Boomers are turning 60 years old, including the first two Baby Boomer presidents, Presidents William J. Clinton and George W. Bush, both born in the first year of the Baby Boom, 1946.

Section Two
Reading One
1. One is rising home prices, which are expected to show big increases in the cost of buying a home compared to a year earlier. The other problem is higher mortgage rates that have pushed some prospective buyers to the sidelines.
2. Omitted.

Reading Two
1. First, the sharp decline in consumer spending on houses, autos and other durables, following the sharp decline in lending to households, will cause a recession as construction of new houses and production of consumer durables nosedive.

Second, many homeowners will default on their mortgage payments and consumer loans, especially as house values fall below the mortgage values.

Third, the banking sector will cut back sharply on its lending in line with the fall in its capital following the write-off of bad mortgage and consumer loans. Those capital losses will push still more financial institutions into bankruptcy or forced mergers with stronger banks.

Fourth, the retrenchment of lending now threatens even the shortest-term loans, which banks and other institutions lend to each other for working capital. Interbank loans and other commercial paper are extremely hard to place.

2. (1) The government and Federal Reserve Board must prevent the collapse of working capital by supplying short-term loans and taking other measures to sustain the commercial paper market, interbank lending and the smooth functioning of money market funds;

(2) The government should also aggressively promote a recapitalization of the banking system so that bank lending is not squeezed for years to come. It can directly inject some public capital into banks, and can both pressure and entice the banks to raise additional private capital.

(3) The government should ease the repayment terms on existing mortgage holders, to reduce the flood of defaults and foreclosures that will otherwise occur.

(4) The government should encourage expansionary monetary and fiscal policies abroad (most notably in cash-rich Asia), so that the decline in U. S. consumer spending is smoothly offset by a rise in spending in other countries.

3. Omitted.

Chapter 13 Education of the U. S. A.

Section One: A Brief Introduction
I. 1~6 AADACD

II.

1. Omitted
2. Middle schools are designed to provide a forum to meet the special needs of adolescents. Team teaching and flexible block scheduling, rather than set 45-or 50-minute classes, are characteristic of middle schools. These schools also place emphasis on small groups, on an interdisciplinary approach to subject matter, and on special projects that can engage 10-to 15-year-olds
3. Through most of the 20th century, high schools were consolidated into larger units to offer wider class choices to more and more students. The rural country school almost disappeared, replaced by countywide high schools. Recent trends: the establishment of smaller schools with lower student-teacher ratios.

Section Two: In-depth Reading
Reading One
1. Concern springs from a number of things: steep rises in fees, increases in the levels of debt of both students and universities, and the declining quality of graduates.
2. States have already cut back dramatically on the amount of financial aid they give universities. Barack Obama has made it clear that he is unhappy about rising tuition fees, and threatens universities with aid cuts if they rise any further.
3. Indeed, evidence from declines in the quality of students and graduates suggests that a degree may now mean less than it once did. For example, a federal survey showed that the literacy of college-educated citizens declined between 1992 and 2003. A remarkable 43% of all grades at four-year universities are As, an increase of 28 percentage points since 1960. Grade point averages rose from about 2.52 in the 1950s to 3.11 in 2006.
4. Another issue is that the salary gap between those with only a high-school diploma and those with a university degree is created by the plummeting value of the diploma, rather than by soaring graduate salaries. After adjusting for inflation, graduates earned no more in 2007 than they did in 1979.
5. The broader significance of MOOCs is that they are part of a trend towards the unbundling of higher education. As online education spreads, universities will come under pressure to move to something more like a "buffet" arrangement, under which they will accept credits from each other—and from students who take courses at home or even at high school, spending much less time on campus.

Reading Two
1. While Secretary Duncan's appearances have naturally soaked up most of the attention—whether he is dancing at a Denver elementary school for "Let's Move" or honoring the Topeka, Kansas site of the Brown vs. Board of Education case—TAFs have been hosting intimate events to ensure that educators' voices are heard.
2. The Teaching Ambassador Fellowship, now in its fifth year, includes six teachers from across the country on leave from their schools to work full-time for a year with the U.S. Department of Education, and six who remain teaching in their local districts while consulting and conducting outreach part-time with ED.
3. "The idea of a 'full teaching load' needs to change. If you asked me what I would ideally be doing, I would teach a 3/5 load full-time, and spend the extra energy on those classes. Class sizes do matter. To think about doing anything else in addition to our full-time load is impossible." "At one point my contract said that I taught 20% mentored 80%, but in reality the teaching part actually took 75% of my time and 90% of my emotional space. Serving as a leader and a

teacher I asked myself the following question, 'If you're teaching, can you do anything else well at the same time?'"

Chapter 14   Media of the U. S. A.

Section One: A Brief Introduction
I. 1~5 DBDCD   6~8 ADC
II.
1. Two newspapers: *The New York Times* and *The Wall Street Journal*. Three newsmagazines: *Time*, *Newsweek* and *U. S. News and World Report*. Four broadcasters: the National Broadcasting Company (NBC), Columbia Broadcasting System (CBS), the American Broadcasting Company (ABC) and Fox.
2. Privately owned. Their revenue derives from advertising, subscriptions and the sale of copyrighted material.
3. Omitted.

Section Two: In-depth Reading
Reading one
1. A free press nurtures democracy. Freedom of the press is essential to democracy because it empowers the citizenry and holds governments accountable.
2. Advances in technology have enhanced the power of the press by increasing the speed and reach of information distribution.
3. Mobile phones with broadband Internet access are promising even more powerful communication possibilities.

Reading Two
1. Literacy: the ability to read or write. Media literacy means the ability to be an active media consumer in today's participatory media.
2. The first four principles of media creation, thoroughness, accuracy, fairness and independence. In this new era, we need to add another: transparency.

Chapter 15   American Literature

Section One: A Brief Introduction
I. 1~5 CAABC   6~10 CACDC
II. 1~5 TFTTT   6~10 FTTTT

III.

1. allegory:（寓言）A specific type of writing in which the settings, characters, and events stand for other specific people, events, or ideas.
2. Alliteration:（头韵）Repetition of the initial sounds of words, as in "Peter Piper picked a peck of pickled peppers".
3. anti-hero:（反英雄）The antihero or antiheroine is a leading character in a film, book or play who lacks the traditional heroic qualities, such as idealism, courage, nobility, fortitude, moral goodness, and altruism.
4. ballad:（民谣）A ballad is a form of verse, often a narrative set to music.
5. epic poetry:（史诗）A long poem that narrates the victories and adventures of a hero. It can be identified by lofty or elegant diction.
6. iambic pentameter:（五音步抑扬格）The word "iambic" describes the type of foot that is used (in English, an unstressed syllable followed by a stressed syllable). The word "pentameter" indicates that a line has five of these "feet".
7. lyric:（抒情诗，歌词）It is a short poem with a song-like quality, or designed to be set to music; often conveying feelings, emotions, or personal thoughts.
8. Naturalism:（自然主义）A theory or practice in literature emphasizing scientific observation of life without idealization and often including elements of determinism.
9. ode:（颂歌）A lyrical poem, sometimes sung, that focuses on the glorification of a single subject and its meaning. Often has an irregular stanza structure.
10. sonnet:（十四行诗）A 14 line poem written in iambic pentameter. There are two types of sonnets: Shakespearean and Italian. The Shakespearean sonnet is written with 3 quatrain and a couplet in abab, cdcd, efef, gg rhythmic pattern. An Italian sonnet is written in 2 stanzas with an octave followed by a septet in abba, abba, cdecde or cdcdcd rhythmic pattern.

Section Two: In-depth Reading
Reading One

There are many similarities between Hemingway and the character, Frederic. Obvious similarities are that:

(1) Both author and character were ambulance drivers, were wounded from the waist down, stayed in a hospital in Milan, got a medal for his courage, and had relations with a nurse.

(2) Frederic also acquired some of Hemingway's little traits and memories. For instance, when Hemingway was injured he said, "My feet felt like I had rubber boots full of water on. And my knee cap was acting queer." When Frederic was injured, he said, "My legs felt warm and wet and my shoes were wet and warm inside. I knew that I was hit and leaned over and put my hand on my knee. My

knee wasn't there." Hemingway even said that the passage from *A Farewell to Arms* was an accurate account of what had happened to him.

(3) Even though the end of the story was different than Hemingway's life, both stories are tragic. Both Hemingway and Frederic get left alone and hurt, without their love.

Reading Two
omitted

Appendix: Canada, Australia and New Zealand

Canada
I. 1~5 DCBDB   6~10 DCAAD
II. 1~4 TTTF
III.
1. Multiculturalism exists when people accept and encourage many cultures to thrive in a society. Multiculturalism can lead to many great outcomes, including racial and ethnic harmony, which simply means that people from different backgrounds get along well together. Living with and accepting different cultures helps us understand each other and discourage hatred and violence.

    Canada officially became a multicultural society in 1971 when the government began to recognize the value and dignity of Canadians of all races and ethnic groups, all languages and all religions. At this time, the government also recognized the value and dignity of Aboriginal peoples and the equal status of Canada's two official languages: English and French. Canada promotes multiculturalism by encouraging all Canadians to take part in all aspects of life. People of every race and ethic background can join in social, cultural, economic and political affairs. Everyone in Canada is equal. Everyone has a right to be heard.

Australia
I. 1~5 BCDAC   6~10 CDABC
II. 1~4 TFFT
III.
1. Australia is a developed country and one of the wealthiest in the world, with the world's 12th-largest economy. In 2012 Australia had the world's fifth-highest per capita income, Australia's military expenditure is the world's 13th-largest. With the second-highest human development index globally, Australia ranks highly in many international comparisons of national performance, such as quality of life, health, education, economic freedom, and the protection of civil liberties and political rights. Australia is a member of the United Nations, G20,

Commonwealth of Nations, ANZUS, Organisation for Economic Co-operation and Development (OECD), World Trade Organization, Asia-Pacific Economic Cooperation, and the Pacific Islands Forum.

New Zealand

Ⅰ. 1~5 DABBB   6~10 AADC C

Ⅱ. 1~4 TFTT

Ⅲ.

1. Maori culture is the culture of the Maori of New Zealand (an Eastern Polynesian people) and forms a distinctive part of New Zealand culture. There have been three distinct but overlapping cultural eras—before widespread European contact, the 1800s in which Maori began interacting with European visitors and settlers, and the modern era since the beginning of the 20th century. The present culture of the Maori has been strongly influenced by western European culture but remnants of the old culture have been retained and revived, though often in a modified modern form. Maori speak fluent English but the New Zealand government has established government funding, organizations and schooling systems to encourage the learning and usage of the Maori language. As a result there is now more awareness of their culture by young Maori.